Professional JavaScript

Fast-track your web development career using the powerful features of advanced JavaScript

Hugo Di Francesco

Siyuan Gao

Vinicius Isola

Philip Kirkbride

D1227643

Professional JavaScript

Authors: Hugo Di Francesco, Siyuan Gao, Vinicius Isola, and Philip Kirkbride

Technical Reviewer: Archit Agarwal

Managing Editor: Aditya Shah

Acquisitions Editors: Koushik Sen and Anindya Sil

Production Editor: Shantanu Zagade

Editorial Board: Shubhopriya Banerjee, Ewan Buckingham, Mahesh Dhyani, Taabish Khan, Manasa Kumar, Alex Mazonowicz, Pramod Menon, Bridget Neale, Dominic Pereira, Shiny Poojary, Erol Staveley, Ankita Thakur, Nitesh Thakur, and Jonathan Wray

First Published: September 2019

Production Reference: 1300919

ISBN: 978-1-83882-021-3

Published by Packt Publishing Ltd.

Livery Place, 35 Livery Street

Birmingham B3 2PB, UK

Table of Contents

Chapter 4: RESTful APIs with Node.js

Chapter 5: Modular JavaScript

Chapter 6: Code Quality   255

Chapter 9: Event-Driven Programming and Built-In Modules

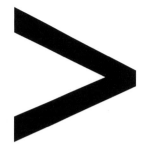

Preface

About

This section briefly introduces the authors, the coverage of this book, the technical skills you'll need to get started, and the hardware and software requirements required to complete all of the included activities and exercises.

About the Book

In depth knowledge of JavaScript makes it easier to learn a variety of other frameworks, including React, Angular, and related tools and libraries. This book is designed to help you cover the core JavaScript concepts you need to build modern applications.

You'll start by learning how to represent an HTML document in the Document Object Model (DOM). Then, you'll combine your knowledge of the DOM and Node.js to create a web scraper for practical situations. As you read through further chapters, you'll create a Node.js-based RESTful API using the Express library for Node.js. You'll also understand how modular designs can be used for better reusability and collaboration with multiple developers on a single project. Later chapters will guide you through building unit tests, which ensure that the core functionality of your program is not affected over time. The book will also demonstrate how constructors, async/await, and events can load your applications quickly and efficiently. Finally, you'll gain useful insights into functional programming concepts such as immutability, pure functions, and higher-order functions.

By the end of this book, you'll have the skills you need to tackle any real-world JavaScript development problem using a modern JavaScript approach, both for the client and server sides.

About the Authors

Hugo Di Francesco is a software engineer who has worked extensively with JavaScript. He holds a MEng degree in mathematical computation from University College London (UCL). He has used JavaScript across the stack to create scalable and performant platforms at companies such as Canon and Elsevier. He is currently tackling problems in the retail operations space with Node.js, React, and Kubernetes while running the eponymous Code with Hugo website. Outside of work, he is an international fencer, in the pursuit of which he trains and competes across the globe.

Siyuan Gao is a software engineer at Electronic Arts. He has a bachelor's degree in computer science from Purdue University. He has worked with JavaScript and Node.js for over 4 years, mainly building efficient backend solutions for high-availability systems. He is also a contributor to the Node.js Core project and has had many npm modules published. In his spare time, he enjoys learning about video game design and machine learning.

Vinicius Isola started programming back in 1999 using Macromedia Flash and ActionScript. In 2005, he took the Java Certification and specialized in building web and enterprise applications. Always working on all parts of the stack, JavaScript and web technologies have always been present in his many job roles and the companies he has worked for. In his free time, he likes to work on open-source projects and mentor new developers.

Philip Kirkbride has over 5 years of experience with JavaScript and is based in Montreal. He graduated from a technical college in 2011 and since then he has been working with web technologies in various roles. He worked with 2Klic, an IoT company contracted by the major electrical heating company Convectair to create smart heaters powered by Z-Wave technology. His role consisted of writing microservices in Node.js and Bash. He has also had a chance to make some contributions to the open-source projects SteemIt (a blockchain-based blogging platform) and DuckDuckGo (a privacy-based search engine).

Learning Objectives

By the end of this book, you will be able to:

- Apply the core concepts of functional programming
- Build a Node.js project that uses the Express.js library to host an API
- Create unit tests for a Node.js project to validate it
- Use the Cheerio library with Node.js to create a basic web scraper
- Develop a React interface to build processing flows
- Use callbacks as a basic way to bring control back

Audience

If you want to advance from being a frontend developer to a full-stack developer and learn how Node.js can be used for hosting full-stack applications, this is an ideal book for you. After reading this book, you'll be able to write better JavaScript code and learn about the latest trends in the language. To easily grasp the concepts explained here, you should know the basic syntax of JavaScript and should've worked with popular frontend libraries such as jQuery. You should have also used JavaScript with HTML and CSS but not necessarily Node.js.

Approach

Each section of this book has been explicitly designed to engage and stimulate you so that you can retain and apply what you learn in a practical context with maximum impact. You'll learn how to tackle intellectually stimulating programming challenges that will prepare you for real-world topics through functional programming and test-driven development practices. Each chapter has been explicitly designed to build upon JavaScript as a core language.

Hardware Requirements

For the optimal experience, we recommend the following hardware configuration:

- Processor: Intel Core i5 or equivalent

- Memory: 4 GB of RAM

- Storage: 5 GB of available space

Software Requirements

We also recommend that you have the following software installed in advance:

- Git latest version

- Node.js 10.16.3 LTS (https://nodejs.org/en/)

Conventions

Code words in the text, database table names, folder names, filenames, file extensions, pathnames, dummy URLs, user input, and Twitter handles are shown as follows:

"The ES6 **import** function also allows you to import a subsection of a module, rather than importing the whole thing. This is one capability ES6's **import** has over the Node.js **require** function. SUSE"

A block of code is set as follows:

```
let myString = "hello";
console.log(myString.toUpperCase()); // returns HELLO
console.log(myString.length); // returns 5
```

Installation and Setup

Before we can do awesome things with data, we need to be prepared with the most productive environment. In this short section, we will see how to do that.

Installing Node.js and npm

Installations of Node.js come with npm (Node.js's default package manager) included.

Installing Node.js on Windows:

1. Find your desired version of Node.js on the official installation page at https://nodejs.org/en/download/current/.

2. Ensure you select Node.js 12 (the current version).

JavaScript, HTML, and the DOM

Learning Objectives

By the end of this chapter, you will be able to:

- Describe the HTML **Document Object Model** (**DOM**)
- Use the Chrome DevTools source tab to explore the DOM of a web page
- Implement JavaScript to query and manipulate the DOM
- Build custom components using Shadow DOM

In this chapter, we will learn about the DOM and how to interact with and manipulate it using JavaScript. We will also learn how to build dynamic applications using reusable custom components.

Introduction

HTML started as a markup language for static documents that was easy to use and could be written using any text editor. After JavaScript became a major player in the internet world, there was a need to expose the HTML documents to the JavaScript runtime. That's when the DOM, was created. The DOM is HTML mapped to a tree of objects that can be queried and manipulated using JavaScript.

In this chapter, you'll learn what the DOM is and how to use JavaScript to interact with it. You'll learn how to find elements and data in a document, how to manipulate elements states, and how to modify their content. You'll also learn how to create DOM elements and append them to a page.

After learning about the DOM and how to manipulate it, you'll build a dynamic application using some sample data. Lastly, you'll learn how to create custom HTML elements to build reusable components using Shadow DOM.

HTML and the DOM

When a browser loads an HTML page, it creates a tree that represents that page. This tree is based on the DOM specification. It uses tags to determine where each node starts and ends.

Consider the following piece of HTML code:

```html
<html>
  <head>
    <title>Sample Page</title>
  </head>
  <body>
    <p>This is a paragraph.</p>
    <div>
      <p>This is a paragraph inside a div.</p>
    </div>
    <button>Click me!</button>
  </body>
</html>
```

The browser will create the following hierarchy of nodes:

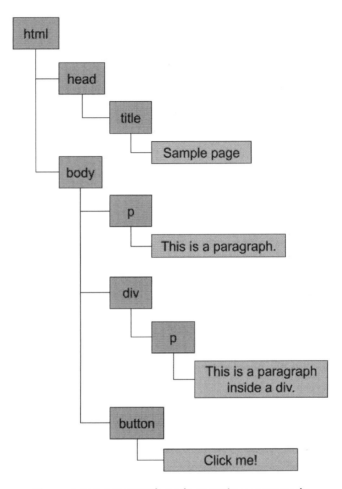

Figure 1.1: A paragraph node contains a text node

Everything becomes a node. Texts, elements, and comments, all the way up to the root of the tree. This tree is used to match styles from CSS and render the page. It's also transformed into an object and made available to the JavaScript runtime.

But why is it called the DOM? Because HTML was originally designed to share documents and not to design the rich dynamic applications we have today. That means that every HTML DOM starts with a document element, to which all elements are attached. With that in mind, the previous illustration of the DOM tree actually becomes the following:

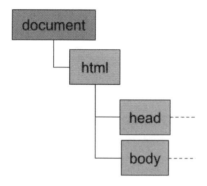

Figure 1.2: All DOM trees have a document element at the root

What does it mean when I say that the browser makes the DOM available to the JavaScript runtime? It means that if you write some JavaScript code in your HTML page, you can access that tree and do some pretty interesting things with it. For example, you can easily access the document root element and access all of the nodes on a page, which is what you're going to do in the next exercise.

Exercise 1: Iterating over Nodes in a Document

In this exercise, we'll write JavaScript code to query the DOM to find a button and add an event listener to it so that we can execute some code when the user clicks on it. When the event happens, we'll query for all paragraph elements, count and store their content, then show an alert at the end.

The code files for this exercise can be found at https://github.com/TrainingByPackt/ Professional-JavaScript/tree/master/Lesson01/Exercise01.

Perform the following steps to complete the exercise:

1. Open the text editor of your preference and create a new file called **alert_paragraphs.html** containing the sample HTML from the previous section (which can be found on GitHub: https://bit.ly/2maW0Sx):

```
<html>
  <head>
    <title>Sample Page</title>
  </head>
  <body>
```

```
  <p>This is a paragraph.</p>
  <div>
    <p>This is a paragraph inside a div.</p>
  </div>
  <button>Click me!</button>
</body>
</html>
```

2. At the end of the **body** element, add a **script** tag such that the last few lines look like the following:

```
  </div>
  <button>Click me!</button>
  <script>
  </script>
</body>
</html>
```

3. Inside the **script** tag, add an event listener for the click event of the button. To do that, you query the document object for all elements with the **button** tag, get the first one (there's only one button on the page), then call **addEventListener**:

```
document.getElementsByTagName('button')[0].addEventListener('click', () =>
{});
```

4. Inside the event listener, query the document again to find all paragraph elements:

```
const allParagraphs = document.getElementsByTagName('p');
```

5. After that, create two variables inside the event listener to store how many paragraph elements you found and another to store their content:

```
let allContent = "";
let count = 0;
```

6. Iterate over all paragraph elements, count them, and store their content:

```
for (let i = 0; i < allParagraphs.length; i++) {  const node =
allParagraphs[i];
  count++;
  allContent += `${count} - ${node.textContent}\n`;
}
```

7. After the loop, show an alert that contains the number of paragraphs that were found and a list with all their content:

    ```
    alert(`Found ${count} paragraphs. Their content:\n${allContent}`);
    ```

    You can see how the final code should look here: https://github.com/ TrainingByPackt/Professional-JavaScript/blob/master/Lesson01/Exercise01/ alert_paragraphs.html.

    Opening the HTML document in the browser and clicking the button, you should see the following alert:

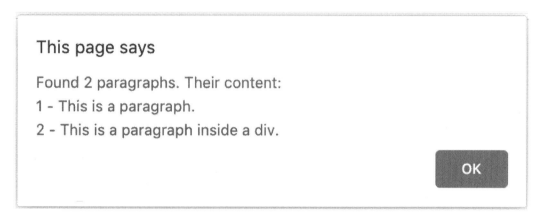

Figure 1.3: Alert box showing information about paragraphs on the page

In this exercise, we wrote some JavaScript code that queried the DOM for specific elements. We collected the contents of the elements to show them in an alert box.

We're going to explore other ways to query the DOM and iterate over nodes in later sections of this chapter. But from this exercise, you can already see how powerful this is and start imagining the possibilities this opens up. For example, I frequently use this to count things or extract data that I need from web pages all around the internet.

Developer Tools

Now that we understand the relationship between the HTML source and the DOM, we can explore it in more detail using a very powerful tool: browser developer tools. In this book, we're going to explore Google Chrome's **DevTools**, but you can easily find equivalent tools in all other browsers.

The first thing we're going to do is explore the page we created in the previous section. When you open it in Google Chrome, you can find the developer tools by opening the **Chrome** menu. Then select **More Tools** and **Developer Tools** to open the developer tools:

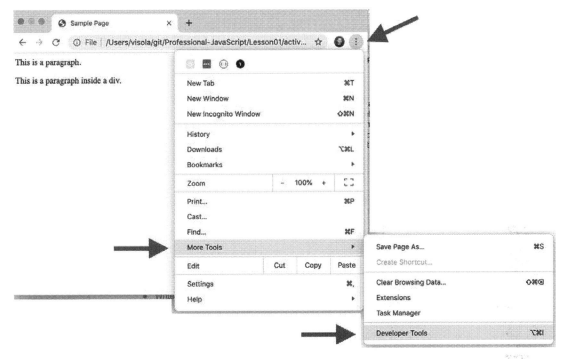

Figure 1.4: Accessing the developer tools in Google Chrome

Developer Tools will open a panel at the bottom of the page:

Figure 1.5: Google Chrome DevTools panel when open

You can see at the top the various tabs that provide different perspectives on what's happening on the loaded page. For this chapter, we're going to be focusing mostly on three tabs:

- **Elements** – Shows the DOM tree as the browser sees it. You can check how the browser is looking at your HTML, how CSS is being applied, and what selectors activated each style. You can also change the state of the nodes to simulate specific states such as `hover` or `visited`:

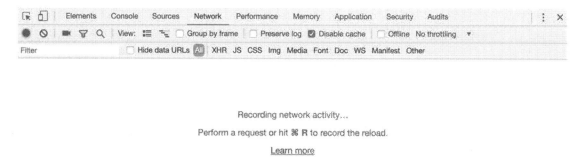

Figure 1.6: View of the Elements tab

- **Console** – Gives access to a JavaScript runtime in the context of the page. The console can be used after loading the page to test short snippets of code. It can also be used to print important debugging information:

Figure 1.7: View of the Console tab

- **Sources** – Shows all the source code loaded for the current page. This view can be used to set breakpoints and start a debugging session:

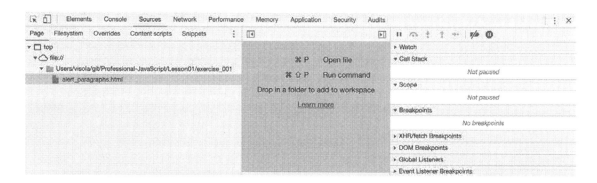

Figure 1.8: View of the Sources tab

Perform the following steps to complete the exercise:

1. The first thing you'll need to do is select the **Sources** tab in the **Developer Tools** panel. Then, open the one source file we have so far. You do that by clicking on it in the left-hand side panel:

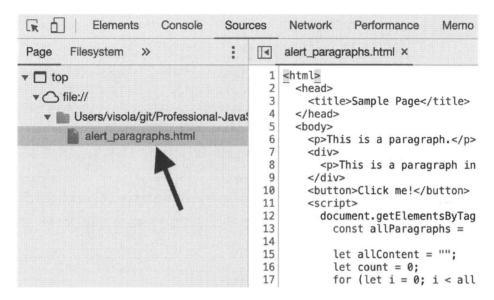

Figure 1.17: Sources tab showing where to find your source files

2. To set a breakpoint in the source, you click on the gutter where the line numbers are, at the line you want to set a breakpoint at. For this exercise, we'll set a breakpoint at the first line inside the event handler. A blue arrow-like symbol will appear on that line:

```
11       <script>
12          document.getEleme
13             const allParagr
14
15          let allContent
16          let count = 0;
```

Figure 1.18: Breakpoints show as arrow-like markers on the gutter of the source file

3. Click the **Click me!** button on the page to trigger the code execution. You'll notice that two things happen – the browser window freezes and there's a message indicating that the code is paused:

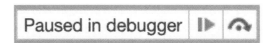

Figure 1.19: The browser pauses the execution when it hits a breakpoint

4. Also, the line of code being executed gets highlighted in the **Sources** tab:

```
11    <script>
12        document.getElementsByTagName('button')[0].addEventListener('click
13        const allParagraphs = ▶document. getElementsByTagName('p');
14
15            let allContent = "";
16            let count = 0;
```

Figure 1.20: Execution paused in the source code, highlighting the line that will be executed next

5. In the side panel, notice the currently executing stack and everything that's in the current scope, both globally and locally. This is the view of the right-hand panel, showing all the important information about the running code:

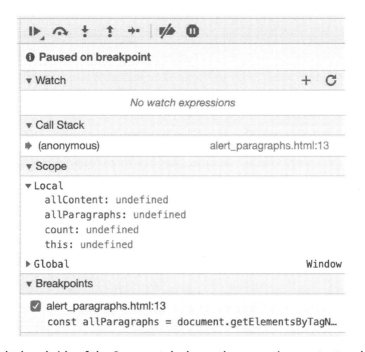

Figure 1.21: The right-hand side of the Sources tab shows the execution context and stack trace of the currently paused execution

6. The bar at the top can be used to control code execution. This is what each button can do:

    The **play** button ends the pause and continues execution normally.

    The **step over** button executes the current line through completion and pauses again at the next line.

    The **step in** button will execute the current line and step in any function call, which means it will pause at the first line inside any function being called on that line.

    The **step out** button will execute all of the steps required to exit the current function.

    The **step button** will execute the next action. If it's a function call, it will step in. If not, it will continue execution on the next line.

7. Press the **step over** the button until the execution gets to line 20:

```
18            const node = allParagraphs[i];
19            count++;   count = 1
20            allContent += `${count} - ${node.textContent}\n`;
21          }
22          alert(`Found ${count} paragraphs. Their content:\n${allCc
```

Figure 1.22: The highlighted line shows the execution paused for debugging

8. In the **Scope** panel on the right-hand side, you'll see four scopes: two scopes for **Block**, then one **Local** and one **Global**. The scopes will vary depending on where you are in the code. In this case, the first **Block** scope includes only what's inside the **for** loop. The second **Block** scope is the scope for the whole loop, including the variable defined in the **for** statement. **Local** is the function scope and **Global** is the browser scope. This is what you should see:

```
▼ Scope
▼ Block
  ▶ node: p
▼ Block
    i: 0
▼ Local
    allContent: ""
  ▶ allParagraphs: HTMLCollection(2) [p, p]
    count: 1
    this: undefined
▶ Global                                    Window
```

Figure 1.23: The Scope panel shows all the variables in the different scopes for the current execution context

9. Another interesting thing to notice at this point is that if you hover your mouse over a variable that is an HTML element in the current page, Chrome will highlight that element in the page for you:

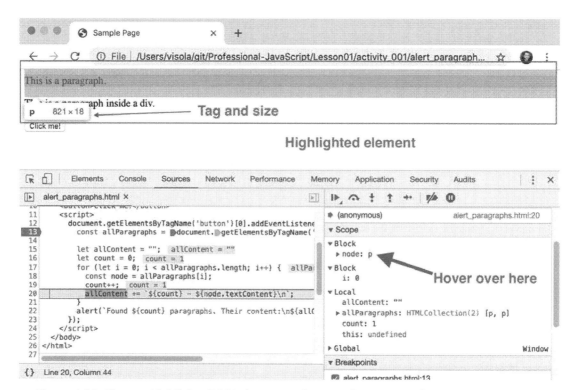

Figure 1.24: Chrome highlights DOM elements when you hover over them in various places

Debugging code using the **Sources** tab is one of the most important things you'll do as a web developer. Understanding how the browser sees your code and what the values of variables in each line are is the easiest way to get to the root of problems in complex applications.

> **Note**
>
> In-line values: As you step over the code in the **Sources** tab while debugging, you'll notice that Chrome adds some light-orange highlights on the side of each line, showing the current values for variables that are being affected in that line.

5. Again, from the **product** element, query for the name.

6. Append all information to the variable initialized in step 1, separating the values with commas. Don't forget to add newline characters to each line you append.

7. Print the variable containing the accumulated data using the **console.log** function.

8. Run the code in the **Console** tab with the storefront page open.

You should see the following content in the **Console** tab:

```
name,price,unit
Apples,$3.99,lb
Avocados,$4.99,lb
Blueberry Muffin,$2.50,each
Butter,$1.39,lb

...
```

> **Note**
>
> The solution for this activity can be found on page 582.

In this activity, you were able to use the **Console** tab to query an existing page to extract data from it. Sometimes, extracting data from a page is very complicated and scraping can get very brittle. Depending on how frequently you'll need data from the page, it might be easier to run a script from the **Console** tab instead of writing a full-fledged application.

Nodes and Elements

In previous sections, we learned about the DOM and how to interact with it. We saw that there's a global document object in the browser that represents the root of the tree. Then, we observed how to query it to fetch nodes and access their content.

But while exploring the DOM in the previous sections, there were some object names, attributes, and functions that were accessed and called without introduction. In this section, we'll dig deeper into those and learn how to find the available properties and methods in each of those objects.

The best place to find documentation about what's going to be discussed in this section is the Mozilla Developer Network web documentation. You can find that at developer. mozilla.org. They have detailed documentation about all the JavaScript and DOM APIs.

The node is where everything starts. The node is an interface that represents in the DOM tree. As mentioned before, everything in the tree is a node. All nodes have a **nodeType** property, which describes what type of node it is. It is a read-only property with a value that is a number. The node interface has a constant for each of the possible values. The most frequently seen node types are the following:

- **Node.ELEMENT_NODE** – HTML and SVG elements are of this type. In the storefront code, if you fetch the **description** element from the product, you'll see its **nodeType** property is **1**, which means it's an element:

```
> document.getElementsByClassName('description')[0].nodeType === Node.ELEMENT_NODE
< true
```

Figure 1.29: The description element node type is Node.ELEMENT_NODE

This is the element we fetched from the DOM as viewed in the **Elements** tab:

```
  ▶<div class="meta">…</div>
  ▼<div class="description"> == $0
      "Lorem ipsum dolor sit amet, consectetur adipiscing elit, sed do eiusmod tempor
      incididunt ut labore et dolore magna aliqua. Ut enim ad minim veniam, quis nostrud
      exercitation ullamco laboris nisi ut aliquip ex ea commodo consequat. Duis aute irure
      dolor in reprehenderit in voluptate velit esse cillum dolore eu fugiat nulla pariatur.
      Excepteur sint occaecat cupidatat non proident, sunt in culpa qui officia deserunt
      mollit anim id est laborum."
  </div>
```

Figure 1.30: The description node as seen in the Elements tab

- **Node.TEXT_NODE** – The text inside tags becomes text nodes. If you get the first child from the **description** node, you can see that it is of type **TEXT_NODE**:

```
> document.getElementsByClassName('description')[0].firstChild
<   "Lorem ipsum dolor sit amet, consectetur adipiscing elit, sed do eiusmod tempor incididun
    exercitation ullamco laboris nisi ut aliquip ex ea commodo consequat. Duis aute irure dol
    pariatur. Excepteur sint occaecat cupidatat non proident, sunt in culpa qui officia deser
> document.getElementsByClassName('description')[0].firstChild.nodeType === Node.TEXT_NODE
< true
```

Figure 1.31: The text inside tags becomes text nodes

This is the node as viewed in the **Elements** tab:

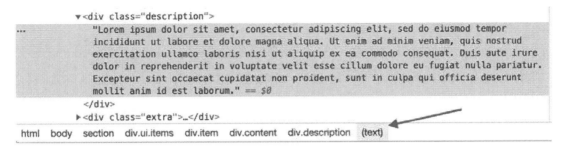

Figure 1.32: The text node selected in the Elements tab

- `Node.DOCUMENT_NODE` – The root of every DOM tree is a **document** node:

```
> document.nodeType === Node.DOCUMENT_NODE
< true
```

Figure 1.33: The root of the tree is always a document node

One important thing to notice is that the **html** node is not the root. When a DOM is created, the **document** node is the root and it contains the **html** node. You can confirm that by fetching the first child of the **document** node:

```
> document
<   ▶ #document
> document.nodeType === Node.DOCUMENT_NODE
< true
> document.nodeName
< "#document"
> document.firstChild
<    <html>
       ▶ <head>…</head>
       ▶ <body>…</body>
     </html>
> document.firstChild.nodeType === Node.ELEMENT_NODE
< true
> document.firstChild.nodeName
< "HTML"
> |
```

Figure 1.34: The html node is the first child of the document node

nodeName is another important property that nodes have. In **element** nodes, **nodeName** will give you the HTML tag for them. Other node types will return different things. The **document** node will always return **#document** (as seen in the preceding figure) and **Text** nodes will always return **#text**.

For text-like nodes such as **TEXT_NODE**, **CDATA_SECTION_NODE**, and **COMMENT_NODE**, you can use **nodeValue** to get the text that they hold.

But the most interesting thing about nodes is that you can traverse them like a tree. They have child nodes and siblings. Let's practice using these properties a little bit in the following exercise.

Exercise 4: Traversing the DOM Tree

In this exercise, we will traverse all the nodes in the sample page from *Figure 1.1*. We'll use a recursive strategy to iterate over all nodes and print the whole tree.

Perform the following steps to complete the exercise:

1. The first step is to open your text editor and set it up to write some JavaScript code.

2. To use a recursive strategy, we'll need a function that will be called for each node in the tree. This function will receive two arguments: the node to print and the depth that the node is at in the DOM tree. Here is how the declaration of the function looks:

```
function printNodes(node, level) {
}
```

3. The first thing we'll do inside the function is to start the message that will identify the opening of this node. For that, we'll use **nodeName**, which for **HTMLElements** will give the tag, and for other types of nodes will give us a reasonable identifier:

```
let message = `${"-".repeat(4 * level)}Node: ${node.nodeName}`;
```

4. If the node also has **nodeValue** associated with it, like **Text** and other text-line nodes, we'll also append that to the message and then print it to the console:

```
if (node.nodeValue) {
  message += `, content: '${node.nodeValue.trim()}'`;
}
console.log(message);
```

And last but not least, there's the **className** attribute, which gives you access to the classes applied to an element:

```
> document.getElementsByClassName('image')[0]
< ▶<div class="image">…</div>
> document.getElementsByClassName('image')[0].className
< "image"
```

Figure 1.40: className gives access to the classes the element has

What's more important about these attributes is that they are read/write, which means you can use them to modify the DOM, adding classes and changing the content of an element. In the upcoming sections, we will use what we've looked at here to create dynamic pages that change based on user interaction.

Special Objects

So far, we've accessed the **document** object in many of our examples and exercises. But what exactly is it and what else can it do? A document is a global object that represents the page loaded in the browser. And as we have seen, it serves as an entry point to the elements in the DOM tree.

Another important role it has that we haven't discussed so far is the ability to create new nodes and elements in a page. These elements can then be attached to the tree in different positions to modify it after the page is already loaded. We're going to explore this ability in upcoming sections.

Besides **document**, there's another object that is part of the DOM specification, which is the **window** object. A **window** object is a global object that is also the bind target for all JavaScript code running in the browser that doesn't have a bind target explicitly defined. That means that the variable is a pointer to the **window** object:

```
> window === this
< true
```

Figure 1.41: The global scope and default bind target in the browser is the window object

The **window** object contains everything you need to access from the browser: location, navigation history, other windows (popups), local storage, and much more. The **document** and **console** objects are also attributed to the **window** object. When you access the **document** object, you're actually using the **window.document** object, but the binding is implicit, so you don't need to write **window** all the time. And because the **window** is a global object, it means that it has to contain a reference to itself:

```
> window.window === this
< true
> window.window.window.window.window.window.window.window === this
< true
```

Figure 1.42: The window object contains a reference to itself

Using JavaScript to Query the DOM

We have been talking about querying the DOM through the **document** object. But all the methods we've used to query the DOM can also be called from elements in the DOM. The ones introduced in this section are also available from the elements in the DOM. We'll also see some that are only available in elements and not in the **document** object.

Querying from elements is very handy since the scope of the query is limited to where it gets executed. As we saw in *Activity 1, Extracting Data from the DOM*, we can start with a query that finds all base elements – the product element, in that specific case, then we can execute a new query from the element that will only search for elements inside the element that query was executed from.

The methods we used to query the DOM in the previous section include accessing elements from the DOM directly using the **childNodes** list, or using the **getElementsByTagName** and **getElementsByClassName** methods. Besides these methods, the DOM provides some other very powerful ways of querying for elements.

5. To solve the problem using the second approach, we will need a function to find all the siblings of a specified element. Open your text editor and let's start by declaring the function with an array to store all the siblings we find. Then, we'll return the array:

```
function getAllSiblings(element) {
  const siblings = [];
  // rest of the code goes here
  return siblings;
}
```

6. Then, we'll iterate over all previous sibling elements using a **while** loop and the **previousElementSibling** attribute. As we iterate over the siblings, we'll push them into the array:

```
let previous = element.previousElementSibling;
while (previous) {
  siblings.push(previous);
  previous = previous.previousElementSibling;
}
```

> **Note: Mind the gap, again**
>
> We use **previousElementSibling** instead of **previousNode** because that will exclude all text nodes and other nodes to avoid having to check **nodeType** for each one.

7. We do the same for all the siblings coming after the specified element:

```
let next = element.nextElementSibling;
while (next) {
  siblings.push(next);
  next = next.nextElementSibling;
}
```

8. Now that we have our **getAllSiblings** function, we can start looking for the products. We can use the **querySelectorAll** function, and some array mapping and filtering to find and print the data that we want:

```
//Start by finding all the labels with content 'organic'
Array.from(document.querySelectorAll('.label'))
.filter(e => e.innerHTML === 'organic')

//Filter the ones that don't have a sibling label 'fruit'
.filter(e => getAllSiblings(e).filter(s => s.innerHTML === 'fruit').length >
0)

//Find root product element
.map(e => e.closest('.item'))

//Find product name
.map(p => p.querySelector('.content a.header').innerHTML)

//Print to the console
.forEach(console.log);
```

9. Executing the code in the **Console** tab in **Developer Tools**, you'll see the following output:

```
Apples 0 ▶ (5) ["Apples", "Avocados", "Grapes", "Pears", "Strawberries"]
Avocados 1 ▶ (5) ["Apples", "Avocados", "Grapes", "Pears", "Strawberries"]
Grapes 2 ▶ (5) ["Apples", "Avocados", "Grapes", "Pears", "Strawberries"]
Pears 3 ▶ (5) ["Apples", "Avocados", "Grapes", "Pears", "Strawberries"]
Strawberries 4 ▶ (5) ["Apples", "Avocados", "Grapes", "Pears", "Strawberries"]
```

Figure 1.47: Output of the code from the exercise. Prints the names of all organic fruits.

> **Note**
>
> The code for this exercise can be found on GitHub. This is the path for the file that contains the code for the first approach: https://github.com/TrainingByPackt/Professional-JavaScript/blob/master/Lesson01/Exercise05/first_approach.js.
>
> The path for the file that contains the code for the second approach is this: https://github.com/TrainingByPackt/Professional-JavaScript/blob/master/Lesson01/Exercise05/second_approach.js.

In this exercise, we used two different techniques to fetch data from a page. We used many querying and node navigation methods and attributes to find elements and move around the DOM tree.

These techniques are essential to know when building modern web applications. Navigating the DOM and fetching data are the most common tasks in this type of application.

Manipulating the DOM

Now that we know what the DOM is and how to query for elements and navigate around it, it's time to learn how to change it using JavaScript. In this section, we're going to rewrite the storefront to be more interactive by loading the list of products and creating the page elements using JavaScript.

The sample code for this section can be found on GitHub at https://bit.ly/2mMje1K.

The first thing we need to know when creating dynamic applications using JavaScript is how to create new DOM elements and append them to the tree. Since the DOM specification is all based on interfaces, there's no concrete class to instantiate. When you want to create DOM elements, you need to use the **document** object. The **document** object has a method called **createElement**, which receives a tag name as a string. The following is an example of code that creates a **div** element:

```
const root = document.createElement('div');
```

The **product** item element has an **item** class. To add that class to it, we can just set the **className** attribute, as follows:

```
root.className = 'item';
```

And now we can attach the element to where it needs to go. But first, we need to find where it needs to go. The HTML for this sample code can be found on GitHub at https://bit.ly/2nKucVo. You can see that it has an empty **div** element where the product items will be added:

```
<div class="ui items"></div>
```

We can use **querySelector** to find that element and then call the **appendChild** method on it, which is a method that every node has, and pass the element node we just created to it so that it gets added to the DOM tree:

```
const itemsEl = document.querySelector('.items');
products.forEach((product) => {
  itemsEl.appendChild(createProductItem(product));
});
```

Here, `createProductItem` is the function that receives a product and creates the DOM element for it using the `createElement` function mentioned previously.

Creating one DOM element is not very useful. For the dynamic storefront example, we have an array of objects with all the data we need to build the page. For each one of them, we need to create all the DOM elements and glue them together in the right place and order. But first, let's take a look at how the data looks. The following shows how each **product** object looks:

```
{
    "price": 3.99,
    "unit": "lb",
    "name": "Apples",
    "description": "Lorem ipsum dolor sit amet, ...",
    "image": "../images/products/apples.jpg",
    "tags": [ "fruit", "organic" ]
}
```

And the following is how the DOM for the same product looks in the static storefront code we used in previous sections:

```
▼<div class="item">
   ▼<div class="image">
      <img src="../images/products/apples.jpg">
   </div>
   ▼<div class="content">
      <a class="header">Apples</a>
      ▼<div class="meta">
         <span>$3.99 / lb</span>
      </div>
      ▶<div class="description">...</div>
      ▼<div class="extra">
         <div class="ui label teal">fruit</div>
         <div class="ui label teal">organic</div>
         ::after
      </div>
      ::after
   </div>
   ::after
</div>
```

Figure 1.48: The DOM tree section for a product

You can see that there are a lot of nested elements that need to be created to get to the desired final DOM tree. So, let's take a look at a few techniques that are very helpful when building complex applications using JavaScript.

Let's get started by taking a look at **createProductItem** in the sample code:

```
function createProductItem(product) {

  const root = document.createElement('div');

  root.className = 'item';


  root.appendChild(createProductImage(product.image));

  root.appendChild(createContent(product));

  return root;

}
```

We start this method by creating the root element for the product tree, which is a **div** element. From the preceding screenshot, you see that this **div** needs an **item** class and that's what is happening on the next line after the element gets created, as described at the beginning of this section.

After the element is ready, it's time to start adding its children to it. Instead of doing everything in the same method, we create other functions that are responsible for creating each child and call them directly, appending the result of each function to the root element:

```
root.appendChild(createProductImage(product.image));

root.appendChild(createContent(product));
```

This technique is useful because it isolates the logic for each child in its own place.

Now let's take a look at the **createProductImage** function. From the previous sample code, you can see that the function receives the path for the **product** image. This is the code for the function:

```
function createProductImage(imageSrc) {

  const imageContainer = document.createElement('div');

  imageContainer.className = 'image';


  const image = document.createElement('img');
```

```
    image.setAttribute('src', imageSrc);
    imageContainer.appendChild(image);


    return imageContainer;
}
```

The function is divided into two major parts:

1. It creates the container element for the image. From the DOM screenshot, you can see that the **img** element is inside a **div** with an **image** class.

2. It creates the **img** element, sets the **src** attribute, and then appends it to the **container** element.

This style of code is simple, readable, and easy to understand. But that's because the HTML that needs to be generated is quite short. It's one **img** tag inside a **div** tag.

Sometimes, though, the tree becomes pretty complex and using this strategy makes the code almost unreadable. So, let's take a look at another strategy. The other child element appended to the product root is the **content** element. That is a **div** tag that has many children, including some nested ones.

We could have approached it the same way as the **createProductImage** function. But the method would have to do the following:

1. Create a **container** element and add a class to it.

2. Create the anchor element that stores the product name and append it to the container.

3. Create the container for the price and append it to the root container.

4. Create the **span** element with the price and append it to the element created in the previous step.

5. Create the element that contains the description and append it to the container.

6. Create a **container** element for the **tag** element and append it to the root container.

7. For each tag, create the **tag** element and append it to the container from the previous step.

It sounds like a long list of steps, doesn't it? Instead of trying to write all that code, we can use a template string to generate the HTML and then set **innerHTML** for the **container** element. So, the steps would, instead, look like the following:

1. Create the **container** element and add a class to it.

2. Create the HTML for the inner content using a string template.

3. Set **innerHTML** on the **container** element.

That sounds much simpler than the previous method. And, as we'll see, it's going to be much more readable too. Let's take a look at the code.

As stated before, the first step is to create the root container and add the class for it:

```
function createContent(product) {
  const content = document.createElement('div');
  content.className = 'content';
```

Then, we start by generating the HTML for the **tag** elements. For that, we have a function that receives the tag as a string and returns an HTML element for it. We use that to map all tags to elements using the **map** function on the **tags** array. Then, we map the element to HTML by using the **outerHTML** attribute from it:

```
const tagsHTML = product.tags.map(createTagElement)
    .map(el => el.outerHTML)
    .join('');
```

With the **container** element created and the HTML for the tags ready, we can set the **innerHTML** attribute of the **content** element using a template string and return it:

```
content.innerHTML = `
  <a class="header">${product.name}</a>
  <div class="meta"><span>$${product.price} / ${product.unit}</span></div>
  <div class="description">${product.description}</div>
  <div class="extra">${tagsHTML}</div>
  `;

  return content;
}
```

This code is much shorter and easier to reason about compared to the many steps that generating HTML elements and appending them would require. When writing your dynamic applications, it is up to you to decide what's best in each case. In this case, the trade-offs are basically readability and conciseness. But for others, trade-offs can also be requirements to cache elements to add event listeners or to hide/show them based on some filter, for example.

Exercise 6: Filtering and Searching Products

In this exercise, we'll add two features to our storefront application to help our customers to find products faster. First, we'll start by making labels clickable, which will filter the list of products by the selected label. Then, we'll add a search box at the top, for users to query by text in the name or description. This is how the page will look:

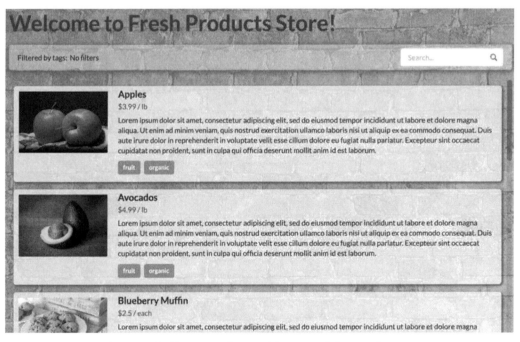

Figure 1.49: New storefront with a search bar at the top

In this new storefront, users can click on tags to filter products that have the same tag. When they do that, the tags being used to filter the list will show at the top, in orange. The user can click on the label in the search bar to remove the filter. This is how it looks:

Figure 1.50: How the tag filtering at the top works

Users can also use the search box on the right-hand side to search for products by name or description. The list will be filtered as they type.

The code for this exercise can be found on GitHub at https://github.com/ TrainingByPackt/Professional-JavaScript/tree/master/Lesson01/Exercise06.

Perform the following steps to complete the exercise:

1. The first thing we'll do is write the base HTML code where all the other elements will be added later using JavaScript. This HTML now contains a base **div** container, where all the content will be. The content inside it is then divided into two parts: a section with the header, which contains the title and the search bar, and a **div**, which will contain all the product items. Create a file called **dynamic_storefront. html** and add the following code in it:

```
<html>
  <head>
    <link rel="stylesheet" type="text/css" href="../css/semantic.min.css"
/>
    <link rel="stylesheet" type="text/css" href="../css/store_with_header.
css" />
  </head>
  <body>
    <div id="content">
      <section class="header">
        <h1 class="title">Welcome to Fresh Products Store!</h1>

        <div class="ui menu">
```

```
        <div class="right item">
          <div class="ui icon input">
            <input type="text" placeholder="Search..." />
            <i class="search icon"></i>
          </div>
        </div>
      </section>

      <div class="ui items"></div>
    </div>
    <script src="../data/products.js"></script>
    <script src="../sample_003/create_elements.js"></script>
    <script src="filter_and_search.js"></script>
  </body>
</html>
```

This HTML uses the **products.js** and **create_elements.js** scripts, which are the same as the sample code used in this section. It also uses the CSS files in the **Lesson01** folder. You can refer to them directly if you are in the same folder or copy and paste them into your project.

2. Create a file called **filter_and_search.js**, which is the last JavaScript code loaded in the HTML code. This is where we'll be adding all the code for this exercise. The first thing we need to do is to store the filter state. There will be two possible filters the user can apply to the page: selecting a tag and/or typing some text. To store them, we'll use an array and a string variable:

```
const tagsToFilterBy = [];
let textToSearch = '';
```

3. Now we'll create a function that will add an event listener for all the tags in the page. This function will find all the **tag** elements, wrap them in an array, and add an event listener using the **addEventListener** method in **Element** to respond to the **click** event:

```
function addTagFilter() {
  Array.from(document.querySelectorAll('.extra .label')).forEach(tagEl =>
  {
    tagEl.addEventListener('click', () => {
      // code for next step goes here
    });
  });
}
```

4. Inside the event listener, we will check whether the tag is already in the array of tags to filter by. If not, we'll add it and call another function, called **applyTagFilters**:

```
if (!tagsToFilterBy.includes(tagEl.innerHTML)) {
  tagsToFilterBy.push(tagEl.innerHTML);
  applyFilters();
}
```

5. **applyFilters** is just a catch-all function that will contain all the logic related to updating the page when the filtering conditions change. You'll just be calling functions we're going to write in the next steps:

```
function applyFilters() {
  createListForProducts(filterByText(filterByTags(products)));
  addTagFilter();
  updateTagFilterList();
}
```

6. Before we continue with the **applyFilters** function, we'll add another function to handle the events on the input box for the text search. This handler will listen to **keyup** events, which are triggered when the user finishes typing each letter. The handler will just get the current text in the input, set the value to the **textToSearch** variable, and call the **applyFilters** function:

```
function addTextSearchFilter() {
  document.querySelector('.menu .right input'
.addEventListener('keyup', (e) => {
      textToSearch = e.target.value;
      applyFilters();
    });
}
```

7. Now, back to the **applyFilters** function. The first function called in there is almost hidden. It's the **filterByTags** function, which filters the list of products using the **tagsToFilterBy** array. It recursively filters the list of products passed in using the selected tags:

```
function filterByTags() {
  let filtered = products;
  tagsToFilterBy
    .forEach((t) => filtered = filtered.filter(p => p.tags.includes(t)));
  return filtered;
}
```

8. Whatever comes out of the filter function is passed to another filter function, the one that filters the products based on the text search. The **filterByText** function transforms all text to lowercase before comparing. That way, the search will always be case-insensitive:

```javascript
function filterByText(products) {
  const txt = (textToSearch || '').toLowerCase();
  return products.filter((p) => {
    return p.name.toLowerCase().includes(txt)
      || p.description.toLowerCase().includes(txt);
  });
}
```

After filtering by the selected tags and filtering by the typed text, we pass the filtered values to **createListForProducts**, which is a function inside **create_ elements.js** and was described during this section, before the exercise.

9. Now that we have the new list of products already showing on the page, we need to re-register the tag filter event listener because the DOM tree elements were recreated. So, we call **addTagFilter** again. As shown previously, this is how the **applyFilters** function looks:

```javascript
function applyFilters() {
  createListForProducts(filterByText(filterByTags(products)));
  addTagFilter();
  updateTagFilterList();
}
```

10. The last function called in the **applyTagFilter** function is **updateTagFilterList**. This function will find the element that will hold the filter indicator, check whether there are tags selected to filter by, and update it accordingly, either setting the text to **No filters** or adding an indicator for each tag applied:

```javascript
function updateTagFilterList() {
  const tagHolder = document.querySelector('.item span.tags');
  if (tagsToFilterBy.length == 0) {
    tagHolder.innerHTML = 'No filters';
  } else {
    tagHolder.innerHTML = '';
    tagsToFilterBy.sort();
    tagsToFilterBy.map(createTagFilterLabel)
      .forEach((tEl) => tagHolder.appendChild(tEl));
  }
}
```

11. The last function we need to tie all of this together is the **createTagFilterLabel** function, which is used to create the indicator that a tag is selected in the search bar. This function will create the DOM element and add an event listener that, when clicked, will remove the tag from the array and call the **applyTagFilter** function again:

```
function createTagFilterLabel(tag) {
  const el = document.createElement('span');
  el.className = 'ui label orange';
  el.innerText = tag;

  el.addEventListener('click', () => {
    const index = tagsToFilterBy.indexOf(tag);
    tagsToFilterBy.splice(index, 1);
    applyTagFilter();
  });

  return el;
}
```

12. The last step you need to take to make the page work is to call the **applyTagFilter** function so that it will update the page to the initial state, which is no tags selected. Also, it will call **addTextSearchFilter** to add the event handler for the textbox:

```
addTextSearchFilter();
applyFilters();
```

Open the page in Chrome and you'll see that the filter is empty at the top and all products are shown in the list. It looks like the screenshot at the beginning of this exercise. Click on a tag or type something in the textbox and you'll see the page change to reflect the new state. For example, selecting the two **cookie** and **bakery** labels and typing **chocolate** in the textbox will make the page only show the products that have those two labels and **chocolate** in their name or description:

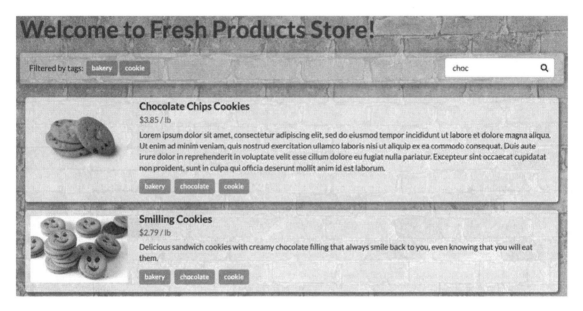

Figure 1.51: The storefront filtered by the two bakery and cookie tags and the word chocolate

In this exercise, you've learned how to respond to user events and change the page accordingly to reflect the state the user wants the page to be in. You've also learned that when elements get removed and re-added to the page, event handlers get lost and need to be re-registered.

Shadow DOM and Web Components

In previous sections, we've seen that a simple web application can require complex coding. When applications get bigger and bigger, they get harder and harder to maintain. The code starts to become tangled and a change in one place affects other unexpected places. That's because of the global nature of HTML, CSS, and JavaScript.

A lot of solutions have been created to try to circumvent this problem, and the **World Wide Web Consortium** (**W3C**) started to work on proposals for a standard way of creating custom, isolated components that could have their own styles and DOM root. Shadow DOM and custom components are two standards born from that initiative.

Shadow DOM is a way for you to create an isolated DOM subtree that can have its own styles and is not affected by styles added to the parent tree. It also isolates the HTML, which means IDs used on the document tree can be reused multiple times in each shadow tree.

The following figure illustrates the concepts involved when dealing with Shadow DOM:

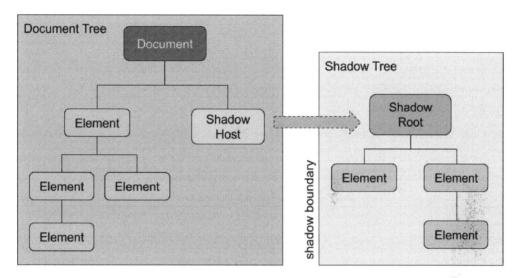

Figure 1.52: Shadow DOM concepts

Let's describe what these concepts mean:

- **Document Tree** is the main DOM tree for the page.
- **Shadow Host** is the node where the shadow tree is attached.
- **Shadow Tree** is an isolated DOM tree attached to the document tree.
- **Shadow Root** is the root element in the shadow tree.

The Shadow Host is an element in the document tree where the shadow tree is attached. The Shadow Root element is a node that is not displayed on the page, just like the document object in the main document tree.

To understand how this works, let's start with some HTML with some strange styles:

```
<style>
  p {
    background: #ccc;
    color: #003366;
  }
</style>
```

This would make every paragraph on the page have a greyish background with some blue color text in it. This is how a paragraph on this page would look:

This is a normal paragraph.

Figure 1.53: Paragraph with the styles applied

Let's add a shadow tree and add a paragraph into it to see how it behaves. We will wrap the paragraph element with a **div** element and add some text to it:

```
<div><p>I'm in a Shadow DOM tree.</p></div>
```

Then we can use the **attachShadow** method in an element to create a shadow root element:

```
const shadowHost = document.querySelector('div');
const shadowRoot = shadowHost.attachShadow({ mode: 'open' });
```

The preceding code selects the **div** element from the page and then calls the **attachShadow** method, passing a configuration object to it. The configuration says that this shadow tree is open, which means the shadow root for it can be accessed through the **shadowRoot** property of the element the shadow tree was attached to – **div**, in this case:

```
> document.querySelector('div').shadowRoot
<· ▶ #shadow-root (open)
```

Figure 1.54: Open shadow trees can be accessed through the element where the tree is attached

Shadow trees can be closed, but taking that approach is not recommended since it gives a false sense of security and it makes the user's life much harder.

After we attach a shadow tree to the document tree, we can start manipulating it. Let's copy the HTML from the shadow host into the shadow root and see what happens:

```
shadowRoot.innerHTML = shadowHost.innerHTML;
```

Now, if you load the page in Chrome, you'll see the following:

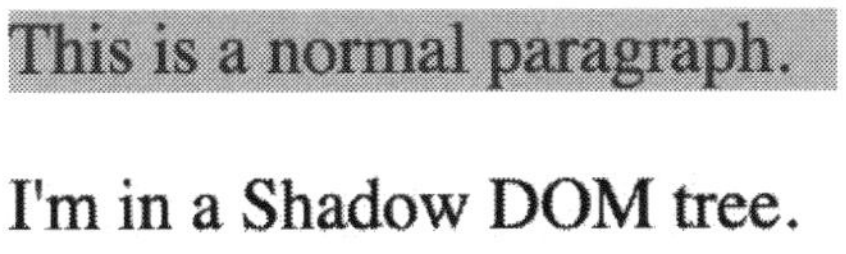

This is a normal paragraph.

I'm in a Shadow DOM tree.

Figure 1.55: Page with the shadow DOM loaded

You can see that even though the styles added to the page are selecting all paragraphs, the paragraph added to the shadow tree is not affected by it. The elements in the Shadow DOM are completely isolated from the document tree.

If you look at the DOM now, you'll see that something looks strange. The shadow tree replaces and wraps the paragraph that was inside the **div** element, which is the shadow host:

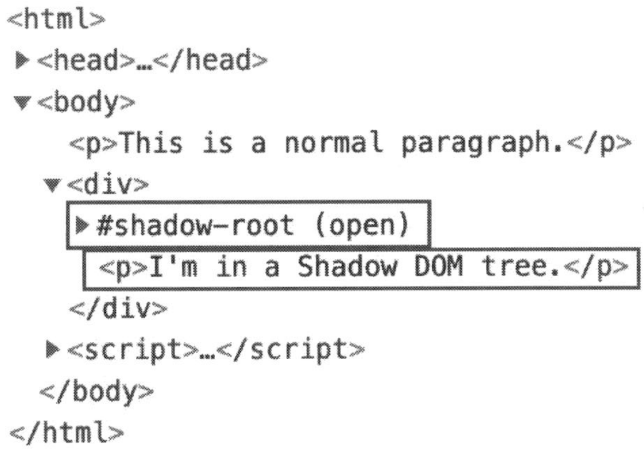

```
<html>
  ▶ <head>…</head>
  ▼ <body>
      <p>This is a normal paragraph.</p>
    ▼ <div>
        ▶ #shadow-root (open)
          <p>I'm in a Shadow DOM tree.</p>
      </div>
    ▶ <script>…</script>
    </body>
</html>
```

Figure 1.56: The shadow tree is at the same level as the other nodes in the shadow host

But the original paragraph inside the shadow host is not rendered on the page. That is because when the browser renders the page, if the element contains a shadow tree with new content, it will replace the current tree under the host. That process is called flattening and the following diagram depicts how it works:

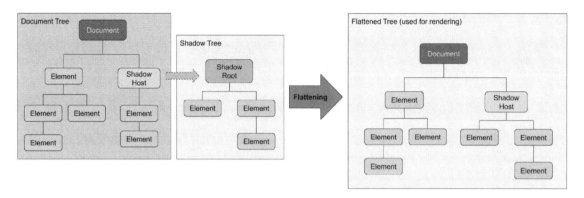

Figure 1.57: When flattened, the browser ignores the nodes under the shadow host

Now that we understand what Shadow DOM is, we can start using it to build or own HTML elements. That's right! With custom component APIs, you can create your own HTML element and then use it just like any other element.

In the rest of this section, we'll build a custom component called **counter**, which has two buttons and text in between. You can click the buttons to increment or decrement the value stored. You can also configure it to have an initial value and a different increment value. The following screenshot shows how the component will look when we are finished. The code for this lives on GitHub at https://bit.ly/2mVy1XP:

```
▶ <counter-component>…</counter-component>
▶ <counter-component value="7" increment="3">…</counter-component>
```

Figure 1.58: The counter component and how it is used in HTML

To define your custom component, you need to call the **define** method in the custom components registry. There's a global instance of the registry called **customElements**. To register your component you call **define**, passing the string that your component will be referenced by. It needs to have at least one dash. You also need to pass the constructor that instantiates your component. Here is the code:

```
customElements.define('counter-component', Counter);
```

Your constructor can be a normal function or, as in this example, you can use the new JavaScript **class** definition. It needs to extend **HTMLElement**:

```
class Counter extends HTMLElement {

}
```

For custom components to be isolated from the rest of the page, you use a shadow tree where the shadow host is your components element. You don't need to use Shadow DOM to build custom components, but it is recommended for more complex components that will also wrap some styles.

In the constructor of your element, you create the shadow root by calling **attachShadow** to your own instance:

```
constructor() {

    super(); // always call super first

    // Creates the shadow DOM to attach the parts of this component

    this.attachShadow({mode: 'open'});

    // ... more code here

}
```

Remember that when you attach a shadow DOM to an element using the **open** mode, the element stores that shadow root in a **shadowRoot** property. So, we can refer to it using **this.shadowRoot** from now on.

In the preceding figure, you saw that the **counter** component has two attributes that it uses to configure itself: **value** and **increment**. Those are set in the beginning of the constructor using the **getAttribute** method of **Element** and setting reasonable defaults, if they are not available:

```
this.value = parseInt(this.getAttribute('value') || 0);

this.increment = parseInt(this.getAttribute('increment') || 1);
```

After that, we create all the DOM elements for this component and append them to the shadow root. We're not going to dig into the details since you've seen enough DOM manipulation for now. In the constructor, we just call the functions that create those elements and append them using **this.shadowRoot.appendChild**:

```
// Create and attach the parts of this component

this.addStyles();

this.createButton('-', () => this.decrementValue());

this.createValueSpan();

this.createButton('+', () => this.incrementValue());
```

The first method creates a **link** element that imports the CSS file for the **counter** component. The second and fourth methods create the **decrement** and **increment** buttons and attach the event handlers. The third method creates a **span** element and keeps a reference to it under the **property** span.

The **incrementValue** and **decrementValue** methods increment the current value by the specified amount and then call an **updateState** method, which synchronizes the state of the values to the DOM (the Shadow DOM, in this case). The code for the **incrementValue** and **updateState** methods is as follows:

```
incrementValue() {
    this.value += this.increment;
    this.triggerValueChangedEvent();
    this.updateState();
}


updateState() {
    this.span.innerText = `Value is: ${this.value}`;
}
```

In the **incrementValue** function, we also call the function to trigger the event to notify users that the value changed. This function will be discussed later.

Now that you have your new **HTMLElement** defined and registered, you can use it just like any other existing HTML element. You can add it via tags in the HTML code as follows:

```
<counter-component></counter-component>
<counter-component value="7" increment="3"></counter-component>
```

Or, via JavaScript, by creating an element and appending it to the DOM:

```
const newCounter = document.createElement('counter-component');
newCounter.setAttribute('increment', '2');
newCounter.setAttribute('value', '3');
document.querySelector('div').appendChild(newCounter);
```

To completely understand the power of web components, there are two last things you need to know about: callbacks and events.

4. To expose the current state, we'll add a getter to the **_searchText** field:

    ```
    get searchText() {
        return this._searchText;
    ```

5. Still in the class, create a method called **render**, which will set **shadowRoot. innerHTML** to the template component we want. In this case, it will be the existing HTML for the search box plus a link to the semantic UI styles, so that we can reuse them:

    ```
    render() {
        this.shadowRoot.innerHTML = '
          <link rel="stylesheet" type="text/css" href="../css/semantic.min.css"
    />
          <div class="ui icon input">
            <input type="text" placeholder="Search..." />
            <i class="search icon"></i>
          </div>
        ';
    }
    ```

6. Create another method called **triggerTextChanged**, which will trigger an event to notify listeners that the search text changed. It receives the new text value and passes it to the listeners:

    ```
    triggerTextChanged(text) {
        const event = new CustomEvent('changed', {
            bubbles: true,
            detail: { text },
        });
        this.dispatchEvent(event);
    }
    ```

7. In the constructor, after attaching the shadow root, call the **render** method and register a listener to the input box so that we can trigger the changed event for our component. The constructor should now look like this:

    ```
    constructor() {
        super();
        this.attachShadow({ mode: 'open' });
        this._searchText = '';

        this.render();
        this.shadowRoot.querySelector('input').addEventListener('keyup', (e) =>
        {
    ```

```
            this._searchText = e.target.value;
            this.triggerTextChanged(this._searchText);
        });
    }
```

8. With our web component ready, we can replace the old search box with it. In the **dynamic_storefront.html** HTML, replace the **div** tag with the **ui**, **icon**, and **input** classes, and all their content, with the new component we created: **search-box**. Also, add the new JavaScript file to the HTML, before all other scripts. You can see the final HTML on GitHub at https://github.com/TrainingByPackt/Professional-JavaScript/blob/master/Lesson01/Exercise07/dynamic_storefront.html.

9. Save a reference to the **search-box** component by using the **querySelector** method from the document:

    ```
    const searchBoxElement = document.querySelector('search-box');
    ```

10. Register an event listener for the changed event so that we know when a new value is available and call **applyFilters**:

    ```
    searchBoxElement.addEventListener('changed', (e) => applyFilters());
    ```

11. Now we can clean the **filter_and_search.js** JavaScript since part of the logic was moved to the new component. We'll do the following cleanup:

    Remove the **textToSearch** variable (line 2) and replace it with **searchBoxElement. searchText** (line 40).

    Remove the **addTextSearchFilter** function (lines 16-22) and the call to it at the end of the script (line 70).

    If everything went fine, opening the file in Chrome will result in the exact same storefront, which is exactly what we wanted.

Now the logic to handle the search box and the search text is encapsulated, which means if we need to change it, we won't need to go around looking for pieces of code spread all around. And when we need to know the value of the search text, we can query the component that holds it for us.

Activity 2: Replacing the Tag Filter with a Web Component

Now that we've replaced the search box with a web component, let's replace the tag filter using the same technique. The idea is that we'll have a component that will store a list of selected tags.

This component will encapsulate the list of selected tags that can be modified by using **mutator** methods (**addTag** and **removeTag**). When the internal state mutates, a changed event gets triggered. Also, when a tag in the list is clicked, a **tag-clicked** event will be triggered.

Steps:

1. Start by copying the code from Exercise 7 into a new folder.

2. Create a new file called **tags_holder.js** and in it add a class called **TagsHolder** that extends **HTMLElement**, then define a new custom component called **tags-holder**.

3. Create two **render** methods: one to render the base state and one to render the tags or some text indicating that no tags are selected for filtering.

4. In the constructor, call **super**, attach the component to the shadow root, initialize the list of selected tags, and call both **render** methods.

5. Create a getter to expose the list of selected tags.

6. Create two trigger methods: one to trigger the **changed** event and one to trigger the **tag-clicked** event.

7. Create two **mutator** methods: **addTag** and **removeTag**. These methods receive the tag name and add tag if not present, or remove the tag if present, in the list of selected tags. If the list was modified, trigger the **changed** event and call the method to re-render the list of tags.

8. In the HTML, replace the existing code with the new component and add the new script file to it.

9. In **filter_and_search.js**, remove the **tagsToFilterBy** variable and replace it with the new **mutator** methods and events in the newly created component.

> ### Note
> The solution for this activity can be found on page 584.

Summary

In this chapter, we explored the DOM specification by learning about its base interfaces, its properties, and its methods. We learned about the relationship between the HTML you write and the tree the browser generates from it. We queried the DOM and navigated the DOM tree. We learned how to create new elements, add them to the tree, and manipulate existing elements. Lastly, we learned how to use Shadow DOM to create isolated DOM trees and custom components that can be easily reused in HTML pages.

In the next chapter, we'll switch gears to the backend world. We'll start learning about Node.js and the basic concepts around it. We'll go through how to install and manage multiple versions of Node.js using **nvm**, and last but not least, we'll also learn about **npm** and how to find and use external modules.

2

Node.js and npm

Learning Objectives

By the end of this chapter, you will be able to:

- Install and use Node.js to build applications

- Run JavaScript code using the Node.js execution environment

- Install and manage multiple Node.js versions using nvm

- Identify and use modules developed by other developers using npm

- Create and configure your own npm package

In this chapter, we will switch gears to the backend world by learning about Node.js and the basic concepts around it. We will go through how to install and manage multiple versions of Node.js using nvm, and then we will learn about npm and how to find and use external modules.

Introduction

In the previous chapter, we learned about how HTML becomes the DOM and how to use JavaScript to query and manipulate the content of a page.

Before JavaScript, all pages were static. After Netscape introduced the scripting environment to its browser, developers started using it to create dynamic and responsive applications. The applications started to become more and more complex but the only place where JavaScript was running was inside the browser. Then, in 2009, Ryan Dahl, the original developer of Node.js, decided to create a way to run JavaScript on the server side, simplifying the web developer's life by allowing them to build applications without having to depend on other languages.

In this chapter, you will learn how Node.js works and how to use it to create scripts using JavaScript. You will learn about the basics of the Node.js core APIs, where to find their documentation, and how to use their **read-eval-print loop** (**REPL**) command line.

With the skills to build JavaScript code, you will then learn how to manage multiple versions of Node.js and understand the importance of Node.js. You will also learn what npm is and how to import and use packages from other developers and build Node.js applications.

What is Node.js?

Node.js is an execution environment that runs on top of the V8 JavaScript engine. Its base premise is that it is asynchronous and event-driven. This means that all the blocking operations, such as reading data from a file, can be handled in the background while the other parts of the application continue to do their work. When the data has finished loading, an event is emitted and whoever was waiting for the data can now execute and do the work.

From its inception, Node.js was designed to serve as an efficient backend for web applications. Because of that, it was widely adopted by companies of all sizes and industry types. Trello, LinkedIn, PayPal, and NASA are some of the companies that use Node.js in multiple parts of their technology stack.

But what is an execution environment? An execution environment provides basic functionality, such as APIs, for a programmer to write applications. Think about the browser, for example – it has the DOM, objects such as documents and windows, functions such as `setTimeout` and `fetch`, and so many other things you can do in the frontend world. All of that is part of the browser's execution environment. Since that execution environment is focused on the browser, it provides ways for you to interact with the DOM and to communicate with the server, which is all that exists in it.

Node.js focuses on creating an environment for developers to build the backend part of web applications in an efficient way. It provides APIs to create HTTP(S) servers, read/write files, manipulate processes, and so on.

Node.js, as we mentioned previously, uses the V8 JavaScript engine underneath the hood. This means that to transform the JavaScript text into executable code for the computer to process, it uses V8, the open source JavaScript engine built by Google to power the Chromium and Chrome browsers. The following is an illustration of this process:

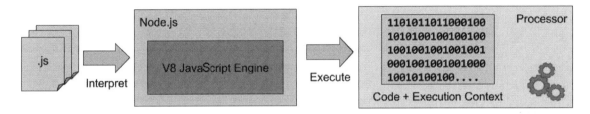

Figure 2.1: Node.js uses the V8 engine to transform JavaScript source code into executable code that runs in the processor

The execution environment that Node.js provides is single-threaded. This means that only one piece of JavaScript code can execute at each given moment. But Node.js has something called an event loop, which is a way to take code that is waiting for something, such as reading data from a file, and put it in a queue while another piece of code can execute.

Reading or writing data from files and sending or receiving data through the network are all tasks that are handled by the system kernel, which is multithreaded in most modern systems. Due to this, some of the work ends up being distributed in multiple threads. But for developers who are working in the Node.js execution environment, that is all hidden away in the form of a programming paradigm called asynchronous programming.

Asynchronous programming means that you are going to ask some tasks to be executed and when the result is available, your code will be executed. Let's go back to the read data from a file example. In most programming languages and paradigms, you would just write some pseudocode, like so:

```
var file = // open file here
var data = file.read(); // do something with data here
```

With the asynchronous programming model, this works in a different way. You open the file and tell Node.js that you want to read it. You also give it a callback function, which will be called when the data is available to you. This is what the pseudocode looks like:

```
var file = // open file here

file.read((data) => {

   // do something with data here

});
```

In this example, the script would be loaded, and execution would start. The script would execute line by line and open the file. When it gets to the read operation, it starts reading the file and schedules the callback to be executed later. After that, it reaches the end of the script.

When Node.js reaches the end of the script, it starts processing the event loop. The event loop is divided into phases. Each phase has a queue that stores code that's scheduled to run in them. I/O operations get scheduled in the poll phase, for example. There are six phases, and they are executed in the following order:

1. **Timers**: Code that's scheduled using `setTimeout` or `setInterval`

2. **Pending Callbacks**: Deferred callbacks for the I/O from the previous cycle

3. **Idle, Prepare**: Internal only

4. **Poll**: Code that's scheduled for I/O handling

5. **Check**: The `setImmediate` callbacks are executed here

6. **Close callbacks**: Code that's scheduled on closing sockets, for example

Node.js has two methods of execution. The most used one is when you pass in the path of a file, from where the JavaScript code will be loaded and executed. The second method is in the REPL. If you execute the Node.js command without giving it any arguments, it will start in REPL mode, which is like the Console from the Dev Tools, which we looked at in the previous chapter. Let's explore this in detail in the next exercise.

Exercise 8: Running Your First Node.js Commands

In this exercise, you will download and install Node.js on your computer, create your first script, and run it. Then, we will use the REPL tool that comes with Node.js and run some commands in there.

> **Note**
>
> To be able to run Node.js applications, you need to have it installed on your machine. For that, you can go to **nodejs.org** and download a Node.js package. It is recommended to download the latest **Long-Term Support** (**LTS**) version, which will give you the most stable and longest support time for security and bug patches. At the time of this writing, that version is **10.16.0**.

Perform the following steps to complete this exercise:

1. After downloading and installing Node.js, go to the command line and check the version you have installed:

    ```
    $ node -version
    v10.16.0
    ```

2. Now, create a new text file called **event_loop.js** and add an extended version of the code (event loop example), as shown previously. This is what it looks like:

    ```
    console.log('First');

    const start = Date.now();
    setTimeout(() => {
      console.log(`Last, after: ${Date.now() - start}ms`);
    }, 100);

    console.log('Second');
    ```

3. To run JavaScript using Node.js, call **node** and pass the path to the file you want to execute. To run the file you just created, execute the following code in the command line from the directory where you created the file:

```
$ node event_loop.js
```

You will see the following output:

```
$ node event_loop.js
First
Second
Last, after: 106ms
```

The time you see in the end will vary on every run. This is because **setTimeout** only ensures that the code will run after the specified time, but it can't guarantee that it will execute exactly at the time you asked it to.

4. Run the **node** command without any argument; you will go into REPL mode:

```
$ node
>
```

The > indicates that you are now inside the Node.js execution environment.

5. In the REPL command line, type in a command and press *Enter* to execute it. Let's try the first one:

```
> console.log('First');
First
Undefined
```

You can see that it prints the string you passed into the **console.log** call. It also prints **Undefined**. This is the return value of the last executed statement. Since **console.log** doesn't return anything, it printed undefined.

6. Create the constant that stores the current time:

```
> const start = Date.now()
undefined
```

7. Declaring a variable also doesn't return anything, so it prints **undefined** again:

```
> start
1564326469948
```

If you want to know what the value of a variable is, you can just type the name of the variable and press *Enter*. The return statement of the variable name is the variable value, so it prints the value for it.

8. Now, type the **setTimeout** call, just like it was in your file. If you press *Enter* and your statement is incomplete because you are starting a function or opening parenthesis, Node.js will print an ellipsis indicating that it is waiting for the rest of the command:

```
> setTimeout(() => {
...
```

9. You can continue typing until all of the commands have been typed out. The **setTimeout** function returns a **Timeout** object, and you can see it in the console. You can also see the text that's printed when the callback is executed:

```
> setTimeout(() => {
...     console.log('Last, after: ${Date.now() - start}ms');
... }, 100);
```

The following is the output of the preceding code:

```
Timeout {
  _called: false,
  _idleTimeout: 100,
  _idlePrev: [TimersList],
  _idleNext: [TimersList],
  _idleStart: 490704,
  _onTimeout: [Function],
  _timerArgs: undefined,
  _repeat: null,
  _destroyed: false,
  domain: [Domain],
  [Symbol(unrefed)]: false,
  [Symbol(asyncId)]: 492,
  [Symbol(triggerId)]: 5 }
> Last, after: 13252ms
```

You can see that the time that's printed is much longer than **100** ms. This is because the **start** variable was declared some time ago and it is subtracting the current time from that initial value. So, that time indicates the **100** ms, plus the time it took for you to type and execute the command.

10. Try changing the value of **start**. You will observe that Node.js won't let you do it since we declared it as a constant:

```
> start = Date.now();
Thrown:
TypeError: Assignment to constant variable.
```

We could try to redeclare it as a variable but Node.js won't let us since it was already declared in the current environment:

```
> let start = Date.now()
Thrown:
SyntaxError: Identifier 'start' has already been declared
```

11. Declare the whole scheduling of the timeout inside another function to get a new scope every time the function is executed:

```
> const scheduleTimeout = () => {
... const start = Date.now();
... setTimeout(() => {
..... console.log('Later, after: ${Date.now() - start}');
..... }, 100);
... };
```

Every time you call the function, it will schedule it and execute it after **100** ms, just like in your script. This would output the following:

```
Undefined
> scheduleTimeout
[Function: scheduleTimeout]
> scheduleTimeout()
Undefined
> Later, after: 104
```

12. To exit the REPL tool, you can press *Ctrl* + *C* twice or type **.exit** and then press *Enter*:

```
>
(To exit, press ^C again or type .exit)
>
```

It is easy to install Node.js and start using it. Its REPL tool allows you to quickly prototype and test things. Knowing how to use both can boost your productivity and help you a lot in the day-to-day development of JavaScript applications.

In this exercise, you installed Node.js, wrote a simple program, and learned how to run it using Node.js. You also used the REPL tool to explore the Node.js execution environment and run some code.

Node Version Manager (nvm)

Node.js and JavaScript have a huge community and a very fast-paced development cycle. Because of this rapid development and its release cycles, it is very easy to become out of date (check Node.js's previous releases page for more information: https://nodejs.org/en/download/releases/).

Can you imagine working on a project that uses Node.js and is a few years old? By the time you come back to fix a bug, you will notice that the version you have installed can't run the code anymore because of some compatibility issues. Or, you will find that you can't change the code using your current version since what is running in production is a couple of years old and doesn't have async/await or some other lifesaving feature you use a lot in the most recent version.

That issue happens with all programming languages and development environments, but in Node.js, this is prominent because of the extremely fast release cycles.

To solve this, it is common to use a version management tool so that you can quickly switch between versions of Node.js. **Node Version Manager** (**nvm**) is a widely used tool that's used to manage installed versions of Node.js. You can find instructions on how to download and install it at https://github.com/nvm-sh/nvm.

> **Note**
>
> If you are using Windows, you can try nvm-windows (https://github.com/coreybutler/nvm-windows), which provides similar functionality for nvm in Linux and Mac. Also, in this chapter, many commands are specific to Mac and Linux. For Windows, please refer to the help section of **nvm-windows**.

The installer script does two things in your system:

1. Creates a .nvm directory inside your home directory where it puts all the scripts that are necessary for working with and keeping all the managed versions of Node. js

2. Adds some configuration to make nvm available in all Terminal sessions

nvm is very simple to use and very well-documented. The idea behind it is that you will have multiple versions of Node.js running in your machine and you can quickly install new versions and switch between them.

In my computer, I initially only had the Node.js version I downloaded some time ago (10.16.0). After installing nvm, I ran the command to list all the versions. The following is the output:

```
$ nvm ls


->system
iojs -> N/A (default)
node -> stable (-> N/A) (default)
unstable -> N/A (default)
```

You can see that I have no other versions available. I also have a system version, which is whatever version you have installed in your system. I could check the current Node.js version by running **node --version**:

```
$ node --version
v10.16.0
```

As an example of how to use nvm, let's say you wanted to test some experimental features on the latest version. The first thing you need to do is find out which version that is. So, you run the **nvm ls-remote** command (or the **nvm list** command for a Windows system), which is the list remote versions command:

```
$ nvm ls-remote
        v0.1.14
        v0.1.15
        v0.1.16

   . . .

    v10.15.3    (LTS: Dubnium)
    v10.16.0    (Latest LTS: Dubnium)

   . . .

     v12.6.0
     v12.7.0
```

That prints a long list with all the versions available. The last one, 12.7.0, at the time of writing, is the latest, so let's install that one. To install any version, run the **nvm install <version>** command. This will download the Node.js binaries for the specified version, verify that the package is not corrupted, and set it as the current version in your Terminal:

```
$ nvm install 12.7.0

Downloading and installing node v12.7.0...

Downloading https://nodejs.org/dist/v12.7.0/node-v12.7.0-darwin-x64.tar.
xz...

#####################################################################
100.0%

Computing checksum with shasum -a 256

Checksums matched!

Now using node v12.7.0 (npm v6.10.0)
```

Now, you can verify that you have the latest version installed and ready to be used in your Terminal:

```
$ node --version

v12.7.0
```

Alternatively, you could just use the alias **node**, which is an alias to the latest version. But for Windows, you will need to mention the specific version that needs to be installed:

```
$ nvm install node

v12.7.0 is already installed.

Now using node v12.7.0 (npm v6.10.0)
```

It is common for widely used frameworks and languages (such as Node.js) to have LTS for specific versions. These LTS versions are considered more stable and guaranteed to have longer support for bug and security fixes, which is important for companies or teams that can't migrate to new versions as fast as the normal release cycles. If you want to use the most latest LTS version, you can use the **--lts** option:

```
$ nvm install --lts

Installing the latest LTS version.

Downloading and installing node v10.16.0...

Downloading https://nodejs.org/dist/v10.16.0/node-v10.16.0-darwin-x64.tar.
xz...

#####################################################################
100.0%
```

```
Computing checksum with shasum -a 256

Checksums matched!

Now using node v10.16.0 (npm v6.9.0)
```

After installing multiple versions of Node.js using nvm, you can switch between them by using the **use** command:

```
$ nvm use system --version

Now using system version of node: v10.16.0 (npm v6.9.0)


$ nvm use node

Now using node v12.7.0 (npm v6.10.0)


$ nvm use 7

Now using node v7.10.1 (npm v4.2.0)
```

When you have multiple projects and you switch between them frequently, it is hard to remember the Node.js version you are using for each one. To make our lives easier, nvm supports a configuration file in the project's directory. You can just add a **.nvmrc** file in the root of the project and it will use the version that is in the file. You can also have an **.nvmrc** file in any parent directory of the project. So, if you want to group projects by Node.js version in a parent directory, you could add the configuration file in that parent directory.

For example, if you have a **.nvmrc** file in a folder that's version **12.7.0**, when you change into the folder and run **nvm use**, it will automatically pick that version:

```
$ cat .nvmrc

12.7.0


$ nvm use

Found '.../Lesson02/Exercise09/.nvmrc' with version <12.7.0>

Now using node v12.7.0 (npm v6.10.0)
```

Exercise 9: Using nvm to Manage Versions

As we mentioned previously, Node.js releases have a very short cycle. If you look for the URL class, for example (https://nodejs.org/dist/latest-v12.x/docs/api/url.html#url_class_url), you will see that only recently has it become available in the global scope. This happened in version 10.0.0, which is only about a year old at the time of writing.

In this exercise, we will write an **.nvmrc** file, install multiple versions of Node.js using nvm, and experiment with different versions to see what type of error you get when you are using the wrong version of Node.js.

Perform the following steps to complete this exercise:

1. Add an **.nvmrc** file to your project. In an empty folder, create a file called **.nvmrc** and add the number 12.7.0 to it. You can do that in one command by using the **echo** command and redirecting the output to the file:

   ```
   $ echo '12.7.0' > .nvmrc
   ```

2. You can check that the file has the content you want by using **cat**:

   ```
   $ cat .nvmrc
   12.7.0
   ```

3. Let's use **nvm use** command, which will try to use the version from inside the **.nvmrc** file:

   ```
   $ nvm use
   Found '.../Lesson02/Exercise09/.nvmrc' with version <12.7.0>
   N/A: version "12.7.0 -> N/A" is not yet installed.
   ```

   You need to run **nvm install 12.7.0** to install it before using it. If you don't have the specified version installed, nvm will give you a clear message.

4. Call **nvm install** to install the version the project needs:

   ```
   $ nvm install
   Found '.../Lesson02/Exercise09/.nvmrc' with version <12.7.0>
   Downloading and installing node v12.7.0...
   Downloading https://nodejs.org/dist/v12.7.0/node-v12.7.0-darwin-x64.tar.
   xz...
   ############################################################################
   100.0%
   Computing checksum with shasum -a 256
   Checksums matched!
   Now using node v12.7.0 (npm v6.10.0)
   ```

Notice that you don't have to pass the version you want since nvm will pick this up from the **.nvmrc** file.

5. Now, create a file called **url_explorer.js**. In it, create an instance of the URL by passing a complete URL to it. Let's also add some calls to explore the parts of a URL:

```
const url = new URL('https://www.someserver.com/not/a/
path?param1=value1&param2=value2`);
console.log(`URL is: ${url.href}`);
console.log(`Hostname: ${url.hostname}`);
console.log(`Path: ${url.pathname}`);


console.log(`Query string is: ${url.search}`);
console.log(`Query parameters:`)
Array.from(url.searchParams.entries())
   .forEach((entry) => console.log(`\t- ${entry[0]} = ${entry[1]}`));
```

6. Run the script. You will see that the URL is parsed correctly and that all the details about it are printed to the console correctly:

```
$ node url_explorer.js
URL is: https://www.someserver.com/not/a/path?param1=value1&param2=value2
Hostname: www.someserver.com
Path: /not/a/path
Query string is: ?param1=value1&param2=value2
Query parameters:
      - param1 = value1
      - param2 = value2
```

7. Now, let's experiment with the wrong version of Node.js. Install version **9.11.2** using **nvm**:

```
$ nvm install 9.11.2
Downloading and installing node v9.11.2...
Downloading https://nodejs.org/dist/v9.11.2/node-v9.11.2-darwin-x64.tar.
xz...
######################################################################## 100.0%
Computing checksum with shasum -a 256
Checksums matched!
Now using node v9.11.2 (npm v5.6.0)
```

8. Now, you can run **url_explorer.js** again and see what happens:

```
$ node url_explorer.js
.../Exercise09/url_explorer.js:1 ... { const url = new URL('...');^
ReferenceError: URL is not defined
    at Object.<anonymous> (.../Exercise09/url_explorer.js:1:75)
    at Module._compile (internal/modules/cjs/loader.js:654:30)
    at Object.Module._extensions..js (internal/modules/cjs/loader.
js:665:10)
    at Module.load (internal/modules/cjs/loader.js:566:32)
    at tryModuleLoad (internal/modules/cjs/loader.js:506:12)
    at Function.Module._load (internal/modules/cjs/loader.js:498:3)
    at Function.Module.runMain (internal/modules/cjs/loader.js:695:10)
    at startup (internal/bootstrap/node.js:201:19)
    at bootstrapNodeJSCore (internal/bootstrap/node.js:516:3)
```

You should see an error similar to the one in the preceding code. It is telling you that the URL is not defined. That is because, as we mentioned previously, the URL class only became globally available in version 10.0.0.

9. Fix the version of Node.js and run the script again to see the correct output:

```
$ nvm use
Found '.../Lesson02/Exercise09/.nvmrc' with version <12.7.0>
Now using node v12.7.0 (npm v6.10.0)

$ node url_explorer.js
URL is: https://www.someserver.com/not/a/path?param1=value1&param2=value2
Hostname: www.someserver.com
Path: /not/a/path
Query string is: ?param1=value1&param2=value2
Query parameters:
    - param1 = value1
    - param2 = value2
```

The error message in step 7 doesn't mention the Node.js version. It is just some cryptic error about a missing class. Errors like these are hard to identify and take a lot of effort in terms of history hunting. This is why having .**nvmrc** in the root of your project is important. It makes it easy for other developers to quickly identify and use the correct version.

In this exercise, you learned how to install and use multiple versions of Node.js, and also learned how to create a .**nvmrc** file for a project. Finally, you looked at the type of errors you expect to see when you use the wrong version, as well as the importance of the .**nvmrc** files.

Node Package Manager (npm)

When someone talks about **Node Package Manager** or npm for short, they can be referring to one or more of the following three things:

- A command-line application that manages packages for a Node.js application
- The repository where developers and companies publish their packages for others to use
- The website where people manage their profile and search for packages

Most programming languages offer at least one way for developers to share packages with each other: Java has Maven, C# has NuGet, Python has PIP, and so on. Node.js started to ship with its own package manager just a few months after its initial release.

Packages can include any type of code that developers think would be useful to others. And sometimes, they also include tools to aid developers in terms of local development.

As the packaged code needs to be shared, there needs to be a repository where all the packages are stored. And to publish their packages, authors need to sign up and register themselves and their packages. This explains the repository and the website part.

The third part, that is, the command-line tool, is the actual package manager for your application. It comes with Node.js and can be used to set up a new project, manage dependencies, and manage scripts for your application, such as build and test scripts.

> **Note**
>
> A Node.js project or application is also considered a package since it contains a **package.json** file that represents what is in the package. So, it is common to use the following terms interchangeably: application, package, and project.

Every Node.js package has a **package.json** file that describes the project and its dependencies. To create one for your project, you can use the **npm init** command. Just run it inside the folder where you want your project to live:

```
$ cd sample_npm

$ npm init

This utility will walk you through creating a package.json file.

It only covers the most common items and tries to guess sensible defaults.

See 'npm help json' for definitive documentation on these fields and exactly what they do.

Use 'npm install <pkg>' afterwards to install a package and save it as a dependency in the package.json file.

Press ^C at any time to quit.

package name: (sample_npm)

version: (1.0.0)

description: Sample project for the Professional JavaScript.

entry point: (index.js)

test command:

git repository: https://github.com/TrainingByPackt/Professional-JavaScript/

keywords:

author:

license: (ISC) MIT

About to write to .../Lesson02/sample_npm/package.json:

{
  "name": "sample_npm",
  "version": "1.0.0",
  "description": "Sample project for the Professional JavaScript.",
  "main": "index.js",
```

```
  "scripts": {
    "test": "echo \"Error: no test specified\" && exit 1"
  },
  "repository": {
    "type": "git",
    "url": "git+https://github.com/TrainingByPackt/Professional-JavaScript.
git"
  },
  "author": "",
  "license": "MIT",
  "bugs": {
    "url": "https://github.com/TrainingByPackt/Professional-JavaScript/
issues"
  },
  "homepage": "https://github.com/TrainingByPackt/Professional-
JavaScript#readme"
}
Is this OK? (yes) yes
```

The command will ask you a few questions, guiding you regarding the creation of your **package.json** file. In the end, it will print the generated file and ask you to confirm it. It contains all the information about the project, including where to find the code, what license it uses, and who the author is.

Now that we have an npm package, we can start looking for external modules we can use. Let's go to https://npmjs.com and look for a package to help us parse command-line arguments. Typing **command line** into the search box and pressing *Enter* gives us a list of packages to choose from:

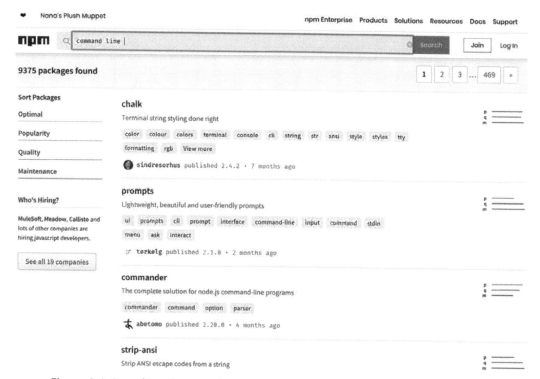

Figure 2.4: Searching for a package to help us build a command-line application

Since we are looking for a tool to help us parse command-line arguments, **commander** sounds like a good solution. Its short description is **The complete solution for node.js command-line programs**. Let's install that in an application and use it to understand how this flow works.

To add a package as a dependency to your package, you ask npm to install it by name from the command line:

```
$ npm install commander
```

npm notice created a lockfile as package-lock.json. You should commit this file.

```
+ commander@2.20.0
```

added 1 package from 1 contributor and audited 1 package in 1.964s

found 0 vulnerabilities

You can see that npm found the package and downloaded the latest version, which is 2.20.0 as of this writing. It also mentions something about a **package-lock.json** file. We are going to talk more about that later, so don't worry about it for now.

Another cool feature that was added to npm recently is vulnerability checks. At the end of the **install** command output, you can see a note about vulnerabilities found, or better, no vulnerabilities found. The npm team is doing a great job of increasing the vulnerability checks and security scans for all the packages in their repository.

> **Note**
>
> It is so easy to use packages from npm that a lot of people out there are pushing malicious code to catch the least-attentive developers. It is highly recommended that you pay a lot of attention when installing packages from npm. Check the spelling, the download count, and the vulnerability reports and make sure that the package you are going to install is really the one you want. You also need to ensure that it is from a trusted party.

After running **npm install**, you will notice that a new section has been added to your **package.json** file. It is the **dependencies** section and contains the package you just asked for:

```
"dependencies": {
    "commander": "^2.20.0"
}
```

That is what the + sign in front of **commander** in the output of the **install** command meant: that the package was added as a dependency to your project.

The **dependencies** section is used to automatically detect and install all the packages that your project needs. When you are working on a Node.js application that has a **package.json** file, you don't have to manually install each dependency. You can just run **npm install** and it will figure everything out based on the **dependencies** section of the **package.json** file. Here is an example:

```
$ npm install
added 1 package from 1 contributor and audited 1 package in 0.707s
found 0 vulnerabilities
```

Even though no package was specified, npm assumes you want to install all the dependencies for the current package, which reads from **package.json**.

Besides adding the **dependencies** section to your **package.json** file, it also created a **node_modules** folder. That is where it downloads and keep all the packages for your project. You can check what is inside **node_modules** by using the list command (**ls**):

```
$ ls node_modules/

commander
```

```
$ ls node_modules/commander/

CHANGELOG.md  LICENSE  Readme.md  index.js  package.json  typings
```

If you run **npm install** again to install the commander, you will notice that npm won't install the package again. It only shows the package as updated and audited:

```
$ npm install commander

+ commander@2.20.0

updated 1 package and audited 1 package in 0.485s

found 0 vulnerabilities
```

In the next exercise, we will build an npm package that uses commander as a dependency and then creates a command-line HTML generator.

Exercise 10: Creating a Command-Line HTML Generator

Now that you have learned the basics of using npm to create a package and how to install some dependencies, let's put this all together and build a command-line tool that can generate HTML templates for your next website project.

In this exercise, you will create an npm package that uses commander as a dependency to process command-line arguments. Then, you will explore the tool that you have created and generate some HTML files.

The code for this exercise can be found on GitHub at https://github.com/TrainingByPackt/Professional-JavaScript/tree/master/Lesson02/Exercise10.

Perform the following steps to complete this exercise:

1. Create a new folder where you are going to put all the files for this exercise.

2. In the command line, change to the new folder and run **npm init** to initialize a **package.json** file. Picking all the default options should be enough:

```
$ npm init
This utility will walk you through creating a package.json file.
...
Press ^C at any time to quit.
package name: (Exercise10)
version: (1.0.0)
...
About to write to .../Lesson02/Exercise10/package.json:

{
  "name": "Exercise10",
  "version": "1.0.0",
  "description": "",
  "main": "index.js",
  "scripts": {
    "test": "echo \"Error: no test specified\" && exit 1"
  },
  "author": "",
  "license": "ISC"
}

Is this OK? (yes)
```

3. Install the **commander** package as a dependency:

```
$ npm install commander
npm notice created a lockfile as package-lock.json. You should commit this
file.
+ commander@2.20.0
added 1 package from 1 contributor and audited 1 package in 0.842s
found 0 vulnerabilities
```

In your **package.json**, add the following:

```
"main": "index.js"
```

This means that the entry point for our application is the **index.js** file.

4. Run an npm package that has an entry point and use the **node** command, passing the directory that contains the **package.json** file in it. The following is an example that runs the package in **Lesson02/sample_npm**, which is available at https://github. com/TrainingByPackt/Professional-JavaScript/tree/master/Lesson02/sample_ npm:

```
$ node sample_npm/
I'm an npm package running from sample_npm
```

5. Create a file called **index.js** and in it, load the **commander** package using the **require** function:

```
const program = require('commander');
```

That is all you need to start using an external package.

Commander parses the arguments that are passed into your Node.js application. You can configure it to tell it what type of parameters you are expecting. For this application, we will have three options: **-b** or **--add-bootstrap**, which adds bootstrap 4 to the generated output; **-c** or **--add-container**, which adds a **<div>** tag with the ID container in the body; and **-t** or **--title**, which adds a **<title>** to the page that accepts the text to add in the title.

6. To configure commander, we call the version method and then the option method multiple times to add each option that our application will support. Lastly, we call **parse**, which will verify that the arguments that are passed in (**process.argv** will be discussed in detail in the next chapter) match the expected options:

```
program.version('0.1.0')
    .option('-b, --add-bootstrap', 'Add Bootstrap 4 to the page.')
    .option('-c, --add-container', 'Adds a div with container id in the
body.')
    .option('-t, --title [title]', 'Add a title to the page.')
    .parse(process.argv);
```

7. Now, you can run your application and check out the results so far:

```
$ node . -help
```

We will receive the following output:

```
Usage: Exercise10 [options]
Options:
  -V, --version           output the version number
  -b, --add-bootstrap     Add Bootstrap 4 to the page.
  -c, --add-container     Adds a div with container id in the body.
  -t, --title [title]     Add a title to the page.
  -h, --help              output usage information
```

You can see that commander gives you a nice help message explaining how your tool is supposed to be used.

8. Now, let's use these options to generate the HTML. The first thing we need to do is declare a variable that will hold all the HTML:

```
let html = '<html><head>';
```

We can initialize it with the **<html>** and **<head>** opening tags.

9. Then, check whether the program received the **title** option. If it did, add a **<title>** tag with the content passed in the tag:

```
if (program.title) {
    html += `<title>${program.title}</title>`;
}
```

10. Do the same thing for the **Bootstrap** option. In this case, the option is just a Boolean, so you just check and add a **<link>** tag pointing to the **Bootstrap.css** file:

```
if (program.addBootstrap) {
    html += '<link';
    html += ' rel="stylesheet"';
    html += ' href="https://stackpath.bootstrapcdn.com';
    html += '/bootstrap/4.3.1/css/bootstrap.min.css"';
    html += '/>';
}
```

11. Close the **<head>** tag and open the **<body>** tag:

```
html += '</head><body>';
```

12. Check for the container **<div>** option and add it if enabled:

```
if (program.addContainer) {
    html += '<div id="container"></div>';
}
```

13. Finally, close the **\<body>** and **\<html>** tags and print the HTML to the console:

```
html += '</body></html>';
console.log(html);
```

14. Running the application with no options will give us a very simple HTML:

```
$ node .
<html><head></head><body></body></html>
```

15. Run the application, enabling all the options:

```
$ node . -b -t Title -c

This will return a more elaborate HTML:

<html><head><title>Title</title><link rel="stylesheet" href="https://
stackpath.bootstrapcdn.com/bootstrap/4.3.1/css/bootstrap.min.css"/></
head><body><div id="container"></div></body></html>
```

npm makes it really easy to use packages in your applications. Packages such as commander and the other hundreds of thousands in the npm repository make Node. js a great alternative for building powerful and complex applications with very little code. Exploring and learning how to use packages can save you a lot of time and effort, making the difference between a project that never sees the light of day and a successful application that's used by millions of users.

In this exercise, you created an npm package that uses an external package to parse command-line arguments, which in general is a laborious task. You have configured the commander to parse the arguments into a nice useable format and also learned how to use the parsed arguments to build an application that makes decisions based on input from the user.

Dependencies

In the previous section, we saw how npm uses the **dependencies** section of your **package.json** file to keep track of the dependencies your package has. Dependencies are a complex topic, but what you must keep in mind is that npm supports the semantic version, or semver, format for version numbers and that it can use interval and other complicated operators to determine what versions of other packages yours can accept.

By default, as we saw in the previous exercise, npm marks all the package versions with a caret, such as 2.20.0. That caret means that your package can use any version that's compatible with 2.20.0. Compatibility, in the sense of semver, means that new minor or patch versions are considered valid since they are backward compatible:

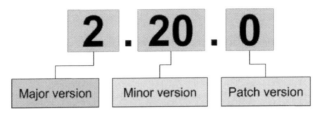

Figure 2.5: Semantic format considering minor and patch versions as valid

Compatible versions with 2.20.0 are 2.21.0 or 2.21.5, or even 2.150.47!

Every now and then, you will want to update the versions of your packages to improve security or move to a version that has a fix for some issue you hit in one of your dependencies. That is the reason why npm adds the caret for versions of packages you install. With one command, you can update all your dependencies to newer compatible versions.

Let's say, for example, that a command-line application that was started a long time ago was using version 2.0.0 of commander. When the developer ran the **install** command, they got version 2.0.0 in their **package.json** file. A few years later, they go back and notice that there are some security vulnerabilities in commander. They can just run the **npm update** command to take care of that:

```
$ npm update
+ commander@2.20.0
added 1 package from 1 contributor and audited 1 package in 0.32s
found 0 vulnerabilities
```

Most of the time, developers follow the semver convention and do not make breaking changes with minor or patch version changes. But when projects grow, the number of dependencies quickly gets to the thousands or even tens of thousands, and the probability of breaking changes or compatibility issues grows exponentially.

To help you in times when you get complicated dependency trees, npm also generates a **package-lock.json** file. This file contains a representation of the packages in your **node_modules** directory, as they were when you last changed the packages you depend on. This can happen when you install a new dependency using the **install** command or update versions using the **update** command.

The **package-lock.json** file should be checked in with the rest of your code because it keeps track of your dependency tree and is useful for debugging complicated compatibility issues. **node_modules**, on the other hand, should always be added to your **.gitignore** file since npm can recreate that folder any time using information from your **package.json** and **package-lock.json** files and downloading the packages from the npm repository.

Besides the **dependencies** section, your **package.json** file can also contain a **devDependencies** section. This section is a way for developers to keep dependencies they use during building or testing the package, but others won't need it. This can include tools such as **babel** to **transpile** code or testing frameworks such as **jest**.

Dependencies in **devDependencies** don't get pulled when your package is pulled by other packages to use. Some frameworks, such as Webpack or **Parcel.js**, also have a production model that will ignore these dependencies when creating the final bundle.

npm Scripts

When you run the **npm init** command, the **package.json** file that gets created has a **scripts** section in it. By default, a test script is added to it. This is what it looks like:

```
"scripts": {
  "test": "echo \"Error: no test specified\" && exit 1"
},
```

Scripts can be used to run any type of command that a developer may need when working on a package. Common examples of scripts are testing, linting, and other code analysis tools. It is also possible to have scripts to start an application or any other thing you can do from the command line.

To define a script, you add an attribute to the **scripts** section, where the value is the script that will be executed, as in the following:

```
"scripts": {
  "myscript": "echo 'Hello world!'"
},
```

The preceding code creates a script called **myscript**. When invoked, it will print the text "Hello World!".

To invoke a script, you can use the **npm run** or run-script command, passing in the name of the script:

```
$ npm run myscript
```

```
> sample_scripts@1.0.0 myscript .../Lesson02/sample_scripts

> echo 'Hello World!'
```

```
Hello World!
```

npm will output all the details of what is being executed to let you know what it is doing. You can ask it to be silent by using the **--silent** (or **-s**) option:

```
$ npm run myscript --silent
```
```
Hello World!
```
```
$ npm run myscript -s
```
```
Hello World!
```

```
$ npm run-script myscript -s
```
```
Hello World!
```

One interesting thing about scripts is that you can use the prefixes "pre" and "post" to invoke other scripts before and after you do setup and/or cleanup tasks. The following is an example of such usage:

```
"scripts": {

  "preexec": "echo 'John Doe' > name.txt",

  "exec": "node index.js",

  "postexec": "rm -v name.txt"

}
```

index.js is a Node.js script that reads a name from a name.txt file and prints a hello message. The exec script will execute the index.js file. The pre and post exec scripts will be automatically called before and after the exec one, creating and deleting the name.txt file (in Windows, you can use the del command instead of rm). Running the exec script will result in the following output:

```
$ ls

index.js package.json


$ npm run exec


> sample_scripts@1.0.0 preexec ../Lesson02/sample_scripts
> echo 'John Doe' > name.txt


> sample_scripts@1.0.0 exec ../Lesson02/sample_scripts
> node index.js


Hello John Doe!


> sample_scripts@1.0.0 postexec ../Lesson02/sample_scripts
> rm -v name.txt


name.txt


$ ls

index.js          package.json
```

You can see that, before invoking the exec script, the name.txt file didn't exist. The preexec script is invoked, which creates the file with the name inside. Then, the JavaScript is called and prints the hello message. Finally, the postexec script is invoked, which deletes the file. You can see that the name.txt file doesn't exist after npm's execution has finished.

npm also comes with some predefined script names. Some of them are published, install, pack, test, stop, and start. The advantage of these predefined names is that you don't need to use the **run** or **run-script** command; you can directly invoke the script by name. For example, to invoke the default test script created by **npm init**, you can just call **npm test**:

```
$ npm test
```

```
> sample_scripts@1.0.0 test .../Lesson02/sample_scripts
> echo "Error: no test specified" && exit 1
```

```
Error: no test specified
npm ERR! Test failed.  See above for more details.
```

Here, you can see that it fails since it has an **exit 1** command, which makes the npm script's execution fail since any command that exits with a non-zero status will make the invocation stop immediately.

start is a widely used script to start web servers for local frontend development. The exec example in the preceding code could be rewritten to look like the following:

```
"scripts": {
    "prestart": "echo 'John Doe' > name.txt",
    "start": "node index.js",
    "poststart": "rm -v name.txt"
}
```

Then, it can be be run just by calling **npm start**:

```
$ npm start
```

```
> sample_scripts@1.0.0 prestart .../Lesson02/sample_scripts
> echo 'John Doe' > name.txt
```

```
> sample_scripts@1.0.0 start .../Lesson02/sample_scripts
```

```
> node index.js

Hello John Doe!

> sample_scripts@1.0.0 poststart .../Lesson02/sample_scripts
> rm -v name.txt

name.txt
```

> **Note**
>
> One important thing to keep in mind when writing npm scripts is whether there is a need to make them platform independent. For example, if you are working with a big group of developers and some of them use Windows machines and some use Mac and/or Linux, scripts that are written to run in Windows will probably fail in the Unix world, and vice versa. JavaScript is a perfect use case for this since Node.js abstracts platform dependency away for you.

As we saw in the previous chapter, sometimes we want to extract data from a web page. In that chapter, we used some JavaScript that was injected into the page from the Developer Tools Console tab to do that so that didn't need to write an application for it. Now, you will write a Node.js application to do something similar.

Activity 3: Creating an npm Package to Parse HTML

In this activity, you will use npm to create a new package. Then, you will write some Node.js code to load and parse the HTML code using a library called **cheerio**. With the loaded HTML, you will query and manipulate it. In the end, you will print the manipulated HTML to see the results.

The steps to perform are as follows:

1. Use npm to create a new package inside a new folder.

2. Install a library called **cheerio** using **npm install** (https://www.npmjs.com/package/cheerio).

3. Create a new entry file called **index.js** and inside it, load the **cheerio** library.

4. Create a variable that stores the HTML from the first sample from *Chapter 1, JavaScript, HTML, and the DOM* (the file can be found in GitHub: https://github.com/TrainingByPackt/Professional-JavaScript/blob/master/Lesson01/Example/sample_001/sample-page.html).

5. Use cheerio to load and parse the HTML.

6. Add a paragraph element with some text into the **div** in the loaded HTML.

7. Using cheerio, iterate over all the paragraphs in the current page, and print their content to the console.

8. Print the manipulated version of the console.

9. Run your application.

The output should look something like the following:

```
$ node index.js
0 - This is a paragraph.
1 - This is a paragraph inside a div.
2 - This is another paragraph.
<html><head>
    <title>Sample Page</title>
  </head>
  <body>
    <p>This is a paragraph.</p>
    <div>
      <p>This is a paragraph inside a div.</p>
      <p>This is another paragraph.</p></div>
    <button>Click me!</button>

</body></html>
```

Figure 2.6: Expected output after calling the application from Node.js

> **Note**
>
> The solution for this activity can be found on page 588.

In this activity, you created a Node.js application by using the npm init command. Then, you imported an HTML parser library. You used it to manipulate and query the parsed HTML. In the next chapter, we will continue to explore techniques that will help us scrape web pages faster and we will actually use against a website.

Summary

In this chapter, we learned about what Node.js is and how its single-threaded, asynchronous, event-driven programming model can be used to build simple and efficient applications. We also learned about nvm and how to manage multiple versions of Node.js. Then, we studied npm and used external libraries in our Node.js applications. Finally, we learned what npm scripts are and some basic concepts related to them.

To help you understand what you learned about in this chapter, you can go to the npm repository, find some projects, and explore their code bases. The best way to learn about npm, Node.js, and the packages and libraries that exist out there is to explore other people's code and see what and how they are building and also what libraries they use.

In the next chapter, we will explore the Node.js APIs and learn how to use them to build a real web scraping application. In future chapters, you will learn how to use npm scripts and packages to improve the quality of your code through linting and automated tests.

3

Node.js APIs and Web Scraping

Learning Objectives

By the end of this chapter, you will be able to:

- Implement Node.js applications using global objects
- Create readable and writable Streams
- Read and write to files using asynchronous and synchronous APIs
- Create static and dynamic web servers using the http module
- Download content from websites using the http/https modules
- Query and extract data from parsed HTML content

In this chapter, we will learn about global objects and functions. Then, we will learn how to write efficient web servers, both static and dynamic, using the http module. Finally, we will use the http and https modules to scrape web pages and extract data from them.

Introduction

From the outset, Node.js was created to provide an alternative to the thread-per-request model of the first generation of HTTP servers. The event loop and the asynchronous nature of Node.js make it ideal for I/O-intensive servers that need to provide high throughput for a high number of concurrent clients. Because of that, it came armed with powerful and simple-to-use APIs to build HTTP servers out of the box.

In the previous chapter, we talked about what Node.js and NPM are and how they work. In this chapter, you will learn about the basic global objects that are available to every script in Node.js. You will learn about readable and writable streams and how you can use them to read and write to files asynchronously. You will also learn how to read and write to files using the synchronous filesystem APIs.

In the last couple of sections, you will learn how to use the HTTP module to write web servers and make HTTP requests. You will build a static and a dynamic web server. Then, you will learn the basics of web scraping and how to use it to extract data from websites.

Globals

The Node.js execution context contains a few **global** variables and functions that can be used from anywhere in any script. The most widely used of all is the `require` function, since it is the function that helps you load other modules and access the non-global functions, classes, and variables that are available from the Node.js APIs.

You must have noticed this function being used in the previous chapter when we loaded the `commander` module from the package you installed in your application:

```
const program = require('commander');
```

It receives one parameter, which is a string representing the ID of the module you want to load, and returns the module's content. Internal modules, such as the ones we will discuss in this chapter, and the modules that are loaded from packages and installed by npm, are identified directly by their names, such as commander, fs, and http. In *Chapter 5, Modular JavaScript*, you will see how to create your own modules and how to use this function to load them.

Another important and widely used global is the console. Just like in the Chrome Developer tools, the console can be used to print text to the Terminal using standard output and standard error. It can also be used to print text to files for logging.

So far, you have used console many times, like in the last exercise of the previous chapter, where you printed the following manipulated HTML:

```
console.log(html);
```

In the browser, **setTimeout** returns a timer ID, which is an integer and can't do more than canceling the timer through the **clearTimeout** function. In Node.js, **setTimeout** returns a **Timeout** object that has some methods itself. An interesting one is the **refresh** method, which resets the start time of the timer to the current time and restarts counting the timer as if it had been scheduled at that moment. Take a look at the following example code:

```
const secondTimer = setTimeout(() => {

  console.log(`I am ${Date.now() - start}ms late.');

}, 3000);


setTimeout(() => {

  console.log(`Refreshing second timer at ${Date.now() - start}ms`);

  secondTimer.refresh();

}, 2000);
```

This prints the following:

```
Refreshing second timer at 2002ms

I am 5004ms late.
```

From the output, you can see that even though **secondTimer** was scheduled to run 3 seconds in the future, it ran 5 seconds in the future. That's because the second **setTimeout**, which was set to 2 seconds, refreshes it, restarting the count at that time, adding 2 seconds to the 3-second timer.

As we mentioned previously, you can use the **Timeout** instance to cancel the timer using the **clearTimeout** function. The following code is an example of this:

```
const thirdTimer = setTimeout(() => {

  console.log('I am never going to be executed.');

}, 5000);


setTimeout(() => {
```

```
    console.log('Cancelling third timer at ${Date.now() - start}ms');
    clearTimeout(thirdTimer);
}, 2000);
```

The output for this code would be as follows:

```
Cancelling third timer at 2007ms
```

setTimeout executes only once. You can use **setInterval** to do a specific task every specific amount of time. **setInterval** also returns a **Timeout** instance that can be used to cancel the timer using **clearInterval**. The following example sets a timer to run every second and keeps track of the number of times it ran. After a certain number of executions, it cancels the timer:

```
let counter = 0;
const MAX = 5;
const start = Date.now();
const timeout = setInterval(() => {
    console.log(`Executing ${Date.now() - start}ms in the future.`);
    counter++
    if (counter >= MAX) {
        console.log(`Ran for too long, cancelling it at ${Date.now() - start}
ms`);
        clearInterval(timeout);
    }
}, 1000);
```

The output for this code looks something like the following:

```
Executing 1004ms in the future.
Executing 2009ms in the future.
Executing 3013ms in the future.
Executing 4018ms in the future.
Executing 5023ms in the future.
Ran for too long, cancelling it at 5023ms
```

In the browser, we have a global object called window that represents the browser. In Node.js, we have process, which represents the currently running application. Through it, we can access the arguments that are passed into the application, including standard inputs and outputs and other information about the process, such as version or process ID.

To access the arguments that are passed into the process, you can use the **argv** attribute of the global variable process. **argv** is an array that contains each argument in a position. It includes the path to the Node.js binary and the full path of the script as the first two elements. After that, all the other extra arguments are passed in.

The following code would print all the arguments passed in, each in one line:

```
console.log(`Arguments are:\n${process.argv.join('\n')}`);
```

Let's go over some sample outputs for this single-line application.

No extra argument:

```
$ node argv.js

Arguments are:

/usr/local/bin/node

/Users/visola/git/Professional-JavaScript/Lesson03/sample_globals/argv.js
```

Many arguments separated one by one:

```
$ node argv.js this is a test

Arguments are:

/usr/local/bin/node

/Users/visola/git/Professional-JavaScript/Lesson03/sample_globals/argv.js

this

is

a

test
```

One argument all in one string:

```
$ node argv.js 'this is a test'

Arguments are:

/usr/local/bin/node

/Users/visola/git/Professional-JavaScript/Lesson03/sample_globals/argv.js

this is a test
```

In the previous chapter, we used the **commander** library to parse command-line arguments. When configuring **commander**, the last call to it was **parse(process.argv)**, which gave **commander** access to all the options that were passed in:

```
program.version('0.1.0')
  .option('-b, --add-bootstrap', 'Add Bootstrap 4 to the page.')
  .option('-c, --add-container', 'Adds a div with container id in the
body.')
  .option('-t, --title [title]', 'Add a title to the page.')
  .parse(process.argv);
```

Another important role that the process variable holds is access to standard inputs and outputs. If you want to print something to the console, you can use **stdout** and **stderr**. These two attributes are what **console.log** and all the other methods in the console use under the hood. The difference is that **stdout** and **stderr** do not add a new line at the end of each call, so you have to do that yourself if you want each output to go into its own line:

```
process.stdout.write(`You typed: '${text}'\n`);
process.stderr.write('Exiting your application now.\n');
```

These are two examples that print something with a new line at the end. For most cases, it is recommended to use the console since it gives you some extra stuff on top, such as logging levels and formatting.

If you want to read input from the command line, you can use **process.stdin**. **stdin** is a Stream, which we're going to talk more about in the next section. For now, you just need to know that Streams are based on events. That means that when input comes in, it will arrive in the form of a data event. To receive input from the user, you need to listen to that event:

```
process.stdin.addListener('data', (data) => {

  ...

});
```

When there's no more code to be executed, the event loop will block, waiting for input from standard input. When the input is read, it will be passed into the callback function as a Buffer of bytes. You can convert it into a string by calling its **toString** method, as shown in the following code:

```
const text = data.toString().trim();
```

```
        write(`Sorry, '${input}' is not valid. Try again. > `);
        return;
    }

    amount = number;
    setTimerAndRestart();
  }
```

6. At the end of the **askForAmount** function, it calls the **setTimerAndRestart** function. Let's create that function, which creates the timer and resets all states so that the loop can start again, and the user can create new timers. This is what the **setTimerAndRestart** function looks like:

```
function setTimerAndRestart() {
  const currentMessage = message;
  write(`Setting reminder: '${message}' in ${amount} ${unit} from now.\
n`);

  let timerMessage = `\n\x07Time to '${currentMessage}'\n> `;
  setTimeout(() => write(timerMessage), amount * multipliers[timeUnit]);

  amount = message = timeUnit = null;
  askForMessage();
}
```

One important bit here is the special character, **\x07**. This will cause your Terminal to make a beep and then print the text set in the message. Also, the text is specially formatted with new lines at the beginning and end so that it doesn't disrupt the usage of the tool that much since the timers will print while the user continues to use the application.

7. The final piece of the application needs to register the listener to the data event in standard input and start the cycle by asking the user for the message:

```
process.stdin.on('data', (data) => processInput(data.toString().trim()));
askForMessage();
```

8. Now, you can run the application from your Terminal, set up a couple of reminds, and hear it beep back at you as the timers expire:

```
$ node .
What do you want to be reminded of? > Buy milk
What unit?
1 - Seconds
2 - Minutes
3 - Hours
> 2
Picked: Minutes
In how many Minutes? > 2
Setting reminder: 'Buy milk' in 2 Minutes from now.
What do you want to be reminded of? > Call my boss
What unit?
1 - Seconds
2 - Minutes
3 - Hours
> 1
Picked: Seconds
In how many Seconds? > 30
Setting reminder: 'Call my boss' in 30 Seconds from now.
What do you want to be reminded of? >
Time to 'Call my boss'
>
Time to 'Buy milk'
>
```

Figure 3.3: Output after running the application

You will notice that the only way to exit the application is to send the interrupt signal by pressing the *Ctrl+C* keys at the same time. As an extra challenge, try adding some code that will create an exit point so that the user can exit in a friendlier way.

Dealing with user inputs is fundamental for every command-line application. In this exercise, you learned how to master the asynchronous nature of Node.js so that you could handle a complex set of inputs to guide the user in the decision-making process of creating a reminder.

FileSystem APIs

In the previous section, we learned about the global variables available to us in the Node.js execution context. In this section, we will learn about the FileSystem APIs, which are the APIs that are used to access files and directories, read and write data to files, and much more.

But before we dig into the FileSystem APIs, we need to understand streams. In Node.js, a Stream is an abstract interface that represents streaming data. In the previous section, we used the standard I/O and briefly mentioned that they are streams, so let's understand them in detail.

Streams can be readable, writable, or both. They are event emitters, which means that to receive data, you need to register event listeners, just like we did with standard input in the previous section:

```
process.stdin.addListener('data', (data) => {

    ...

});
```

In the next section, we will continue to build on our understanding of the previous sections and see that streams are used as an abstraction to represent all the things that data can flow through, including standard input and outputs, files, and network sockets.

To start understanding how this works, we will write an application that reads its own code by using **createReadStream** from the filesystem package. To use the FileSystem APIs, we need to import them, since they are not globally available:

```
const fs = require('fs');
```

Then, we can create a readable stream that points to the script file itself:

```
const readStream = fs.createReadStream(__filename);
```

Finally, we register for the events of the stream so that we can understand what's going on. The read stream has four events that you should care about: ready, data, close, and error.

Ready tells you when the file is ready to start reading, although when you create a readable stream that points to a file, it will start reading the file immediately when it is available.

Data, as we saw with standard input, will be called by passing in the data that was read from the stream as a byte buffer. The buffer needs to be transformed into a string by either calling its **toString** method or by concatenating it with another string.

Close is called when all the bytes have been read, and the stream is not readable anymore.

Error is called if an error occurs while reading from the stream.

The following code demonstrates how we can register for the events by printing content to the console as the events occur:

```
readStream.on('data', (data) => console.log(`--data--\n${data}`));

readStream.on('ready', () => console.log(`--ready--`));

readStream.on('close', () => console.log(`--close--`));
```

The output of this application appears as follows:

```
$ node read_stream.js

--ready--

--data--

const fs = require('fs');

const readStream = fs.createReadStream(__filename);


readStream.on('data', (data) => console.log(`--data--\n${data}`));

readStream.on('ready', () => console.log(`--ready--`));

readStream.on('close', () => console.log(`--close--`));


--close--
```

Now that you know how to read a file and how to use read streams, let's take a look at writable streams in more detail. You saw some of their usage in the previous section, since standard output is a writable stream:

```
process.stdout.write('You typed: '${text}'\n');

process.stderr.write('Exiting your application now.\n');
```

The **write** method is the one most frequently used in writable streams. If you want to create a writable stream that writes to a file, you just need to pass the name of the filename:

```
const fs = require('fs');

const writable = fs.createWriteStream('todo.txt');
```

Then, you can start writing to it:

```
writable.write('- Buy milk\n');

writable.write('- Buy eggs\n');

writable.write('- Buy cheese\n');
```

Don't forget to add the newline character at the end, otherwise everything will be printed in the same line.

After you're done writing to the file, you call the **end** method to close it:

```
writable.end();
```

Writable streams also have events you can listen to. The two most important ones are **error** and **close**. The error event will be triggered when an error occurs while writing to the stream. The **close** event will be called when the stream is closed. There's also the **finish** event, which will be triggered when the **end** method is called. The following code is the final part of the sample code that can be found on GitHub: https://github.com/TrainingByPackt/Professional-JavaScript/blob/master/Lesson03/sample_filesystem/write_stream.js:

```
writable.on('finish', () => console.log("-- finish --"));

writable.on('close', () => console.log("-- close --"));
```

After running the application, you will see that it will create the **todo.txt** file with the expected content in it:

```
$ node write_stream.js

-- finish --

-- close --


$ cat todo.txt

- Buy milk

- Buy eggs

- Buy cheese
```

> **Note**
>
> Creating a stream that points to a file will create a stream that overwrites the file content by default. To create a stream to append to the file, you need to pass an option object with the "a" flag, as in append, like so:

```
const writable = fs.createWriteStream('todo.txt', { flags: 'a'});
```

Another interesting thing about streams is that you can pipe them. This means that you can send all the bytes from a read stream to a write stream. You could easily copy the content of one file to another with the following code:

```
const fs = require('fs');

fs.createReadStream('somefile.txt')

  .pipe(fs.createWriteStream('copy.txt'));
```

Besides reading and writing to files, the FileSystem APIs also provide methods so that you can list files in directories, check a file's status, watch a directory or file for changes, copy, delete, change file permissions, and so on.

When dealing with filesystem operations, you have to remember that the operations are asynchronous. This means that all the operations receive a callback that gets called when the operation has finished. When making a directory, for example, you could write the following code:

```
const firstDirectory = 'first';

fs.mkdir(firstDirectory, (error) => {
  if (error != null) {
    console.error(`Error: ${error.message}`, error);
    return;
  }
  console.log(`Directory created: ${firstDirectory}`);
});
```

The callback receives an error argument if something goes wrong while trying to create a directory, for example, if the directory already exists. Running the code for the first time would work:

```
$ node directories_and_files.js

. . .

Directory created: first
```

But when running it for the second time, it would fail as the directory has already been created:

```
$ node directories_and_files.js

Error: EEXIST: file already exists, mkdir 'first' { [Error: EEXIST: file
already exists, mkdir 'first'] errno: -17, code: 'EEXIST', syscall: 'mkdir',
path: 'first' }

. . .
```

If you want to create a file in the directory you just created, you need to create the file inside the callback that is passed into **mkdir**. Doing it the following way can fail:

```
const firstDirectory = 'first';
fs.mkdir(firstDirectory, (error) => {

  ...

});


fs.writeFile(`${firstDirectory}/test.txt`, 'Some content', (error) => {
  console.assert(error == null, 'Error while creating file.', error);
});
```

This happens when you try to run it:

```
$ node directories_and_files.js
Assertion failed: Error while creating file. { [Error: ENOENT: no such file or
directory, open 'first/test.txt']

  ...
```

That's because when the call to **writeFile** happens, there's a chance that the directory still doesn't exist. The correct way to do it is to call **writeFile** inside the callback that's passed into **mkdir**:

```
const firstDirectory = 'first';
fs.mkdir(firstDirectory, (error) => {

  ...


  fs.writeFile(`${firstDirectory}/test.txt`, 'Some content', (error) => {
    console.assert(error == null, 'Error while creating file.', error);
  });
});
```

Since dealing with the preceding asynchronous calls is complicated and not all cases require high-performance asynchronous operations, in the filesystem module, almost all operations include a synchronous version of the same API. So, if you wanted to make a directory and create a file with some content in it, and there's nothing else your application can be doing while the directory doesn't exist, you could write the code in the following way:

```
const thirdDirectory = 'third';

fs.mkdirSync(thirdDirectory);

console.log(`Directory created: ${thirdDirectory}`);


const thirdFile = `${thirdDirectory}/test.txt`;

fs.writeFileSync(thirdFile, 'Some content');

console.log(`File created: ${thirdFile}`);
```

Notice the **Sync** word at the end of each method name. The output of the preceding code is as follows:

```
$ node directories_and_files.js

Directory created: third

File created: third/test.txt
```

In Node.js 10, a promise-based API was also added to the filesystem module. Promises and other techniques that deal with asynchronous operations will be discussed in further chapters, so we will skip this for now.

Now that you know how to create directories and read and write data to files, let's move on to the next most frequently used filesystem operation: listing directories.

To list files in a directory, you can use the **readdir** method. The callback that's passed to the function will receive an error object if something goes wrong when you're trying to read the directory and a list of filenames. The following code will print the names of all the files in the current directory:

```
fs.readdir('./', (error, files) => {
  if (error != null) {
    console.error('Error while reading directory.', error);
    return;
  }

  console.log('-- File names --');
```

```
    console.log(files.join('\n'));
  });
```

This is a sample output:

```
$ node list_dir.js
-- File names --
.gitignore
copy_file.js
directories_and_files.js
first
list_dir.js
read_stream.js
second
third
write_stream.js

...
```

But sometimes, you want more than just filenames. Here, the **readdir** function accepts an options object, which can be provided with the **withFileTypes** flag. If the flag is passed, then what the callback gets, instead of filenames, is an array of **Dirents**, which contains some extra information about the file, such as if it is a directory or a file. The following example will print the filenames in the current directory and prepend it with a (D) or (F), depending on whether it is a directory or file, respectively:

```
fs.readdir('./', { withFileTypes: true }, (error, files) => {
  if (error != null) {
    console.error('Error while reading directory.', error);
    return;
  }

  console.log('-- File infos --');
  console.log(files.map(d => `(${d.isDirectory() ? 'D': 'F'}) ${d.name}`)
    .sort()
    .join('\n'));
});
```

The sample output looks like this:

```
$ node list_dir.js

...

-- File infos --

(D) first

(D) second

(D) third

(F) .gitignore

(F) copy_file.js

(F) directories_and_files.js

(F) list_dir.js

(F) read_stream.js

(F) write_stream.js
```

The last operation of the FileSystem APIs that is important to be aware of is concerned with how to check the status of a file. If you just need to know whether a file exists and is readable, you can use the **access** function, which receives the path to the file and a set of status flags to check for. If the file state matches the specified flags, then no error will be passed to the callback. Let's take a look at an example:

```
const fs = require('fs');

const filename = process.argv[2];

fs.access(filename, fs.constants.F_OK | fs.constants.R_OK, (error) => {
  if (error == null) {
    console.log('File exists and is readable');
  } else {
    console.log(error.message);
  }
});
```

In this example, we're combining two flags, **F_OK** and **R_OK**. The first checks whether the file exists, while the second checks whether it's readable. You can combine multiple flags with the **|** (or) operator.

After executing the preceding code, you would see the following output if the file exists:

```
$ node file_status.js test.txt

File exists and is readable
```

If the file doesn't exist, then you would see the following output:

```
$ node file_status.js not.txt

ENOENT: no such file or directory, access 'not.txt'
```

Finally, if the file exists but is not readable, you would receive the following message:

```
$ node file_status.js not.txt

EACCES: permission denied, access 'not.txt'
```

All of this looks interesting, but if you need to know whether a path is a file or a directory, when it was last modified, and so on, then you need to use the **lstat** function, which will return a Stats instance. Stats contains everything you need to know about a path.

The following example checks whether the path is a file or directory, when it was created and last modified, and prints that information to the console:

```
fs.lstat(filename, (statError, stat) => {

  if (statError != null) {

    console.error('Error while file status.', statError);

    return;

  }


  console.log(`Is file: ${stat.isFile()}`);

  console.log(`Is directory: ${stat.isDirectory()}`);

  console.log(`Created at: ${stat.birthtime}`);

  console.log(`Last modified at: ${stat.mtime}`);

});
```

This is a sample output:

```
$ node file_status.js first/test.txt

...

Is file: true

Is directory: false

Created at: Tue Aug 13 2019 20:39:37 GMT-0400 (Eastern Daylight Time)

Last modified at: Tue Aug 13 2019 21:26:53 GMT-0400 (Eastern Daylight Time)
```

Globs are path-like strings that contain parts of the path replaced by wildcards, represented by *. When you have two *, for example, **, this means any directory or subdirectory. A simple example is to search for all the .txt files in any subdirectory of the current directory:

```
$ search '**/*.txt'
```

Exercise 12: Searching for a File through a Directory Using Glob Pattern

In this exercise, we will create an application that will scan through a directory tree and search for files based on glob. To achieve this, we will recursively call the synchronous version of the **readdir** function and use the **commander** and the **glob-to-regexp** modules to help us with processing the user's input.

Perform the following steps to complete this exercise:

1. In an empty directory, start a new application using **npm init** and add an **index.js** file, which will be our entry point.

2. Install the two external modules that we will be using: **commander** and **glob-to-regexp**. For that, execute the **npm install** command:

```
$ npm install commander glob-to-regexp
npm notice created a lockfile as package-lock.json. You should commit this
file.
+ glob-to-regexp@0.4.1
+ commander@3.0.0
added 2 packages from 2 contributors and audited 2 packages in 0.534s
found 0 vulnerabilities
```

3. Inside the **index.js** file, using your favorite editor, import all the necessary modules for this project at the beginning of the file:

```
const fs = require('fs');
const globToRegExp = require('glob-to-regexp');
const join = require('path').join;
const program = require('commander');
```

We are already aware of the **fs** and commander modules. The **globToRegExp** module and **join** function will be explained in the upcoming steps.

4. Initialize the **counter** and **found** variables. These will be used to show some statistics relating to the search being executed:

```
let counter = 0;
let found = 0;
const start = Date.now();
```

5. Configure the **commander** to receive the glob as the argument and an extra option for the user to set the initial directory to start the search from:

```
    program.version('1.0.0')
    .arguments('<glob>')
    .option('-b, --base-dir <dir>', 'Base directory to start the search.',
    './')
    .parse(process.argv);
```

6. For this exercise, we will use a recursive function to walk through the directory tree. The **walkDirectory** function calls **readdirSync**, with the **withFileTypes** flag set to **true**. The **walkDirectory** function receives two arguments: the path to start reading from and the callback to be called for each file. When a directory is found, it is passed to the **walkDirectory** function so that the recursion continues:

```
function walkDirectory(path, callback) {
  const dirents = fs.readdirSync(path, { withFileTypes: true });
  dirents.forEach(dirent => {
    if (dirent.isDirectory()) {
      walkDirectory(join(path, dirent.name), callback);
    } else {
      counter++;
      callback(join(path, dirent.name));
    }
  });
}
```

When a file is found, the path is passed to the callback and the counter is incremented. Here, we use the **path.join** function to join the filename to the parent path to reconstruct the whole path to the file.

7. Now that we have the **walkDirectory** tree function, we will validate the arguments that have been passed to the application:

```
const glob = program.args[0];
if (typeof glob === 'undefined') {
  program.help();
  process.exit(-1);
}
```

8. Then, we use the **globToRegExp** module to transform the glob to a **RegExp** that can be used to test files:

```
const matcher = globToRegExp(program.args[0], { globstar: true });
```

9. With the matcher and the walk directory tree function ready, we can now walk the directory tree and test each file we find:

```
walkDirectory(program.baseDir, (f) => {
  if (matcher.test(f)) {
    found++;
    console.log(`${found} - ${f}`);
  }
});
```

10. Finally, since all the code is executing synchronously, after the call to **walkDirectory** finishes, all the directories and subdirectories will have been processed. Now, we can print the statistics of what we found:

```
console.log('-- Done --');
console.log(`Found ${found} files`);
console.log(`Searched ${counter} files in ${Date.now() - start}ms`);
Execute the application to search for JavaScript files in the current
directory:
$ node . '**/*.js'
1 - index.js
2 - node_modules/commander/index.js
3 - node_modules/glob-to-regexp/index.js
4 - node_modules/glob-to-regexp/test.js
-- Done -
Found 4 files
Searched 14 files in 7ms
```

Figure 3.4: Statistics of the files found

You can execute the search by starting in the parent directory:

```
$ node . -b ../ '**/*.js'
1 - ../exercise_001/index.js
2 - ../exercise_002/index.js
3 - ../exercise_002/node_modules/commander/index.js
4 - ../exercise_002/node_modules/glob-to-regexp/index.js
5 - ../exercise_002/node_modules/glob-to-regexp/test.js
6 - ../sample_filesystem/copy_file.js
7 - ../sample_filesystem/directories_and_files.js
8 - ../sample_filesystem/file_status.js
9 - ../sample_filesystem/list_dir.js
10 - ../sample_filesystem/read_stream.js
11 - ../sample_filesystem/write_stream.js
12 - ../sample_globals/argv.js
13 - ../sample_globals/console.js
14 - ../sample_globals/dir_and_filename.js
15 - ../sample_globals/read_input.js
16 - ../sample_globals/setInterval.js
17 - ../sample_globals/setTimeout.js
-- Done -
Found 17 files
Searched 32 files in 18ms
```

Figure 3.5: Executing the search in the parent directory

In this exercise, you learned how to use the FileSystem APIs to traverse a directory tree. You also used regular expressions to filter files by name.

The FileSystem APIs provide the foundation for almost every application. Learning how to use them synchronously and asynchronously is fundamental for anything you will be doing in the backend world. In the next section, we will use these APIs to build a basic web server to serve files to the browser.

HTTP APIs

In the beginning, Node.js was created with the objective of replacing old web servers that used the traditional model of one thread per connection. In the thread-per-request model, the server keeps a port open, and when a new connection comes in, it uses a thread from the pool or creates a new one to execute the work the user asked for. All of the operations on the server side happen synchronously, which means that while a file is being read from disk or a record from the database, the thread sleeps. The following illustration depicts this model:

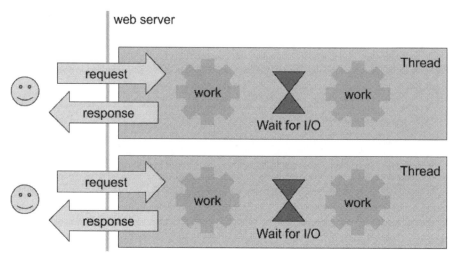

Figure 3.6: On the thread-per-request model, threads sleep while the I/O and other blocking operations happen

The problem with the thread-per-request model is that threads are expensive to create, and having them sleep while there's more work to do means a waste of resources. Another issue is that when the number of threads is higher than the number of CPUs, they start losing their most precious value: concurrency.

Because of these issues, web servers that used the thread-per-request model would have a thread pool that's not big enough so that the server can still respond to many requests in parallel. And because the number of threads is limited when the number of concurrent users making requests grows too much, the server runs out of threads and the users now have to wait:

```
      }
    });
  }
```

4. Then, we will pick the root directory, which can be passed as an argument. Otherwise, we will just assume it is the directory from where we're running the script:

```
const rootDirectory = path.resolve(process.argv[2] || './');
```

5. Now, we can scan the directory tree and store the path to all files in a **Set**, which will make the process of checking the availability of the file quicker:

```
const files = new Set();
walkDirectory(rootDirectory, (file) => {
  file = file.substr(rootDirectory.length);
    files.add(file);
});
console.log(`Found ${files.size} in '${rootDirectory}'...`);
```

6. With the list of files ready to serve, we will create the HTTP server instance:

```
const server = http.createServer();
```

7. Start the request handler function:

```
server.on('request', (request, response) => {
```

8. Inside the handler function, parse what the user is requesting to a URL. For this, we will use the url module and, from the parsed URL, we will fetch the pathname that points to the file the client wants:

```
const requestUrl = url.parse(request.url);
const requestedPath = path.join(requestUrl.pathname);
```

9. With the path to the file, we will check whether the file is in the list we collected before and, if not, respond with a 404 (not found) error message, log the result of the request, and return it:

```
if (!files.has(requestedPath)) {
  console.log('404 %s', requestUrl.href);
  response.writeHead(404);
  response.end();
  return;
}
```

10. If the file is in the **Set**, we will use the path module to extract its extension and resolve the content type using the **mime** module. Then, we will respond with a 200 (ok) error message, create a read stream to the file, and pipe it to the response:

```
const contentType = mime.getType(path.extname(requestedPath));

console.log('200 %s', requestUrl.href);
response.writeHead(200, { 'Content-type': contentType });
fs.createReadStream(path.join(rootDirectory, requestedPath))
    .pipe(response);
});
```

11. That's all for the handler function. After that, we can start the server by picking a port, letting the user know what that is, and calling what to listen to the method in the http server:

```
const port = 3000;
console.log('Starting server on port %d.', port);
console.log('Go to: http://localhost:%d', port);
server.listen(port);
```

12. You can start the server by running the following command:

```
$ node .
Found 23 in '/Path/to/Folder'...
Starting server on port 3000.
o to: http://localhost:3000
```

13. From another Terminal window, we can use the command-line HTTP client curl to call our server and see the response:

```
$ curl -i localhost:3000/index.js
HTTP/1.1 200 OK
Content-type: application/javascript
Date: Fri, 16 Aug 2019 02:06:05 GMT
Connection: keep-alive
Transfer-Encoding: chunked

const fs = require('fs');
const http = require('http');
const mime = require('mime');
... rest of content here....
```

We can also do the same from the browser:

```
const fs = require('fs');
const http = require('http');
const mime = require('mime');
const path = require('path');
const url = require('url');

function walkDirectory(dirPath, callback) {
  const dirents = fs.readdirSync(dirPath, { withFileTypes: true });

  dirents.forEach(dirent => {
    if (dirent.isDirectory()) {
      walkDirectory(path.join(dirPath, dirent.name), callback);
    } else {
      callback(path.join(dirPath, dirent.name));
    }
  });
}

const rootDirectory = path.resolve(process.argv[2] || './');

const files = new Set();
walkDirectory(rootDirectory, (file) => {
  file = file.substr(rootDirectory.length);
  files.add(file);
});
console.log(`Found ${files.size} in '${rootDirectory}'...`);

const server = http.createServer();
server.on('request', (request, response) => {
  const requestUrl = url.parse(request.url);
  const requestedPath = path.join(requestUrl.pathname);
```

Figure 3.11: Static index.js served from our HTTP server as viewed from the browser

You can also try this with a file that doesn't exist to see the result:

```
$ curl -i localhost:3000/not_real.js
HTTP/1.1 404 Not Found
Date: Fri, 16 Aug 2019 02:07:14 GMT
Connection: keep-alive
Transfer-Encoding: chunked
```

From the browser, the 404 response looks like an error page:

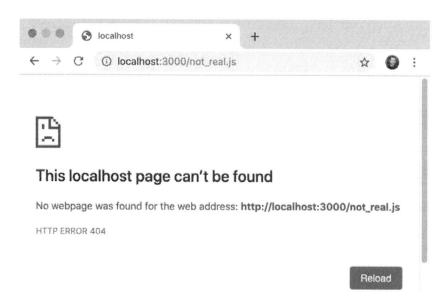

Figure 3.12: The server responds with a 404 error when asked for a file that doesn't exist

On the Terminal where you're running the server, you can see that it prints information about what's being served:

```
$ node .
Found 23 in '/Path/to/Folder'...
Starting server on port 3000
Go to: http://localhost:3000
200 /index.js
404 /not_real.js
```

With just a few lines of code, you were able to build an HTTP server that serves static content.

An HTTP server is one of the fundamental components of the internet. Node.js makes it simple to build powerful servers. In this exercise, with just a few lines of code, we have built a static HTTP server. In the rest of this section, we will learn how to build a dynamic server that can generate HTML using templates and data that have passed in the request and also loaded from other data sources, such as a JSON file.

Before we move on to building a dynamic HTTP server, let's take a look at the HTTP client APIs that are available in Node.js. To test the HTTP client APIs, we will be using HTTP Bin, a free service that can be used to test HTTP requests. You can read more about it here: https://httpbin.org.

13. Open a browser window and go to **http://localhost:3000**. You should see the storefront:

Figure 3.13: Storefront served from the dynamic web server

In this exercise, we transformed the storefront application into a dynamic web application that reads data from a JSON file and renders an HTML request when the user requests it.

Dynamic web servers are the basis of all online applications, from Uber to Facebook. You can summarize the work as loading data/processing data to generate HTML. In *Chapter 2, Node.js and npm*, we used some simple HTML and did the processing in the frontend. In this exercise, you learned how to do the same work on the backend using a template engine. Each methodology has its pros and cons and most applications end up with a combination of both.

You can add filtering options to the storefront web page as an improvement. Let's say the users want to filter the products by tag or a combination of them. In your **handleProductsPage** function, you could use query parameters to filter the list of products you're passing to the template for rendering. See if you can make this improvement yourself.

What is Scraping?

For the remainder of this chapter, we will be talking about web **scraping**. But what exactly is web scraping? It's the process of downloading a page and processing its content to execute some repetitive automated tasks that would otherwise take too long to do manually.

For example, if you want to get car insurance, you need to go to each insurance company website and get a quote. That process normally takes hours since you have to fill in a form, submit it, wait for them to send you an email on each website, compare prices, and pick the one you want:

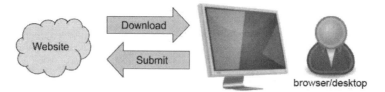

Figure 3.14: The user downloads content, types data in, submits it, and then wait for the results

So why not make a program that can do that for you? That's what web scraping is all about. A program downloads a page as if it were a human, scrapes information from it, and makes decisions based on some algorithm, and submits the necessary data back to the website.

When you're getting insurance for your car, it doesn't seem like automating would bring much value. Writing an application that does that correctly for different websites would take many hours – more than doing it yourself manually. But what if you were an insurance broker? Then you would have to do this hundreds of times a day, maybe more.

If you are an insurance broker company, and if you spend your time building one robot (that's what these applications are called), you will start to become more efficient. That's because, for that one website, you won't be spending time filling out the forms. With the efficiency that you got from building your first robot, you can save time and be able to build a second one, then a third one, and so forth:

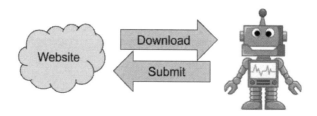

Figure 3.15: Robot executing the task automatically by downloading content and making decisions based on an algorithm

Web scraping started in the early days of the internet when Yahoo! was trying to manually index all the websites that existed. Then, a start-up, out of two college students' garages, started using robots to pull the data and index everything. In a very short amount of time, Google became the number one search website, a position that only gets harder and harder for competitors to challenge.

Web scraping is a widely used technique to extract data from websites that do not provide APIs, such as most insurance companies and banks. Search and indexing is also another very common case. Some companies use scraping to analyze a website's performance and grade them, such as HubSpot (https://website.grader.com).

There are many techniques for web scraping, depending on what goal you're trying to achieve. The most basic one is to download the base HTML from a website and read the content from there. If you only need to download data or fill in a form, this might be more than enough:

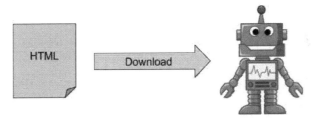

Figure 3.16: The basic scraping technique involves downloading and processing the base HTML file

But sometimes, websites use Ajax to dynamically load the content after the HTML has been rendered. For those cases, just downloading the HTML wouldn't be enough since it would just be an empty template. To solve that, you can use a headless browser, which works like a browser, parsing all HTML, downloading and parsing the related files (CSS, JavaScript, and so on), rendering everything together, and executing the dynamic code. That way, you can wait for the data to be available:

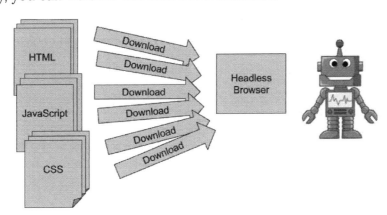

Figure 3.17: Depending on the use case, scraping requires a simulated or a fully headless browser to download and render the page more accurately

The second technique is much slower since it requires the whole page to download, parse, and render. It is also much more brittle since executing the extra calls can fail, and waiting for JavaScript to finish processing the data can be hard to predict.

Downloading and Parsing Web Pages

Let's examine the simpler approach to web scraping. Suppose we wanted to follow the latest posts about JavaScript in Medium. We could write an application to download the JavaScript topic page, then search for anchors (links), and use that to navigate around.

To start, having a generic download function that will do some basic wrapping on the HTTP client is a good idea. We could use an external library, such as request, but let's see how we would go about wrapping that kind of logic.

We will need the http module, but in this case, we will use the https version of it, since most websites these days will redirect you to their secure version if you try to reach the plain HTTP version. The https module provides the same APIs except it understands HTTPS protocol, which is the secure version of HTTP:

```
const http = require('https');
```

The **downloadPage** function receives a URL to download and a callback function that will be called after the content of the page has finished downloading:

```
function downloadPage(urlToDownload, callback) {

}
```

Inside that function, we will start by making a request and ensuring that we are calling the end function to complete the request:

```
const request = http.get(urlToDownload, (response) => {

});
request.end();
```

In the callback we pass to the get function, the first thing we will do is check for the response status and print an error message if it doesn't match 200, which is the HTTP code that means we have a successful request. We also stop everything by returning from the callback since the body will probably not be what we're expecting if this happens:

```
if (response.statusCode != 200) {
    console.error('Error while downloading page %s.', urlToDownload);
```

This means that for each anchor element, we can get that DIV, query for an anchor, and fetch its text as the description for the article.

8. Set the article information in the result object using the title as the key. We use the title of the article as the key because that will automatically deduplicate articles from the result:

```
.forEach(el => {
  const description = el.parentNode.nextSibling.querySelector('p a').text;
  articles[el.text] = {
    description: description,
    link: url.parse(el.href).pathname,
    title: el.text,
  };
});
```

9. Lastly, from the **findArticles** function, we return the array containing all the articles:

```
  return articles;
}
```

The other function we call inside the callback passed to **downloadPage** is **printArticle**. It is also the last piece of code to make this application.

10. Let's write the **printArticle** function, which receives an article object and prints it to the console in a pretty way:

```
function printArticle(article) {
  console.log('-----');
  console.log(` ${article.title}`);
  console.log(` ${article.description}`);
  console.log(` https://medium.com${article.link}`);
}
```

Run the application to print the articles to the console with the extra information in a nice format:

```
$ node .
-----
 NBA Statistics and the Golden State Warriors: Part 2
 Exploratory analysis in Python https://medium.com/better-programming/nba-
statistics-and-the-golden-state-warriors-during-their-championship-runs-
part-2-bf7240ddbbd4
-----
 12 Things That Destroy Developer Creativity
 A lot of articles address the role of tech leads and engineering managers.
One common theme we often come across is how to increase a…
https://medium.com/@AdelHanyads/12-things-that-destroy-developer-creativity-
4cbc574f556a
-----
 Apigee Shared Flow and API Proxy to Access Salesforce APIs using mutual
TLS.
 In this tutorial I am going to show you how to build from scratch an Apigee
Shared Flow that uses the Salesforce OAuth 2.0 API to retrieve…
https://medium.com/@micovery/apigee-shared-flow-and-api-proxy-to-access-
salesforce-apis-using-mutual-tls-bafc2a854261
-----
 NBA Statistics and the Golden State Warriors: Part 1
 Data resources and data wrangling in Python  https://medium.com/better-
programming/nba-statistics-and-the-golden-state-warriors-during-their-
championship-runs-part-1-cafc5d8042a8
```

Figure 3.19: Article printed to the console after running the application

In this exercise, we wrote an application that pulls data from Medium and prints a summary of the articles found to the console.

Web scraping is a powerful way of fetching data when no API is available. Many companies use scraping to sync data between systems, to analyze the performance of websites, and to optimize processes that otherwise would not scale, thus blocking some important business needs. Understanding the concepts behind scraping allows you to build systems that would otherwise be impossible to build.

Activity 4: Scraping Products and Prices from Storefront

In *Chapter 2, Node.js and npm*, we wrote some code that would fetch information about the products in the storefront example page. At the time, we said that the site wasn't going to be updated that frequently, so manually doing it from the Chrome Developer Console was fine. For some scenarios, this is fine, but when the content is dynamically generated, like in the newer version of the storefront that we wrote in this chapter, we might need to eliminate all manual intervention.

In this activity, you will write an application that will scrape the storefront web page by downloading it using the http module and parsing it using **jsdom**. Then, you will extract the data from the DOM and generate a **CSV** file with the data.

You will need to perform the following steps to complete this activity:

1. Use the previous code you built or use a copy of it to serve the storefront website in **localhost:3000**. The code can be found on GitHub at https://github.com/ TrainingByPackt/Professional-JavaScript/tree/master/Lesson03/Activity04.

2. Create a new **npm** package, install the **jsdom** library, and create an entry file called **index.js**.

3. In the entry file, call the **require()** method to load all the modules that are needed in the project.

4. Make an HTTP request to **localhost:3000**.

5. Ensure a successful response and collect data from the body.

6. Parse the HTML using **jsdom**.

7. Extract the product data from DOM; you will want the name, price, and unit.

8. Open the **CSV** file where the data will be written to.

9. Write the product data to a **CSV** file, which is one product line.

10. Run the application and check the results.

The output should look something like this:

```
$ node .
Downloading http://localhost:3000...
Download finished.
Parsing product data...
....................
Found 21 products.
Writing data to products.csv...
Done.

$ cat products.csv
name,price,unit
Apples,3.99,lb
Avocados,4.99,lb
Blueberry Muffin,2.5,each
Butter,1.39,lb
Cherries,4.29,lb
Chocolate Chips Cookies,3.85,lb
Christmas Cookies,3.89,lb
Croissant,0.79,each
Dark Chocolate,3.49,lb
Eggs,2.99,lb
Grapes,2.99,lb
Milk Chocolate,3.29,lb
Nacho Chips,2.39,lb
Parmesan Cheese,8.99,lb
```

```
Pears,4.89,lb

Petit French Baguette,0.39,each

Smiling Cookies,2.79,lb

Strawberries,7.29,lb

Swiss Cheese,2.59,lb

White Chocolate,3.49,lb

Whole Wheat Bread,0.89,each
```

> **Note**
> The solution for this activity can be found on page 591.

Summary

In this chapter, we learned about the global variables that are available to every Node.js script. We learned how to set timers and read from, and write to, the console. After that, we learned about streams and how to use them to read and write data from files. We also learned how to use the synchronous filesystem APIs. Then, we learned how to use the HTTP module to build web servers and scrape content from web pages.

Now that you are well acquainted with the web scraping concept, you are ready to explore opportunities where you can build your own web applications and build automated robots to scrape content from other web applications. A good idea is to try and build a simple content management application to serve your blog, where you're going to write about all the new things you just learned about.

In the next chapter, you will learn about REST APIs and use some frameworks to help you build them. In further chapters, you will learn about techniques you can use to manage asynchronous operations to make your Node.js applications powerful, but keep the code easy to write and maintain.

RESTful APIs with Node.js

Learning Objectives

By the end of this chapter, you will be able to:

- Set up the project structure for an Express.js API

- Design an API with endpoints using different HTTP methods

- Run the API on the localhost and interact with it via cURL or a GUI-based tool

- Parse user inputs for endpoints and consider different ways of dealing with errors

- Set up an endpoint that requires user authentication

In this chapter, we will use Express.js and Node.js to set up an API that can be used by frontend applications.

Introduction

Application Program Interfaces (**APIs**) have become more important than ever. The use of an API allows for a single server-side program to be used by multiple scripts and applications. Due to its usefulness, API management has become one of the most common tasks for backend developers using Node.js.

Let's take the example of a company with both a website and a mobile app. Both of these front-facing interfaces require essentially the same functionality from the server. By wrapping this functionality in an API, we allow for clean separation and reuse of the server-side code. Gone are the days of clunky PHP applications that embed backend functionality directly into the interface code of a website.

We'll use Node.js to set up a **Representational State Transfer** (**REST**) API. Our API will run on Express.js, a popular web application framework with routing functionality. With these tools, we can quickly have an endpoint running on our localhost. We'll look at the best practices for setting up an API as well as the specific syntax that is used in the Express.js library. In addition to this, we will also consider the basics of API design, simplifying its use for the developers and services that use it.

What is an API?

An API is a standardized way of interacting with a software application. APIs allow different software applications to interact with each other without having to understand the inner workings of the underlying functions.

APIs have become popular in modern software engineering as they allow organizations to be more effective by reusing code. Take the use of maps as an example: before the popularization of APIs, organizations needing map functionality would have to maintain map widgets internally. Often, these map widgets would perform poorly, as they were only a secondary concern of their business and engineering teams.

Now it's rare for a website or application that uses a map to maintain it internally. Many applications for the web and mobile phones are utilizing map APIs from either Google or alternatives such as OpenStreetMap. This allows each company to focus on its core competency by not having to create and maintain their own map widgets.

There are several successful start-ups whose business models revolve around providing a service via an API. Some examples include well-known companies such as Twilio, Mailgun, and Sentry. In addition to this, there are several smaller companies that offer unique services via APIs, such as Lob, which can send physical letters and postcards on request via their API. Here, developers simply send the contents of the letter and the destination address to Lob's API and it will automatically be printed and sent in the mail on the developer's behalf. Here are a few examples of the API services provided by a number of well-known companies.

Company	API Service
Twilio	Provides an API for phone calls and text messaging. Messages and calls can be sent or received. Users can create their own interactive phone systems by using this paid API service.
Mailgun	Provides an API for sending emails. Allows application developers to make use of emails without hosting a mail server or worrying about email-specific issues.
Sentry	Provides an API for error tracking.
Lob	Allows users of the API to print and send physical mail from a software application or server.
Stripe	Widely used payment API that can be integrated into other projects. Used by both and small and large companies; companies include Spotify, Lyft, and Target.
OpenStreetMap	Provides map data and maps using OpenData licensing and Creative Commons-licensed cartography.
IBM Watson	Provides artificial intelligence as a service made available by an API. Current services include voice recognition, intent recognition, and tone analysis.
Microsoft Cognitive Services	Another API providing artificial intelligence-related services. Current services include image analysis, natural language recognition, and decision recommendation.

Figure 4.1: API-based company examples

These companies enable developers to make apps better and faster by providing building blocks that can be used to provide a particular service. The proof of its effectiveness can be seen in the widespread adoption of these services. Companies that use Twilio to provide text or phone integration include Coca-Cola, Airbnb, Uber, Twitch, and many others. Many of those companies, in turn, provide their own APIs for other companies and developers to build upon. This trend is referred to as the API economy.

Another thing these services all have in common is that they use REST via HTTP. New developers often assume that all APIs are used via HTTP; however, when we talk about an API, there is no restriction on the protocol or medium used. The interface of an API could theoretically be anything from a button to a radio wave. While there are many interface options to choose from, HTTP is still the most widely used medium. In the next section, we'll discuss REST in more detail.

What is REST?

REST is a software architecture pattern for creating web-based services. This means that resources are represented by a specific URL endpoint, for example, `website.com/post/12459`, where a website's post can be accessed by using its specific ID. REST is the method of mapping resources to URL endpoints.

A related concept in the area of database management is that of **CRUD** (**create, read, update, and delete**). These are the four ways in which you can interact with database resources. Similarly, there are also four ways in which we generally interact with resource objects defined by our API endpoints. The HTTP protocol has built-in methods that facilitate tasks such as `POST`, `GET`, `PUT`, and `DELETE`.

The functionalities of the previously mentioned tasks are as follows:

- `POST`: Creates an object resource
- `GET`: Retrieves information about the object resource
- `PUT`: Updates a specific object's information
- `DELETE`: Removes a specific object

Additional Methods: In addition to the four main methods, there are some other less frequently used methods. We won't use them here and you shouldn't worry about them as they are rarely used by clients and servers:

- `HEAD`: This is the same as `GET` but only retrieves headers and not the body.
- `OPTIONS`: This returns a list of allowed options for the server or API.
- `CONNECT`: This is used for creating an HTTP tunnel.
- `TRACE`: This is a message loopback used for debugging.
- `PATCH`: This is similar to `PUT` but is used for updating a single value. Note that `PUT` can be used instead of `PATCH`.

Express.js for RESTful APIs on Node.js

The good news is that if you understand basic JavaScript, you're already halfway to creating your first API. Using Express.js, we can easily construct HTTP endpoints. Express is a popular and minimal web framework that is used for creating and hosting web applications on a node. It includes several built-in routing methods that allow us to map incoming requests. There are many middleware packages that make common tasks easier. We will use a validation package later in this chapter.

In this chapter, we'll be creating various aspects of a hypothetical smart-house API. This will require adding endpoints for various devices that have logic to change the state of the devices. Some of the endpoints will be open to anyone in the network, for example, a smart light, while others, such as a heater, will require authentication.

> **Note**
>
> What is a smart house? A smart house is a house that contains internet-connected devices, which you can interact with via a cloud-based control system. The trend of devices that are connected to the internet and communicate with users and other devices is often referred to as the **Internet of Things (IoT)**.
>
> In this chapter, we'll write an API for a house that contains smart devices, including a smart lightbulb and a heater. The code files for this exercise are available at https://github.com/TrainingByPackt/Professional-JavaScript/tree/master/Lesson04/Exercise16.

Exercise 16: Creating an Express Project with an Index Route

In this exercise, our aim is to create a new node project, install Express, and then create an index route that returns a JSON object with a single attribute of the message. Once it's running, we can test it by making a cURL request to our localhost. To do this, perform the following steps:

1. Create a folder called **smartHouse** and initiate an **npm** project:

    ```
    mkdir smartHouse
    cd smartHouse
    npm init
    ```

2. Install the **express** library, using the **-s** flag to have it saved to our **package.json** file:

    ```
    npm install -s express
    ```

3. Create a file called **server.js** that imports **express** and makes an **app** object:

    ```
    const express = require('express');
    const app = express();
    ```

4. Add an **app.get** method that specifies **'/'** for our index route in **server.js**:

```
app.get('/', (req, res) => {
  let info = {};
  info.message = "Welcome home! Our first endpoint.";
  res.json(info);
});
```

The preceding code creates an **HTTP GET** function that returns an object called **info** with a single attribute of **message**.

5. Add an **app.listen** function that tells our application to listen on **port 3000**:

```
// Start our application on port 3000
app.listen(3000, () => console.log('API running on port 3000'));
```

The preceding steps are all that is needed for a simple example of the Node.js Express API. By running the preceding code, we'll create an application on our localhost that returns a simple JSON object.

6. In another Terminal window, return to the root of your **smartHouse** folder and run the following command:

```
npm start
```

7. Confirm the application is running correctly by going to **localhost:3000** in your web browser:

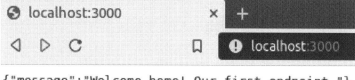

Figure 4.2: Showing localhost:3000 in the web browser

If you've copied the code correctly, you should see a JSON object being served at **localhost:3000**, as displayed in the preceding screenshot.

> **Note**
>
> If, during any step, you're having trouble or aren't sure what the project files should look like, you can use the project folders to move your code back in line with the project. The folders will be named based on which step they're associated with, for example, **Exercise01, Exercise02**, and so on. When you first go into a folder, make sure to run **npm install** to install any modules used by the project.

Interacting with Your API via HTTP

In this section, we'll interact with the server created in *Exercise 16, Creating an Express Project with an Index Route*. Therefore, make sure you keep a Terminal window open with the server running. If you've since closed that window or turned it off, simply return to the `smartHouse` folder and run `npm start`.

We verified that our API is running by using the web browser. A web browser is the easiest way to look at a route, but it is limited and only works for `GET` requests. In this section, we'll look at two other methods for interacting with the API in a more advanced way, both of which allow for more advanced requests including the following:

- Requests beyond `GET`, including `PUT`, `POST`, and `DELETE`

- Adding header information to your requests

- Including authorization information for protected endpoints

My preferred method is to use the command-line tool cURL. cURL stands for Client for URLs. It comes installed on most versions of macOS, Linux, and Windows 10 (for versions released in 2018 and later). It is a command-line tool for making HTTP requests. For a very simple command, run the following:

```
curl localhost:3000
```

The following is the output of the preceding code:

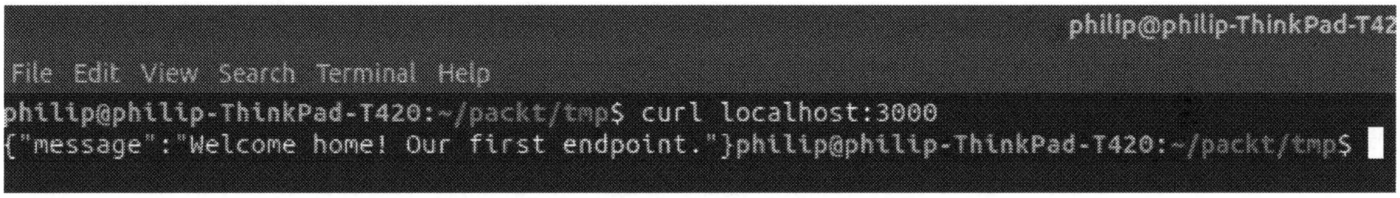

Figure 4.3: Showing cURL localhost:3000

> **Note**
>
> The command-line program **jq** will be used throughout this chapter to format cURL requests. **jq** is a lightweight and flexible command-line JSON processor. The program is available for macOS, Linux, and Windows. If you cannot get it installed on your system, you can still use **curl** without **jq**. To do so, simply remove the **|** **jq** command from the end of any curl command in this chapter.
>
> Instructions for installing **jq** can be found at https://github.com/stedolan/jq.

By using **curl** with **jq**, we can make reading the output a bit easier, which will be especially useful once our JSON becomes more complex. In the following, we'll repeat the same curl command as in the preceding example, but this time using a Unix pipe (|) to feed the output into **jq**:

```
curl -s localhost:3000 | jq
```

When piping **curl** into **jq** as in the preceding command, we'll use the **-s** flag, which stands for "silent." If **curl** is piped without this flag, you'll also see unwanted information about the speed of the request.

Assuming that you've done everything correctly, you should observe some cleanly displayed JSON as the output:

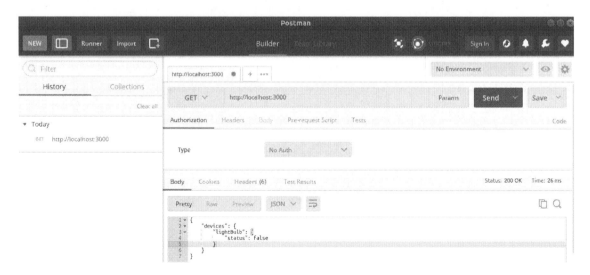

Figure 4.4: cURL piped to jq

If you prefer using a GUI-based application, you can use Postman, which is a Chrome extension that can easily send HTTP requests in a straightforward manner. Generally, I prefer cURL and jq for quick use on the command line. However, for more complex use cases, I may open up Postman, as the GUI makes dealing with headers and authorization a bit easier. For instructions on installing Postman, check out the website at https://www.getpostman.com:

Figure 4.5: Screenshot of the cURL request in Postman

Exercise 17: Creating and Importing a Route File

Currently, our application is running with a single endpoint at the root URL. Typically, an API will have many routes, and keeping them all in the main **server.js** file will quickly cause the project to become unorganized. To prevent this, we'll separate each of our routes into modules and import each one into our **server.js** file.

> **Note**
>
> The complete code for this example can be found at https://github.com/ TrainingByPackt/Professional-JavaScript/tree/master/Lesson04/Exercise17.

Perform the following steps to complete the exercise:

1. To get started, create a new folder in the **smartHouse** folder:

   ```
   mkdir routes
   ```

2. Create the **routes/index.js** file and move the **import** statements and **main** function from **server.js** into that file. Then, below that, we'll add a line that exports the **router** object as a module:

   ```
   const express = require('express');
   const router = express.Router();

   router.get('/', function(req, res, next) {
     let info = {};
     info.message = "Welcome home! Our first endpoint.";
     res.json(info);
   });

   // Export route so it is available to import
   module.exports = router;
   ```

   The preceding code is essentially the code we wrote in the first exercise being moved to a different file. The crucial difference is the very bottom line where it says **module.exports = router;**. This line takes the **router** object we create and makes it available for importing into another file. Every time we create a new route file, it will contain that same bottom line for exporting.

3. Open **server.js** and delete lines 3 to 8, as the **app.get** method has been moved to the **/routes/index.js** file. Then, we'll import the **path** and **fs** (filesystem) libraries. We'll also import a library called **http-errors**, which will be used later on for managing HTTP errors. The top nine lines of **server.js** will read as follows:

```
const express = require('express');
const app = express();

// Import path and file system libraries for importing our route files
const path = require('path');
const fs = require('fs');

// Import library for handling HTTP errors
const createError = require('http-errors');
```

4. Below that, also in **server.js**, we'll turn on URL encoding and tell **express** to use JSON:

```
// Tell express to enable url encoding
app.use(express.urlencoded({extended: true}));
app.use(express.json());
```

5. Next, we will import our index route and associate it with a path. After we've done that and the preceding steps, **server.js** should contain the following:

```
// Import our index route
let index = require('./routes/index');

// Tell Express to use our index module for root URL
app.use('/', index);
```

6. We can create a catch-all **404** error for any URL that is visited that doesn't have a corresponding function. Inside the **app.use** method, we'll set the HTTP status code to **404** and then use the **http-errors** library we imported in *step* 2 to create a catch-all **404** error (it's important that the following code is underneath all other route declarations):

```
// catch 404 and forward to error handler
app.use(function(req, res, next) {
  res.status(404);
  res.json(createError(404));
});
```

7. The final line in the file should exist from our previous exercise:

```
// Start our application on port 3000
app.listen(3000, () => console.log('API running on port 3000'));
```

With this done, running our code should produce the following output, which is identical to the result in *Exercise 16, Creating an Express Project with an Index Route*:

Figure 4.6: Output message

The advantage of having a **routes** folder is that it makes organizing our API easier as it grows. Every time we want to create a new route, we just have to make a new file in the **routes** folder, import it using **require** in **server.js**, and then use the Express **app.use** function to associate the file with an endpoint.

Templating Engines: In the preceding two lines where we used **app.use**, we were modifying the settings of **express** to use extended URL encoding and JSON. It can also be used to set a templating engine; for example, the **Embedded JavaScript (EJS)** templating engine:

```
app.set('view engine', 'ejs');
```

Templating engines allow Express to generate and serve dynamic HTML code for websites. Popular templating engines include EJS, Pug (Jade), and Handlebars. By using EJS, for example, we could generate HTML dynamically using a user object passed from a route to a view:

```
<p><%= user.name %></p>
```

In our case, we will not need to make use of **view** or templating engines. Our API will return and accept standard JSON exclusively. If you are interested in using Express for HTML-based websites, we encourage you to research the templating engines that are compatible with Express.

HTTP Status Codes

In *step 6* of *Exercise 17, Creating and Importing a Route File*, we set the HTTP status code for our response to **404**. Most people have heard of a 404 error as it is commonly seen when a page can't be found on a website. However, most people don't know what a status code is, or of any codes beyond **404**. So, we will start by explaining the concept of status codes and going over some of the most commonly used codes.

A status code is a three-digit number that is returned from a server in response to a client request over HTTP. Each three-digit code corresponds to a standardized status, for example, **not found**, **success**, and **server error**. These standardized codes make dealing with servers easier and more standardized. Often, a status code will be accompanied by some additional message text. These messages can be useful for humans, but when writing a script to deal with HTTP responses, it's much easier to simply account for status codes. For example, creating a case statement based on the status code returned.

Response codes fall into categories that are determined by the first digit in a three-digit number:

100-199	Information response codes
200-299	Successful response codes
300-399	Redirection message codes
400-499	Client error codes
500-599	Server error codes

Figure 4.7: Table of HTTP response code categories

Each of the categories of HTTP codes contains several specific codes that are to be used in certain situations. These standardized codes will help clients deal with responses even if they involve an unfamiliar API. For example, any 400-series client error code indicates to the client that the problem was with the request, whereas a 500-series error code indicates that the issue may be with the server itself.

Let's take a look at some of the specific HTTP status codes that exist in each of the categories from the following figure:

Information Response Codes:	
Information response codes are the least used of the five types. This type of code is rarely used and was not included in the original HTTP 1.0 specification. It can be used when a successful request has been received from the client but more time is needed for processing. Note: Information response codes are rarely used and are shown only for informational purposes.	
100 – Continue	Used in a situation where a very large payload is being sent that will take multiple requests. In this case, the server will respond with 100 to tell the client to continue uploading via continued
101 – Switching Protocols	Used when the client has requested a change of protocol and the server has agreed.
Successful Response Codes:	
Successful response codes are used when the request has been successfully received and processed by the server. Popular success codes include:	
200 – OK	Request successfully received and processed
201 – Created	Request successfully received, processed, and a new resource was
202 – Accepted	Request successfully received, and to be processed at some later
Redirection Message Codes: These codes are used when the client must take additional action to complete the request; most often used for URL redirects. Popular redirection message codes include:	
301 – Moved Permanently	Indicates that the resource has changed location permanently.
303 – See Other	The server cannot retrieve the resource but it may be found at some other URL.

Figure 4.8: Table of HTTP response codes

In the following figure, we can see a few more specific HTTP status codes:

Client Error Codes:	
Client error codes are used when an error has occurred due to a mistake made by the client.	
403 – Forbidden	The request was received and understood but the client doesn't have permission.
404 - Not Found	The resource indicated by the URL does not exist on the
422 – Unprocessable Entity	Request received and understood but unable to process.
Server Error Codes:	
Server error codes are used when the server has received the request and encountered an error while processing it. Popular server error codes include:	
500 – Internal Server Error	Indicates a general server error without specific cause
503 – Service Unavailable	Indicates service is not available due to overload or

Figure 4.9: Table of HTTP response codes continued

The codes that are listed here are only a handful of the dozens of HTTP status codes that are available. When writing your API, it is useful to use status codes where appropriate. Status codes make responses easier to understand for both users and machines. When testing our application, we may want to write a script that matches a list of requests with the expected response status codes.

When using Express, the default status code is always **200**, so if you don't specify a code in your result, it will be **200**, which indicates a successful response. A full list of HTTP status codes can be found at https://developer.mozilla.org/en-US/docs/Web/HTTP/Status.

To set a status code error, use the preceding code section and replace **404** with any error code supported by the **http-errors** library, which is a sub-dependency of Express. A list of all supported error codes can be found in the project's GitHub at https://github.com/jshttp/http-errors.

You can also pass an additional string to **createError()** to set a custom message:

```
res.status(404);

res.json(createError(401, 'Please login to view this page.'));
```

If you're using a success code, simply use **res.status** and return your JSON object as you would with the default **200** status:

```
res.status(201); // Set 201 instead of 200 to indicate resource created

res.json(messageObject); // An object containing your response
```

> **Note**
>
> There are many status codes that are rarely used; among these are some joke codes created throughout internet history:
>
> 418 – I'm a teapot: Made as an April Fool's joke in 1998. It indicates that the server refuses to brew coffee because it's a teapot.
>
> 420 – Enhance your calm: Used in the original version of Twitter when an app is being rate-limited. It is a reference to the movie Demolition Man.

Designing Your API

It's important to consider the design of your API early on in the software design process. Changing the endpoints of your API after release will require updating any service that relies on those endpoints. If an API is released for public use, it is often required that it maintain backward compatibility. Time spent on planning endpoints, accepted HTTP methods, required input types, and structures of JSON returned will be saved in the long run.

Often, guidelines relating to your specific use case or industry can be found, so be sure to do your research on this beforehand. In our example of a smart-home API, we'll take inspiration from the **World Wide Web Consortium's** (**WC3's**) recommendation related to IoT devices. The WC3 is one of the most influential organizations working to develop web standards, and their IoT initiative is known as **Web of Things** (**WoT**). You can find out more about this at https://www.w3.org/WoT/.

According to the WoT guidelines, each device should contain information about the model as well as a list of possible actions that can be used with the device. Here are some endpoints that are recommended by the WoT standard:

URL	Description
{wt}	Root resource URL
{wt}/model/	Information on the device model
{wt}/properties/	List of device properties
{wt}/properties/{id}	Information on specific property
{wt}/actions/	List of actions
{wt}/actions/{id}	Information on specific action
{wt}/actions/{id}/{actionId}	Execution of specific action
{wt}/.../	....

Figure 4.10: Table of standard WoT routes

This design is useful for two reasons – firstly, because it conforms to a standard, which gives users a set of expectations. Secondly, the use of helper endpoints such as **/properties/** and **/actions/** give users the ability to discover how the API can be used by requesting additional information at those endpoints.

Each device added to the house should have the **/model/**, **/properties/**, and **/actions/** endpoints. We'll map the endpoints shown in the preceding table onto each device in our API. The following tree diagram shows a map of our API stemming from the root endpoint.

The third level in the following figure shows the **/devices/light/** endpoint, and, stemming from that endpoint, we have the endpoints listed in the preceding table:

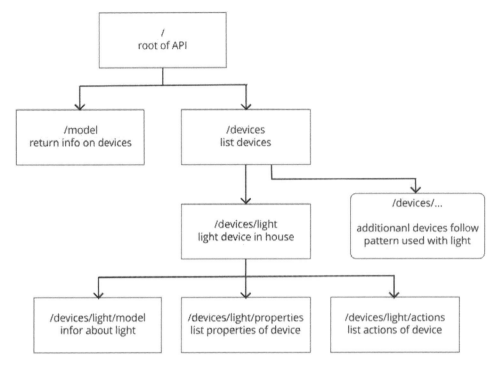

Figure 4.11: A tree chart of the smart-house API design

As an example of the kind of JSON that would be returned by an endpoint, we'll look more closely at the **/devices/light/actions** route defined in the preceding diagram. The following example shows the object of an action that contains a single action called **Fade**:

```
"actions": {
  "fade": {
    "title": "Fade Light",
    "description": "Dim light brightness to a specified level",
    "input": {
      "type": "object",
      "properties": {
```

```
      "level": {
        "type": "integer",
        "minimum": 0,
        "maximum": 100
      },
      "duration": {
        "type": "integer",
        "minimum": 0,
        "unit": "milliseconds"
      }
    }
  },
  "links": [{"href": "/light/actions/fade"}]
  }
}
```

We're basing our **fade** action on the suggestions made by Mozilla in their WoT documentation at https://iot.mozilla.org/wot. They've created this documentation with the goal of complementing the standard proposed by W3C and have included many examples of JSON representing IoT devices and their associated actions.

Notice that the object contains the name of the action, a description of the action, and the accepted values to use the action. It's also always a good idea to include the unit of measurement where applicable. With the duration, we know that it's measured in milliseconds; without this information, we'd have no idea what "1" really means.

By reading the preceding JSON, we can see that we need to send a request with a number for the desired lighting level (0 to 100) and another number to specify the length of time for the dimming. Using **curl**, we might fade the lights as follows:

```
curl -sd "level=80&duration=500" -X PUT localhost:3000/lightBulb/actions/
fade
```

According to the API action description, the preceding request should cause the lightbulb to fade to 80% brightness over a period of 500 milliseconds.

> **Note**
>
> **Documentation with Swagger**: Although it won't be covered in this book, another project you should look into is Swagger. This project helps automate the process of creating, updating, and displaying your API documentation and works well with Node.js and Express.
>
> An example of the kind of interactive documentation generated by Swagger can be seen at https://petstore.swagger.io/.

Exercise 18: Creating Action Routes

In this exercise, our aim is to create a new route file that returns information about the **fade** action, which we looked at in the previous section. The starting point for this exercise will be where we left off at the end of *Exercise 17, Creating and Importing a Route File*.

> **Note**
>
> The complete code for this example can be found at https://github.com/TrainingByPackt/Professional-JavaScript/tree/master/Lesson04/Exercise18.

Perform the following steps to complete the exercise:

1. Create a sub-folder in the **routes** folder called **devices**:

    ```
    mkdir routes/devices
    ```

2. Copy **routes/index.js** to **routes/devices/light.js**:

    ```
    cp routes/index.js routes/devices/light.js
    ```

3. Next, we'll open up **/routes/devices/light.js** from the previous exercise and modify it. Find line 6, which should contain the following:

```
info.message = "Welcome home! Our first endpoint.";
```

We will replace the preceding line with a large block of JSON that represents a list of all the device actions:

```
let info =    {
  "actions": {
    "fade": {
      "title": "Fade Light",
      "description": "Dim light brightness to a specified level",
      "input": {
        "type": "object",
        "properties": {
          "level": {
            "type": "integer",
            "minimum": 0,
            "maximum": 100
          },
```

In our case, the only action is **fade**. This action will change the lightbulb's level of brightness over a defined period of time (measured in milliseconds). This endpoint won't contain the logic to implement the function, but it will return the details needed to interact with it.

4. In the **server.js** file, import our newly created device route:

```
let light = require('./routes/devices/light');
```

5. We'll now use the preceding route by telling Express to use our **light** object for the **/devices/light** route:

```
app.use('/devices/light', light);
```

6. Run the program with **npm start**:

```
npm start
```

7. Test the route by using **curl** and **jq**:

```
curl -s localhost:3000/devices/light | jq
```

If you copied the preceding code correctly, you should get a formatted JSON object representing the **fade** action as follows:

```
> curl -s localhost:3000/devices/light | jq
{
  "actions": {
    "fade": {
      "title": "Fade Light",
      "description": "Dim light brightness to a specified level",
      "input": {
        "type": "object",
        "properties": {
          "level": {
            "type": "integer",
            "minimum": 0,
            "maximum": 100
          },
          "duration": {
            "type": "integer",
            "minimum": 0,
            "unit": "milliseconds"
          }
        }
      }
    },
    "links": [
      {
        "href": "/devices/light/actions/fade"
      }
    ]
  }
}
```

Figure 4.12: The cURL response for localhost:3000/devices/light

Further Modularizing

In the project files, we'll separate the light route further by making a **lightStructure.js** file, which contains only a JSON object representing the light. We won't include the long string of JSON that includes **model**, **properties**, and **action** descriptions.

> **Note**
>
> There won't be an exercise for the changes made in this section, but you can find the code at https://github.com/TrainingByPackt/Professional-JavaScript/tree/master/Lesson04/Example/Example18b.
>
> *Exercise 19* will start off using the code found in the **Example18b** folder.

It's useful to separate static data such as the endpoint object and the functions of separate files. **lightStructure.js** will contain the data representing the model, properties, and actions. This allows us to focus on the logic of endpoints in **light.js**. With this, we'll have four endpoints that each return the relevant section of the JSON light object:

```
// Light structure is imported at the top of the file
const lightStructure = require('./lightStructure.js');


// Create four routes each displaying a different aspect of the JSON object
router.get('/', function(req, res, next) {
  let info = lightStructure;
  res.json(info);
});


router.get('/properties', function(req, res, next) {
  let info = lightStructure.properties;
  res.json(info);
});


router.get('/model', function(req, res, next) {
  let info = lightStructure.model;
  res.json(info);
});


router.get('/actions', function(req, res, next) {
  let info = lightStructure.actions;
  res.json(info);
});
```

When working on a large block of JSON like the one found in `lightStructure.js`, it can be useful to use a GUI visualization tool. One example is https://jsoneditoronline.org/, which provides a tool that allows you to paste a block of JSON on the left-hand section of a page, and, on the right-hand side, visualize it as a tree-like object:

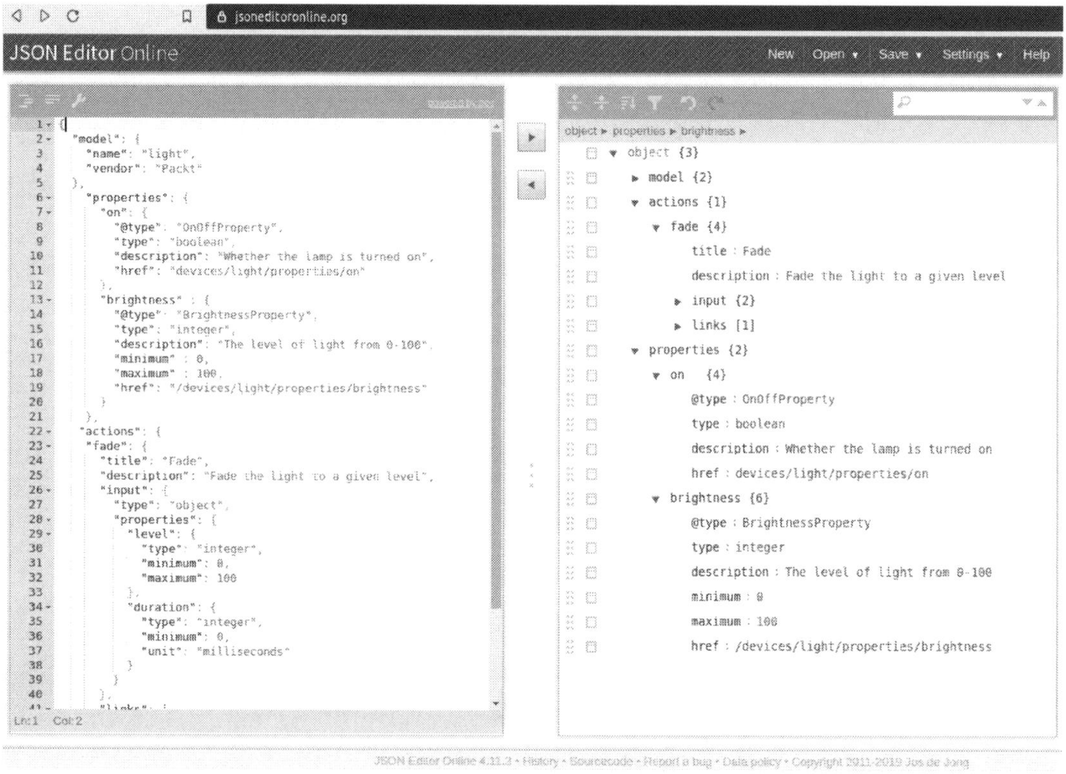

Figure 4.13: Online JSON explorer/editor

Changes can be made on either side of the visualization and copied to the other. This is useful because the more complex a JSON object becomes, the more difficult it is to see how many levels exist within a property.

Type Checking and Validating the Input Sent to an Endpoint

While type checking and validation are not strictly required for the creation of an API, using them can cut down on debugging time and help to avoid bugs. Having a guaranteed input for an endpoint means that code can be written with a focus on returning the desired result without considering the many edge cases that can be created by input outside that which is expected.

Since this task is so common with the creation of APIs, a library has been created to make verifying the input of Express endpoints easy. With the **express-validator** middleware, we can simply pass the input requirements to our endpoint as an argument. For example, the requirements described by the JSON object returned in *Exercise 18* for our lightbulb's **fade** action can be represented with the following array:

```
    check('level').isNumeric().isLength({ min: 0, max: 100 }),
    check('duration').isNumeric().isLength({ min: 0 })
]
```

As you can see, it contains an entry for each expected input. For each of these inputs, we perform two checks. The first is .**isNumeric()**, which checks that the input is a number. The second is .**isLength()**, which checks that the length is within the specified minimum to maximum range.

Exercise 19: Creating a Route with Type Checking and Validation

> **Note**
>
> The complete code for this example can be found at https://github.com/
> TrainingByPackt/Professional-JavaScript/tree/master/Lesson04/Exercise19.

In this exercise, we'll expand on our **routes/devices/light.js** file by adding a route that accepts **PUT** requests in **/actions/fade**.

The route will check that the request conforms to the standards specified by the **fade** action object, which we added to the **devices/light** endpoint in *Exercise 18, Returning JSON Representing Action Routes*. This includes the following aspects:

- The request contains level and duration values.
- The level and duration values are integers.
- The level value is between 0 and 100.
- The duration value is above 0.

Execute the following steps to complete the exercise:

1. Install **express-validator**, which is a middleware that wraps **validator.js** for the easy use of the **validation** and **sanitization** functions with **express**:

    ```
    npm install -s express-validator
    ```

2. Import the **check** and **validationResult** functions from the **express-validator** library by putting **routes/devices/light** on line 2, just below the **require** statement for **express**:

    ```
    const { check, validationResult } = require('express-validator/check');
    ```

3. Below the **route.get** function we wrote in the last exercise, create the following function that will handle **PUT** requests:

    ```
    // Function to run if the user sends a PUT request
    router.put('/actions/fade', [
        check('level').isNumeric().isLength({ min: 0, max: 100 }),
        check('duration').isNumeric().isLength({ min: 0 })
      ],
      (req, res) => {
        const errors = validationResult(req);
        if (!errors.isEmpty()) {
          return res.status(422).json({ errors: errors.array() });
        }
        res.json({"message": "success"});
    });
    ```

4. Run the API with **npm start**:

    ```
    npm start
    ```

5. Make a **PUT** request to **/devices/light/actions/fade** with the incorrect value **(na)** to test the validation:

    ```
    curl -sd "level=na&duration=na" -X PUT \
    http://localhost:3000/devices/light/actions/fade | jq
    ```

    The **-d** flag indicates "data" values to be passed to the endpoint. The **-X** flag indicates the HTTP request type.

If the preceding steps were done correctly, we should get an error when we make a **PUT** request to **/devices/light/actions/fade** with non-numeric values for the level and duration:

```
philip@philip-ThinkPad-T420:~/packt/steps/smartHouse$ \
> curl -sd "level=na&duration=na" -X PUT \
> http://localhost:3000/devices/light/actions/fade | jq
{
  "errors": [
    {
      "location": "body",
      "param": "level",
      "value": "na",
      "msg": "Invalid value"
    },
    {
      "location": "body",
      "param": "duration",
      "value": "na",
      "msg": "Invalid value"
    }
  ]
}
philip@philip-ThinkPad-T420:~/packt/steps/smartHouse$
```

Figure 4.14: The cURL error response for the /device/light/actions/fade route with incorrect data

6. Next, we'll make a **PUT** request like before, but with the correct values of **50** and **60**:

    ```
    curl -sd "level=50&duration=60" -X PUT \
    http://localhost:3000/devices/light/actions/fade | jq
    ```

    Sending a **PUT** request with values in the correct range should return the following:

```
philip@philip-ThinkPad-T420:~/packt/final/exercise_5$ \
> curl -sd "level=50&duration=60" -X PUT \
> http://localhost:3000/devices/light/actions/fade | jq
{
  "message": "success"
}
philip@philip-ThinkPad-T420:~/packt/final/exercise_5$
```

Figure 4.15: The cURL response for the /device/light/actions/fade route with correct data

The preceding screenshot indicates that the **PUT** request was successful.

Useful Defaults and Easy Inputs

So, we've seen how enforcing restrictions on inputs to an endpoint can be helpful. However, excessive restrictions and requirements can hinder the user experience of an API. Let's take a closer look at the lightbulb fade action. In order to allow for the feature of fading over a period of time, we require the user to pass a value for the duration. Many people already have experience of using a fade action on a physical lightbulb.

With a physical lightbulb, we know that we input our desired brightness level by adjusting a physical switch or other input. The duration is not necessarily part of that process or consciously thought about by the user. This creates the expectation that you should be able to fade the light by only the desired level.

For this reason, we should consider making the **duration** value optional. In the case that a **duration** value is not received, the script will fall back to a default value. This allows us to meet user expectations while still allowing fine-grained control for users who want to specify a duration.

Exercise 20: Making the Duration Input Optional

> **Note**
>
> The complete code for this example can be found at https://github.com/TrainingByPackt/Professional-JavaScript/tree/master/Lesson04/Exercise20.

In this exercise, we'll modify the fade action to make the duration an optional input. We'll modify our fade action endpoint to use a default value of 500 milliseconds if no duration value is provided:

1. In **routes/devices/light.js**, modify the line that validates **duration** by adding **.optional()** to the chain of functions. It should look like this:

   ```
   check('duration').isNumeric().optional().isLength({ min: 0 })
   ```

2. In **routes/devices/light.js**, delete the **return** statement and add the following in the same location:

   ```
   let level = req.body.level;
   let duration;

   if(req.body.duration) {
   ```

```
    duration = req.body.duration;
  } else {
    duration = 500;
  }
```

The preceding code creates a **level** variable using **level** input and initializes an empty variable for the duration. Next, we check whether the user provided a **duration** input. If so, we set the duration to that value. If not, we set **duration** to **500**.

3. Now, we'll create a **message** object called **message** using our **level** and **duration** variables. Then, we'll return that **message** object to the client:

```
let message = `success: level to ${level} over ${duration} milliseconds`;
res.json({"message": message});
```

4. Finally, we'll associate a second route with our function so that sending a **PUT** request to **/devices/light** executes the same function as **/devices/light/actions/fade**. This is accomplished by changing the first argument of **router.put** with an array that contains the old value and a new one of **/**. The opening of the **router.put** section should look like this:

```
// Function to run if user sends a PUT request
router.put(['/', '/actions/fade'], [
    check('level').isNumeric().isLength({ min: 0, max: 100 }),
    check('duration').isNumeric().optional().isLength({ min: 0 })
  ],
  (req, res) => {
```

5. Now that we're done with the coding part, we'll turn on the server for testing:

```
npm start
```

6. With the server running in one Terminal, open another to perform a few tests using **curl**. In the first command, we'll check that our new default endpoint is working and that our default value for the duration is used when no duration is provided:

```
curl -sd "level=50" -X PUT http://localhost:3000/devices/light | jq
```

If you've copied everything correctly, you should see an output like this:

```
philip@philip-ThinkPad-T420:~/packt/steps/smartHouse$ \
> curl -sd "level=50" -X PUT http://localhost:3000/devices/light | jq
{
   "message": "success: level to 50 over 500 ms"
}
philip@philip-ThinkPad-T420:~/packt/steps/smartHouse$
```

Figure 4.16: The cURL response for the /device/light route without a specified duration

7. We'll also want to make sure that providing a **duration** value overrides the default value. We can test this by making a cURL request that specifies a **duration** value:

    ```
    curl -sd "level=50&duration=250" -X PUT http://localhost:3000/devices/
    light | jq
    ```

    When specifying **250** as the **duration** value, we should see a confirmation that **level** will change to over 250 milliseconds in the response:

```
philip@philip-ThinkPad-T420:~/packt/steps/smartHouse$ \
> curl -sd "level=50&duration=250" -X PUT http://localhost:3000/devices/light | jq
{
   "message": "success: level to 50 over 250 ms"
}
philip@philip-ThinkPad-T420:~/packt/steps/smartHouse$
```

Figure 4.17: The cURL response for the /device/light route with a specified duration

With these changes, we've now made fade the default action for **/devices/light** and given the duration input a default value if not provided. It's worth noting that we now have two functions associated with the **/devices/light** endpoint:

- **HTTP GET /devices/light**: This returns information about interacting with the light.

- **HTTP PUT /devices/light**: This performs the default action of the light.

The reuse of the same endpoint with multiple methods is a good practice. Another common example is that of blog entries, where an API might have a single endpoint with four functions based on the method used:

- **HTTP POST /blog/post/42**: This creates a blog post with an ID of 42.

- **HTTP GET /blog/post/42**: This returns blog post #42 as a JSON object.

- **HTTP PUT /blog/post/42**: This edits blog post #42 by sending new content.

- **HTTP DELETE /blog/post/42**: This deletes blog post #42.

This makes sense logically using the REST model, where each endpoint represents a resource that can be interacted with in various ways.

In our case, we have made a **PUT** request to the **/devices/light** route that triggers the **fade** function. Arguably, a **switch** function that turns the light on and off would be more in line with most people's expectations of the default action of light. In addition to this, the switch would be a better default because it requires no inputs from the client. Fade was only chosen for this project because the switch was thought to be too simplistic.

We won't go into much depth on the **switch** function, but it would likely contain something like the following code section, which allows the client to specify the desired state. If no state is specified, it becomes the opposite of the current value:

```
if(req.body.state) {
  state = req.body.state;
} else {
  state = !state;
}
```

Middleware

Middleware functions in Express are functions that run before the function associated with an endpoint. Some common examples of this include logging a request or checking for authentication before running the main function of an endpoint. In these cases, the logging and authentication functions will be common among all the endpoints that use them. By using middleware, we can reuse code that is common across endpoints.

With Express, we can have middleware functions that run for all endpoints by using **app.use()**. For example, if we wanted to create a function that logs a request to the console before running the main route, we could write a **logger** middleware:

```
var logger = function (req, res, next) {
  // Request is logged
  console.log(req);
  // Call the special next function which passes the request to next function
  next();
}
```

To have the logger run with all endpoints, we tell our app to use it with the following:

```
app.use(logger);
```

If, instead, we want our middleware function to run on only some routes, we could attach it directly:

```
app.use('/devices/light', logger, light);
```

There is no limit to the number of middleware functions that can be used for some or all routes. When multiple middleware functions are used, they are called in the order that they are declared in your code. When one middleware function finishes, it passes the **req** and **res** objects on to the next function in the chain:

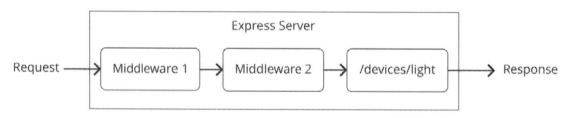

Figure 4.18: Diagram of middleware chaining

The preceding diagram visualizes a request process where once a request has been received by the server, it runs the first middleware function, passes the results to a second middleware function, and, when that is complete, our **/devices/light** destination route is finally run.

In the next section, we'll create our own middleware for checking whether guests have checked in to get an authentication token.

Exercise 21: Setting Up an Endpoint that Requires Authentication

> **Note**
>
> The complete code for this example can be found at https://github.com/
> TrainingByPackt/Professional-JavaScript/tree/master/Lesson04/Exercise21.

In the following exercise, we'll build on our project by adding an endpoint that requires authentication with a **JSON Web Token** (**JWT**). We'll create two new endpoints: the first, `restricted light`, will be identical to `light` but requires authentication. The second endpoint, `check-in`, allows clients to get a token by sending the server their name.

> **Note**
>
> **JWT and Security**: This exercise is meant to highlight how JWT authentication works. It wouldn't be secure in production as there is no means of verifying that the name supplied by the client is authentic.
>
> In production, a JWT should also contain an expiry date by which a client has to renew the token for continued use. For instance, a token given to a mobile app client might have an expiry date of 7 days. The client might check on startup whether the token is expiring soon. If so, it would request an updated token and the user of the application wouldn't notice the process.
>
> If, however, the user of the mobile app hadn't opened it in many days, the app would require the user to sign in again. This adds security, since any third party that might find a JWT only has a very short period of time in which to use it. For example, in the case that a cell phone is lost and found several days later, many applications using JWTs with expiry dates will require signing in again to interact with the owner's account.

Perform the following steps to complete the exercise:

1. Create a **config.js** file with a random secret value:

    ```
    let config = {};
    config.secret = "LfL0qpg91/ugndUKLWvS6ENutE5Q82ixpRe9MSkX58E=";
    module.exports = config;
    ```

    The preceding code creates a **config** object. It sets the secret attribute of **config** to a random string. Then, it exports the **config** object.

    It's important to remember that the secret is random and so yours should be unique to the one that is shown here. There is no set method for generating the random string but an easy way on the command line is to use **openssl**, which should be installed by default on most Linux and Mac operating systems:

    ```
    openssl rand -base64 32
    ```

2. Install **jwt-simple** with **npm**:

    ```
    npm install -s jwt-simple
    ```

3. Create the **routes/check-in.js** file for the **check-in** endpoint. Import the following modules, which we will need to make use of:

    ```
    const express = require('express');
    const jwt = require('jwt-simple');
    const { check, validationResult } = require('express-validator/check');
    const router = express.Router();

    // import our config file and get the secret value
    const config = require('../config');
    const secret = config.secret;
    ```

4. Below the import, in **routes/check-in.js**, we'll create a **post** route that requires a string value for **name**. We'll then encode all the information that has been sent into a JWT. This JWT is then returned to the client to use for authentication:

    ```
    router.post('/', [
        check('name').isString()
      ],
      (req, res) => {

        // If errors return 422, client didn't provide required values
        const errors = validationResult(req);
    ```

```
    if (!errors.isEmpty()) {
      return res.status(422).json({ errors: errors.array() });
    }

    // Otherwise use the server secret to encode the user's request as a
  JWT
    let info = {};
    info.token = jwt.encode(req.body, secret);
    res.json(info);
  });

  // Export route so it is available to import
  module.exports = router;
```

5. In **server.js**, also import **config.js** and **jwt-simple**, and set the secret value:

```
// Import library for working with JWT tokens
const jwt = require('jwt-simple');

// import our config file and get the secret value
const config = require('../config');
const secret = config.secret;
```

6. In **server.js**, add a middleware function to see whether a user has a valid token:

```
// Check if the requesting client has checked in
function isCheckedIn(req, res, next) {
  // Check that authorization header was sent
  if (req.headers.authorization) {
    // Get token from "Bearer: Token" string
    let token = req.headers.authorization.split(" ")[1];
    // Try decoding the client's JWT using the server secret
    try {
      req._guest = jwt.decode(token, secret);
    } catch {
      res.status(403).json({ error: 'Token is not valid.' });
    }
    // If the decoded object has a name protected route can be used
    if (req._guest.name) return next();
  }
  // If no authorization header or guest has no name return a 403 error
  res.status(403).json({ error: 'Please check-in to recieve a token.' });
}
```

7. In **server.js**, add the **check-in** endpoint and a second light to the **restricted-light** endpoint:

```
// Import our index route
let index = require('./routes/index');
let checkIn = require('./routes/check-in');
let light = require('./routes/devices/light');

// Tell Express to use our index module for root URL
app.use('/', index);
app.use('/check-in', checkIn);
app.use('/devices/light', light);
app.use('/devices/restricted-light', isCheckedIn, light);
```

The section of **server.js** where routes are imported and set up should look like the preceding code, with three new lines added. You can see that there is one line to import the **check-in** route and two for creating our new routes. Notice that we don't need to import **restricted-light** as it reuses the **light** object. The crucial difference with **restricted-light** is the use of the **isCheckedIn** middleware function. This tells **express** to run that function before serving the light route.

8. Turn the server on with **npm start**:

```
npm start
```

9. Open another Terminal window and run the following command to get a signed JWT token:

```
TOKEN=$(curl -sd "name=john" -X POST http://localhost:3000/check-in \
    | jq -r ".token")
```

The preceding command uses **curl** to post a name to the **check-in** endpoint. It takes the result from the server and saves it to a Bash variable called **TOKEN**. The **TOKEN** variable is local to the Terminal window in which the command was run; so, if you close the Terminal, you'll need to run it again. To check that it was saved correctly, tell the Bash shell to print the value:

```
echo $TOKEN
```

The following is the output of the preceding code:

Figure 4.19: Checking the value of $TOKEN in the Bash shell

You should see a JWT token, as shown in the preceding figure.

10. Send a cURL request to **restricted-light**, with an authentication token, by running the following command in your Terminal:

```
curl -sd "level=50&duration=250" -X PUT \
  -H "Authorization: Bearer ${TOKEN}" \
  http://localhost:3000/devices/restricted-light \
  | jq
```

It should return a successful fade, as shown in the following figure:

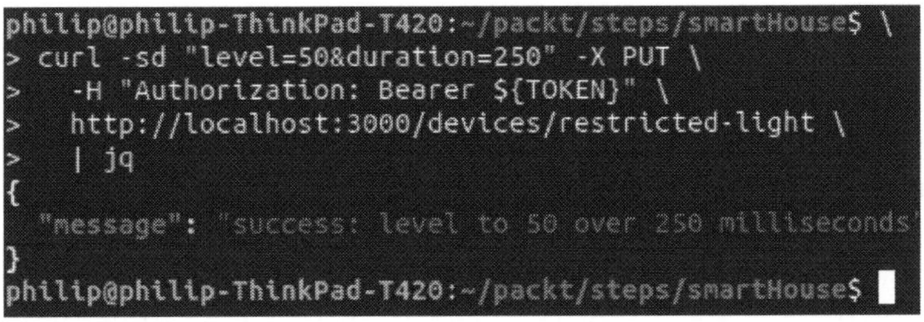

Figure 4.20: A successful cURL request to restricted-light using JWT

11. Send a **curl** request to **restricted-light**, without an authentication token, in your Terminal:

```
curl -sd "level=50&duration=250" -X PUT \
  http://localhost:3000/devices/restricted-light \
  | jq
```

In comparison, sending the same request without the endpoint returns an error:

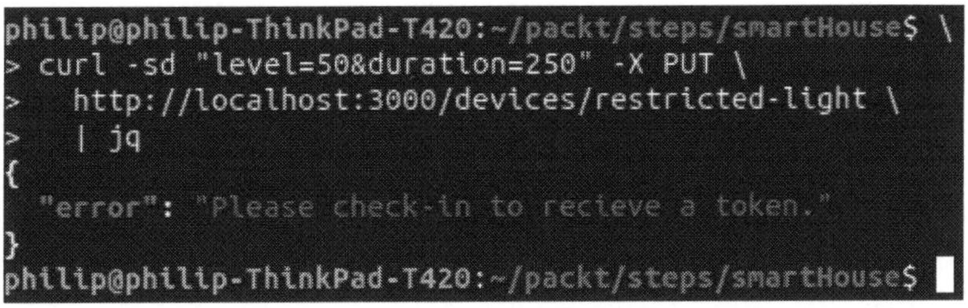

Figure 4.21: Trying to cURL restricted-light without a JWT

We now have an endpoint set up to distribute authentication tokens and a protected endpoint that requires them. We can now add additional routes that require authentication tokens by reusing our **isCheckedIn** function with any new endpoint. We just need to pass the function to Express as the second argument, as done in **server.js**.

The Contents of a JWT

In the previous exercise, during *step* 7, we requested a token from the server and saved the value to our local Terminal session. For the exercise to have worked, the JWT should have the three parts separated by a period. If we take the JWT that was returned from our **echo $TOKEN** command and put it into the website jwt.io, we can look at the contents of the JWT more closely.

Additionally, paste your secret value into the bottom-right corner of the GUI, which should display **Signature Verified** in the bottom-left corner. This tells us that the JWT being viewed was created using the private signature:

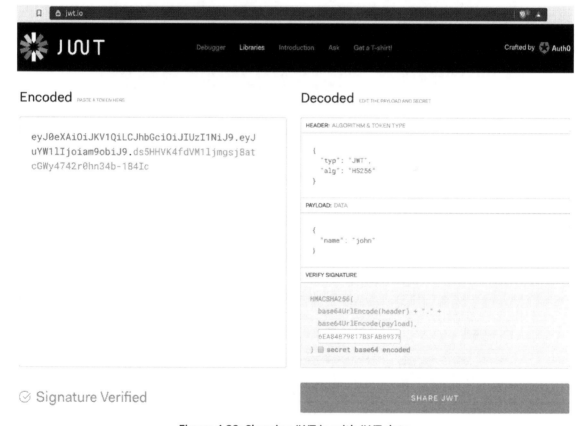

Figure 4.22: Showing JWT.io with JWT data

The JWT website allows us to easily visualize what the three sections of the JWT represent. The first section in red is the header, that is, information that describes the encoding standard used. The purple section is the payload – it contains the data that was verified by the server when the token was created, which, in our case, is just a name. Finally, the blue section is the signature, which is the result of hashing the contents of the other two sections with the server's secret.

In the preceding example, the **PAYLOAD** section is the smallest of the three. This won't always be the case as the red and blue sections are fixed in size, while the purple section is dependent on the size of the payload. If we request another token from our server using the **check-in** endpoint, then instead of just providing a name, we also provide an email and phone number. This means we will see a resulting token that has a larger purple section:

Figure 4.23: JWT.io with a token that has a larger payload

MongoDB

Many APIs make use of a database for keeping track of the underlying data being read and written by the API. In other cases, such as IoT, the functions at endpoints may update a real object. Even when a real object or event is being tracked or triggered, it is a good idea to track the expected state in a database. A database representation can be accessed and manipulated quickly.

We won't go into depth on the use and design of a database; however, we'll briefly talk about how you could use one to extend the functionality of an API. It is rare that you will have an API that goes beyond **hello world** without making use of a database of some sort.

The most popular database used with Node.js is MongoDB. MongoDB is an object-oriented library with a convenient syntax for working with JSON objects. In addition to storing data as JSON-like objects, it doesn't require the use of a schema. This means that the attributes for an object can change over time without you having to do any configuration on the database.

For example, we may start tracking events in our database that simply contain the request body and a timestamp:

```
{
   "timestamp": 1556116316288,
   "body" : { "level" : "50", "duration" : "250" }
}
```

We might start out with a very simple event log, and later decide that additional details should be saved along with each event. For example, if we include authorization data and the exact path of the request, our log objects would look like the following:

```
{
   "timestamp": 1556116712777,
   "body" : { "level" : "20", "duration" : "500" },
   "path" : "/devices/light",
   "token" : null
}
```

If a SQL database was used instead, we would first need to add **path** and **token** columns to the database schema. The flexibility of MongoDB is one of its great features along with the simplicity of adding it to a project that already uses JSON for data manipulation.

Often, APIs will be completely based around a database, as is the case for most social-media style apps. For example, with Twitter, Facebook, and Instagram, each user, post, and comment is ultimately an entry in a database that is made accessible to the client-side software through an API.

We won't go into depth on the use of databases with an API, but an extra folder explaining how to set up MongoDB and use it with this API for logging events has been included with the project files (see the following note).

The use of event logging with JWT would allow us to associate any malicious use of restricted endpoints with a specific JWT. By using a logging system and enforcing the use of JWTs on all endpoints, we could associate any requested action to `smartHouse` with a specific user. In the case of malicious use, a JWT could be blacklisted. Of course, this would require more stringent requirements for issuing a JWT; for example, requiring a guest to present government-issued photo identification.

> **Note**
>
> **Middleware with MongoDB logging example**: You can refer to the folder called `extra/mongo_logger_middleware` in the project file for an example of creating a catch-all middleware that logs information about each request including the methods, data, and user information. Something like this could be used to track which requests were made by who.
>
> When running this code, you'll need to first run **npm install**. In addition to this, make sure you have MongoDB installed locally and running. For more details, see the README file in the folder at https://github.com/TrainingByPackt/Professional-JavaScript/tree/master/Lesson04/Example/extra/mongo_logger_middleware.

Activity 5: Creating an API Endpoint for a Keypad Door Lock

In this activity, you need to create an API endpoint for a keypad door lock. The device needs a new endpoint to support the use case of authenticated users being able to create one-time passcodes to open the door.

Perform the following steps to complete the activity:

1. Create a new project folder and change directories going to it.

2. Initialize an **npm** project and install **express**, **express-validator**, and **jwt-simple**. Then, make a directory for **routes**.

3. Create a **config.js** file, which should contain a randomly generated secret value.

4. Make the **routes/check-in.js** file, in order to create a check-in route.

5. Create a second route file called **routes/lock.js**. Start the file off by importing the required libraries and modules, and create an empty array to hold our valid passcodes.

6. Below the code in **routes/lock.js**, create a **GET** route for **/code** that requires a **name** value.

7. Create another route in **routes/lock.js**. This one will be for **/open** and requires a four-digit code that will be checked against the **passCodes** array to see whether it is valid. Below that route, make sure to export **router**, so that it can be used in **server.js**.

8. Create the main file where our routes will be used in **server.js**. Start by importing the libraries needed and also setting URL encoding the JSON.

9. Next, in **server.js**, import the two routes, implement a **404** catch-all, and tell the API to listen on port **3000**.

10. Test the API to ensure it was done correctly. Start by running your program.

11. With the program running, open a second Terminal window and use the **/check-in** endpoint to get a JWT and save the value as **TOKEN**. Then, echo that value to ensure it was successful.

12. Use our JWT to use the **/lock/code** endpoint to get a one-time passcode for a new name.

13. Send the code to the **/lock/open** endpoint twice to get an error for the second instance.

> **Note**
>
> The solution to this activity can be found on page 594.

Summary

In this chapter, we've explored the use of Node.js for creating RESTful APIs. We've considered various uses of APIs and some techniques for designing them. Looking at aspects such as HTTP codes and input validation, we've considered common problems that are dealt with when creating and maintaining APIs. Despite this, there are still many areas of API design and development that haven't been considered.

The best way to continue improving your knowledge about API design and creation is to start making your own, whether at work or through personal projects. The code we've created throughout the exercises in this chapter can be used as a jumping-off point. Try expanding on what we've done here to create your own endpoints and eventually your own APIs.

In the next chapter, we'll talk about code quality. This will include techniques for writing readable code as well as techniques that can be used to test our code. Those techniques can be used in conjunction with what you've learned here to ensure that the endpoints you create continue to return the correct values as your project grows.

5

Modular JavaScript

Learning Objectives

By the end of this chapter, you will be able to:

- Import and export functions and objects in JavaScript for code reusability
- Use JavaScript ES6 classes to reduce code complexity
- Implement object-oriented programming concepts in JavaScript
- Create private variables for an object using encapsulation
- Convert ES6 to generic JavaScript using Babel
- Create and publish an npm package in JavaScript
- Combine modules using composability and strategies to create higher-level modules

In this chapter, we will learn about the importance of reusable code in modern JavaScript and how ES6 has introduced syntax for easily creating and using modules. We will create a JavaScript module that can be imported and used by different endpoints of our API.

Introduction

In the previous chapter, we built an API using Node.js and Express. We talked about designing the API structure, HTTP methods, and **JSON Web Token** (**JWT**) authentication. In this chapter, we'll be looking at various aspects of JavaScript modules and module-based design.

Modules are important for programming productivity, breaking software into reusable modules. The modular design encourages developers to build software out of small, single-focus components. You may be familiar with popular UI libraries, such as Bootstrap, Material-UI, and jQuery UI. These are all sets of components – minimal graphical elements purposefully built so that they can be used in many situations.

Due to the extensive use of external libraries for both graphical elements and programming aspects, most developers are already familiar with the use of modules. That said, it is much easier to use a module than to create one or to write your application in a modular way.

> ### Note Components, Modules, and ES6 Modules
>
> There are various opinions as to the exact usage and relation of these terms. In this chapter, we refer to components as visual widgets that can be used on a website.
>
> We'll refer to a module as a source code that is written in one file to be imported and used in another. As most components exist as reusable code, often imported by a script tag, we'll consider them modules. Of course, when you import the Bootstrap library, for example, you import all the components. That said, most libraries offer the ability to compile and import the specific components that are needed – for example, https://getbootstrap.com/docs/3.4/customize/.
>
> When we refer to ES6 modules, we're talking about the specific syntax added to JavaScript in ES6 that allows for exporting a module in one file and importing it in another. While ES6 modules are part of the ES6 standard, it's important to remember that they're not currently supported by browsers. Making use of them requires a pre-compile step, which we will cover in this chapter.

The recent explosion in the popularity and productivity of JavaScript is in part due to the **node package manager** (**npm**) ecosystem. Whether doing frontend or backend development with JavaScript, you're bound to use npm at some point. Hundreds of useful packages are made available to developers through the simple `npm install` command.

npm has become the largest source of modularized code on the internet, out of any programming language. npm now contains nearly a half a billion packages.

All packages on npm are, at their core, modules. By grouping related functions as a module, we make that functionality reusable across multiple projects or multiple aspects of a single project.

All great packages on npm have been built in a way that makes reuse across many projects easy. A good datetime picker widget, for example, can be used across thousands of projects, saving many hours of development time and likely yielding a better end product.

In this section, we'll look at modular JavaScript and how we can improve our code by writing JavaScript in a modular way. This includes the basic syntax of exporting and importing, but, beyond that, there are several patterns and techniques that can be used to write better modules, such as concepts from object-oriented programming that are useful in module development. However, JavaScript is technically prototype-oriented, which is a specific style of object-oriented programming that differs from the classic object-oriented style in its use of prototypes as opposed to classes. We'll discuss prototypes and classes later in the chapter.

Dependencies and Security

While modules are a powerful technique, they can also get out of hand if not used with care. Each package added to a `node.js` project, for example, contains its own dependencies. So, it's important to keep an eye on the packages you're using to make sure you don't import anything malicious. There is a useful tool at the website http://npm.broofa.com, where you can upload a `package.json` file and get a visualization of the dependencies.

If we take the **package.json** file from *Exercise 1*, *Creating an Express Project with an Index Route*, in *Chapter 4*, *RESTful APIs with Node.js*, as an example, it contained only four **dependencies**:

```
"dependencies": {

  "express": "^4.16.4",

  "express-validator": "^5.3.1",

  "jwt-simple": "^0.5.6",

  "mongodb": "^3.2.3"

}
```

Yet, when we upload this **package.json** file, we can see that our 4 dependencies balloon out to over 60 when accounting for sub-dependencies:

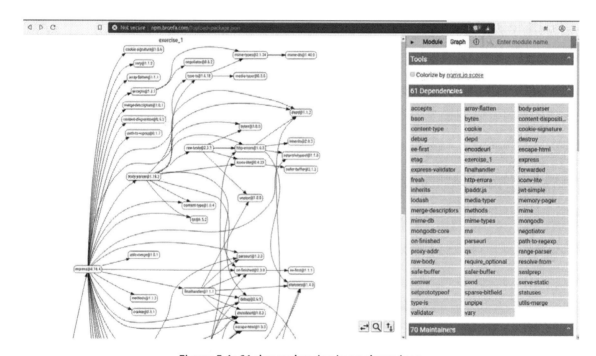

Figure 5.1: 61 dependencies in package.json

This highlights the risk associated with module-based design and the need for thoughtful design when making and using modules. Badly written packages or modules can have unintended consequences. In recent years, there have been stories of widely used packages becoming malicious. For example, the **event-stream** package was downloaded over 8 million times in 2.5 months in 2018. It was found that the once-legitimate module had been updated in an attempt to steal cryptocurrency from users' machines. Aside from security risks and bugs, there is also the risk of polluting the global namespace or lowering the performance of the parent project.

> **Note npm audit**
>
> As a response to cases of malicious dependencies or sub-dependencies, npm added an **audit** command, which can be used to check a package's dependencies for modules known to be malicious. Run **npm audit** in the directory of a Node. js project to check your project's dependencies. The command also runs automatically as part of **npm install** when you're installing projects downloaded from places such as GitHub.

Other Costs of Modularity

Other costs associated with modular design include:

- The cost of loading multiple parts
- The cost of bad modules (security and performance)
- A quick increase in the total amount of modules used

Overall, these costs are generally acceptable, but caution should be used. When it comes to the overhead associated with loading many modules, pre-compilers such as **webpack** and **babel** can help by converting your whole program to a single file.

A few things to bear in mind when you're creating a module or importing one are the following:

- Does using a module hide significant complexity or save a significant amount of work?
- Is the module from a trusted source?
- Does it have a lot of sub-dependencies?

Take the npm package, `isarray`, for example. The package contains a single function, which simply runs:

```
return toString.call(arr) == '[object Array]';
```

This is an example where the answer to the first question, "Does using a module hide significant complexity?", is no. The second question – "Is it a trusted source?" Not particularly. Finally, in answer to the last question about sub-dependencies, it does not – and this is a good thing. Given the simplicity of this module, it is recommended to just write your own function based on the preceding single line.

Carelessly installing packages that add little benefit while increasing the complexity of the project should be avoided. If you consider the three points mentioned, you likely won't find it worth it to import packages such as `isarray`.

Reviewing Imports and Exports

In the last section, we made use of importing and exporting without going into depth on the topic. Whenever we created a new route, we made sure to put it in its own file in the **routes** folder. If you recall, all of our route files ended with a line exporting a **router** object:

```
module.exports = router;
```

We also made use of our routes using the built-in **require** function from Node.js:

```
let light = require('./routes/devices/light');
```

Separation of Concerns

When it comes to designing a module, one of the key concepts is the **separation of concerns**. Separation of concerns means we should separate our software into parts that deal with a single concern of the program. A good module will focus on doing a single aspect of functionality well. Popular examples include:

- MySQL – A package with several methods for connecting to and using MySQL databases

- Lodash – A package for efficiently parsing and working with arrays, objects, and strings

- Moment – A popular package for working with dates and times

Within these packages or within our own projects, there is often a further separation into sub-modules.

> **Note ES6**
>
> We've already used some ES6 features in prior chapters, but, as a reminder, ES6, or the longer ECMAScript, is short for European Computer Manufacturer's Association Script. ECMA is the organization responsible for the standardization of standards, including the new version of JavaScript, which was standardized in 2015.

ES6 Modules

When writing JavaScript with Node.js, the ability to import modules using the built-in `require()` function has long been used. As this feature was useful, many frontend developers began making use of it by pre-processing their JavaScript with compilers such as Babel. A JavaScript pre-compiler processes code that normally wouldn't work on most browsers and generates a new JavaScript file that is compatible.

As there was a large demand for an import style function in JavaScript, it was eventually added to the language in the ES6 version. At the time of writing, the latest version of most browsers is almost completely ES6 compatible. Yet the use of **import** can't be taken for granted, as many devices will continue to run older versions for years.

The rapid standardization of ES6 shows us that, going forward, ES6 imports will be the most popular method.

In the last chapter, we made use of the Node.js **require** method for importing a module. For example, take this line:

```
const express = require('express');
```

The ES6 **import** function, on the other hand, has the following syntax:

```
import React from 'react';
```

The ES6 **import** function also allows you to import a subsection of a module, rather than importing the whole thing. This is one capability ES6's **import** has over Node.js' **require** function. Importing single components helps to save memory in your application. If we wanted to use just the **button** component from the React version of Bootstrap, for example, we could import just that:

```
import { Button } from 'reactstrap';
```

If we want to import additional components, we just add them to the list:

```
import { Button, Dropdown, Card } from 'reactstrap';
```

> **Note React**
>
> You've probably seen this style of importing if you've ever used the popular frontend framework React. The framework is known for its focus on modularity. It takes interactive frontend elements and packages them as components.
>
> In traditional vanilla JavaScript/HTML, projects are often split into HTML/CSS/JavaScript with various components spread out across those files. React instead packages the related HTML/CSS/JavaScript of an element into a single file. That component is then imported into another React file and used as an element in the application.

Exercise 22: Writing a Simple ES6 Module

> **Note**
>
> This chapter has a starting point directory, which can be found at https://github.com/TrainingByPackt/Professional-JavaScript/tree/master/Lesson05/start.
>
> The finished code for this exercise can be found at https://github.com/TrainingByPackt/Professional-JavaScript/tree/master/Lesson05/Exercise22.

In this exercise, we'll export and import a module using ES6 syntax:

1. Change directories to **/Lesson_05/start/**; we'll use this as our starting point.
2. Install project dependencies using **npm install**.
3. Create the **js/light.js** file with the following code:

```
let light = {};
light.state = true;
light.level = 0.5;

var log = function () {
```

```
        console.log(light);
    };
```

```
    export default log;
```

4. Open the file called **js/viewer.js**. This is the JavaScript that will run on our page. At the top of the file, add:

```
    import light from './light.js';
```

5. At the bottom of **js/viewer.js**, add:

```
    light();
```

6. **js/viewer.js** is already being included in **index.html**, so we can now start the program with **npm start**.

7. With the server running, open a web browser and go to **localhost:8000**. Once there, press F12 to open the developer tools.

If you've done everything right, you should see our object being logged in the Google Chrome console:

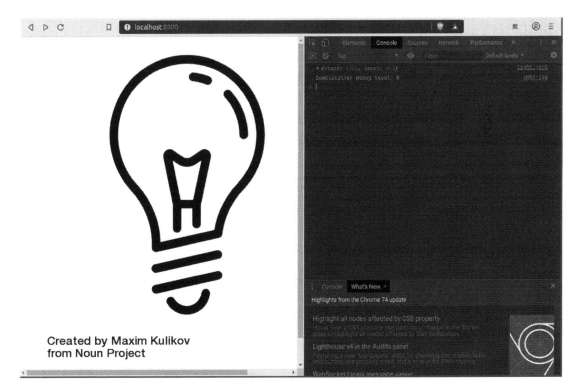

Figure 5.2: Object logged in the Google Chrome console

Objects in JavaScript

If you've been writing JavaScript for even a short time, you'll quickly come across the **object** type. JavaScript is designed using prototypes, a type of object-based programming. An object in JavaScript is a variable that can contain multiple properties. These properties can point to values, sub-objects, or even functions.

Every variable in a JavaScript program is either an object or a primitive. A primitive is a more basic type that contains only a single piece of information, with no properties or methods. What complicates JavaScript and makes objects even more important is that even most basic types such as strings and numbers are wrapped in an object once assigned to a variable.

For example:

```
let myString = "hello";

console.log(myString.toUpperCase()); // returns HELLO

console.log(myString.length); // returns 5
```

The preceding code shows that even a basic string variable in JavaScript has properties and methods.

A true primitive has no properties or methods. For example, numbers declared directly are primitives:

```
5.toString(); // this doesn't work because 5 is a primitive integer

let num = 5;

num.toString(); // this works because num is a Number object
```

Prototypes

As mentioned earlier, JavaScript is a prototype-oriented language. This is a variation on object-oriented programming where prototypes are used instead of classes. A prototype is an object that is used as a starting point for another. For example, in the last section, we looked at a simple string variable:

```
let myString = "hello";
```

As we saw in the last section, **myString** comes with some built-in functions, such as **toUpperCase()**, and attributes, such as **length**. Behind the scenes, **myString** is an object that is being created from the string prototype. This means that all the properties and functions that exist in the string prototype also exist in **myString**.

JavaScript objects contain a special attribute called **__proto__** property, which contains the parent prototype for an object. To look at this, let's run **console.dir(myString)** in the Google Chrome Developer Console:

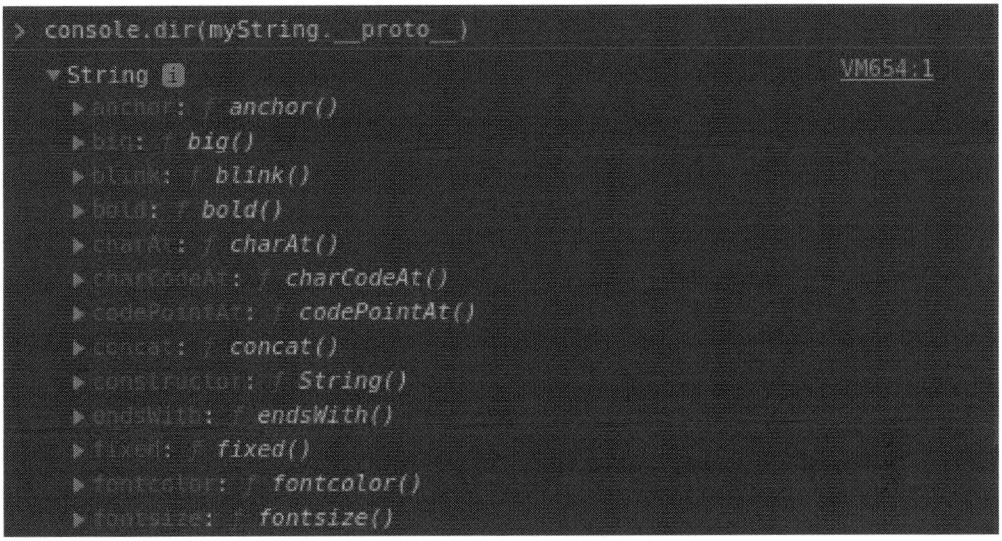

Figure 5.3: Prototypes in JavaScript (String)

Running the command returns **String**, an object that contains several methods. The built-in **String** object itself has a prototype. Next, run **console.dir(myString.__proto__.__proto__)**:

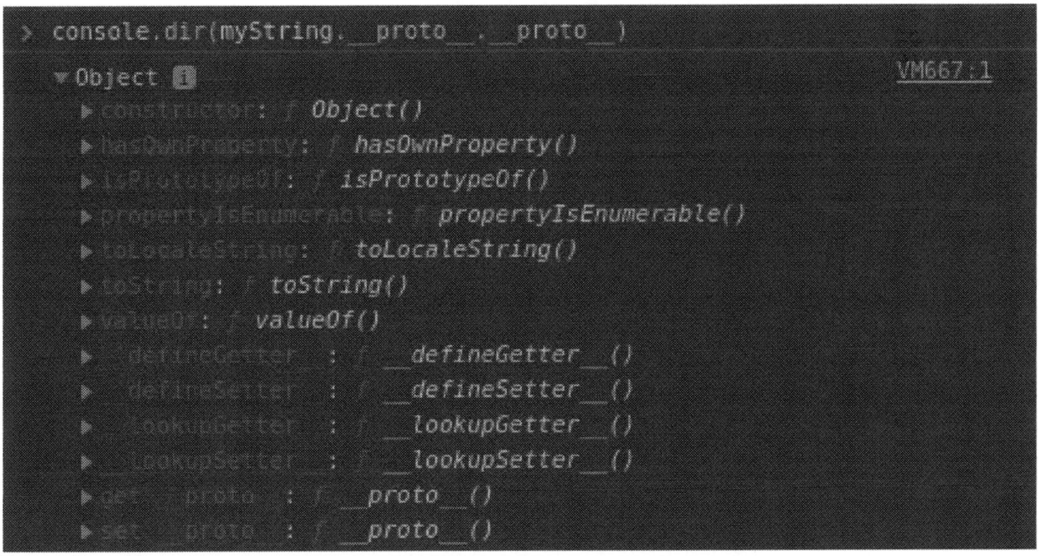

Figure 5.4: Prototypes in JavaScript (Object)

Running it again with an additional **__proto__** property will return **null**. All prototypes in JavaScript eventually lead to **null**, which is the only prototype that itself does not have a prototype:

```
> console.dir(myString.__proto__.__proto__.__proto__)
  null
```

Figure 5.5: Additional _proto_ returning null

This relationship, where one prototype leads to another and so on, is referred to as the prototype chain:

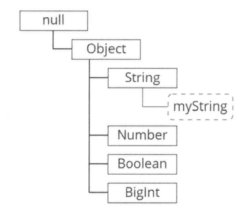

Figure 5.6: Prototype chain

Whenever you use an attribute of a variable in JavaScript, it starts at the current object, and, if it doesn't find it, it looks in the parent prototype. So, when we run **myString. toUpperCase()**, it first looks in **myString**. After not finding a method of that name, it checks **String**, where it finds the method. In the case that **String** did not contain the method, it would check the **Object** prototype, and then it would reach **null**, at which point a **not found error** is returned.

JavaScript provides the syntax to redefine the behavior of any prototype function, whether built-in or user defined. This can be done using the following command:

```
Number.prototype.functionName = function () {
    console.log("do something here");
}
```

In the next exercise, we'll modify the built-in **Number** prototype to give it some extra functionality. Remember that this technique can be applied to both built-in and custom-built prototypes.

Exercise 23: Extending the Number Prototype

In this exercise, we'll look at an example of extending one of JavaScript's built-in prototypes, **Number**, to include some additional functions. After *step 1*, see whether you can come up with the second solution yourself:

- double (returns the value multiplied by two)

- square (returns the number multiplied by itself)

- Fibonacci (returns **n** in Fibonacci sequence, where each number is the sum of the previous two numbers)

- factorial (returns the result of multiplying all numbers between 1 and **n**)

Here are the steps to follow:

1. In a new folder, create a file called **number.js**. We'll start by adding a **double** function to the **Number** prototype. Notice the use of **this.valueOf()** to retrieve the value of the number:

   ```
   Number.prototype.double = function () {
      return this.valueOf()*2;
   }
   ```

2. Next, following the same pattern, we'll add a solution for the square of any number:

   ```
   Number.prototype.square = function () {
      return this.valueOf()*this.valueOf();
   }
   ```

3. Again, we'll follow the same pattern, though the solution to this one is a bit trickier, as it uses recursion with memorization, and the use of the **BigInt** prototype:

   ```
   Number.prototype.fibonacci = function () {
      function iterator(a, b, n) {
         return n == 0n ? b : iterator((a+b), a, (n-1n))
      }
   ```

```
    function fibonacci(n) {
      n = BigInt(n);
      return iterator(1n, 0n, n);
    }
    return fibonacci(this.valueOf());
  }
```

Note BigInt (Big Integer)

You'll notice in the preceding step that we used the **BigInt** keyword. **BigInt**, like
Number, is another prototype built into JavaScript. It was the first new primitive in
ES6. The main difference is that **BigInt** is safe for dealing with very large numbers.
The **Number** prototype starts to fail with any value greater than **9007199254740991**.

A number can be converted to **BigInt** either by wrapping it with **BigInt()** or by
appending **n**; notice the use of **0n** and **1n**.

4. Next, we'll add a solution for the factorial using the same pattern and **BigInt**:

```
Number.prototype.factorial = function () {
  factorial = (n) => {
    n = BigInt(n);
    return (n>1) ? n * factorial(n-1n) : n;
  }
  return factorial(this.valueOf());
}
```

5. To demonstrate, define a number and call the functions:

```
let n = 100;

console.log(
  "for number " + n +"\n",
  "double is " + n.double() + "\n",
  "square is " + n.square() + "\n",
  "fibonacci is " + n.fibonacci() + "\n",
  "factorial is " + n.factorial() + "\n"
);
```

6. Run the script using Node.js:

```
node number.js
```

You should get back a similar result to the following:

```
> node number.js
for number 100
 double is 200
 square is 10000
 fibonacci is 354224848179261915075
 factorial is 93326215443944152681699238856266700490715968264381
6214686925293895217599993229915608941463976156518286253697920827223
758251185210916864000000000000000000000000000000
```

Figure 5.7: Output after extending JavaScript's built-in prototype

ES6 Classes

As mentioned earlier, one of the key differences between prototype-based languages and classic object-oriented languages is the use of prototypes instead of classes. However, ES6 has introduced built-in classes. We will start by comparing and creating an object using prototype syntax to ES6 class syntax by creating a **Vehicle** prototype/class and a **Car** prototype/class.

First, the prototype way:

```
function Vehicle(name, color, sound) {
    this.name = name;
    this.color = color;
    this.sound = sound;
    this.makeSound = function() {console.log(this.sound);};
}


var car = new Vehicle("car", "red", "beep");
car.makeSound();
```

Then, the same thing with ES6 classes:

```
class Vehicle {

    constructor(name, color, sound) {

        this.name = name;

        this.color = color;

        this.sound = sound;

        this.makeSound = () => console.log(this.sound);

    }

}


const car = new Vehicle("car", "red", "beep");

car.makeSound();
```

The ES6 syntax for class syntax allows us to write code in an object-oriented way. At a lower level in the language, classes are simply syntactic styling for creating prototypes.

In the coming section, we'll discuss programming in an object-oriented style using ES6 classes.

Object-Oriented Programming (OOP)

It is important to make a clear distinction between JavaScript objects and **object-oriented programming** (**OOP**). These are two very different things. The JavaScript object is simply a key-value pair that contains properties and methods. OOP, on the other hand, is a set of principles that can be used to write more organized and efficient code.

OOP is not required for modular JavaScript, but it contains many concepts relevant to modular JavaScript. The use of classes is an essential aspect of OOP that allows us to reuse code by creating classes and subclasses.

It teaches us to group related aspects of a program in a way that makes maintenance and debugging easier. It has a focus on classes and subclasses that makes reusing code more practical.

Historically, OOP became a popular way to deal with spaghetti code (messy, hard-to-read code) that was being commonly written in procedural code. Often, unorganized procedural code became fragile and rigid due to the interdependence of functions. A change in one aspect of the program may cause completely unrelated bugs to appear.

Imagine we're fixing a car and changing the headlight caused a problem with the engine. We would consider this to be bad architecture on the part of the designer of the car. Modular programming embraces the grouping of common aspects of a program.

There are four core concepts of OOP:

- Abstraction
- Encapsulation
- Inheritance
- Polymorphism

Throughout this chapter, we'll look at these four principles and how they can be used in the JavaScript programming language using ES6 syntax. We'll try to focus on practical application in this chapter but relate back to the core concepts above.

Abstraction

Abstraction is a high-level concept used throughout programming and is the foundation of OOP. It allows us to create complex systems by not having to deal with the specific implementation. When we use JavaScript, many things are abstracted by default. For example, consider the following array and the use of the built-in **includes()** function:

```
let list = ["car", "boat", "plane"];

let answer = list.includes("car") ? "yes" : "no";

console.log(answer);
```

We don't need to know the algorithm or code that is used when we run **includes()**. All we need to know is that it will return **true** if the **car** is in the array and **false** if it is not. This is an example of abstraction. It is possible that as versions of JavaScript change, the inner workings of the algorithm for **include()** may change. It may get faster or smarter in some way, but because it has been abstracted, we don't need to worry about the program breaking. We simply have to know the condition upon which it will return **true** or **false**.

We don't need to consider how our computer converts binary to visuals on the screen, or how pressing a key creates an event in our browser. Even the keywords that make up the JavaScript language are themselves code.

It is possible to look at the lower-level code that executes when we use built-in JavaScript functions, which will differ between browser engines. With **JSON.stringify()**.

Let's take a moment to think about what an abstract object is. Consider an apple on your desk sitting next to you; this is a specific apple. It's an instance of the idea or classification of an apple. We can also talk about the idea of the apple and what makes an apple an apple; what attributes are common in apples and which are required to make an apple.

When I say the word *apple*, a picture of the fruit comes into your mind. The exact details of how you imagine the apple is based on your mind's version of the idea of an apple. When we define an apple class in a computer program, we are defining how the program defines the class of an apple. As in our imagination, an idea of a thing can be as specific or unspecific as we desire. It may contain only a few factors, such as shape and color, or dozens, including weight, origin, and flavor.

Classes and Constructors

In the first exercise, we created a light module. While it is a module, it isn't object-oriented. In this section, we'll go about redesigning that module in an object-oriented way.

One of the most essential aspects of a class is its constructor. The constructor is a built-in function that is called when an instance of a class is created. Often, the constructor is used to define the attributes of an object. For example, you'll often see something like this:

```
class Apple {
  constructor(color, weight) {
    this.color = color;
    this.weight = weight;
  }
}
```

The passed arguments are saved to the instance for later use. You also might add some additional attributes not based on the passed arguments. For example, say we want to give our apple a birthdate by attaching a datetime stamp. We could add a third line inside our constructor:

```
this.birthdate = Date.now();
```

Or we may want to call some other function within the light module. Imagine a game where every apple that enters the world has a 1 in 10 chance of being rotten:

```
this.checkIfRotten();
```

Our class would need to contain a **checkIfRotten** function, which would set the **isRotten** attribute to **true** 1 out of 10 times:

```
checkIfRotten() {
  If (Math.floor(Math.random() * Math.floor(10)) == 0) {
    this.isRotten = true;
  } else {
    this.isRotten = false;
  }
}
```

Exercise 24: Converting a Light Module to a Class

> **Note**
>
> This exercise uses the end product of *Exercise 22, Writing a Simple ES6 Module* of this chapter, as a starting point. The state of the code after completing this exercise can be found at https://github.com/TrainingByPackt/Professional-JavaScript/tree/master/Lesson05/Exercise24.

Let's return to our light example from *Exercise 22, Writing a Simple ES6 Module*, of this chapter. We'll take the attributes defined in the previous chapter for the light module and assign them at creation. In addition, we'll write functions that check the format of the light attributes. If a light was created with an invalid attribute value, we'll set it to a default value.

The following are the steps to perform the exercise:

1. Open up **js/light.js** and delete the code from the previous exercise.

2. Create a class declaration for our **Light** class:

```
class Light  {

}
```

3. Add the **constructor** function to the class and set the attributes from the arguments as well as a **datetime** attribute. Instead of setting **state** and **brightness** directly, we'll first pass arguments to two functions to check the correct format. The logic for these functions will be written in the following steps:

```
class Light  {
  constructor(state, brightness) {
    // Check that inputs are the right types
    this.state = this.checkStateFormat(state);
    this.brightness = this.checkBrightnessFormat(brightness);
    this.createdAt = Date.now();
  }
}
```

4. Add the **checkStateFormat** and **checkBrightnessFormat** functions to the class declaration:

```
checkStateFormat(state) {
  // state must be true or false
  if(state) {
    return true;
  } else {
    return false;
  }
}

checkBrightnessFormat(brightness) {
  // brightness must be a number between 0.01 and 1
  if(isNaN(brightness)) {
    brightness = 1;
  } else if(brightness > 1) {
    brightness = 1;
  } else if(brightness < 0.01) {
    brightness = 0.01;
  }
  return brightness;
}
```

5. Add a **toggle** function and a **test** function, which we'll use for debugging. Both of these functions should also be within the class declaration. The **toggle** function will simply turn the light's state to the opposite of its current state; for example, on to off, and vice versa:

```
toggle() {
  this.state = !this.state;
}

test() {
  alert("state is " + this.state);
}
```

6. In **js/lightBulb.js**, below your class declaration, add a module export as we did in the previous exercise:

```
export default Light;
```

7. Open **js/viewer.js** and replace the **light()** line we wrote in *Exercise 22, Writing a Simple ES6 Module*, with a variable containing an instance of the **Light** class:

```
let light = new Light(true, 0.5);
```

8. Below the preceding line in **js/viewer.js**, add the following code. This code connects the source of the image to **state**, and the opacity of the image to **brightness**:

```
// Set image based on light state
bulb.src = light.state ? onImage : offImage;

// Set opacity based on brightness
bulb.style.opacity = light.brightness;

// Set slider value to brightness
slider.value = light.brightness;

bulb.onclick = function () {
  light.toggle();
  bulb.src = light.state ? onImage : offImage;
}

slider.onchange = function () {
  light.brightness = this.value;
  bulb.style.opacity = light.brightness;
}
```

9. Return to the project directory and run **npm start**. With the project running, open **localhost:8000** in your browser. You should see a new picture for the light indicating that it's on:

Figure 5.8: Light with a state of true

With the page open, click the image and ensure that doing so causes the image to change. Also, notice the input slider at the bottom of the page. Try changing the value to confirm that doing so updates the opacity of the image.

Note Naming Convention of Classes

In the preceding code, we created a **Light** class. Notice that we're using a capital "L" rather than the usual camelcase used in JavaScript. It is common practice to capitalize the names of classes; refer to Google's JavaScript styling guide for more details on naming conventions: https://google.github.io/styleguide/javascriptguide.xml#Naming.

Camelcase is the most popular naming style in JavaScript. Other styles include snake_case, kebab-case, and PascalCase.

Default Attributes

One of the most common things you'll want to make use of with classes is default attribute values. Often, you want to create an instance of your class but don't care about the specifics of the attributes – without specifying arguments, for example:

```
myLight = new Light();
```

Both **state** and **brightness** will default to **undefined**.

With the code we've written, calling **light** without attributes won't raise an error because we've written **checkStateFormat** and **checkBrightnessFormat** to account for all invalid values. However, in many cases, you can simplify your code by providing default values in the constructor as follows:

```
constructor(state=false, brightness=100) {
```

The preceding syntax isn't specific to the class **constructor** and can be used to set the default arguments of any function, assuming you're using ES6, ES2015, or a newer version of JavaScript. Default parameters are not available in versions before ES2015.

Encapsulation

Encapsulation is the idea that modules should only make object properties available for consumption when necessary. Furthermore, properties should be accessed and modified using functions rather than directly. As an example, let's go back to our light module. Inside the **constructor** function, we made sure that we first ran the values through state checkers:

```
constructor(state, brightness) {
    // Check that input has the right format
    this.brightness = this.checkBrightnessFormat(brightness);
}
```

Let's say you develop the preceding module and release it to be used by your colleagues. You don't have to worry about them initializing the class with the wrong values, because if they do, **checkBrightnessFormat()** will automatically correct the value. However, once an instance of our class exists, nothing is stopping others from modifying that value directly:

```
let light = new Light();
light.brightness = "hello";
```

In a single command, our **Light** class's **checkBrightnessFormat** function has been sidestepped and we have a light with a **brightness** value of **hello**.

Encapsulation is the idea of writing our code in a way that makes this impossible. Languages such as C# and Java make encapsulation easy. Unfortunately, even with the ES6 update, the use of encapsulation in JavaScript is not obvious. There are a few ways to do this; one of the most popular takes advantage of the built-in **WeakMap** object type, which is also new to ES6.

WeakMap

The **WeakMap** object is a key-value pair collection where a key is an object. WeakMap has a special characteristic where, if an object that is a key in WeakMap is removed from the program and no reference exists to it, WeakMap removes the associated pair from its collection. This process of removing the pair is known as garbage collection. Thus, the element is particularly useful in cases where the use of a map could cause a memory leak.

An example where WeakMap would be used over Map is that of a script that keeps track of each element in a dynamically changing HTML page. Say that each element in the DOM is iterated and we create some extra data about each element in our Map. Then, as time goes on, elements are added and removed from the DOM. With Map, all the old DOM elements will continue to be referenced, causing the memory used to increase over time, by storing useless information relating to deleted DOM elements. With WeakMap, the deletion of the DOM element (which is the key object in the collection) causes the associated entry in the collection to be removed during garbage collection.

Here, we will make use of **WeakMap()**. First, we create an empty **map** variable, and then create a **light** object with some attributes. Then, we associate the object itself with a string, **kitchen light**. This isn't a case of adding a property to **light**; rather, we are using the object as if it was a property name in the map:

```
var map = new WeakMap();
var light = {state: true, brightness: 100};
map.set(light, "kitchen light");
console.log(map.get(light));
```

Also, it's important to note that the key object is based on the specific reference to the object. If we create a second light with the same attribute values, that counts as a new key:

```
let light2 = {state: true, brightness: 100};

map.set(light2, "bedroom light");

// above has not changed kitchen light reference

console.log(map.get(light));
```

If we update the properties of an object, that doesn't change the mapping:

```
light.state = false;

// reference does not change

console.log(map.get(light));
```

The mapping will exist until the key object goes out of scope, or until it is set to null and garbage collected; for example:

```
light = null;

// value will not be returned here

console.log(map.get(light));
```

Exercise 25: WeakMap for Encapsulation

> **Note**
>
> This exercise uses the end product of *Exercise 24, Converting a Light Module to a Class*, of this chapter as a starting point. The state of the code after completing this exercise can be found at https://github.com/TrainingByPackt/Professional-JavaScript/tree/master/Lesson05/Exercise25.

In this exercise, we will use **WeakMap** to create private variables that can't be accessed directly from outside a module. Perform the following steps to complete the exercise:

1. Open **js/light.js** and, at the very top of the file, add a **WeakMap** object called **privateVars**:

    ```
    let privateVars = new WeakMap();
    ```

2. In **js/light.js**, modify the **constructor** function so that the object properties are saved to **privateVars** using the **set** method, instead of directly on the object:

```
constructor(state, brightness) {
    // Parse values
    state = this.checkStateFormat(state);
    brightness = this.checkBrightnessFormat(brightness);

    // Create info object
    let info = {
        "state": state,
        "brightness": brightness,
        "createdAt": Date.now()
    };
    // Save info into privateVars
    privateVars.set(this, info);
}
```

3. Now, in **js/light.js**, modify the **toggle** function so that we're getting state info from our **WeakMap** object named **privateVars**. Notice that when we set the variable, we are sending back an object that contains all info, not just **state**. In our example, each instance of **light** has a single **info** object associated with **WeakMap**:

```
toggle() {
    let info = privateVars.get(this);
    info.state = !info.state;
    privateVars.set(this, info);
}
```

4. We also need to modify the **test** function in **js/light.js** in a similar way. We'll change the source of **state** that is sent to the user in an alert to **WeakMap**:

```
test() {
    let info = privateVars.get(this);
    alert("state is " + privateVars.get(this).state);
}
```

5. Since encapsulation takes away the ability to change state and brightness directly, we need to add methods that allow for this. We'll start by adding a **setState** function in **js/light.js**. Notice that it is almost identical to our **toggle** function:

```
setState(state) {
    let info = privateVars.get(this);
    info.state = checkStateFormat(state);
    privateVars.set(this, info);
}
```

6. Next, add the getter method in **js/light.js**:

```
getState() {
    let info = privateVars.get(this);
    return info.state;
}
```

7. Follow the pattern from the last two steps to add getter and setter functions for the **brightness** property in **js/light.js**:

```
setBrightness(brightness) {
    let info = privateVars.get(this);
    info.brightness = checkBrightnessFormat(brightness);
    privateVars.set(this, info);
}

getBrightness() {
    let info = privateVars.get(this);
    return info.brightness;
}
```

8. The last change we need to make is in **js/viewer.js**. Below where the variables are declared, change each reference to light brightness and state to use the getter methods we created:

```
// Set image based on light state
bulb.src = light.getState() ? onImage : offImage;

// Set opacity based on brightness
```

```
  bulb.style.opacity = light.getBrightness();

  // Set slider value to brightness
  slider.value = light.getBrightness();

  bulb.onclick = function () {
    light.toggle();
    bulb.src = light.getState() ? onImage : offImage;
  }

  slider.onchange = function () {
    light.setBrightness(this.value);
    bulb.style.opacity = light.getBrightness();
  }
```

9. Run the code with **npm start** and view the page project in your browser at **localhost:8000**. Check to make sure clicking the image works, as well as changing brightness using the input slider:

Created by Maxim Kulikov
from Noun Project

Figure 5.9: Correctly rendering the site with click and slider functions

Getters and Setters

When using encapsulation, most objects will end up having getter and setter functions for some or all of their properties, since we no longer allow users to access properties directly:

```
console.log(light.brightness);

// will return undefined
```

Instead, we specifically create functions that allow getting and setting the property. These are known as getters and setters, and they are a popular design pattern, especially in languages such as Java and C++. If you completed step 7 in the last exercise, you should have added setters and getters for **brightness**:

```
setBrightness(brightness) {

  let info = privateVars.get(this);

  info.brightness = checkBrightnessFormat(state);

  privateVars.set(this, info);

}


getBrightness() {

  let info = privateVars.get(this);

  return info.brightness;

}
```

Inheritance

Inheritance is the concept of having one class inherit the properties and methods of another class. A class that inherits from another is known as a subclass, and a class that is inherited from is known as a superclass.

It's from the term **superclass** that we get the built-in **super()** function, which can be used to call the constructor of a subclass's superclass. We'll use **super()** later in this chapter to make our own subclass.

It should be noted that a class can be both a subclass and a superclass. For example, say we have a program that simulates different types of animals. In our program, we have a mammal class, which is a subclass of animal class and a superclass to the dog class.

By organizing our program this way, we can put properties and methods that are relevant to all animals in the animal class. The mammal subclass contains methods relevant to mammals, but not reptiles; for example:

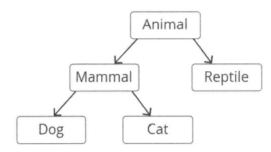

Figure 5.10: Inheritance in JavaScript

This may sound complex at first, but it often saves a significant amount of coding. Without the use of classes, we would end up copying and pasting methods from one animal to another. With that comes the difficulty of having to update a function in multiple places.

Going back to our smart house scenario, say we have received a new colored lightbulb device. We want our colored lightbulb to have all the attributes and functions that are contained in a lightbulb. In addition, the colored light should have an extra attribute of **color**, containing a hex color code, a color format checker, and functions related to changing color.

Our code should also be written in a way that if we make changes to the underlying **Light** class, the colored lightbulb will automatically gain any added functionality.

Exercise 26: Extending a Class

Note

This exercise uses the end product of *Exercise 25, WeakMap for Encapsulation*, as a starting point. The state of the code after completing this exercise can be found at https://github.com/TrainingByPackt/Professional-JavaScript/tree/master/Lesson05/Exercise26.

To extend the **Light** class written in the previous exercise, we will create a new **ColorLight** class:

1. Create a new file at **/js/colorLight.js**. On the first line, we'll import **./light.js**, which we'll use as a starting point:

   ```
   import Light from './light.js';
   ```

2. Next, we'll create **WeakMap** for private variables. Then, we'll create a class statement for our **ColorLight** class, and use the **extends** keyword to tell JavaScript that it will use **Light** as a starting point:

   ```
   let privateVars = new WeakMap();

   class ColorLight extends Light {

   }
   ```

3. Inside the **ColorLight** class statement, we'll create a new **constructor** that uses the built-in **super()** function, which runs the **constructor()** function of our base class, **Light**:

   ```
   class ColorLight extends Light {
     constructor(state=false, brightness=100, color="ffffff") {
       super(state, brightness);

       // Create info object
       let info = {"color": this.checkColorFormat(color)};

       // Save info into privateVars
       privateVars.set(this, info);
     }
   }
   ```

4. Notice in the preceding constructor that we make a call to **checkColorFormat()**, a function that will check that the color value provided is a valid hex value. If not, we'll set the value to the hex value of white (#FFFFFF). The function should be inside the **ColorLight** class statement:

```
checkColorFormat(color) {
    // color must be a valid hex color
    var isHexColor  = /^#[0-9A-F]{6}$/i.test('#'+color);
    if(!isHexColor) {
        // if invalid make white
        color = "ffffff";
    }
    return color;
}
```

5. Add getter and setter functions, like we did in the later exercise:

```
getColor() {
    let info = privateVars.get(this);
    return info.color;
}

setColor(color) {
    let info = privateVars.get(this);
    info.color = this.checkColorFormat(color);
    privateVars.set(this, info);
}
```

6. At the bottom of **js/colorLight.js**, add an **export** statement to make the module available for import:

```
export default ColorLight;
```

7. Open **js/viewer.js** at the top of the file and switch the **Light** import with one for **ColorLight**. Below that, we will import a pre-written script called **changeColor.js**:

```
import ColorLight from './colorLight.js';
import changeColor from './__extra__/changeColor.js';
```

8. Further below, in **js/viewer.js**, find the line where we initialize the **light** variable and replace it with this:

```
let light = new ColorLight(true, 1, "61AD85");
```

9. At the bottom of **js/viewer.js**, add the following:

```
// Update image color
changeColor(light.getColor());
```

10. Start the program again using **npm start** and go to **localhost:8000** in your browser:

    If you've followed the instructions correctly, you should now see the light in a light green color, as demonstrated in the following diagram. Try opening **js/viewer.js** and changing the hex value; doing so should result in a different color for the light image:

Created by Maxim Kulikov
from Noun Project

Figure 5.11: The change-color function applying a CSS filter to make the lightbulb green

Polymorphism

Polymorphism is simply overriding the default behavior of a parent class. In strongly typed languages such as Java and C#, polymorphism can take a bit of effort. With JavaScript, polymorphism is straightforward. You simply overwrite a function.

For example, in the previous exercise, we took **Light** and extended it with the **ColorLight** class. Say we wanted to take the **test()** function that was written in **Light** and override it so that instead of alerting the state of the light, we alert the current color value of the light.

So, our **js/light.js** file would contain this:

```
test() {
  let info = privateVars.get(this);
  alert("state is " + privateVars.get(this).state);
}
```

Then all we have to do is create a new function in js/colorLight.js which has the same name, and replace state with color:

```
test() {
  let info = privateVars.get(this);
  alert("color is " + privateVars.get(this).color);
}
```

Exercise 27: LightBulb Builder

> **Note**
>
> This exercise uses the end product of *Exercise 26, Extending a Class*, as a starting point. The state of the code after completing this exercise can be found at https://github.com/TrainingByPackt/Professional-JavaScript/tree/master/Lesson05/Exercise27.

In this exercise, we will use the concepts we've learned so far to enhance our example project. Instead of having a single lightbulb, we will modify the project to allow us to create unlimited instances of the **lightbulb** class, choosing the color, brightness, and state:

1. Open **js/light.js** and add two values for the image source just below the **WeakMap** reference:

```
let onImage = "images/bulb_on.png";
let offImage = "images/bulb_off.png";
```

2. Next, in **js/light.js**, below where the **info** variable is defined, add the following:

```
// Create html element
let div = document.createElement("div");
let img = document.createElement("img");
let slider = document.createElement("input");

// Save reference to element as private variable
info.div = div;
info.img = img;
info.slider = slider;
this.createDiv(div, img, slider, state, brightness);
```

3. In the last step in **js/light.js**, we made a reference to **this.createDiv**. In this step, we'll create that function below the constructor in **js/light.js**. This function creates HTML for every instance of the **Light** class:

```
createDiv(div, img, slider, state, brightness) {
    // make it so we can access this in a lower scope
    let that = this;

    // modify html
    div.style.width = "200px";
    div.style.float = "left";
    img.onclick = function () { that.toggle() };
    img.width = "200";
    img.src = state ? onImage : offImage;
    img.style.opacity = brightness;
    slider.onchange = function () { that.setBrightness(this.value) };
    slider.type = "range";
    slider.min = 0.01;
    slider.max = 1;
    slider.step = 0.01;
    slider.value = brightness;
    div.appendChild(img);
    div.appendChild(slider);

    // append to document
    document.body.appendChild(div);
}
```

4. Next, in **js/light.js**, find the **setState** function and add the following line within the function:

```
info.img.src = info.state ? onImage : offImage;
```

5. Add the same line to the **toggle** function in **js/light.js**:

```
info.img.src = info.state ? onImage : offImage;
```

6. Similarly, we will update the **setBrightness** function in **js/light.js** to set the opacity of the image based on brightness:

```
info.img.style.opacity = brightness;
```

7. The last change in **js/light.js** is to add a getter function for the **img** HTML object. We will place it between the **getBrightness** and **toggle** functions:

```
getImg() {
    let info = privateVars.get(this);
    return info.img;
}
```

8. In **js/colorLight.js**, we'll import the pre-built **colorChange** function. This should go with your imports just under the **Light** import:

```
import changeLight from './__extra__/changeColor.js';
```

9. Next, in **js/colorLight.js**, we're going to update the constructor by adding the following lines:

```
let img = this.getImg();
img.style.webkitFilter = changeLight(color);
```

10. In **js/viewer.js**, delete all the code and replace it with the following:

```
import ColorLight from './colorLight.js';

let slider = document.getElementById("brightnessSlider");
let color = document.getElementById("color");
let button = document.getElementById("build");

button.onclick = function () {
    new ColorLight(true, slider.value, color.value);
}
```

11. The final change is **index.html**; remove the **img** and **input** tags and replace them with the following:

```
<div style="position: 'fixed', top: 0, left: 0">
    <input type="color" id="color" name="head" value="#e66465">
    <input id="brightnessSlider" min="0.01" max="1" step="0.01"
type="range"/>
    <button id="build">build</button>
</div>
```

12. With all the changes made, run **npm start** and open your browser to **localhost:8000**. If you've done everything correctly, hitting the **build** button should add a new element to the page based on the color chosen:

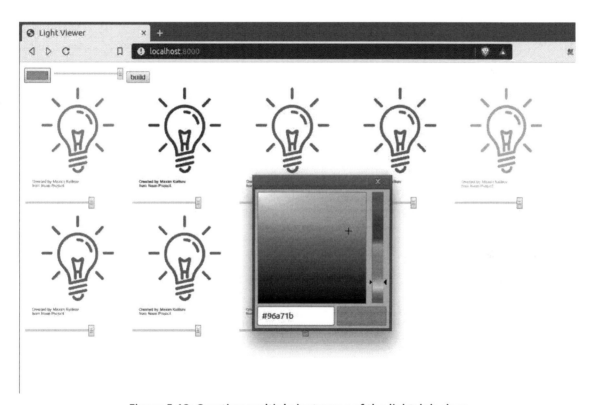

Figure 5.12: Creating multiple instances of the lightclub class

As you can see, classes really start to come in handy once you're creating many instances of a single thing. In the next section, we'll look at npm packages and how we can export our **Light** class as one.

npm Package

An **npm package** is a JavaScript module that has been packaged and uploaded to the npm server. Once a module has been uploaded to npm, it can quickly be installed and used by anyone.

This probably isn't new to you, as anyone who has used Node.js quickly ends up installing a package. What is less commonly done and known about is how to create and upload a package. It's easy to spend years as a developer without having the need to publish a public module, yet it is something worth knowing. It will help not only when you want to export your own module, but when you want to read and understand the packages that your project uses.

The first step in creating an npm module is making sure you have a complete **package.json** file. When running a project locally, it is normal to not worry much about fields such as **author** and **description**. It's a different story when you prepare a module for public use. You should take the time to fill out all fields relevant to your package.

The following is a table that includes the common properties recommended by npm. Many of these are optional. For more information and a complete list, refer to https:// docs.npmjs.com/files/package.json.

At the very minimum, metadata should include a name, version, and description. In addition, most packages will need a **dependencies** property; however, this should be generated automatically by using the **--save** or **-s** option whenever installing a dependency using **npm install**:

Name	Name of your package
Version	Version number.
Description	A description of what the module does and is used for.
Keywords	An array of keywords related to the package.
Homepage	A URL to the project home page.
Bugs	An object containing properties for the URL and email. The URL should point to the project's bug tracker if one exists.
License	A string with the license type for the project.
Author OR Contributors	Projects usually include an author, which is a single string containing the author's name. Alternatively, a contributor's property is used, which is an array of people objects that have properties for name, email, and URL
Files	An optional property that can be used to specify the specific files in the directory that should be packaged, instead of automatically including all files in the directory.
Main	Specifies the entry point file of the project – for example, server.js or index.js.
Browser	If the package is meant to be used on the client-side, the browser field should be used in place of the `main` field to specify the entry point

Figure 5.13: npm properties table

The following table shows some more properties of npm:

Bin	The bin field refers to the bin directory on the Unix system where executables are stored. npm allows for a package to add a shortcut to npm's path to have a keyword associated with a script. For example, we might allow users to run checkWeather by associating it with a file at js/weather.js. The format used for bin is an object that maps keywords to script locations.
Man	Refers to Unix's man, which is short for manuals. This property should be used to provide either a string with a path to the document file OR an array of file locations. File specified in man should be of the man file type.
Repository	An object with type and url properties specifying where the version control for the project is hosted.
Scripts	A dictionary including lists of scripts and locations.
Dependencies	An object that describes the external packages required and specific versions. This should be generated automatically.
DevDependencies	Similar to dependencies, but lists those required for development but not needed for release.

Figure 5.14: npm properties table continued

npm Link Command

Once you have your **package.json** complete, and the first version of your package that you want to test, you can make use of the **npm link** command. The link command will associate your local npm project with a namespace. For example, first navigate to the project folder where you want to use a local **npm** package:

```
cd ~/projects/helloWorld
npm link
```

Then, go into another project folder where you want to make use of that package, and run **npm link helloWorld**, where **helloWorld** is the name of the package you are testing:

```
cd ~/projects/otherProject

npm link helloWorld
```

These two steps will allow you to work as if you had installed **helloWorld** using **npm install helloWorld**. By doing this, you can ensure that your package is working locally when used in another project.

Npm Publish Command

Once you are satisfied with the results of testing your package locally, you can easily upload it to npm with the **npm publish** command. To make use of the **publish** command, you will first need to create an account at https://www.npmjs.com/. Once you have an account, you can log in to it locally by running **npm login** on your command line.

Once logged in, it is very simple to publish your package. Simply navigate to your **project** folder and run **npm publish**. Here is an example of a package being successfully uploaded to npm for others to use:

```
> npm publish
npm notice
npm notice         projs-l5@1.0.2
npm notice === Tarball Contents ===
npm notice 994B      package.json
npm notice 39B       .babelrc
npm notice 195B      webpack.config.js
npm notice 25.8kB    build/bundle.js
npm notice 23.7kB    build/images/bulb_off.png
npm notice 23.2kB    build/images/bulb_on.png
npm notice 404B      build/index.html
npm notice 10.9kB    build/js/__extra__/changeColor.js
npm notice 4.2kB     build/js/colorLight.js
npm notice 4.4kB     build/js/light.js
npm notice 433B      build/js/viewer.js
npm notice 23.7kB    src/images/bulb_off.png
npm notice 23.2kB    src/images/bulb_on.png
npm notice 421B      src/index.html
npm notice 8.0kB     src/js/__extra__/changeColor.js
npm notice 970B      src/js/colorLight.js
npm notice 4.0kB     src/js/light.js
npm notice 279B      src/js/viewer.js
npm notice === Tarball Details ===
npm notice name:          projs-l5
npm notice version:       1.0.2
npm notice package size:  107.2 kB
npm notice unpacked size: 154.7 kB
npm notice shasum:        b1674942006ef0013234d4d436614c6fbe3c52d7
npm notice integrity:     sha512-h7M2W/QeONhfn[...]KBEotpgxkq5tw==
npm notice total files:   18
npm notice
+ projs-l5@1.0.2
```

Figure 5.15: Example of an npm package published

ESM versus CommonJS

ESM is short for ECMAScript Modules, which is the standard used for modules in ES6. So, you may hear "ES6 Modules" referred to as ESM. This is due to the fact that the ESM standard has been in development before ES6 was a standard.

You've likely seen the CommonJS format that was used in the previous chapter:

```
const express = require('express');
```

The same code in the ES6 module style would be like this:

```
import express from 'express';
```

ES6 modules are great because they give JavaScript developers more control over their imports. However, it is important to note that, currently, JavaScript is in a transition period. ES6 has given a definite standard as to how ES6 modules should work. While most browsers have implemented it, npm is still using its own standard CommonJS.

That said, the introduction of ES6 is being quickly accepted. npm now ships with an experimental flag, `--experimental-modules`, which allows the use of ES6-style modules. However, use of this flag is not recommended, as it adds unneeded complexity, such as having to change your file extensions from `.js` to `.mjs`.

Babel

The more common and recommended way to use ES6 modules with Node.js is to run a JavaScript compiler. The most popular compiler is `Babel.js`, which takes ES6 code and compiles it down to older versions of JavaScript that can run anywhere.

Babel is a widely used tool in the Node.js ecosystem. Often, projects use starter templates that have Babel and other bundling tools, such as webpack, built in. These starter projects allow developers to start using ES6 imports without thinking about the fact that a compile step is required. For example, there's Facebook's create-react-app, which compiles and displays your application every time a change is made to a file.

React is one of the largest communities pushing ES6. In the React ecosystem, the standard import used is ES6. The following is taken from the React documentation on creating a component:

```
import React, { Component } from 'react';


class Button extends Component {
  render() {
    // ...

  }
```

```
}
```

```
export default Button; // Don't forget to use export default!
```

Note the similarity between the preceding code and what we've been working on. It's an example of inheritance, where **Button** inherits the properties of **Component**, just like **ColorLight** inherited those of **Light**. React is a component-based framework that makes heavy use of ES6 features such as imports and classes.

webpack

Another common JavaScript compiler is webpack. webpack takes multiple JavaScript files and compiles them into a single bundled file. In addition, webpack can take steps to improve performance, such as minifying code to reduce the total size. webpack is particularly useful when using modules, as each separate file loaded into an HTML site increases load time due to making an extra HTTP call.

With webpack, we can very simply specify the entry point for the JavaScript we want to compile, and it will automatically merge any referenced files. For example, if we want to compile the code from our last exercise, we would create a **webpack.config.js** file to specify the entry point:

```
const path = require("path");

module.exports = {
  mode: 'development',
  entry: "./src/js/viewer.js",
  output: {
    path: path.resolve(__dirname, "build"),
    filename: "bundle.js"
  }
};
```

Notice where **entry** is defined above; this would be the starting point of our program from where webpack will automatically find all referenced files. The other important value to take note of is **output**. This defines the location and filename of the resulting bundled JavaScript file created by the compiler.

In the next exercise, we'll make use of Babel to convert our code from ES6 to generic JavaScript. Once we've converted our JavaScript, we'll use webpack to compile the resulting files into a single bundled JavaScript file.

Exercise 28: Converting ES6 and Packages with webpack and Babel

> **Note**
>
> This exercise uses the end product of *Exercise 27, LightBulb Builder*, as a starting point. The state of the code after completing this exercise can be found at https://github.com/TrainingByPackt/Professional-JavaScript/tree/master/Lesson05/Exercise28.

In this exercise, we will use Babel to convert our ES6 to generic JavaScript that is compatible with older browsers such as Internet Explorer. The second thing we'll do is run webpack to compile all our JavaScript files into a single file:

1. Create two new folders in the base of your project, one called **build** and the other **src**:

   ```
   mkdir src build
   ```

2. Move the **images**, **index.html**, and **js** folders into the new **src** folder. The source folder will be used to generate the contents of the **build** folder later:

   ```
   mv images index.html js src
   ```

3. Install **babel-cli** and **babel preset** as developer dependencies:

   ```
   npm install --save-dev webpack webpack-cli @babel/core @babel/cli @babel/preset-env
   ```

4. Add a file called **.babelrc** to the root directory. In it, we will tell Babel to use the preset settings:

   ```
   {
     "presets": ["@babel/preset-env"]
   }
   ```

5. Add a webpack configuration file at **webpack.config.js** in the root directory:

```
const path = require("path");

module.exports = {
  mode: 'development',
  entry: "./build/js/viewer.js",
  output: {
    path: path.resolve(__dirname, "build"),
    filename: "bundle.js"
  }
};
```

6. To generate the contents of the **build** folder from **src**, we need to add a new script command to our project. Open up **package.json** and look for the section that lists scripts. In that section, we'll add a **build** command that runs Babel and webpack and copies our **image** files to the **build** folder. We will also modify the **start** command to reference our **build** folder, so we can test it after building:

```
"scripts": {
  "start": "ws --directory build",
  "build": "babel src -d build && cp -r src/index.html src/images build
&& webpack --config webpack.config.js"
},
```

> **Note**
>
> Windows users should use the following command:
>
> **"build": "babel src -d build && copy src build && webpack --config webpack.config.js"**

7. To make sure the command has been added properly, run **npm run build** on the command line. You should see output like this:

```
philip@philip-ThinkPad-T420:~/packt/Professional-JavaScript/Lesson05/exercise_7$ npm run build

> projs-l5@1.0.0 build /home/philip/packt/Professional-JavaScript/Lesson05/exercise_7
> babel src -d build && cp -r src/index.html src/images build && webpack --config webpack.config.js

Successfully compiled 5 files with Babel.
Hash: 49b007a37b8ad578065f
Version: webpack 4.35.3
Time: 145ms
Built at: 07/14/2019 12:37:50 PM
    Asset       Size  Chunks                 Chunk Names
bundle.js   25.1 KiB    main  [emitted]  main
Entrypoint main = bundle.js
[./build/js/__extra__/changeColor.js] 10.6 KiB {main} [built]
[./build/js/colorLight.js] 4.06 KiB {main} [built]
[./build/js/light.js] 4.34 KiB {main} [built]
[./build/js/viewer.js] 433 bytes {main} [built]
```

Figure 5.16: npm run build output

8. Next, open up **build/index.html** and change the **script** tag to import our newly created file, **bundle.js**:

```
<script src="bundle.js"></script>
```

9. To test, run **npm start** and open **localhost:8000** in the browser. You should see the same website as the last exercise. Press the **build** button a few times to ensure that it is working as expected:

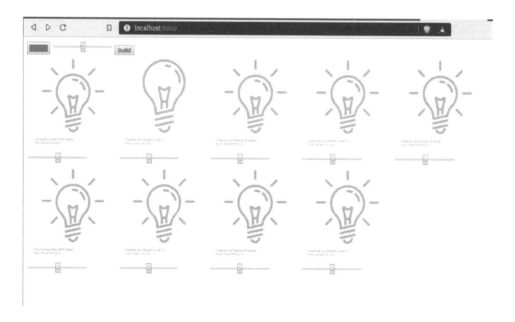

Figure 5.17: Test run using the build button

10. To double check that everything has compiled correctly, go to `localhost:8000/bundle.js` in the browser. You should see a large file that contains the compiled version of all our JavaScript source files:

```
/******/ (function(modules) { // webpackBootstrap
/******/      // The module cache
/******/      var installedModules = {};
/******/
/******/      // The require function
/******/      function __webpack_require__(moduleId) {
/******/
/******/          // Check if module is in cache
/******/          if(installedModules[moduleId]) {
/******/              return installedModules[moduleId].exports;
/******/          }
/******/          // Create a new module (and put it into the cache)
/******/          var module = installedModules[moduleId] = {
/******/              i: moduleId,
/******/              l: false,
/******/              exports: {}
/******/          };
/******/
/******/          // Execute the module function
/******/          modules[moduleId].call(module.exports, module, module.exports, __webpack_require__);
/******/
/******/          // Flag the module as loaded
/******/          module.l = true;
/******/
/******/          // Return the exports of the module
/******/          return module.exports;
/******/      }
/******/
/******/
/******/      // expose the modules object (__webpack_modules__)
/******/      __webpack_require__.m = modules;
/******/
/******/      // expose the module cache
/******/      __webpack_require__.c = installedModules;
/******/
/******/      // define getter function for harmony exports
/******/      __webpack_require__.d = function(exports, name, getter) {
/******/          if(!__webpack_require__.o(exports, name)) {
```

Figure 5.18: A complied version of all our JavaScript source files

If you've done everything right, you should have a `bundle.js` file that contains all our JavaScript code compiled into a single file.

Composability and Strategies for Combining Modules

We've seen how a module can be an extension of another, as `ColorLight` was to `Light`. Another common strategy when a project grows is to have modules that are themselves made up of multiple sub-modules.

The use of sub-modules is a simple as importing a module in the module file itself. For example, say we wanted to improve the brightness slider in our light modules. It may be that if we created a new `Slider` module, we could use it in multiple cases besides just the `Light` class. This is the kind of situation where it would be advised to make our "advanced slider input" a sub-module.

If, on the other hand, you think your new slider will only ever be used in the **Light** class, then adding it is a new class will only create more overhead. Don't fall into the trap of over-modularizing simply because you can. The key factor here is reusability and utility.

Activity 6: Creating a Lightbulb with a Flash Mode

The lightbulb company you work for has asked you to work on a version of their product. They want a lightbulb with a special "flash mode" that can be used at events and concerts. The flash mode light should allow people to put the light in flash mode and have it automatically turned on and off at a given time interval.

Create a **FlashingLight** class that extends **Light**. The class should be the same as **Light**, except it has a property called **flashMode**. If **flashMode** is on, then the value of the state should switch every five seconds.

Once you've created this new component, add it to the package exports in **js/index.js** and compile the project using Babel.

Perform the following steps to complete the activity:

1. Install the **babel-cli** and **babel** presets as developer dependencies.

2. Add .**babelrc** to tell Babel to use **preset-env**.

3. Add a webpack configuration file that specifies the mode, entry, and output location.

4. Create a new file called **js/flashingLight.js**; it should start as a blank ES6 component that extends **Light**.

5. At the top of the file, add a **privateVars** variable of the **weakMap** type.

6. In the constructor, set the **flashMode** property and save it to **privateVars** within the constructor.

7. Add a setter method for the **FlashingLight** object.

8. Add a getter method for the **FlashingLight** object.

9. On line 2, add an empty variable that will keep track of the flashing timer at the global level of the class.

10. Create a **startFlashing** function that references the parent class's **lightSwitch()** function. This step is tricky because we have to bind it to **setInterval**.

11. Create a **stopFlashing** function that can be used to turn off the timer.

12. In the constructor, check whether **flashMode** is true, and, if it is, run **startFlashing**.

13. Also, check **flashMode** when setting **mode** – if true, **startFlashing**; or else, **stopFlashing**.

14. Import and export the new component in **index.js**.

15. Compile the code by running our **build** function with npm.

Expected output:

Figure 5.19: Lightbulb with flash mode

> **Note**
>
> The solution to this activity can be found on page 599.

Summary

In this chapter, we've explored concepts of modular design, ES6 modules, and their use with node. The principles of object-oriented design can be useful when designing programs that have several layers of modules composed as a complex system.

ES6 classes allow us to create classes much more easily than previous versions of JavaScript. These classes can be built by using the **extends** keyword. This allows for layers of complexity where more complex objects can be built on top of simple ones and so on.

We also saw how the new ES6 **WeakMap** type allows us to create private variables. This pattern limits the number of errors in modules that will be used by others. For example, by requiring properties to be changed, we can check the format and value before allowing the change. This was the case with the light example, where we wanted to check that **state** was a Boolean value before allowing it to be set. We did this by creating getter and setter methods for each private variable that we wanted to make available to other parts of our code.

After that, we talked about how ES6 modules aren't currently supported natively in Node.js, even though big-name projects such as Facebook-backed React make use of them extensively. As a solution to this limitation, we installed Babel, an ES6-to-JavaScript compiler, and used it to convert our **src** folder to the final build code.

We also talked about how, once you have a project working locally, you can convert it to an npm package that can be shared and updated via npm. This process involved testing locally using **npm link**. Then, once satisfied with how the package works, publish it using **npm publish**.

In the next chapter, we will look at code quality and how automated testing can be implemented to defend against regression as we update our code.

6

Code Quality

Learning Objectives

By the end of this chapter, you will be able to:

- Identify the best practices for writing clean JavaScript code

- Perform linting and add a lint command to your node project

- Use unit, integration, and end-to-end testing methods on your code

- Automate linting and tests using Git hooks

In this chapter, we will focus on improving code quality, setting up tests, and automating tests to run before a Git commit. These techniques can be used to ensure that mistakes or errors are found early on and never make it to production.

Introduction

In the previous chapter, we explored the concepts of modular design, ES6 modules, and their use with Node.js. We took our compiled ES6 JavaScript and converted it into a compatible script using Babel.

In this chapter, we'll discuss code quality, which is one of the key qualities of professional JavaScript development. When we start writing code, we tend to focus on solving simple problems and evaluating the outcome. When it comes to the small pet projects that most developers start with, there is little need to communicate with others or work as part of a large team.

As the projects, you work on becoming larger in scope, the importance of code quality increases. In addition to ensuring that the code works, we have to consider other developers who will use the components we create or update the code we write.

There are several aspects of quality code. The first and most obvious is that it does what it is intended to do. This is often easier said than done. Often, it can be difficult to meet the requirements of a large project. To make matters more complex, often adding a new feature can cause an error in some existing part of the application. We can reduce these mistakes through good design but, even so, these types of breakages are bound to happen.

As agile development becomes more popular, the speed at which code changes have also increased. As a result, tests are more important than ever. We'll demonstrate how you can use unit tests to confirm the proper functioning of functions and classes. In addition to unit tests, we'll look at integration testing, which ensures that all aspects of the program function together correctly as expected.

The second component of code quality is performance. The algorithms in our code may produce the desired result, but do they do so efficiently? We'll look at how you can test functions for performance to ensure that algorithms can return results in an acceptable amount of time when processing a large input. As an example, you may have a sorting algorithm that works great with 10 rows of data but takes several minutes once you try processing 100.

The third aspect of code quality we'll talk about in this chapter is readability. Readability is a measure of how easy it is for a human to read and understand your code. Have you ever looked at code written with vague functions and variable names or variable names that are misleading? When writing code, consider that others may have to read or modify it. Following some basic guidelines can help to improve your readability.

Clear Naming

One of the easiest ways to make code more readable is **<u>clear naming</u>**. Make using variables and functions as obvious as possible. Even on a one-man project, it's easy to come back to your own code after 6 months and have trouble remembering what every function does. When you're reading someone else's code, this is doubly true.

Make sure your names are clear and pronounceable. Consider the following example, where a developer has created a function that returns the date in **yymm** format:

```
function yymm() {
  let date = new Date();
  Return date.getFullYear() + "/" + date.getMonth();
}
```

When we're given the context and explanation of what this function does, it's obvious. But for an outside developer skimming over the code for the first time, **yymm** can easily cause some confusion.

Vague functions should be renamed in a way that makes their use obvious:

```
function getYearAndMonth() {
  let date = new Date();
  return date.getFullYear() + "/" + date.getMonth();
}
```

When the correct naming of functions and variables is used, it becomes easy to compose code that is easily readable. Consider another example, in which we want to turn on a light if it's nighttime:

```
if(time>1600 || time<600) {
  light.state = true;
}
```

It's not at all clear what's going on in the preceding code. What exactly is meant by **1600** and **600**, and what does it mean if the light's state is **true**? Now consider the same function rewritten as follows:

```
if(time.isNight) {
  light.turnOn;
}
```

The preceding code makes the same process clear. Instead of asking whether the time is between 600 and 1600, we simply ask whether it is night, and, if so, we turn the light on.

In addition to being more readable, we have also put the definition of when it is nighttime into a central location, `isNight`. If we want to make night end at 5:00 instead of 6:00, we only have to change a single line within `isNight` instead of finding all instances of `time<600` in our code.

Convention

When it comes to the **convention** of how to format or write code, there are two categories: industry- or language-wide convention and company/organization-wide convention. The industry- or language-specific conventions are generally accepted by most programmers using a language. For example, in JavaScript, an industry-wide convention is the use of camel case for variable names.

Good sources for industry-wide conventions include W3 JavaScript Style Guide and Mozilla MDN Web Docs.

In addition to industry-wide conventions, software development teams or projects will often have a further set of conventions. Sometimes, these conventions are compiled into a style guide document; in other cases, these conventions are undocumented.

If you're part of a team that has a relatively large code base, documenting the specific style choices can be useful. This will help you to consider what aspects you'd like to keep and enforce new updates, and which aspects you may want to change. It also helps onboarding new employees who may be familiar with JavaScript but not familiar with the specifics of the company.

A good example of a company-specific style guide is Google JavaScript Style Guide (https://google.github.io/styleguide/jsguide.html). It contains some information that is useful in general. For example, *Section 2.3.3* discusses the use of non-ASCII in code. It suggests the following:

```
const units = 'μs';
```

Is preferable to using something like:

```
const units = '\u03bcs'; // 'μs'
```

Using `\u03bcs` without the comment would be even worse. The more obvious the meaning of your code, the better.

Companies often have a set of libraries they favor for doing things such as logging, working with time values (for example, the Moment.js library), and testing. This can be useful for compatibility and the reuse of code. Having multiple dependencies that do similar things, used by different developers, increases the size of the compiled project, for example, if a project is already using Bunyan for logging, and someone else decides to install an alternative library such as Morgan.

> **Note: Style Guides**
>
> It's worth taking the time to read over some of the more popular style guides for JavaScript. Don't feel obligated to follow every single rule or suggestion, but get accustomed to the thinking behind why rules are created and enforced. Some popular guides worth checking out include the following:
>
> MSDN Style Guide: https://developer.mozilla.org/en-US/docs/Web/JavaScript/Guide

Opinionated versus Non-Opinionated

When it comes to convention, the term "opinionated" is one you will likely come across. When exploring existing libraries and frameworks, you will often see phrases such as "an opinionated framework." In this context, "opinionated" is a measure of how strictly a convention is enforced:

Opinionated: Strictly enforces its chosen conventions and methods of doing things

Non-opinionated: Does not enforce convention, that is, as long as the code is valid, it can be used

Linting

Linting is an automated process where code is examined and validated against a standard of style guidelines. For example, a project that has linting set up to ensure two

spaces instead of tabs will detect instances of tabs and prompt the developer to make the change.

It's important to be aware of linting, but it's not a strict requirement for your projects. When I'm working on a project, the main points I consider when deciding whether linting is needed are the size of the project and the size of the team working on the project.

Linting really comes in handy on long-term projects with medium- to large-sized teams. Often, new people join the project with experience of using some other styling convention. This means that you start getting mixed styles between files or even within the same file. This leads to the project becoming less organized and harder to read.

If you're writing a prototype for a hackathon, on the other hand, I would suggest that you skip the linting. It adds overhead to a project, that is unless you're using a boilerplate project as your starting point, which comes with your preferred linting installed.

There is also the risk of linting systems that are too restrictive and end up slowing down development.

Good linting should consider the project and find a balance between enforcing a common style and not being too restrictive.

Exercise 29: Setting up ESLint and Prettier to Monitor Errors in Code

In this exercise, we will install and set up ESLint and Prettier to monitor our code for styling and syntax errors. We will use a popular ESLint convention that was developed by Airbnb and has become somewhat of a standard.

> **Note**
>
> The code files for this exercise can be found at https://github.com/TrainingByPackt/ Professional-JavaScript/tree/master/Lesson06/Exercise29/result.

Perform the following steps to complete the exercise:

1. Create a new folder and initialize an **npm** project:

    ```
    mkdir Exercise29
    cd Exercise29
    npm init -y
    npm install --save-dev eslint prettier eslint-config-airbnb-base eslint-
    config-prettier eslint-plugin-jest eslint-plugin-import
    ```

    We're installing several developer dependencies here. In addition to **eslint** and **prettier**, we're also installing a starting config made by Airbnb, a config to work with Prettier, and an extension that adds style exceptions for our Jest-based test files.

2. Create a **.eslintrc** file:

```
{
  "extends": ["airbnb-base", "prettier"],
  "parserOptions": {
    "ecmaVersion": 2018,
    "sourceType": "module"
  },
  "env": {
    "browser": true,
    "node": true,
    "es6": true,
    "mocha": true,
    "jest": true,
  },
  "plugins": [],
  "rules": {
    "no-unused-vars": [
      "error",
      {
        "vars": "local",
        "args": "none"
      }
    ],
    "no-plusplus": "off",
  }
}
```

3. Create a **.prettierignore** file (similar to the **.gitignore** file, this just lists the files that should be ignored by Prettier). Your **.prettierignore** file should contain the following:

```
node_modules
build
dist
```

4. Create a **src** folder and, inside it, create a file called **square.js** that contains the following code. Make sure that you include the out-of-place tab:

```
var square = x => x * x;
    console.log(square(5));
```

5. Create a **lint** script in your npm **package.json** file:

```
"scripts": {
  "lint": "prettier --write src/**/*.js"
},
```

6. Next, we will test and demonstrate **prettier --write** by running our new script from the command line:

```
npm run lint
```

7. Open **src/square.js** in a text editor; you can see that the out-of-place tab was removed:

```
let square = x => x * x;
console.log(square(5));
```

Figure 6.1: The out-of-place tab was removed

8. Next, go back to **package.json** and extend our lint script to run **eslint** after **prettier** is complete:

```
"scripts": {
  "lint": "prettier --write src/**/*.js && eslint src/*.js"
},
```

9. In the command line, run **npm run lint** again. You will encounter a linting error due to the code format in **square.js**:

```
> prettier --write src/**/*.js && eslint src/*.js

src/square.js 49ms

/home/philip/packt/lesson_6/lint/src/square.js
  1:1  error    Unexpected var, use let or const instead  no-var
  2:1  warning  Unexpected console statement               no-console

  2 problems (1 error, 1 warning)
  1 error and 0 warnings potentially fixable with the --fix option.
```

The preceding script produces one error and one warning. The error is due to the use of **var** when **let** or **const** could be used. Although, in this particular case, **const** should be used, as the value of **square** is not reassigned. The warning is in regard to our use of **console.log**, which generally shouldn't be shipped in production code, as it will make it hard to debug the console output when an error occurs.

10. Open **src/example.js** and change **var** to **const** on line 1, as shown in the following figure:

```
const square = x => x * x;
console.log(square(5));
```

Figure 6.2: The var statement replaced to const

11. Now run **npm run lint** again. You should now only get back the warning:

```
> prettier --write src/**/*.js && eslint src/*.js

src/js.js 48ms

/home/philip/packt/lesson_6/lint/src/js.js
  2:1  warning  Unexpected console statement  no-console

1 problem (0 errors, 1 warning)
```

In this exercise, we installed and set up Prettier for automatic code formatting, and ESLint to check our code for common bad practices.

Unit Tests

A **unit test** is an automated software test that checks whether a single aspect or function in some software is working as expected. For example, a calculator application might be split up into functions that deal with the Graphical User Interface (GUI) of the application and another set of functions responsible for each type of mathematical calculation.

In such a calculator, unit tests might be set up to ensure that each mathematical function works as expected. This setup allows us to quickly find any inconsistent results or broken functions caused by any changes. As an example, such a calculator's test file might include the following:

```
test('Check that 5 plus 7 is 12', () => {
  expect(math.add(5, 7)).toBe(12);
});


test('Check that 10 minus 3 is 7', () => {
  expect(math.subtract(10, 3)).toBe(7);
});
```

```
test('Check that 5 multiplied by 3 is 15', () => {
  expect(math.multiply(5, 3).toBe(15);
});


test('Check that 100 divided by 5 is 20', () => {
  expect(math.multiply(100, 5).toBe(20);
});


test('Check that square of 5 is 25', () => {
  expect(math.square(5)).toBe(25);
});
```

The preceding tests would run every time the code base was changed and be checked into version control. Often, errors will arise unexpectedly when a function that is used in multiple places is updated and causes a chain reaction, breaking some other function. If such a change happens and one of the preceding statements becomes false (for example, 5 multiplied by 3 returns 16 instead of 15), we will immediately be able to associate our new code change with the break.

This is a very powerful technique that can be taken for granted in environments where tests are already set up. In work environments without such a system, it's possible that changes from developers or updates in software dependencies that unexpectedly break an existing function are committed to source control. Later, the bug is found, and it becomes difficult to make the association between the broken function and the code change that caused it.

It's also important to remember that unit tests ensure the functionality of some sub-unit of work, but not the functionality of a project as a whole (where multiple functions work together to produce a result). This is where integration testing comes into play. We will explore integration tests later on within this chapter.

Exercise 30: Setting up Jest Tests to Test a Calculator Application

In this exercise, we will demonstrate setting up a unit test using Jest, the most popular testing framework in the JavaScript ecosystem. We will continue with our example of a calculator application and set up automated testing for a function that takes a number and outputs its square.

> **Note**
>
> The code files for this exercise can be found at https://github.com/TrainingByPackt/ Professional-JavaScript/tree/master/Lesson06/Exercise30.

Perform the following steps to complete the exercise:

1. On the command line, navigate to the **Exercise30/start** exercise folder. This folder includes a **src** folder that contains the code we will be running our tests on.

2. Initialize a **npm** project by entering the following command:

```
npm init -y
```

3. Install Jest using the **--save-dev** flag (this indicates that the dependency is required for development but not production) by entering the following command:

```
npm install --save-dev jest
```

4. Create a folder called **__tests__**. This is the default location where Jest looks for tests:

```
mkdir __tests__
```

5. Now we're going to create our first test in **__tests__/math.test.js**. It should import **src/math.js** and ensure that running the **math.square(5)** returns **25**:

```
const math = require('././src/math.js');

test('Check that square of 5 is 25', () => {
  expect(math.square(5)).toBe(25);
});
```

6. Open **package.json** and modify the test script so that it runs **jest**. Notice the **scripts** section in the following screenshot:

```
"name": "jest1",
"version": "1.0.0",
"description": "",
"main": "index.js",
"scripts": {
  "test": "jest"
},
"keywords": [],
"author": "",
"license": "ISC",
"devDependencies": {
  "jest": "^24.8.0"
}
```

Figure 6.3: The test script modified so that it runs Jest

7. On the command line, enter the **npm run test**. This should return a message that tells us the wrong value was found, as shown in the following code:

```
FAIL  __test__/math.test.js
  × Check that square of 5 is 25 (17ms)

  ● Check that square of 5 is 25

    expect(received).toBe(expected) // Object.is equality

    Expected: 25
    Received: 10

      2 |
      3 | test('Check that square of 5 is 25', () => {
    > 4 |   expect(math.square(5)).toBe(25);
        |                          ^
      5 | });
      6 |

      at Object.toBe (__test__/math.test.js:4:26)

Test Suites: 1 failed, 1 total
```

```
Tests:        1 failed, 1 total
Snapshots:    0 total
Time:         1.263s
```

This error triggers because the start code has purposely included an error in the **square** function. Instead of multiplying the number by itself, we have instead doubled the value. Notice that the number of received answers was **10**.

8. Fix the error by opening up the file and fixing the **square** function. It should multiply **x**, as shown in the following code, instead of doubling it:

    ```
    const square = (x) => x * x;
    ```

9. With our code fixed, let's test again with **npm run test**. You should get a success message, as follows:

```
philip@philip-ThinkPad-T420:~/packt/Professional-JavaScript/Lesson06/exercise02/result$ \
> npm run test

> jest1@1.0.0 test /home/philip/packt/Professional-JavaScript/Lesson06/exercise02/result
> jest

 PASS  __test__/math.test.js
  ✓ Check that square of 5 is 25 (5ms)

Test Suites: 1 passed, 1 total
Tests:       1 passed, 1 total
Snapshots:   0 total
Time:        1.625s
Ran all test suites.
philip@philip-ThinkPad-T420:~/packt/Professional-JavaScript/Lesson06/exercise02/result$
```

Figure 6.4: Success message shown after testing with npm run test

In this exercise, we set up a Jest test to ensure that running our **square** function with an input of 5 returns 25. We also looked at what to expect when the wrong value is returned by running our test with a mistake in the code that returned 10 instead of 25.

Integration Tests

So, we have discussed unit tests, which are extremely useful for finding the cause of errors when a project's code changes. However, it's also possible that the project passes all unit tests yet does not work as expected. This is because the whole of the project contains additional logic that glues our functions together, as well as static components such as HTML, data, and other artifacts.

Integration tests can be used to ensure a project works from a higher level. For example, while our unit tests directly call functions such as **math.square**, an integration test will test multiple pieces of functionality working together for a particular result.

Often, this means bringing together multiple modules or interacting with a database or other external components or APIs. Of course, integrating more parts means integration tests take longer, so they should be used more sparingly than unit tests. Another downside of the integration test is that when one fails, there are multiple possibilities as to the cause. In contrast, a failed unit test is generally easy to fix as the code being tested is in a specified location.

Exercise 31: Integration Testing with Jest

In this exercise, we'll continue where we left off in our last Jest exercise, where we tested that the **square** function was returning 25 in response to 5. In this exercise, we'll continue by adding some new tests that use our functions in conjunction with each other:

1. On the command line, navigate to the **Exercise31/start** exercise folder, and install the dependencies with **npm**:

   ```
   npm install
   ```

2. Create a folder called **__tests__**:

   ```
   mkdir __tests__
   ```

3. Create a file called **__tests__/math.test.js**. Then, at the top, import the **math** library:

   ```
   const math = require('./../src/math.js');
   ```

4. Similarly to the last exercise, we'll add a test. The main difference here, however, is that we're combining multiple functions:

   ```
   test('check that square of result from 1 + 1 is 4', () => {
       expect(math.square(math.add(1,1))).toBe(4);
   });
   ```

5. Add a timer to measure performance to the preceding test:

   ```
   test('check that square of result from 1 + 1 is 4', () => {
       const start = new Date();
       expect(math.square(math.add(1,1))).toBe(4);
       expect(new Date() - start).toBeLessThan(5000);
   });
   ```

6. Now, test to make sure everything works by running **npm test**:

```
philip@philip-ThinkPad-T420:~/packt/Professional-JavaScript/Lesson06/exercise03/result$ \
> npm test

> jest1@1.0.0 test /home/philip/packt/Professional-JavaScript/Lesson06/exercise03/result
> jest

 PASS   __test__/math.test.js
  ✓ Check that square of 5 is 25 (4ms)
  ✓ check that square of result from 1 + 1 is 4 (1ms)
  ✓ check that square of result from 1 - 1 is 0
  ✓ check that square of result from 1 + 1 is 4

Test Suites: 1 passed, 1 total
Tests:       4 passed, 4 total
Snapshots:   0 total
Time:        1.103s
Ran all test suites.
philip@philip-ThinkPad-T420:~/packt/Professional-JavaScript/Lesson06/exercise03/result$
```

Figure 6.5: Running npm test to make sure everything is working fine

You should see an output similar to the preceding figure, with each test passing with an expected result.

It should be noted that these integration tests are somewhat simplistic. In a real-world scenario, integration tests combine functions, as we demonstrated previously, but from different sources. For example, when you have multiple components created by different teams, integration testing is there to ensure that everything works together. Often, bugs can be caused by simple things, such as updating an external library.

The idea is that multiple parts of your application are integrated, giving you a greater chance of finding where something breaks.

Code Performance Fibonacci Example

Often, a problem has more than one solution. While all solutions might return the same result, they likely don't have the same performance. Take, for example, the problem of getting the nth number of the Fibonacci sequence. Fibonacci is a mathematical pattern where the next number in the sequence is the sum of the last two numbers (1, 1, 2, 3, 5, 8, 13, …).

Consider the following solution, where Fibonacci calls itself recursively:

```
function fib(n) {

    return (n<=1) ? n : fib(n - 1) + fib(n - 2);

}
```

The preceding example states that if we want to get the nth number of the Fibonacci sequence recursively, then get the Fibonacci of **n** minus one plus the Fibonacci of **n** minus two, unless **n** is 1, in which case, return 1. It works and will return the correct answer for any given number. However, as the value of **n** increases, the execution time increases exponentially.

To see how slow this performs, add the **fib** function to a new file and use the function by console logging the result as follows:

```
console.log(fib(37));
```

Next, on the command line, run the following command (**time** should be available in most Unix- and Mac-based environments):

```
time node test.js
```

On a particular laptop, I got back the following, which indicates the 37th digit of Fibonacci is **24157817** and the execution time took 0.441 seconds:

```
24157817

real 0m0.441s

user 0m0.438s

sys 0m0.004s
```

Now open up that same file and change **37** to **44**. Then, run the same **time node test** command again. In my case, an increase of only 7 caused the execution time to increase up to 20 times:

```
701408733

real 0m10.664s

user 0m10.653s

sys 0m0.012s
```

We can rewrite the same algorithm in a more efficient way to increase speed for larger numbers:

```
function fibonacciIterator(a, b, n) {
  return n === 0 ? b : fibonacciIterator((a+b), a, (n-1));
}


function fibonacci(n) {
  return fibonacciIterator(1, 0, n);
}
```

Even though it appears to be more complex, this method of generating a Fibonacci number is superior due to the speed of execution.

One of the downsides of tests with Jest is that, given the preceding scenario, both the slow and fast versions of Fibonacci will pass. Yet, the slow version would clearly be unacceptable in a real-world application where quick processing has to be done.

To guard against this, you may want to add some performance-based tests that ensure functions are completed within a certain time period. The following is an example of creating a custom timer to ensure that a function finishes within 5 seconds:

```
test('Timer - Slow way of getting Fibonacci of 44', () => {
  const start = new Date();
  expect(fastFib(44)).toBe(701408733);
  expect(new Date() - start).toBeLessThan(5000);
});
```

> **Note: Future versions of Jest**
>
> It can be somewhat cumbersome to manually add timers to all your functions. For this reason, there is discussion within the Jest project to create an easier syntax for accomplishing what has been done previously.
>
> To see the discussion related to this syntax and whether it's been resolved, check issue #6947 for Jest on GitHub at https://github.com/facebook/jest/issues/6947.

Exercise 32: Ensuring Performance with Jest

In this exercise, we'll use the technique described previously to test the performance of two algorithms for getting Fibonacci:

1. On the command line, navigate to the **Exercise32/start** exercise folder and install dependencies with **npm**:

   ```
   npm install
   ```

2. Create a folder called **__tests__**:

   ```
   mkdir __tests__
   ```

3. Create a file called **__tests__/fib.test.js**. At the top, import the fast and slow Fibonacci functions (these are already created in the **start** folder):

   ```
   const fastFib = require('./../fastFib');
   const slowFib = require('./../slowFib');
   ```

4. Add a test for fast Fibonacci that creates a timer and ensures that the timer hasn't run for longer than 5 seconds:

   ```
   test('Fast way of getting Fibonacci of 44', () => {
     const start = new Date();
     expect(fastFib(44)).toBe(701408733);
     expect(new Date() - start).toBeLessThan(5000);
   });
   ```

5. Next, add a test for slow Fibonacci, which also checks the run time is less than 5 seconds:

   ```
   test('Timer - Slow way of getting Fibonacci of 44', () => {
     const start = new Date();
     expect(slowFib(44)).toBe(701408733);
     expect(new Date() - start).toBeLessThan(5000);
   });
   ```

6. From the command line, run the tests using the **npm test** command:

```
philip@philip-ThinkPad-T420:~/packt/chapter_6/exercise04/result$ npm test

> tmp@1.0.0 test /home/philip/packt/chapter_6/exercise04/result
> jest

FAIL   __tests__/fib.test.js (11.545s)
  ✓ Fast way of getting Fibonacci of 44 (5ms)
  ✗ Timer - Slow way of getting Fibonacci of 44 (10963ms)

  ● Timer - Slow way of getting Fibonacci of 44

    expect(received).toBeLessThan(expected)

    Expected: < 5000
    Received:   10961

      11 |    const start = new Date();
      12 |    expect(slowFib(44)).toBe(701408733);
    > 13 |    expect(new Date() - start).toBeLessThan(5000);
         |                                ^
      14 | });
      15 |

      at Object.toBeLessThan (__tests__/fib.test.js:13:30)

Test Suites: 1 failed, 1 total
Tests:       1 failed, 1 passed, 2 total
Snapshots:   0 total
Time:        12.153s, estimated 13s
Ran all test suites.
npm ERR! Test failed.  See above for more details.
```

Figure 6.6: Result from the Fibonacci tests

Notice the preceding error response for the part that mentions the timer. The expected result for the function's running time was under 5,000 milliseconds but, in my case, I actually received 10,961. You'll likely get a different result based on the speed of your computer. If you didn't receive the error, it may be that your computer is so fast that it completed in less than 5,000 milliseconds. If that's the case, try lowering the expected maximum time to trigger the error.

End-to-End Testing

While integration testing combines multiple units or functions of a software project, **end-to-end testing** goes one step further by simulating the actual use of the software.

For example, while our unit tests directly called functions such as **math.square**, an end-to-end test would load the graphical interface of the calculator and simulate pressing a number, say 5, followed by the square button. After a few seconds, the end-to-end test would look at the resulting answer in the graphical interface and ensure it equals 25 as expected.

End-to-end testing should be used more sparingly due to the overhead, but it is a great final step in a testing process to ensure that everything is working as expected. In contrast, unit tests are relatively quick to run and, therefore, can be run more often without slowing down development. The following figure shows a recommended distribution of tests:

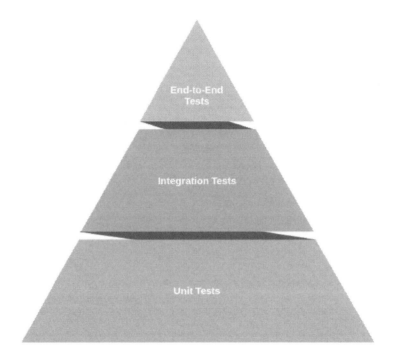

Figure 6.7: Recommended distribution of tests

> **Note: Integration Testing versus End-to-End Testing**
>
> It should be noted that there can be some overlap between what is considered an integration test and what is considered an end-to-end test. The interpretation of what constitutes a test type may vary between one company and another.
>
> Traditionally, tests have been classified as either a unit test or an integration test. Over time, other classifications have become popular, such as system, acceptance, and end-to-end. Due to this, there can be an overlap as to what type a particular test is.

Puppeteer

In 2018, Google released the **Puppeteer** JavaScript library, which has drastically increased the ease with which end-to-end testing can be set up on a JavaScript-based project. Puppeteer is a headless version of the Chrome web browser, meaning that it has no GUI component. This is crucial, as it means we're testing our applications with a full Chrome browser, rather than a simulation.

Puppeteer can be controlled through jQuery-like syntax, where elements on an HTML page are selected by ID or class and interacted with. For example, the following code opens Google News, finds a `.rdp59b` class, clicks on it, waits 3 seconds, and finally takes a screenshot:

```
(async() => {
    const browser = await puppeteer.launch();
    const page = await browser.newPage();
    await page.goto('http://news.google.com');
    const more = await page.$(".rdp59b");
    more.click();
    await page.waitFor(3000);
    await page.screenshot({path: 'news.png'});
    await browser.close();
})();
```

Bear in mind that, in the preceding example, we're selecting a `.rdp59b` class that looks like it was automatically generated; therefore, it is likely that this class will change in the future. In the case that the class name changes, the script will no longer work.

If upon reading this, you find the preceding script does not work, I challenge you to update it. One of the best tools when working with Puppeteer is the Chrome DevTools. My usual workflow is to go to the website I'm writing a script for and right-click on the element that I'll be targeting, as shown in the following figure:

Figure 6.8: Right-click to inspect in Chrome

Once you click on **Inspect**, the DOM explorer will pop up and you'll be able to see any classes or IDs associated with the element:

Figure 6.9: DOM explorer in Chrome DevTools

Note: Puppeteer for Web Scraping and Automation

In addition to being useful for writing end-to-end tests, Puppeteer can also be used for web scraping and automation. Almost anything that can be done in a normal browser can be automated (given the right code).

In addition to being able to select elements on a page via selectors, as we previously looked at, Puppeteer has full access to keyboard and mouse simulation. Thus, more complex things such as automating web-based games and daily tasks are possible. Some have even managed to bypass things such as captchas using it.

Exercise 33: End-to-End Testing with Puppeteer

In this exercise, we're going to use Puppeteer to manually open an HTML/JavaScript-based calculator and use it as an end user would. I didn't want to target a live website as its content often changes or goes offline. So, instead, I have included an HTML calculator in **Exercise33/start** of the project files.

You can view it by installing dependencies with npm, running **npm start**, and then going to **localhost:8080** in your browser:

Figure 6.10: Site showing the demonstration of a calculator created using Puppeteer

In this exercise, we'll be creating a script that opens the site, presses the buttons, and then checks the site for the correct results. Instead of just checking the output of a function, we're listing actions to take on the site and specifying the HTML selector to use as the value to run our tests against.

Perform the following steps to complete the exercise:

1. Open the **Exercise33/start** folder and install the existing dependencies:

   ```
   npm install
   ```

2. Install the required **jest**, **puppeteer**, and **jest-puppeteer** packages:

   ```
   npm install --save-dev jest puppeteer jest-puppeteer
   ```

3. Open **package.json** and configure Jest to use the **jest-puppeteer** presets, which will automatically set up Jest to work with Puppeteer:

   ```
   "jest": {
     "preset": "jest-puppeteer"
   },
   ```

4. Create a file called **jest-puppeteer.config.js** and add the following to it:

   ```
   module.exports = {
     server: {
       command: 'npm start',
       port: 8080,
     },
   }
   ```

   The preceding configuration will make sure the **npm start** command is run before the testing phase. It also tells Puppeteer to look for our web application on **port: 8080**.

5. Make a new folder called **__tests__**, as we did in our previous examples:

   ```
   mkdir __test__
   ```

6. Inside the **__tests__** folder, create a file called **test.test.js** that contains the following:

   ```
   describe('Calculator', () => {
     beforeAll(async () => {
       await page.goto('http://localhost:8080')
   ```

```
    })

    it('Check that 5 times 5 is 25', async () => {
      const five = await page.$("#five");
      const multiply = await page.$("#multiply");
      const equals = await page.$("#equals");
      await five.click();
      await multiply.click();
      await five.click();
      await equals.click();
      const result = await page.$eval('#screen', e => e.innerText);
      expect(result).toMatch('25');
    })
  })
})
```

The preceding code is a complete end-to-end test for multiplying 5 by 5 and confirming that the answer returned within the interface is 25. Here, we're opening the local website, pressing five, pressing multiply, pressing five, pressing equals, and then checking the value of the **div** with the ID of **screen**.

7. Run the tests using **npm**:

```
philip@philip-ThinkPad-T420:~/packt/Professional-JavaScript/Lesson06/exercise05/result$ \
> npm test

> after@1.0.0 test /home/philip/packt/Professional-JavaScript/Lesson06/exercise05/result
> jest

 PASS   __tests__/test.test.js
  Calculator
    ✓ Check that 5 times 5 is 25 (109ms)

Test Suites: 1 passed, 1 total
Tests:       1 passed, 1 total
Snapshots:   0 total
Time:        0.836s
Ran all test suites.
philip@philip-ThinkPad-T420:~/packt/Professional-JavaScript/Lesson06/exercise05/result$
```

Figure 6.11: Output after running the calculator script

You should see a result, as shown in the preceding figure, with the output of 25.

Git Hooks

The tests and linting commands discussed here can be incredibly useful for maintaining and improving your code quality and functionality. However, in the heat of actual development, where our focus is on specific problems and deadlines, it can be easy to forget to run the linting and test commands.

One popular solution to this problem is the use of Git hooks. A Git hook is a feature of the Git version control system. A **Git hook** specifies a terminal command to be run at some specific point in the Git process. A Git hook can be run before a commit; after, when a user updates by pulling; and at many other specific points. A full list of possible Git hooks can be found at https://git-scm.com/docs/githooks.

For our purposes, we'll focus only be using the pre-commit hook. This will allow us to find any formatting issues before we commit our code to the source.

> ### Note: Exploring Git
>
> Another interesting way of exploring the possible Git hooks and how they're used in general is to open any Git version control project and look in the **hooks** folder.
>
> By default, any new `.git` project will contain a large list of samples in the `.git/` **hooks** folder. Explore their contents and have them trigger by renaming them with the following pattern:
>
> `<hook-name>.sample to <hook-name>`

Exercise 34: Setting up a Local Git Hook

In this exercise, we'll set up a local Git hook that runs the **lint** command before we're allowed to commit using Git:

1. On the command line, navigate to the **Exercise34/start** exercise folder and install the dependencies:

   ```
   npm install
   ```

2. Initialize the folder as a Git project:

   ```
   git init
   ```

3. Create the `.git/hooks/pre-commit` file, which contains the following:

```
#!/bin/sh
npm run lint
```

4. If on an OS X- or Linux-based system, make the file executable by running the following (this is not required on Windows):

```
chmod +x .git/hooks/pre-commit
```

5. We'll now test the hook by making a commit:

```
git add package.json
git commit -m "testing git hook"
```

The following is the output of the preceding code:

```
philip@philip-ThinkPad-T420:~/packt/chapter_6/githook$ git add package.json
philip@philip-ThinkPad-T420:~/packt/chapter_6/githook$ git commit -m "testing git hook"

> lint@1.0.0 lint /home/philip/packt/chapter_6/githook
> prettier --write src/**/*.js && eslint src/*.js

src/js.js  64ms

/home/philip/packt/chapter_6/githook/src/js.js
  2:1  warning  Unexpected console statement  no-console

✖ 1 problem (0 errors, 1 warning)

[master (root-commit) 86aa387] testing git hook
 1 file changed, 22 insertions(+)
 create mode 100644 package.json
philip@philip-ThinkPad-T420:~/packt/chapter_6/githook$ 
```

Figure 6.12: Git hook being run before committing to Git

You should see the **lint** command being run before your code is committed to the source, as shown in the preceding screenshot.

6. Next, let's test failure by adding some code that will generate a linting error. Modify your **src/js.js** file by adding the following line:

```
    let number = square(5);
```

Make sure that you keep the unnecessary tab in the preceding line, as this will be what triggers a lint error.

7. Repeat the process of adding the file and committing it:

```
git add src/js.js
git commit -m "testing bad lint"
```

The following is the output of the preceding code:

```
philip@philip-ThinkPad-T420:~/packt/chapter_6/githook$ git add src/js.js
philip@philip-ThinkPad-T420:~/packt/chapter_6/githook$ git commit -m "testing bad lint"

> lint@1.0.0 lint /home/philip/packt/chapter_6/githook
> prettier --write src/**/*.js && eslint src/*.js

src/js.js 75ms

/home/philip/packt/chapter_6/githook/src/js.js
  2:1  warning  Unexpected console statement                        no-console
  3:5  error    'number' is assigned a value but never used         no-unused-vars
  3:5  error    'number' is never reassigned. Use 'const' instead   prefer-const

✖ 3 problems (2 errors, 1 warning)
  1 error and 0 warnings potentially fixable with the `--fix` option.

npm ERR! code ELIFECYCLE
npm ERR! errno 1
npm ERR! lint@1.0.0 lint: `prettier --write src/**/*.js && eslint src/*.js`
npm ERR! Exit status 1
npm ERR!
npm ERR! Failed at the lint@1.0.0 lint script.
npm ERR! This is probably not a problem with npm. There is likely additional logging output above.

npm ERR! A complete log of this run can be found in:
npm ERR!     /home/philip/.npm/_logs/2019-06-05T15_39_23_693Z-debug.log
philip@philip-ThinkPad-T420:~/packt/chapter_6/githook$ 
```

Figure 6.13: A failed linting before committing the code to git

You should see the **lint** command running as before; however, after it runs, the code is not committed like the last time, due to the Git hook returning an error.

Sharing Git Hooks with Husky

An important factor to be aware of with Git hooks is that, because these hooks are within the **.git** folder itself, they are not considered part of the project. Therefore, they will not be shared to your central Git repository for collaborators to use.

However, Git hooks are most useful in collaborative projects where new developers may not be fully aware of a project's conventions. It's a very convenient process when a new developer clones a project, makes some changes, tries to commit, and immediately gets feedback based on linting and tests.

The **husky** node library was created with this in mind. It allows you to keep track of your Git hooks within the source code using a single config file called `.huskyrc`. When a project is installed by a new developer, the hooks will be active without the developer having to do anything.

Exercise 35: Setting up a Commit Hook with Husky

In this exercise, we're going to set up a Git hook that does the same thing as the one in *Exercise 34, Setting up a Local Git Hook*, but has the advantage of being shareable across a team. By using the **husky** library instead of **git** directly, we'll ensure that anyone who clones the project also has the hook that runs **lint** before committing any changes:

1. On the command line, navigate to the **Exercise35/start** exercise folder and install the dependencies:

   ```
   npm install
   ```

2. Create a file called `.huskyrc` that contains the following:

   ```
   {
     "hooks": {

       "pre-commit": "npm run lint"
     }
   }
   ```

   The preceding file is the most important part of this exercise as it defines exactly what command will be run at what point in the Git process. In our case, we're running the **lint** command before any code is committed to the source.

3. Initialize the folder as a Git project by running **git init**:

   ```
   git init
   ```

4. Install Husky using **npm**:

   ```
   npm install --save-dev husky
   ```

5. Make a change to **src/js.js** that will be used for our test commit. As an example, I'll add a comment as follows:

   ```
   // test commit
   const square = x => x * x;
   console.log(square(5));
   ```

   Figure 6.14: The test commit comment

6. Now, we'll run a test ensuring it works like in the previous example:

```
git add src/js.js
git commit -m "test husky hook"
```

The following is the output of the preceding code:

```
philip@philip-ThinkPad-T420:~/packt/Professional-JavaScript/Lesson06/exercise07/start$ git commit -m "test"
husky > pre-commit (node v10.13.0)

> lint@1.0.0 lint /home/philip/packt/Professional-JavaScript/Lesson06/exercise07/result
> prettier --write src/**/*.js && eslint src/*.js

src/js.js 50ms

/home/philip/packt/Professional-JavaScript/Lesson06/exercise07/result/src/js.js
  2:1  warning  Unexpected console statement  no-console

✖ 1 problem (0 errors, 1 warning)

[master 658a9b6] test
 1 file changed, 1 insertion(+)
philip@philip-ThinkPad-T420:~/packt/Professional-JavaScript/Lesson06/exercise07/start$
```

Figure 6.15: Output after committing the test husky hook

We're getting a warning about our use of **console.log**, but you can ignore this for our purposes. The main point is that we have set up our Git hook using Husky, so anyone else who installs the project will also have the hooks set up, as opposed to if we set them up directly in Git.

> ### Note: Initializing Husky
>
> Take note of the fact that **npm install --save-dev husky** was run after our Git repository was created. When you install Husky, it runs the required commands to set up your Git hooks. However, if the project isn't a Git repository, it won't be able to.
>
> If you have any problems related to this, try re-running **npm install --save-dev husky** once you have initialized a Git repository.

Exercise 36: Getting Elements by Text with Puppeteer

In this exercise, we're going to write a Puppeteer test that verifies a small quiz app is working. If you go into the exercise folders and find the starting point for *Exercise 36*, you can run **npm start** to see the quiz we'll be testing:

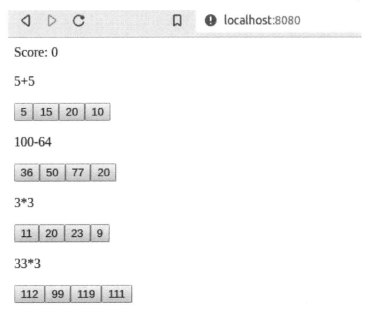

Figure 6.16: Puppeteer showing a small quiz app

In this application, clicking on the correct answer of a question makes the question disappear and the score increment by one:

1. On the command line, navigate to the **Exercise36/start** exercise folder and install the dependencies:

    ```
    npm install --save-dev jest puppeteer jest-puppeteer
    ```

2. Add a test script to **package.json** by modifying the **scripts** section so that it looks like the following:

    ```
    "scripts": {
      "start": "http-server",
      "test": "jest"
    },
    ```

3. Add a Jest section to **package.json** that tells Jest to use Puppeteer presets:

```
"jest": {
  "preset": "jest-puppeteer"
},
```

4. Create a file called **jest-puppeteer.config.js** where we will tell Jest to turn our quiz app on before running any tests:

```
module.exports = {
  server: {
    command: 'npm start',
    port: 8080,
  },
}
```

5. Create a folder called **__test__** where we will put our Jest tests:

```
mkdir __test__
```

6. Create a test in the folder called **quiz.test.js**. It should contain the following to initialize our test:

```
describe('Quiz', () => {
  beforeAll(async () => {
    await page.goto('http://localhost:8080')
  })
  // tests will go here
})
```

7. Next, replace the comment in the preceding code with a test for the first question in our quiz:

```
it('Check question #1', async () => {
  const q1 = await page.$("#q1");
  let rightAnswer = await q1.$x("//button[contains(text(), '10')]");
  await rightAnswer[0].click();
  const result = await page.$eval('#score', e => e.innerText);
  expect(result).toMatch('1');
})
```

Notice our use of **q1.$x("//button[contains(text(), '10')]")**. Instead of using an ID, we're searching the answers for a button that contains the text **10**. This can be very useful when parsing a website that doesn't use IDs on the elements you need to interact with.

8. The following test is added to the last step. We'll add three new tests, one for each question:

```
it('Check question #2', async () => {
    const q2 = await page.$("#q2");
    let rightAnswer = await q2.$x("//button[contains(text(), '36')]");
    await rightAnswer[0].click();
    const result = await page.$eval('#score', e => e.innerText);
    expect(result).toMatch('2');
})

it('Check question #3', async () => {
    const q3 = await page.$("#q3");
    let rightAnswer = await q3.$x("//button[contains(text(), '9')]");
    await rightAnswer[0].click();
    const result = await page.$eval('#score', e => e.innerText);
    expect(result).toMatch('3');
})

it('Check question #4', async () => {
    const q4 = await page.$("#q4");
    let rightAnswer = await q4.$x("//button[contains(text(), '99')]");
    await rightAnswer[0].click();
    const result = await page.$eval('#score', e => e.innerText);
    expect(result).toMatch('4');
})
```

Notice how the line at the bottom of each test has an expected result, one higher than the last; this is us tracking the score on the page. If everything is working properly, the fourth test will find a score of 4.

9. Finally, return to the command line so that we can confirm the correct results. Run the **test** command as follows:

```
npm test
```

The following is the output of the preceding code:

```
> npm test

> before@1.0.0 test /home/philip/packt/Professional-JavaScript/
> jest

 PASS  __test__/quiz.test.js
  Quiz
    ✓ Check question #1 (32ms)
    ✓ Check question #2 (30ms)
    ✓ Check question #3 (37ms)
    ✓ Check question #4 (30ms)

Test Suites: 1 passed, 1 total
Tests:       4 passed, 4 total
Snapshots:   0 total
Time:        0.853s, estimated 1s
Ran all test suites.
```

Figure 6.17: Command line confirming the correct results

If you have done everything correctly, you should see four passing tests as a response to running **npm test**.

Activity 7: Putting It All Together

In this activity, we'll combine several aspects of the chapter. Starting with a pre-built calculator using HTML/JavaScript, your task is the following:

- Create a **lint** command that checks the project against **prettier** and **eslint** using the **eslint-config-airbnb-base** package, as was done in a previous exercise.

- Install **puppeteer** with **jest** and create a **test** command in **package.json** that runs **jest**.

- Create a Puppeteer test that uses the calculator to calculate 777 multiplied by 777, and ensure the answer returned is 603,729.

- Create another Puppeteer test to calculate 3.14 divided by 2, and ensure the answer returned is 1.57.

- Install and set up Husky to run both the linting and testing commands before a commit is made using Git.

Perform the following steps to complete the activity (high-level steps):

1. Install the developer dependencies listed in the linting exercise (**eslint**, **prettier**, **eslint-config-airbnb-base**, **eslint-config-prettier**, **eslint-plugin-jest**, and **eslint-plugin-import**).

2. Add an **eslint** configuration file, **.eslintrc**.

3. Add a **.prettierignore** file.

4. Add a **lint** command to your **package.json** file.

5. Open the **assignment** folder and install the developer dependencies for using Puppeteer with Jest.

6. Modify your **package.json** file by adding an option telling Jest to use the **jest-puppeteer** preset.

7. Add a **test** script to **package.json** that runs **jest**.

8. Create a **jest-puppeteer.config.js** to configure Puppeteer.

9. Create a test file at **__tests__/calculator.js**.

10. Create a Husky file at **.huskyrc**.

11. Install **husky** as a developer dependency by running **npm install --save-dev husky**.

Expected Output

```
philip@philip-ThinkPad-T420:~/packt/Professional-JavaScript/Lesson06/exercise08/result$ npm run lint && npm test

> before@1.0.0 lint /home/philip/packt/Professional-JavaScript/Lesson06/exercise08/result
> prettier --write js/*.js && eslint js/*.js

js/index.js  78ms

> before@1.0.0 test /home/philip/packt/Professional-JavaScript/Lesson06/exercise08/result
> jest

  console.error  node_modules/jest-jasmine2/build/jasmine/Env.js:289
    Unhandled error

  console.error  node_modules/jest-jasmine2/build/jasmine/Env.js:290

 PASS  __tests__/calc.test.js
  Calculator
    ✓ Check that 777 times 777 is 603729 (198ms)
    ✓ Check that 3.14 divided by 2 is 1.57 (133ms)

Test Suites: 1 passed, 1 total
Tests:       2 passed, 2 total
Snapshots:   0 total
Time:        1.001s, estimated 2s
Ran all test suites.
```

Figure 6.18: The final output showing calc.test passed

After completing the assignment, you should be able to run the `npm run lint` command and the `npm test` command and get tests passing like in the preceding screenshot.

> **Note**
>
> The solution for this activity can be found on page 602.

Summary

In this chapter, we looked at aspects of code quality with an emphasis on automated testing. We started with the basics of clear naming and getting familiar with the industry-wide conventions of the language. By following these conventions and writing clearly, we're able to make our code more readable and reusable.

Building from there, we looked at how linting and testing commands can be created with Node.js using a handful of popular tools, including Prettier, ESLint, Jest, Puppeteer, and Husky.

In addition to setting up tests, we talked about the categories of tests and their use cases. We went through unit tests that ensure that individual functions are working as expected, and integration tests that combine multiple functions or aspects of a program to ensure things are working together. Then, we performed end-to-end tests, which open the application's interface and interact with it as an end-user would.

Finally, we looked at how we can tie it all together by having our linting and testing scripts automatically run with Git hooks.

In the next chapter, we'll look at constructors, promises, and async/await. We'll be using some of these techniques to refactor JavaScript in a modern way that takes advantage of the new features available in ES6.

Advanced JavaScript

Learning Objectives

By the end of this chapter, you will be able to:

- Test simple scripts using Node.js REPL
- Construct objects and arrays and modify their content
- Use object methods and operators to get information about the object
- Create simple JavaScript classes and classes that inherit from other classes
- Use advanced built-in methods from Math, RegEx, Date, and String
- Manipulate data in JavaScript using Array, Map, and Set methods
- Implement Symbols, Iterators, Generators, and Proxies

In this chapter, we will work with arrays, classes, and objects in JavaScript, and then we will use inheritance and built-in methods in common JavaScript classes to simplify our code and make it highly reusable.

Introduction

When writing JavaScript code for medium to large projects (10+ files), it is helpful to understand all of the possible features that this language provides. It is always easier and quicker to use what is already there than reinvent the wheel. These built-in methods will not only help you with performing basic functions, but they will also help with code readability and maintainability. These built-in methods range from basic calculations to the complex array and string manipulation that developers face every day. By using these built-in methods, we can reduce our code size and help with the performance of our application.

JavaScript is usually used as a functional language, but you can use it for **Object-Oriented Programming** (**OOP**). In recent years, many new features, such as classes, have been added to the language in response to the growing need for JavaScript to accomplish more complex and data-driven tasks. While it is still possible to create JavaScript using function prototypes, many developers have moved on from doing so since it offers a much closer syntax, similar to popular OOP languages such as C++, Java, and C#.

In this chapter, we will explore the vast number of built-in methods that JavaScript provides us with. We will use Node.js **REPL** (**Read-Eval-Print Loop**) to test our code as this doesn't require us to create any files on the disk or invoke any special commands.

Language Features Supported in ES5, ES6, ES7, ES8, and ES9

Before we dive into the depths of these amazing language features, let's take a look at the different versions of JavaScript. Currently, most websites that you regularly come across that still support legacy browsers use ES5. As of 2019, many mainstream browsers have already added support for ES6. Later versions will only have minimal browser support. Since we will be running and testing our code in a Node.js runtime, we don't have to worry about version compatibility as long as we are using the latest LTS (long term support) version of Node.js. Regarding the materials that will be used in this chapter, here is a breakdown of the minimum ES version your runtime needs to support:

	Compatible Features
ES6	classes
	arrows
	template strings
	enhanced object literals
	generators
	let + const
	proxies
	symbols
	math, string, array, object built-in methods
ES7	Array.prototype.includes()
ES8	Object.values()
ES9	full rest/spread properties

Figure 7.1: Minimum required ES version

In this chapter, we won't be switching runtimes, but in the future, it is best to check the language support on the runtime you are going to be developing for before getting started.

Working in the Node.js REPL

We won't be doing anything too complex in this chapter, so we are going to write our code in the **Node.js** REPL. This allows us to test some ideas before we start coding without the need to create any files. Before we start, make sure you have Node.js installed on your computer and you have opened a Terminal application.

Executing the Node.js REPL

Every Node.js installation includes a node executable that allows you to run local JavaScript files or start the REPL. To run the Node.js executable as a REPL, all you need to do is type the **node** command in your favorite Terminal without any parameters. To test our Node.js installation, you can run the **node -v** command:

```
r1cebank@Hachune-0:~$ node -v
v10.16.0
r1cebank@Hachune-0:~$
```

Figure 7.2: Testing the Node.js installation

If you see an output like this, it means you have **Node.js** installed correctly.

> **Note**
>
> This command outputs the currently running version of the **Node.js** runtime, so it is also a very good way to check the current version. For this book, we will be using the current LTS, that is, v10.16.0.

After we have verified our Node.js installation, to run the node command in REPL mode, all you need to do is type **node** in your Command Prompt:

```
r1cebank@Hachune-0:~$ node -v
v10.16.0
r1cebank@Hachune-0:~$ node
>
```

Figure 7.3: Running the node command in REPL mode

If you can see a cursor waiting for your input, congratulations – you have successfully entered the REPL mode of Node.js! From now on, you can start typing code into the prompt and pressing Enter to evaluate it.

Array Manipulation in JavaScript

Creating arrays and modifying its content in JavaScript is very easy. Unlike other languages, creating arrays in JavaScript doesn't require you to specify the data type or size because these can be changed on request later.

To create a JavaScript array, use the following command:

```
const jsArray = [];
```

Note that, in JavaScript, there is no need to define the size or the type of items in the array.

To create an array with elements predefined, use the following command:

```
const foodList = ['sushi', 'fried chicken', 21];
```

To access and modify items in an array, use the following commands:

```
const sushi = foodList[0];
foodList[2] = 'steak';
```

This is very similar to other programming languages when accessing the array.

Exercise 37: Creating and Modifying an Array

In this exercise, we will be creating a simple array and exploring its value using the REPL. The syntax for creating an array is very similar to many other scripting languages. We will create an array of **singers** in two ways: one is using the **Array** constructor and the other is to use an array literal way. Once we have created the array, we will then manipulate the contents of the array. Let's get started:

1. Use the array literal method to create an empty array and test it is successfully created afterward:

    ```
    > let exampleArray1 = [];
    => undefined
    > Array.isArray(exampleArray1);
    => true
    ```

2. Now, we will use the **Array** constructor to do the same. While they yield the same result, the constructor allows more flexibility:

    ```
    > let exampleArray2 = new Array();
    => undefined
    > Array.isArray(exampleArray2);
    => true
    ```

Notice we are not using **typeof** to check the type of the array because, in JavaScript, array is a type of object. If we were to use **typeof** on the array we just created, we would get an unexpected result:

```
> let exampleArray3 = [];
=> undefined
> typeof exampleArray3
=> 'object'
```

3. Create arrays with a predefined size and items. Note that JavaScript arrays will automatically resize as you add items to the array:

```
> let exampleArray4 = new Array(6)
=> undefined
> exampleArray4
=> [ <6 empty items> ]
```

or

```
> let singers = new Array(6).fill('miku')
=> undefined
> singers
=> [ 'miku', 'miku', 'miku', 'miku', 'miku', 'miku' ]
```

As you can see, we have an array initialized that has an initial size of **6**. We also used the **fill** method to predefine all the items in our array. This is very useful when we want to use the array to keep track of flags in our application.

4. Assign a value to index **0**:

```
> singers[0] = 'miku'
=> 'miku'
> singers
=> [ 'miku' ]
```

5. Assign any arbitrary index for a JavaScript array. The indexes without assignment will simply be **undefined**:

```
> singers[3] = 'luka'
=> 'luka'
> singers[1]
=> undefined
```

6. Modify the item at the end of the array using the array's length:

```
> singers[singers.length - 1] = 'rin'
=> 'rin'
> singers
=> [ 'miku', 'miku', 'miku', 'miku', 'miku', 'rin' ]
```

Thus, we have learned how we can define arrays in JavaScript. These arrays behave similar to other languages and they are also auto-expanded so that you don't have to worry about manually resizing the array. In the next exercise, we will go over how to add items to the array.

Exercise 38: Adding and Removing Items

It's very easy to add and remove items from JavaScript arrays, which we have to do in many applications where we have to accumulate a number of items. In this exercise, we are going to modify the existing **singers** array we created previously. Let's get started:

1. Start with an empty array:

```
> let singers = [];
=> undefined
```

2. Add a new item to the end of an array using **push**:

```
> singers.push('miku')
=> 1
> singers
=> [ 'miku' ]
```

The **push** method will always add the item to the end of the array, even if you have items in the array that are **undefined**:

```
> let food = new Array(3)
=> undefined
> food.push('burger')
=> 4
> food
=> [ <3 empty items>, 'burger' ]
```

As you can see in the preceding code, if you have an array that of a predefined size, using **push** will expand the array and add it to the end of the array instead of just adding it to the beginning

3. Remove an item from the end of an array:

```
> singers.push('me')
=> 2
> singers
=> [ 'miku', 'me' ]
> singers.pop()
=> 'me'
> singers
=> [ 'miku' ]
```

4. Add an item to the beginning of an array:

```
> singers.unshift('rin')
=> 2
> singers
=> [ 'rin', 'miku' ]
```

5. Remove items from the beginning of an array:

```
> singers.shift()
=> 'rin'
> singers
=> [ 'miku' ]
```

These are very useful in a larger scale application, such as if you are building a simple web application that processes images. When a request comes in, you can push the image data, the job ID, and even the client connection to an array, which means that the JavaScript array can be of any type. You can have another worker calling **pop** on the array to retrieve the jobs and then process them.

Exercise 39: Getting Information About the Items in Your Array

In this exercise, we will go over various basic ways to get information about the items in your array. These functions are very helpful when we are working on applications that need to manipulate the data. Let's get started:

1. Create an empty array and push items to it:

```
> let foods = []
=> undefined
> foods.push('burger')
=> 1
```

```
> foods.push('fries')
=> 2
> foods.push('wings')
=> 3
```

2. Find the index of an item:

```
> foods.indexOf('burger')
=> 0
```

3. Find the number of items in the array:

```
> foods.length
=> 3
```

4. Remove an item from a certain index in the array. We will do this by storing the position of the item we want to remove into a variable position. After we know where we want to remove the item, we can call **array.splice** to remove it:

```
> let position = foods.indexOf('burger')
=> undefined
> foods.splice(position, 1) // splice(startIndex, deleteCount)
=> [ 'burger' ]
> foods
=> [ 'fries', 'wings' ]
```

> **Note**
>
> **array.splice** can also be used to insert/replace items into the array at a specific index. We will go over the specifics of that function later. When we are using it, we are supplying it with two parameters. The first one tells splice where to start, and the next one tells it how many items to delete from the start position. Since we only want to remove the item at that index, we are supplying it with 1.

In this exercise, we explored ways to get more information about the array. Trying to locate the index of a specific item is very useful in building applications. Using these built-in methods is very useful because you don't need to iterate through the array to find the item yourself. In the next activity, we will be building a simple user tracker using the ID of the user.

Activity 8: Creating a User Tracker

Suppose you are building a website and you want to track how many people are currently viewing it. In order to do this, you decide to keep a list of users in your backend. When a user opens your website, you will update the list to include that user, and when that user closes your website, you will remove that user from the list.

For this activity, we will have a list called **users**, which stores a list of strings, and a couple of helper functions to help store and remove the users from the list.

In order to do this, we need to define a function that takes our list of users and modifies it to our liking.

Perform the following steps to complete this activity:

1. Create the **Activity08.js** file.

2. Define a **logUser** function, which will add the user to the **userList** argument supplied and make sure no duplicates are added.

3. Define a **userLeft** function. It will remove the user from the **userList** argument supplied in the argument.

4. Define a **numUsers** function, which returns the number of users currently inside the list.

5. Define a function called **runSite**. This will be used to test our implementation.

> **Note**
>
> The solution for this activity can be found on page 607.

In this activity, we explored one of the ways in which we can use arrays to accomplish certain tasks in JavaScript. We can use it to keep track of a list of items and use the built-in methods to add and remove items. The reason we are seeing **user3**, **user5**, and **user6** is because these users were never removed.

Object Manipulation in JavaScript

Creating basic objects in JavaScript is very easy and objects are used in every JavaScript application out there. A JavaScript object also includes a collection of built-in methods for you to use. These methods are very helpful when we are writing our code because it makes developing in JavaScript very easy and fun. In this section, we will examine how to create objects in our code and how we can use them to maximize their potential.

To create an object in JavaScript, use the following command:

```
const myObj = {};
```

By using the {} notation, we are defining an empty object and assigning it to our variable name.

We can use objects to store many numbers of key-value pairs in our application:

```
myObj.item1 = 'item1';
myObj.item2 = 12;
```

If we want to access the value, this is also quite easy:

```
const item = myObj.item1;
```

In JavaScript, creating an object doesn't mean having to follow a specific schema. You can put any number of properties within the object. Just make sure that none of the object keys are duplicated:

```
> dancers = []
=> undefined
> dancers.push({ name: 'joey', age: 30 })
=> undefined
```

Notice that the syntax for a new object is very similar to the JSON notation. There are times where we need to know exactly what kind of information is in our object.

You can create an object user with some properties:

```
> let myConsole = { name: 'PS4', color: 'black', price: 499, library: []}
=> undefined
```

In order to get all the property names, you need to use the **keys** method, as shown here:

```
> Object.keys(myConsole)
=> [ 'name', 'color', 'price', 'library' ]
```

We can also test whether a property exists. Let's check this for a property that has not been defined:

```
> if (myConsole.ramSize) {
... console.log('ram size is defined.');
... }
> undefined
```

Now, let's check this for the properties that we defined previously:

```
> if (myConsole.price) {
... console.log('price is defined.');
... }
> price is defined.
```

This is a very simple way of testing whether the property exists in an object. In a lot of applications, this is used frequently to check the existence of the field and, if it doesn't exist, a default value will be set. Just keep in mind that, in JavaScript, an empty string, an empty array, the number zero, and other falsy values will be evaluated to **false** by the **if** statement. In the following exercise, we will try to create an object with a lot of information and output very useful information from it.

Exercise 40: Creating and Modifying Objects in JavaScript

In this exercise, we will store objects inside an array and modify the array by making changes to the object. We will then check how we can access an object using its properties. We will keep using the **singers** array we defined earlier, but this time instead of only storing a list of strings, we will use objects. Let's get started:

1. Set the **singers** array to an empty array:

    ```
    > singers = []
    => undefined
    ```

2. Push an object to the array:

    ```
    > singers.push({ name: 'miku', age: 16 })
    => undefined
    ```

3. Modify the **name** property of the first object inside the array:

    ```
    > singers[0].name = 'Hatsune Miku'
    => 'Hatsune Miku'
    > singers
    => [ { name: 'Hatsune Miku', age: 16 } ]
    ```

    It's very simple to modify values in an object; for example, you can assign any value to the property, but it doesn't stop there. You can also add properties that weren't originally part of the object to expand its information.

4. Add a property called **birthday** to the object:

```
> singers[0].birthday = 'August 31'
=> 'August 31'
> singers
=> [ { name: 'Hatsune Miku', age: 16, birthday: 'August 31' } ]
```

To add properties to an existing object, simply assign a value to a property name. This will create that property if it doesn't exist. You can assign any value to the property, functions, arrays, or other objects.

5. Read the property in the object by executing the following code:

```
> singers[0].name
=> 'Hatsune Miku'
or
> const propertyName = 'name'
=> undefined
> singers[0][propertyName]
=> 'Hatsune Miku'
```

As you can see, accessing the property value of an object is very simple in JavaScript. If you already know the name of the value, you can just use dot notation. In some cases where the property name is dynamic or from a variable, you can use bracket notation to access the property value of that property name.

In this exercise, we went over ways to create an object in JavaScript and how to modify and add properties to it. JavaScript objects, just like arrays, are very easy to modify and they do not need you to specify a schema. In the next activity, we will build a very interesting utility that can help you understand how objects work across networks and how to efficiently use them.

JSON.stringify

JSON.stringify is a very useful utility that converts a JavaScript object into a formatted string. Later, the string can be transmitted over the network.

For example, let's say we have a **user** object that we want to convert it into a string:

```
const user = {
    name: 'r1cebank',
    favoriteFood: [
        'ramen',
        'sushi',
        'fried chicken'
    ]
};
```

If we want to convert our object into a string, we need to call **JSON.stringify** with this object, as shown in the following code:

```
JSON.stringify(user);
```

We will get a result like this:

Figure 7.4: Result using JSON.stringify

As you can see, calling **JSON.stringify** has converted our object into a string representation of the object.

But because of the way it is implemented, **JSON.stringify** is very inefficient. Although the performance difference is not apparent in most applications, in high-performance applications, a little bit of performance does matter. One way to make a faster **JSON. stringify** utility is to know which property you need in the final output.

Exercise 41: Creating an Efficient JSON.Stringify

Our objective is to write a simple function that takes an object and a list of properties to be included in the final output. The function will then call **JSON.stringify** to create the string version of the object. Let's define a function called **betterStringify** in the **Exercise41.js** file:

1. Create the **betterStringify** function:

   ```
   function betterStringify(item, propertyMap) {
   }
   ```

2. Now, we will create a temporary output. We will store the property we want to be included in **propertyMap**:

   ```
   let output = {};
   ```

3. Iterate through our **propertyMap** argument to cherry-pick the property we want to include:

   ```
   propertyMap.forEach((key) => {
   });
   ```

   Because our **propertyMap** argument is an array, we want to use **forEach** to iterate through it.

4. Assign the value from our item to the temporary output:

   ```
   propertyMap.forEach((key) => {
   if (item[key]) {
       output[key] = item[key];
   }
   });
   ```

   Here, we are checking whether the key in our **propertyMap** argument is set. If it is set, we will store the value in our **output** property.

5. Use a function on a test object:

```
const singer = {
 name: 'Hatsune Miku',
 age: 16,
 birthday: 'August 31',
 birthplace: 'Sapporo, Japan',
 songList: [
   'World is mine',
   'Tell your world',
   'Melt'
 ]
}
console.log(betterStringify(singer, ['name', 'birthday']))
```

After finishing the function, running the file will produce the following output:

```
node v10.15.2 linux/amd64
>
{"name":"Hatsune Miku","birthday":"August 31"}
=> undefined
>
```

Figure 7.5: Output of running Exercise41.js

Now, it's time to answer the tough question: just how fast can you make your code if you did something like this?

If you run a benchmark on this over **JSON.stringify**, you will see a 30% performance gain:

Figure 7.6 Performance difference between JSON.stringify and ouR method

That's 30% more time you can spend calculating more important stuff. Note that this is a very bare-bones example of what you can do if you cherry-pick your properties rather than dumping everything using **JSON.stringify**.

Array and Object Destructuring

In the previous exercises and activities, we went over basic ways to modify values in objects and arrays and ways to get more information from them. There is also a way to retrieve values from the array or object using **destructuring assignment**.

Consider you have been given a list of parameters you need to assign to variables:

```
const param = ['My Name', 12, 'Developer'];
```

One way to assign them is to access each item in the array:

```
const name = param[0];

const age = param[1];

const job = param[2];
```

We can also simplify this into one line by using destructuring:

```
[name, age, job] = param;
```

Exercise 42: Using Destructuring Assignment for an Array

In this exercise, we will declare an array called **userInfo**. It will include basic user information. We will also declare a couple of variables so that we can store the item inside the array by using the destructuring assignment. Let's get started:

1. Create the **userInfo** array:

   ```
   > const userInfo = ['John', 'chef', 34]
   => undefined
   ```

2. Create the variables for storing **name**, **age**, and **job**:

   ```
   > let name, age, job
   => undefined
   ```

3. Use the destructuring assignment syntax to assign values to our variables:

   ```
   > [name, job, age] = userInfo
   => [ 'John', 'chef', 34 ]
   ```

   Check our values:

   ```
   > name
   => 'John'
   > job
   => 'chef'
   > age
   => 34
   ```

4. You can also ignore values inside the array using the following code:

```
> [name, ,age] = userInfo
=> [ 'John', 'chef', 34 ] // we ignored the second element 'chef'
```

The destructuring assignment is very useful when you are dealing with data that is not exactly formatted the way you like. It can also be used to pick items you want inside the array.

Exercise 43: Using Destructuring Assignment for an Object

In the previous exercise, we declared an array with the user's information, and we used destructuring assignment to retrieve some values from it. A similar thing can be done to objects as well. In this exercise, we will try destructuring assignment on objects. Let's get started:

1. Create an object called **userInfo**:

```
> const userInfo = { name: 'John', job: 'chef', age: 34 }
=> undefined
```

2. Create the variables we will use to store the information:

```
> let name, job
=> undefined
```

3. Use the destructuring assignment syntax to assign values:

```
> ({ name, job } = userInfo)
=> { name: 'John', job: 'chef', age: 34 }
```

4. Check the values:

```
> name
=> 'John'
> job
=> 'chef'
```

Note that when using deconstructing assignment on an object, it acts like a filter where the variable name must match, and you can selectively choose which property in the array you want to select. There is also a different way of using this on objects that don't require you to predeclare the variables.

5. Use deconstructing assignment with the arrays:

```
> userInfo = ['John', 'chef', 34]
=> undefined
> [ name, , age] = userInfo
=> undefined
> name
=> 'John'
> age
=> 34
```

6. Use the destructuring operator to create a variable from the object values:

```
> const userInfoObj = { name: 'John', job: 'chef', age: 34 }
=> undefined
> let { job } = userInfoObj
=> undefined
> job
=> 'chef'
```

The following is the output of the preceding code:

Figure 7.7: Output of the job variable

In this exercise, we went over how we can use the destructuring operator to extract specific information from our objects and arrays. This is very useful when we are dealing with a lot of information and we only want to transfer a subset of that information.

Spread Operators

In the previous exercise, we went over some ways in which we can get specific information from objects or arrays. There is another operator that can help us expand arrays or objects. The spread operator was added to the ES6 specification, but in ES9, it also added support for object spread. The spread operator's function is to spread each item into individual items. In the case of arrays, when we use the spread operator, we can treat it as a list of separate values. For objects, they will be spread into key-value pairs. In the next exercise, we will explore different ways we can use the spread operator in our application.

To use the spread operator, we use three dots (...) before any iterrable object, like this:

```
printUser(...userInfo)
```

Exercise 44: Using Spread Operators

In this exercise, we are going to see how the spread operator can help us. We will use the original **userInfo** array from the previous exercise.

Perform the following steps to complete the exercise:

1. Create the **userInfo** array:

   ```
   > const userInfo = ['John', 'chef', 34]
   => undefined
   ```

2. Create a function that prints out the user's information:

   ```
   > function printUser(name, job, age) {
   ... console.log(name + ' is working as ' + job + ' and is ' + age + '
   years old');
   ... }
   => undefined
   ```

3. Spread the array into a list of arguments:

   ```
   > printUser(...userInfo)
   John is working as chef and is 34 years old
   ```

   As you can see, the original way to call this function without the spread operator is to use the array access operator and repeat this for each argument. Since the ordering of the array matches the respective arguments, we can just use the spread operator.

4. Use the spread operator when you want to merge arrays:

   ```
   > const detailedInfo = ['male', ...userInfo, 'July 5']
   => [ 'male', 'John', 'chef', 34, 'July 5' ]
   ```

5. Use the spread operator as a way to copy an array:

   ```
   > let detailedInfoCopy = [ ...detailedInfo ];
   => undefined
   > detailedInfoCopy
   => [ 'male', 'John', 'chef', 34, 'July 5' ]
   ```

Using the spread operator on objects is much more powerful and practical.

6. Create a new object called **userRequest**:

```
> const userRequest = { name: 'username', type: 'update', data: 'newname'}
=> undefined
```

7. Clone the object using the **object** spread:

```
> const newObj = { ...userRequest }
=> undefined
> newObj
=> { name: 'username', type: 'update', data: 'newname' }
```

8. Create an object that includes every property of this object:

```
> const detailedRequestObj = { data: new Date(), new: true,
...userRequest}
=> undefined
> detailedRequestObj
=> { data: 'newname', new: true, name: 'username', type: 'update' }
```

You can see that the spread operator is very useful when you want to copy all the properties over to a new object. You can see this being used in many applications where you want to wrap a user request with some generic properties for further processing.

Rest Operators

In the previous section, we looked at spread operators. The same operator can also be used in a different way. In function declarations, they are called **rest operators**.

Rest operators are mainly used to represent an indefinite number of arguments. Then, the arguments will be placed in an array:

```
function sum(...numbers) {
    console.log(numbers);
}


sum(1, 2, 3, 4, 5, 6, 7, 8, 9);
```

As you can see, we used the same three dots before the name. This tells our code that we are expecting an indefinite number of arguments for this function. When we do call the function with a list of arguments, they will be put inside a JavaScript array:

```
node v10.15.2 linux/amd64
>
[ 1, 2, 3, 4, 5, 6, 7, 8, 9 ]
=> undefined
>
```

Figure 7.8: Output of sum when called with a list of numbers

That doesn't mean you don't have any control over the number of arguments. You can write your function declaration like this to let JavaScript map several parameters to your liking and the rest into an array:

```
function sum(initial, ...numbers) {
    console.log(initial, numbers);
}
```

This maps the first parameter to the variable initial, and the rest to an array called **numbers**:

```
sum(0, 1, 2, 3, 4, 5, 6, 7, 8, 9);
```

The following is the output of the preceding code:

```
node v10.15.2 linux/amd64
>
0 [ 1, 2, 3, 4, 5, 6, 7, 8, 9 ]
=> undefined
>
```

Figure 7.9: Output of sum when called with 0 and 1-9.

OOP in JavaScript

Because of the popularity of JavaScript in web development, it is used mainly in a functional way. This led many developers to the assumption that there is no way to do OOP in JavaScript. Even before the release of the ES6 standard, there was a way to define a class: by using functions. You might have seen this way of defining a class before in legacy frontend code. For example, if you want to create a class called **Food**, you would have to write something like this:

```
function Food(name) {
    this.name = name;
```

```
}
var leek = new Food("leek");


console.log(leek.name); // Outputs "leek"
```

After the release of ES6, an increasing number of developers adopted the modern way of writing JavaScript classes using the **class** keyword. In this chapter, we will be going over ways to declare classes using the ES6 standard.

Defining a Class in JavaScript

Before we dive into the latest syntax to define a class in JavaScript, let's go over how it used to be done before ES6.

The syntax that was used to define a class before ES6 was as follows:

```
function ClassName(param1, param2) {
    // Constructor Logic
}
```

Essentially, we are defining the **constructor** class. The name of the function will be the name of the class.

The syntax to define a class with ES6 is as follows:

```
class ClassName {
    constructor(param1, param2) {
        // Constructor logic
    }
    method1(param) {
        // Method logic
    }
}
```

This is what we usually do with class definitions in other languages. Here, we can define a constructor and a method.

Exercise 45: Declaring an Object Constructor Using Functions

In this exercise, we will create a very simple class called **Food**. Later, we will also add some methods to the class. We will be using the function constructor method here. Let's get started:

1. Define the **Food** constructor function:

```
function Food(name, calories, cost) {
    this.name = name;
    this.calories = calories;
    this.cost = cost;
}
```

2. Add the method to the constructor:

```
Food.prototype.description = function () {
    return this.name + ' calories: ' + this.calories;
}
```

3. Create a new object using the **Food** constructor:

```
let burger = new Food('burger', 1000, 9);
```

4. Call the method we have declared:

```
console.log(burger.description());
```

The following is the output of the preceding code:

```
node v10.16.0
>
burger calories: 1000
=> undefined
>
```

Figure 7.10: Output of the burger.description() method

Many of you might be familiar with this type of declaration of a class. But this also creates issues. First, using functions as constructors gives a developer no clear idea of when to treat a function as a function and when to use it as a constructor. Later, when JavaScript released ES6, it introduced a new way of declaring classes. In the next exercise, we will use the new method to declare the **Food** class.

Exercise 46: Creating a Class in JavaScript

In this exercise, we will create a class definition in JavaScript to store food data. It will include a name, a cost, and a calorie count. Later, we will also create methods that return the description of the food and another static method to output the calories for a certain food. Let's get started:

1. Declare a **Food** class:

```
class Food {
}
```

2. Run **typeof** on the class name to see what type it is:

```
console.log(typeof Food) // should print out 'function'
```

The following is the output of the preceding code:

```
node v10.16.0
>
function
=> undefined
>
```

Figure 7.11: Running the typeof command on the class

As you can see, the type of the new class we just declared is **function** – isn't that interesting? This is because, inside JavaScript, the class we declared is just another way of writing the **constructor** function.

3. Let's add our **constructor**:

```
class Food {
    constructor(name, calories, cost) {
        this.name = name;
        this.calories = calories;
        this.cost = cost;
    }
}
```

Just like any other language, the class definition will include a constructor, which is called using the **new** keyword to create an instance of this class.

4. Write the **description** method inside the class definition:

```
class Food {
    constructor(name, calories, cost) {
        this.name = name;
        this.calories = calories;
        this.cost = cost;
    }
    description() {
        return this.name + ' calories: ' + this.calories;
    }
}
```

5. If you try to invoke the **Food** class constructor like a function, it will throw the following error:

```
Food('burger', 1000, 9);
// TypeError: Class constructor Food2 cannot be invoked without 'new'
```

The following is the output of the preceding code:

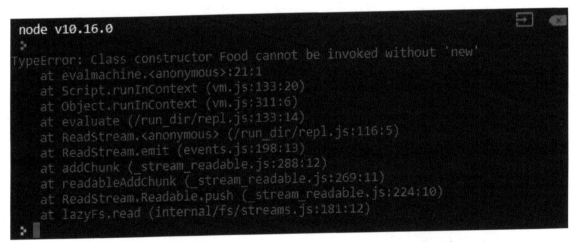

Figure 7.12: TypeError for invoking the constructor as a function

Notice that the runtime throws an error when you are trying to call the constructor like a function. This is very helpful as it prevents the developer from mistakenly calling the constructor as a function.

6. Create a new food object using the class constructor:

```
let friedChicken = new Food('fried chicken', 520, 5);
```

7. Call the method we have declared:

```
console.log(friedChicken.description());
```

8. Declare the **static** method, which returns the number of calories:

```
class Food {
    constructor(name, calories, cost) {
        this.name = name;
        this.calories = calories;
        this.cost = cost;
    }
    static getCalories(food) {
        return food.calories
    }
    description() {
        return this.name + ' calories: ' + this.calories;
    }
}
```

9. Call the **static** method with the object we just created:

```
console.log(Food.getCalories(friedChicken)); /// 520
```

The following is the output of the preceding code:

```
node v10.16.0
>
520
=> undefined
>
```

Figure 7.13: Output generated after calling the static method of the Food class

Like any other programming language, you can call the **static** method without instantiating the object.

Now that we've looked at the new way to declare classes in JavaScript, let's talk about some of the differences of class declarations:

- The constructor method is required. If you do not declare one, JavaScript will add an empty constructor.

- The class declaration is not hoisted, which means that you cannot use it before it is declared. So, it's best to have your class definitions or imports at the top of the code.

Creating a Simple User Information Cache Using Objects

In this section, we will design a simple user info cache. A cache is a temporary location where you can store the most frequently accessed items when fetching them from the original place takes time. Suppose you are designing for a backend application that handles user profiles. Whenever the request comes in, the server needs to call the database to retrieve the user profile and send it back to the handler. As you may know, calling the database is a very costly operation. As a backend developer, you may be asked to improve the read performance of the service.

In the next exercise, you will create a simple cache for storing the user profile so that you can skip the request to the database most of the time.

Exercise 47: Creating a Cache Class to Add/Update/Remove Records from the Data Store

In this exercise, we will create a cache class that includes a local memory data store. It also includes a method that adds/updates/removes a record from the data store.

Perform the following steps to complete this exercise:

1. Create the **MySimpleCache** class:

```
class MySimpleCache {
constructor() {
    // Declare your cache internal properties here
    this.cacheItems = {};
}
}
```

   In the constructor, we will also initialize our internal state for the cache. This will be a simple object.

2. Define **addItem**, which will set the cache item for the key:

```
addItem(key, value) {
// Add an item with the key
this.cacheItems[key] = value;
    }
```

3. Define **updateItem**, which will use the **addItem** we already defined:

```
updateItem(key, value) {
// Update a value use the key
this.addItem(key, value);
    }
```

4. Define **removeItem**. This will remove the object we stored in our cache and invoke the **updateItem** method we created previously:

```
removeItem(key) {
this.updateItem(key, undefined);
}
```

5. Test our cache using **assert()** with **testMycache** by updating and deleting a few users:

```
function testMyCache() {
    const cache = new MySimpleCache ();

    cache.addItem('user1', { name: 'user1', dob: 'Jan 1' });
    cache.addItem('user2', { name: 'user2', dob: 'Jul 21' });
    cache.updateItem('user1', { name: 'user1', dob: 'Jan 2' });
    cache.addItem('user3', { name: 'user3', dob: 'Feb 1' });
    cache.removeItem('user3');

    assert(cache.getItem('user1').dob === 'Jan 2');
    assert(cache.getItem('user2').dob === 'Jul 21');
    assert(cache.getItem('user3') === undefined);

    console.log ('=====TEST PASSED=====')
}

testMyCache();
```

> **Note**
> **assert()** is a built-in Node.js function that takes an expression. It will pass if the expression evaluates to **true** and throw an exception if it is evaluated to **false**.

After running the file, you should see no errors and the following output:

Figure 7.14: Output of simple_cache.js

Class Inheritance

So far, we have only created simple class definitions in JavaScript. In OOP, we can also have a class inherit from another class. Class inheritance is simply making one class's implementation be derived from another class. The child class that's created will have all the attributes and methods of the parent class. This is shown in the following diagram:

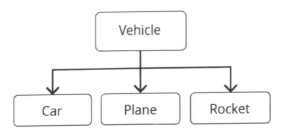

Figure 7.15: Class inheritance

Class inheritance provides some benefits:

- It creates clean, testable, and reusable code.

- It reduces the amount of similar code.

- It reduces maintenance time when writing a new feature that will apply to all subclasses.

In JavaScript, it is very easy to create a subclass that inherits from another class. In order to do so, the **extends** keyword is used:

```
class MySubClass extends ParentClass {



}
```

Exercise 48: Implementing a Subclass

In this exercise, we will define a superclass called **Vehicle** and create our subclasses from it. The superclass will have methods called **start**, **buy**, and **name**, **speed**, and **cost** as its attributes.

The constructor of the superclass will take a name, color, and speed attributes, and then store them inside the object.

The **start** method will simply print out a string, telling you which vehicle you are using and how you are traveling. The **buy** function will print out which vehicle you are about to purchase.

Perform the following steps to complete this exercise:

1. Define the **Vehicle** class:

```
class Vehicle {
    constructor(name, speed, cost) {
        this.name = name;
        this.speed = speed;
        this.cost = cost;
    }
    start() {
        console.log('Starting vehicle, ' + this.name + ' at ' + this.speed
+ 'km/h');
    }
    buy() {
        console.log('Buying for ' + this.cost);
    }
}
```

2. Create a **vehicle** instance and test out its methods:

```
const vehicle = new Vehicle('bicycle', 15, 100);
vehicle.start();
vehicle.buy();
```

You should see the following output:

```
node v10.15.2 linux/amd64
Starting vehicle, at 15km/h
Buying for 100
```

Figure 7.16: Output of the Vehicle class

3. Create the **Car**, **Plane**, and **Rocket** subclasses:

```
class Car extends Vehicle {}
class Plane extends Vehicle {}
class Rocket extends Vehicle {}
```

4. In **Car**, **Plane**, and **Rocket**, override the **start** method:

```
class Car extends Vehicle {
    start() {
        console.log('Driving car, at ' + this.speed + 'km/h');
    }
}
```

```
class Plane extends Vehicle {
    start() {
        console.log('Flying plane, at ' + this.speed + 'km/h');
    }
}
class Rocket extends Vehicle {
    start() {
        console.log('Flying rocket to the moon, at ' + this.speed +
    'km/h');
    }
}
```

5. Create an instance for **Plane**, **Rocket**, and **Car**:

```
const car = new Car('Toyota Corolla', 120, 5000);
const plane = new Plane('Boeing 737', 1000, 26000000);
const rocket = new Rocket('Saturn V', 9920, 6000000000);
```

6. Call the **start** method on all three objects:

```
car.start();
plane.start();
rocket.start();
```

The following is the output of the preceding code:

```
node v10.15.2 linux/amd64
>
Driving car, at 120km/h
Flying plane, at 1000km/h
Flying rocket to the moon, at 9920km/h
=> undefined
>
```

Figure 7.17: Output from the objects

When you call these start methods now, you can clearly see that the output is different. When declaring subclasses, most of the time, we need to override some methods from the parent class. This is very useful when we are reducing the duplicated code while preserving the customization this creates.

The customization doesn't stop here – you are also able to create a new subclass with a different constructor. You are also able to call the parent method from the subclass.

7. For the subclasses we created previously, we will be modifying the **Car** subclass so that it includes extra parameters in the constructor:

```
class Car extends Vehicle {
    constructor(name, speed, cost, tankSize) {
        super(name, speed, cost);
        this.tankSize = tankSize;
    }
    start() {
        console.log('Driving car, at ' + this.speed + 'km/h');
    }
}
```

8. Check to see whether the extra property is set:

```
const car2 = new Car('Toyota Corolla 2', 120, 5000, 2000);
console.log(car2.tankSize); // 2000
```

The following is the output of the preceding code:

```
node v10.16.0
>
2000
=> undefined
>
```

Figure 7.18: Checking the extra property of the Car class

As you can see, declaring a subclass is very easy – you can have a lot of code shared when coding this way. Also, you do not lose the ability of being able to do customization. After the ES6 standard, you can easily define classes just like the other OOP languages out there. It can make your code cleaner, more testable, and more easily maintainable.

Private and Public Methods

In OOP, sometimes, it's useful to separate publicly accessible properties and functions and privately accessible properties and functions. It's a protection layer to prevent developers who are using the class from invoking or accessing some internal states of the class. In JavaScript, that behavior is not possible because ES6 doesn't allow private properties to be declared; all the properties you declare in the class will be publicly accessible. To achieve this type of behavior, some developers have opted to use the underscore prefix, for example, **privateMethod()**, to inform other developers not to use it. However, there are hacks around declaring private methods. In the next exercise, we will explore private methods.

Exercise 49: Private Methods in the Vehicle Class

In this exercise, we will try to declare a private function for the **Car** class we created previously so that we can make sure our private method isn't exposed when we export the class as a module later. Let's get started:

1. Create a function named **printStat**:

```
function printStat() {
    console.log('The car has a tanksize of ', this.tankSize);
}
```

2. Modify the **public** method to use the function we just declared:

```
class Car extends Vehicle {
    constructor(name, speed, cost, tankSize) {
        super(name, speed, cost);
        this.tankSize = tankSize;
    }
    start() {
        console.log('Driving car, at ' + this.speed + 'km/h');
        printStat();
    }
}
```

We called **printStat** from our **start** method directly, but there is no real way to access the method directly without using one of the methods in our class. By having the method declared outside, we made the method **private**.

3. Create another **car** instance and call the **start** method:

```
const car = new Car('Toyota Corolla', 120, 5000, 2000);
car.start();
```

When you run this code, you will realize that this causes an anomaly:

```
node v10.15.2 linux/amd64
>
Driving car, at 120km/h
The car has a tanksize of  undefined
=> undefined
>
```

Figure 7.19: Output of printStat

4. Modify the **start** method so that the function knows about the object instance we are calling it from:

```
start() {
        console.log('Driving car, at ' + this.speed + 'km/h');
        printStat.bind(this)();
    }
```

Notice we used .**bind()**. By using bind, we are binding the current instance to the **this** variable inside this function. This enabled our code to work as expected:

```
node v10.15.2 linux/amd64
>
Driving car, at 120km/h
The car has a tanksize of  2000
=> undefined
>
```

Figure 7.20: Output of printStat after using .bind()

As you can see, currently, there is no way to easily declare a **private** method or properties in JavaScript. This example is just a hack around the issue; it still doesn't provide equal separation like other OOP languages do, such as Java or Python. There are also options online where you can declare private methods using symbols, but they can also be accessed if you know where to look.

Array and Object Built-in Methods

Previously, we talked about basic arrays and objects. They deal with how we store data. Now, we will dive deep into how we take the data we have just stored in them and make advanced calculations and manipulations on them.

array.map(function)

Array map will iterate over each item in the array and return a new array as a result. The function that's passed to the method will take the current item as a parameter and the returned value of the function will be included in the final array's result; for example:

```
const singers = [{ name: 'Miku', age: 16}, { name: 'Kaito', age: 20 }];
```

If we want to create a new array and only include the name property from the object in the list, we can use **array.map** to accomplish this:

```
const names = singers.map((singer) => singer.name);
```

The following is the output of the preceding code:

```
node v10.16.0
>
=> [ 'Miku', 'Kaito' ]
>
```

Figure 7.21: Output using array.map(function)

array.forEach(function)

.forEach is a way of iterating over an array of items. Unlike **.map**, it does not return new values. The function we passed in simply gets called repeatedly with the values in the array; for example:

```
const singers = [{ name: 'Miku', age: 16}, { name: 'Kaito', age: 20 }];

singers.forEach((singer) => {
    console.log(singer.name);
})
```

This will print out every singer's name in the array.

array.find(function)

The **.find** method works just like the **.map** and **.forEach** methods; it takes a function as a parameter. This function will be used to determine whether the current object matches the requirement of the search. If a match is found, it will be used as the returned result for the method. This method is only useful if you have only one match in the array and will not return at all if multiple matches were found. For example, if we want to find the object with the name equal to a string, we can do the following:

```
const singers = [{ name: 'Miku', age: 16}, { name: 'Kaito', age: 20 }];


const miku = singers.find((singer) => singer.name === 'Miku');
```

array.filter(function)

`.filter` works just like `.find`, but it allows multiple items to be returned. If we want to match multiple items in a list, we need to use `.filter`. If we want to find a list of singers with an age less than 30, use the following code:

```
const singers = [{ name: 'Miku', age: 16}, { name: 'Kaito', age: 20 }];

const youngSingers = singers.filter((singer) => singer.age < 30);
```

The **map** method from the array creates a new array while iterating through every item in the array. The **map** method takes a function such as the **forEach** method. When it executes, it will call the function with the first parameter with the current item and the second with the current index. The **map** method also expects the function that's supplied to it to be returned. The returned value will be put inside a new array and returned by the method, like so:

```
const programmingLanguages = ['C', 'Java', 'Python'];


const myMappedArray = programmingLanguages.map((language) => {
    return 'I know ' + language;
});
```

The `.map` method will iterate through the array and our **map** function will return **"I know,"** plus the current language. So, the result of **myMappedArray** will be as follows:

```
node v10.16.0
>
=> [ 'I know C', 'I know Java', 'I know Python' ]
>
```

Figure 7.22: Example output using an array map method

We will go over **array.map** in more detail in *Chapter 10, Functional Programming in JavaScript*.

Another method that we will use in the following exercise is the **forEach** method. The **forEach** method is much cleaner, as there is no need to manage the current index and write the actual call to the function. The **forEach** method is a built-in array method and it takes a function as a parameter. The following is an example of the **forEach** method:

```
foods.forEach(eat_food);
```

In the following exercise, we will use iteration methods on arrays.

Exercise 50: Using Iteration Methods on Arrays

There are many ways to iterate through an array. One is to use the **for** loop with an index, while another is to use one of its built-in methods. In this exercise, we will initialize an array of strings and then explore some of the iteration methods that are available in JavaScript. Let's get started:

1. Create a list of foods as an array:

   ```
   const foods = ['sushi', 'tofu', 'fried chicken'];
   ```

2. Join every item in the array using **join**:

   ```
   foods.join(', ');
   ```

   The following is the output of the preceding code:

   ```
   node v10.16.0
   >
   => 'sushi, tofu, fried chicken'
   >
   ```

   Figure 7.23: Joined items in the array

   Array joining is another way to iterate through every item in the array, combining them into one single string using the separator supplied in between them.

3. Create a function called **eat_food**:

   ```
   function eat_food(food) {
       console.log('I am eating ' + food);
   }
   ```

4. Use the **for** loop to iterate through the array and call the function:

   ```
   const foods = ['sushi', 'tofu', 'fried chicken'];

   function eat_food(food) {
       console.log('I am eating ' + food);
   }

   for(let i = 0; i < foods.length; i++) {
       eat_food(foods[i]);
   }
   ```

The following is the output of the preceding code:

```
node v10.15.2 linux/amd64
>
I am eating sushi
I am eating tofu
I am eating fried chicken
=> undefined
>
```

Figure 7.24: Output of eat_food being called inside a loop

5. Use the **forEach** method to achieve the same:

```
foods.forEach(eat_food);
```

The following is the output of the preceding code:

```
node v10.15.2 linux/amd64
>
I am eating sushi
I am eating tofu
I am eating fried chicken
=> undefined
>
```

Figure 7.25: The same output is generated by using the forEach method

Because **eat_food** is a function and its first parameter references the current item, we can just pass the function name over.

6. Create a new array of calorie numbers:

```
const nutrition = [100, 50, 400]
```

This array includes all the calories for each item in our **food** array. Next, we will use a different iterative function to create a new list of objects, including this information.

7. Create new array of objects:

```
const foodInfo = foods.map((food, index) => {
    return {
        name: food,
        calories: nutrition[index]
    };
});
```

8. Print out **foodInfo** to the console:

```
console.log(foodInfo);
```

The following is the output of the preceding code:

```
node v10.15.2 linux/amd64
:
[ { name: 'sushi', calories: 100 },
  { name: 'tofu', calories: 50 },
  { name: 'fried chicken', calories: 400 } ]
=> undefined
:
```

Figure 7.26: Array containing food and calorie information

After running **array.map**, the new array will be created, which includes information about our food name and its calorie count.

In this exercise, we went over two iteration methods, that is, **forEach** and **map**. Each has its own capabilities and usages. In most applications, maps are generally used to calculate array results by running the same code on each array item. This is very useful if you want to manipulate every item in the array without modifying the array directly.

Exercise 51: Lookups and Filtering the Array

Previously, we talked about ways to iterate through arrays. These ways can also be used for lookups. As we all know, a lookup is very costly when you are iterating the array from start to finish. Luckily, a JavaScript array has some built-in methods for that, so we don't have to write our search function ourselves. In this exercise, we will use **includes** and **filter** to search the items in our array. Let's get started:

1. Create a list of names called **profiles**:

```
let profiles = [
    'Michael Scott',
    'Jim Halpert',
    'Dwight Shrute',
    'Random User',
    'Hatsune Miku',
    'Rin Kagamine'
];
```

2. Try to find out whether the list of profiles includes a person named **Jim Halpert**:

```
let hasJim = profiles.includes('Jim Halpert');
console.log(hasJim);
```

The following is the output of the preceding code:

Figure 7.27: Output of the hasJim method

3. Modify the **profiles** array to include extra information:

```
const profiles = [
    { name: 'Michael Scott', age: 42 },
    { name: 'Jim Halpert', age: 27},
    { name: 'Dwight Shrute', age: 37 },
    { name: 'Random User', age: 10 },
    { name: 'Hatsune Miku', age: 16 },
    { name: 'Rin Kagamine', age: 14 }
]
```

Now, the array is no longer a simple list of strings – it's a list of objects, and things will work a little bit differently when we are dealing with objects.

4. Try to use **includes** to find the **Jim Halpert** profile again:

```
hasJim = profiles.includes({ name: 'Jim Halpert', age: 27});
console.log(hasJim);
```

The following is the output of the preceding code:

Figure 7.28: Output of the hasJim method

5. Find the profile with the name **Jim Halpert**:

```
hasJim = !!profiles.find((profile) => {
    return profile.name === 'Jim Halpert';
}).length;
console.log(hasJim);
```

6. Find all the users with an age older than **18**:

```
const adults = profiles.filter((profile) => {
    return profile.age > 18;
});
console.log(adults);
```

When you run the preceding code, it should output all the users with an age over 18. The difference between **filter** and **find** is that **filter** returns an array:

```
node v10.15.2 linux/amd64
>
[ { name: 'Michael Scott', age: 42 },
  { name: 'Jim Halpert', age: 27 },
  { name: 'Dwight Shrute', age: 37 } ]
=> undefined
>
```

Figure 7.29: Output after using the filter method

In this exercise, we looked at two ways we can locate a specific item in our array. By using these methods, we can avoid rewriting the search algorithm. The difference between **find** and **filter** is that **filter** returns an array of all the objects matching the requirement. In an actual production environment, when we want to test whether the array has an object that matches our requirement, we usually use the **find** method because it stops scanning when it finds one match, whereas **filter** compares with all the objects in the array and will return all the matching occurrences. This is more costly if you are just testing for the existence of something. We also used the double negative operator to cast our result to a Boolean. This notation is very useful if you are using this value later in a conditional.

Sorting

Sorting is one of the biggest challenges that developers face. When we want to sort a number of items in our array, we usually need to define a specific sorting algorithm. These algorithms usually require us to write a lot of logic on sorting and they are not easily reused. In JavaScript, we can use the built-in array methods to sort our custom list of items and write minimal custom code.

Sorting in JavaScript arrays requires us to call the `.sort()` function on the array. The **sort()** function takes one parameter, called the sorting comparator. Based on the comparator, the **sort()** function will make a decision on how to arrange each element.

The following is a brief description of some of the other functions we will use in the upcoming exercise.

The **compareNumber** function only calculates the difference between **a** and **b**. In the **sort** method, we can declare our own custom compare function to be passed down to do the comparison:

```
function compareNumber(a, b) {
    return a - b;
}
```

The **compareAge** function is very similar to the **compareNumber** function. The only difference here is that we are comparing JavaScript objects instead of numbers:

```
function compareAge(a, b) {
    return a.age - b.age;
}
```

Exercise 52: Sorting Arrays in JavaScript

In this exercise, we will go over ways to sort our arrays. Sorting is always complicated in computer science. In JavaScript, the array object has a sorting method built into it where you can do basic sorting on the array.

We will be using the **profiles** array of objects from the previous exercise. Let's get started:

1. Create an array of **numbers**:

   ```
   const numbers = [ 20, 1, 3, 55, 100, 2];
   ```

2. Call **array.sort()** to sort this array:

   ```
   numbers.sort();
   console.log(numbers);
   ```

   When you run the preceding code, you will get the following output:

```
node v10.15.2 linux/amd64
>
[ 1, 100, 2, 20, 3, 55 ]
=> undefined
>
```

Figure 7.30: Output of array.sort()

This is not exactly what we want; it appears that the **sort** function just randomly arranges the values. The reason behind this is that, in JavaScript, **array.sort()** doesn't really support sorting by values. By default, it treats everything as a string. When we called it using the number array, it converted everything into strings and then started sorting. That's why you are seeing numbers with 1 appearing before 2 and 3. To implement the sorting of numbers, we need to do something extra.

3. Define the **compareNumber** function:

```
function compareNumber(a, b) {
    return a - b;
}
```

The function expects to take two values that are going to be compared, and returns a value that must match the following: if **a** is smaller than **b**, return a number less than 0; if **a** is equal to **b**, return 0; and if **a** is larger than **b**, return a number greater than 0.

4. Run the **sort** function and provide the **compareNumber** function as our parameter:

```
numbers.sort(compareNumber);
console.log(numbers);
```

When you run the preceding code, you will see that the function has sorted our array into the order we wanted:

Figure 7.31: Output of array.sort(compareNumber)

Now, the array is sorted correctly from smallest to largest. However, most of the time when we have to do sorting, we need to sort complex objects into order. For the next step, we will use the **profiles** array we created in the previous exercise.

5. Create the **profiles** array if it isn't defined in your workspace:

```
const profiles = [
    { name: 'Michael Scott', age: 42 },
    { name: 'Jim Halpert', age: 27},
    { name: 'Dwight Shrute', age: 37 },
    { name: 'Random User', age: 10 },
    { name: 'Hatsune Miku', age: 16 },
    { name: 'Rin Kagamine', age: 14 }
]
```

6. Call **profiles.sort()**:

```
profiles.sort();
console.log(profiles);
```

The following is the output of the preceding code:

```
node v10.15.2 linux/amd64
>
[ { name: 'Michael Scott', age: 42 },
  { name: 'Jim Halpert', age: 27 },
  { name: 'Dwight Shrute', age: 37 },
  { name: 'Random User', age: 10 },
  { name: 'Hatsune Miku', age: 16 },
  { name: 'Rin Kagamine', age: 14 } ]
=> undefined
>
```

Figure 7.32: Output of the profiles.sort() function

Because our **sort** function has no idea how to compare these objects, the array is left the way it is. In order to make it correctly sort objects, we need a compare function just like last time.

7. Define **compareAge**:

```
function compareAge(a, b) {
    return a.age - b.age;
}
```

The two arguments that are supplied to **compareAge**, **a** and **b**, are objects in our array. So, in order to have them sorted correctly, we need to access the **age** property of these objects and compare them.

8. Call the **sort** function with the **compare** function we just have defined:

```
profiles.sort(compareAge);
console.log(profiles);
```

The following is the output of the preceding code:

```
node v10.15.2 linux/amd64
>
[ { name: 'Random User', age: 10 },
  { name: 'Rin Kagamine', age: 14 },
  { name: 'Hatsune Miku', age: 16 },
  { name: 'Jim Halpert', age: 27 },
  { name: 'Dwight Shrute', age: 37 },
  { name: 'Michael Scott', age: 42 } ]
=> undefined
>
```

Figure 7.33: Result of profile.sort(compareAge)

In this exercise, we went over the ways to sort our arrays. One thing to keep in mind is that, in JavaScript, if you are not sorting string values, you are required to supply the sorting function with a compare function so that it knows how to sort. The space and time complexity for this method varies from platform to platform, but if you are using Node.js, the V8 engine of JavaScript is highly optimized for these types of operations, so you don't have to worry about performance. In the next exercise, we will go over a very interesting, yet useful, array operation in JavaScript, the array reducer. By using the array reducer, we can easily combine items in the array and reduce them into one single value.

Array Reduce

When building backend applications, there are many times where you are given a list of formatted results and you must calculate a single value from them. While this can be done using the traditional loop method, it is much cleaner and much easier to maintain when you are using the JavaScript reducing function. Reducing means taking each element in the array and producing a single value in return.

If we want to reduce an array, we can call the built-in **array.reduce()** method:

```
Array.reduce((previousValue, currentValue) => {
    // reducer
}, initialValue);
```

When we call **array.reduce()**, we need to pass in a function and the initial value. The function will feed a previous value and a current value as arguments and will use the return as the final value.

Exercise 53: Using JavaScript Reduce Method to Make Calculations for a Shopping Cart

In this exercise, we will try to use JavaScript **reduce** method to make calculations for a shopping cart. Let's get started:

1. Create the shopping cart variable:

    ```
    const cart = [];
    ```

2. Push items into the array:

```
cart.push({ name: 'CD', price: 12.00, amount: 2 });
cart.push({ name: 'Book', price: 45.90, amount: 1 });
cart.push({ name: 'Headphones', price: 5.99, amount: 3 });
cart.push({ name: 'Coffee', price: 12.00, amount: 2 });
cart.push({ name: 'Mug', price: 15.45, amount: 1 });
cart.push({ name: 'Sugar', price: 5.00, amount: 1 });
```

3. Calculate the total cost of the shopping cart using the loop method:

```
let total = 0;
cart.forEach((item) => {
    total += item.price * item.amount;
});
console.log('Total amount: ' + total);
```

The following is the output of the preceding code:

```
node v10.15.2 linux/amd64
>
Total amount: 132.32
=> undefined
>
```

Figure 7.34: Result of the loop method of calculating total

4. We write our reducer called **priceReducer**:

```
function priceReducer (accumulator, currentValue) {
    return accumulator += currentValue.price * currentValue.amount;
}
```

5. Call **cart.reduce** with our reducer:

```
total = cart.reduce(priceReducer, 0);
console.log('Total amount: ' + total);
```

Following is the output of the preceding code:

```
node v10.15.2 linux/amd64
>
Total amount: 132.32
=> undefined
>
```

Figure 7.35: Result of cart.reduce

In this exercise, we went over the ways in which we can reduce the array into a single value in JavaScript. While it is perfectly correct to use a loop to iterate through the array and return the accumulator, it makes the code much cleaner when you are using the reduce function. We not only reduced the number of mutable variables in the scope, but we also made the code much cleaner and maintainable. The next person maintaining the code will know that the returned value of that function will be a single value, whereas the `forEach` method may make it unclear what the result of that returned is.

Activity 9: Creating a Student Manager Using JavaScript Arrays and Classes

Suppose you are working for a local school district, and up until now they've been using a paper register to keep track of student information. Now, they've had some funding and want you to develop a piece of computer software to track student information. They have the following requirements for the software:

- It needs to be able to record information about students, including their name, age, grade level, and book information.

- Each student will be assigned a unique ID that will be used to retrieve and modify student record.

- Book information will include the name and the current grade (number grade) of the book for that student.

- There needs to be a way to calculate the average grade for the student.

- There needs to be a way to search for all students with the same age or grade level.

- There needs to be a way to search for a student using their name. When multiples are found, return all of them.

> **Note**
>
> The complete code for this activity can also be found on our GitHub repository, here: https://github.com/TrainingByPackt/Professional-JavaScript/blob/master/Lesson07/Activity09/Activity09.js.

Perform the following steps to complete this activity:

1. Create a **School** class and initialize a list of students in the constructor.

2. Create a **Student** class and store a list of courses, the student's **age**, **name**, and **grade level** in it.

3. Create a **Course** class that will include information about **course**, **name** and **grades**.

4. Create the **addStudent** function in the **School** class to push students into a list in the **school** object.

5. Create the **findByGrade** function in the **School** class, which returns all the students with a given **grade level**.

6. Create the **findByAge** function in the **School** class, which returns a list of students with the same **age**.

7. Create the **findByName** function in the **School** class, which searches for all the students in the school by name.

8. In the **Student** class, create a **calculateAverageGrade** method for calculating the average grade of the student.

9. In the **Student** class, create a **assignGrade** method, which will assign a number grade for a course the student is taking.

> **Note**
>
> The solution for this activity can be found on page 608.

In the previous section, we went over methods that allow us to iterate, look up, and reduce our arrays. These are very useful methods when dealing with arrays. While most of the methods only accomplish basic tasks and they can be easily implemented using loops, using them helps with making our code more usable and testable. Some of the built-in methods are also well optimized by the runtime engine.

In the next section, we will go over some built-in functions for Map and Set. They are very useful if we need to track values in our application.

Maps and Sets

Maps and Sets are very underrated types in JavaScript, but they can be very powerful in some applications. Maps work just like a basic hashmap in JavaScript, and are useful when you need to keep track of a list of key-value pairs. Sets are used when you need to keep a list of unique values. Most developers often use objects for everything while forgetting that, in some cases, using Maps and Sets is way more efficient. In the following section, we will go over Maps and Sets and how to use them.

There are many cases where we must keep track of a list of unique key-value pairs in our application. When programming with other languages, we often need to implement a class called **Hashmap**. In JavaScript, there are two types that can accomplish this: one is Map and the other is Object. Because they seem to do the same thing, many JavaScript developers tend to use Object for everything while ignoring that using Map is sometimes way more effective for their use case.

Exercise 54: Using Maps versus Objects

In this exercise, we will go over ways we can use Maps and how they are different compared to Objects:

1. Create a new Map called **map**:

    ```
    const map = new Map()
    ```

2. Create a list of objects we want to use as keys:

    ```
    const key1 = 'key1';
    const key2 = { name: 'John', age: 18 };
    const key3 = Map;
    ```

3. Use **map.set** to set a value for all the keys we defined earlier:

    ```
    map.set(key1, 'value for key1');
    map.set(key2, 'value for key2');
    map.set(key3, 'value for key3');
    ```

    The following is the output of the preceding code:

```
node v10.15.2 linux/amd64

=> Map {
  'key1' => 'value for key1',
  { name: 'John', age: 18 } => 'value for key2',
  [Function: Map] => 'value for key3' }
```

Figure 7.36: Output after assigning values to map.set

4. Get the values of the keys:

```
console.log(map.get(key1));
console.log(map.get(key2));
console.log(map.get(key3));
```

The following is the output of the preceding code:

```
node v10.15.2 linux/amd64
>
value for key1
value for key2
value for key3
=> undefined
>
```

Figure 7.37: Output of console.log for value retrieval

5. Retrieve the value for **key2** without using the reference:

```
console.log(map.get({ name: 'John', age: 18 }));
```

The following is the output of the preceding code:

```
node v10.15.2 linux/amd64
>
undefined
=> undefined
>
```

Figure 7.38: Output of console.log when using get without reference

While we typed everything correctly, our Map doesn't seem to be able to find the value for that key. This is because, when doing these retrievals, it is using the reference to the object instead of the values.

6. Iterate through the Map using **forEach**:

```
map.forEach((value, key) => {
    console.log('the value for key: ' + key + ' is ' + value);
});
```

The Map can be iterated through like an array. When using the **forEach** method, the function that is passed in will be called with two parameters: the first parameter is the value while the second parameter is the key.

7. Get the list of keys and values as arrays:

    ```
    console.log(map.keys());
    console.log(map.values());
    ```

    The following is the output of the preceding code:

```
node v10.16.0

[Map Iterator] { 'key1', { name: 'John', age: 18 }, [Function: Map] }
[Map Iterator] { 'value for key1', 'value for key2', 'value for key3' }
=> undefined
```

Figure 7.39: List of keys and values as arrays

These methods are useful when you only need a part of the information it stores. If you have a Map tracking the users while using their IDs as keys, calling the **values** method will simply return a list of users.

8. Check whether the Map includes a key:

    ```
    console.log(map.has('non exist')); // false
    ```

    The following is the output of the preceding code:

```
node v10.16.0

false
=> undefined
```

Figure 7.40: Output indicating that Map does not include a key

> **Note**
>
> Here, we can see the first major difference between Maps and Objects, even though both are able to keep track of a list of unique key-value pairs. In Maps, you can have keys that are references of an object or function. This is not possible with Objects in JavaScript. Another thing we can see is that it also preserves the order of the keys according to the order that they are added to the Map. While you might get ordered keys in Objects, JavaScript does not guarantee the order for keys in terms of the order they are added into the Object.

With this exercise, we went over the usage of Maps and its differences compared to Object. When you are dealing with key-value data and you need to do ordering, Map should be always preferred over Objects because not only does it keep the order of your keys, it also allows object references to be used as keys. That's the main difference between the two types. In the next exercise, we will go over another type that is often overlooked by developers: Set.

In mathematics, a set is defined as a collection of distinct objects. In JavaScript, it is rarely used, but we are going to go over one usage of Set regardless.

Exercise 55: Using Sets to Track Unique Values

In this exercise, we will go over the JavaScript Set. We will be building an algorithm to remove all the duplicate values inside an array.

Perform the following steps to complete this exercise:

1. Declare an array string called **planets**:

```
const planets = [
    'Mercury',
    'Uranus',
    'Mars',
    'Venus',
    'Neptune',
    'Saturn',
    'Mars',
    'Jupiter',
    'Earth',
    'Saturn'
]
```

2. Create a new Set using the array:

```
const planetSet = new Set(planets);
```

3. Retrieve the unique values in the **planets** array:

```
console.log(planetSet.values());
```

The following is the output of the preceding code:

```
node v10.15.2 linux/amd64
>
[Set Iterator] {
  'Mercury',
  'Uranus',
  'Mars',
  'Venus',
  'Neptune',
  'Saturn',
  'Jupiter',
  'Earth' }
=> undefined
>
```

Figure 7.41: Unique array values

4. Add more values to the Set using the **add** method:

```
planetSet.add('Venus');
planetSet.add('Kepler-440b');
```

We can use the **add** method to add a new value to our Set, but because Set always maintains the uniqueness of its members, if you add anything that already exists, it will be ignored:

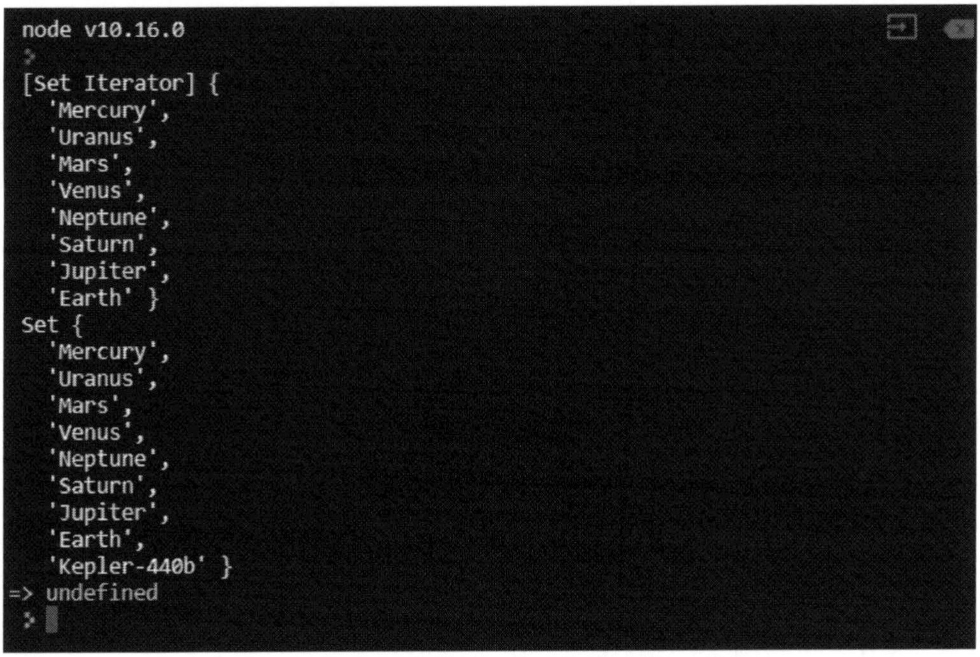

```
node v10.16.0
>
[Set Iterator] {
  'Mercury',
  'Uranus',
  'Mars',
  'Venus',
  'Neptune',
  'Saturn',
  'Jupiter',
  'Earth' }
Set {
  'Mercury',
  'Uranus',
  'Mars',
  'Venus',
  'Neptune',
  'Saturn',
  'Jupiter',
  'Earth',
  'Kepler-440b' }
=> undefined
>
```

Figure 7.42: Failure to add duplicate values

5. Get the size of the Set using the `.size` property:

```
console.log(planetSet.size);
```

6. Clear all the values inside the Set:

```
planetSet.clear();
console.log(planetSet);
```

The following is the output of the preceding code:

Figure 7.43: All values cleared from the set

In this exercise, we went over some ways in which we can use Set as a tool to help us remove duplicate values in our arrays. Sets are very useful when you want to keep a list of unique values with the smallest effort possible while you don't have any need to access them through an index. Otherwise, arrays are still the best choice if you are dealing with a lot of items that may include duplicates. In the next section, we will talk about the Math, Date, and String methods.

Math, Date, and String

When building complex applications using JavaScript, there will be times when you need to deal with string manipulation, math calculations, and dates. Luckily, JavaScript has several built-in methods for this type of data. In the following exercises, we will go over the ways we can utilize these in our applications.

To create a **new Date** object, use the following command:

```
const currentDate = new Date();
```

This will point to the current date.

To create a new string, use the following command:

```
const myString = 'this is a string';
```

To use the **Math** module, we can use the **Math** class:

```
const random = Math.random();
```

Exercise 56: Using String Methods

In this exercise, we will go over some of the ways we can work with strings more easily in our applications. String manipulation and building have always been complex tasks in other languages. In JavaScript, by using String methods, we can create, match, and manipulate strings with ease. In this exercise, we will create various strings and use String methods to manipulate them.

Perform the following steps to complete this exercise:

1. Create a variable called **planet**:

   ```
   let planet = 'Earth';
   ```

2. Create a **sentence** using template strings:

   ```
   let sentence = `We are on the planet ${planet}`;
   ```

   A template strings is a very useful feature that was introduced in ES6. We can create strings by combining templates and variables without the need to create a string build or using string concatenation. String templates are wrapped using `` ` ``, while the variable to be inserted in the string is wrapped with **${}**.

3. Separate our sentence into words:

   ```
   console.log(sentence.split(' '));
   ```

   We can split strings into arrays by using the **split** method and a separator. In the preceding example, JavaScript will split our sentence into an array of words, like so:

   ```
   node v10.15.2 linux/amd64
   >
   [ 'We', 'are', 'on', 'the', 'planet', 'Earth' ]
   => undefined
   >
   ```

   Figure 7.44: Splitting a string into an array of words

4. We can also use **replace** to replace any matched substring with another substring, as follows:

   ```
   sentence = sentence.replace('Earth', 'Venus');
   console.log(sentence);
   ```

The following is the output of the preceding code:

```
node v10.16.0
>
We are on the planet Venus
=> undefined
>
```

Figure 7.45: Replacing a word in a string

In the **replace** method, we will provide the first parameter as the substring to match in the string. The second parameter is the string you want it to be replaced with.

5. Check whether our sentence includes the word **Mars**:

```
console.log(sentence.includes('Mars'));
```

The following is the output of the preceding code:

```
node v10.16.0
>
false
=> undefined
>
```

Figure 7.46: Checking the string for the presence of a character

6. You can also convert the entire string into uppercase or lowercase:

```
sentence.toUpperCase();
sentence.toLowerCase();
```

7. Get a character at index in the string using **charAt**:

```
sentence.charAt(0); // returns W
```

Since sentences are not necessarily arrays, you cannot access a specific character at index such as an array. To do that, you need to call the **charAt** method.

8. Get the length of the string using the **length** property of the string:

```
sentence.length;
```

The following is the output of the preceding code:

Figure 7.47: Length of the sentence after our modification

In this exercise, we went over ways in which we can construct strings using template strings and string methods, which help us manipulate strings. These are very useful in applications that deal with a lot of user input. In the next exercise, we will go over Math and Date methods.

Math and Date

In this section, we will go over Math and Date types. We rarely deal with Math in our applications but when we do, it's very useful to utilize the Math library. Later, we will talk about the Date object and its methods. The Math and Date classes include various useful methods to help us do mathematical calculations and date manipulations.

Exercise 57: Using Math and Date

In this exercise, we will learn how to implement Math and Date types in JavaScript. We will use them to generate random numbers and use their built-in constants for mathematical calculations. We are also going to use the Date object to test the different ways we can treat dates in JavaScript. Let's get started:

1. Create a function called **generateRandomString**:

```
function generateRandomString(length) {

}
```

2. Create a function that generates a random number within a certain range:

```
function generateRandomNumber(min, max) {
    return Math.floor(Math.random() * (max - min + 1)) + min;
}
```

In the preceding function, **Math.random** generates a random number between 0 inclusive and 1 exclusive. When we want a number between the two ranges, we can also use **Math.floor** to round the number down to make sure it doesn't include **max** in our output.

3. Use the random number generator function in **generateRandomString**:

```
function generateRandomString(length) {
    const characters = [];
    const characterSet =
'ABCDEFGHIJKLMNOPQRSTUVWXYZabcdefghijklmnopqrstuvwxyz0123456789';
    for (let i = 0; i < length; i++) {
        characters.push(characterSet.charAt(generateRandomNumber(0,
characterSet.length)));
    }
    return characters.join(');
}
```

The method we need for our random number generation is very simple – we have a character set that we want to include in the random string. Later, we will run a loop to get a random character using the function we created, using **charAt** with a random index passed to it.

4. Test out our function:

```
console.log(generateRandomString(16));
```

The following is the output of the preceding code:

```
node v10.15.2 linux/amd64
>
nDI7sVilzrkLHaAP
=> undefined
>
```

Figure 7.48: Output of our random String function

Every time we run this function, it will give us a totally random string with the size we just passed. It is a really simple way to generate random usernames, but not very suitable for generating IDs as it doesn't really guarantee uniqueness.

5. Use **Math** constants to create a function that calculates circle areas, as follows:

```
function circleArea(radius) {
    return Math.pow(radius, 2) * Math.PI;
}
```

In this function, we used **Math.PI** from the **Math** object. It is assigned to an approximation of the actual **PI** value. We also used the **Math.pow** method to raise the radius from the argument to the power of 2. Next, we will explore the **Date** type in JavaScript.

6. Create a new **Date** object:

    ```
    const now = new Date();
    console.log(now);
    ```

    The following is the output of the preceding code:

    ```
    node v10.15.2 linux/amd64
    >
    2019-06-07T23:20:51.029Z
    => undefined
    >
    ```

Figure 7.49: Output of the new Date object

    When we create the new **Date** object with nothing, it will generate an object that stores the current time.

7. Create a new **Date** object at a specific date and time:

    ```
    const past = new Date('August 31, 2007 00:00:00');
    ```

    The **Date** constructor will take a string argument that can be parsed into a date. When we call the constructor using this string, it will create a **Date** object on that date and time.

8. Get the year, month, and date from our **past** Date object:

    ```
    console.log(past.getFullYear());
    console.log(past.getMonth());
    console.log(past.getDate());
    ```

    The following is the output of the preceding code:

    ```
    node v10.15.2 linux/amd64
    >
    2007
    7
    31
    => undefined
    >
    ```

Figure 7.50: Year, month, and date of the past date object

    The returned month doesn't start from 1, where January is 1. Instead, it started from 0, so August is 7.

9. You can also generate a string represented version of the object by calling **toString**:

```
console.log(past.toString());
```

The following is the output of the preceding code:

```
node v10.15.2 linux/amd64
>
Fri Aug 31 2007 00:00:00 GMT+0000 (Coordinated Universal Time)
=> undefined
>
```

Figure 7.51: Date presented in string form

By using the **toString** method, we can simply use this to keep a record of a timestamp in our applications.

10. If you want to get the Unix time, you can use **Date.now**:

```
console.log(Math.floor(Date.now() / 1000));
```

The reason we are using **Math.floor** again is that we need to divide the output of **Date.now** by 1,000 because it is returned in milliseconds.

In this exercise, we went over a couple ways that Math and Date types can be used in our applications. They are incredibly useful when we want to generate stuff such as pseudorandom IDs or random strings. The **Date** object is also used when we need to keep track of timestamps in our applications. In the next section, we will briefly go over Symbols, Iterators, Generators, and Proxies.

Symbols, Iterators, Generators, and Proxies

In JavaScript development, these types are rarely used, but for some use cases, they can be very useful. In this section, we will go over what these are and how we can use them in our applications.

Symbol

Symbols are unique values; they can be used as an identifier because every time you call **Symbol()**, it returns a unique symbol. Even the function returns a Symbol type. However, it cannot be called using the **new** keyword because it is not a constructor. When stored in objects, they are not included when you iterate through the property list, so if you want to store anything as a property inside the object and do not want them to be exposed when you run **JSON.stringify**, you can use Symbols to achieve that.

Iterator and Generator

Iterator and Generator are often used together. Generator functions are functions whose code is not executed immediately when invoked. When a value is to be returned from the generator, it needs to be called using **yield**. It stops executing after that until the next function is called again. This makes generators perfect for using iterators. In iterators, we need to define the function that has the **next** method and each time it is called, a value will be returned. By using these two together, we can build very powerful iterators with a large amount of reusable code.

Symbols are a hard concept in JavaScript, and they are not used frequently. In this exercise, we will go over a couple of ways we can use Symbols and explore their properties.

Exercise 58: Using Symbols and Exploring Their Properties

In this exercise we will use Symbols and their properties to identify object properties. Let's get started:

1. Create two symbols:

   ```
   let symbol1 = Symbol();
   let symbol2 = Symbol('symbol');
   ```

2. Test their equivalence:

   ```
   console.log(symbol1 === symbol2);
   console.log(symbol1 === Symbol('symbol'));
   ```

   Both statements will be evaluated to false. This is because symbols are unique in JavaScript and even if they have the same name, they are still not equal.

3. Create a test object with some properties:

   ```
   const testObj = {};
   testObj.name = 'test object';
   testObj.included = 'this will be included';
   ```

4. Create a property in the object using symbols as keys:

   ```
   const symbolKey = Symbol();
   testObj[symbolKey] = 'this will be hidden';
   ```

5. Print out the keys in the object:

   ```
   console.log(Object.keys(testObj));
   ```

The following is the output of the preceding code:

node v10.15.2 linux/amd64
>
['name', 'included']
=> undefined
>

Figure 7.52: List of keys printed out using Object.keys

It appears that calling **Object.keys** didn't return our **Symbol** property. The reason behind that is that because Symbols are not enumerable, so they will not be returned by either **Object.keys** or **Object.getOwnPropertyNames**.

6. Let's try to get the value of our **Symbol** property:

```
console.log(testObj[Symbol()]); // Will return undefined
console.log(testObj[symbolKey]); // Will return our hidden property
```

7. Use the **Symbol** registry:

```
const anotherSymbolKey = Symbol.for('key');
const copyOfAnotherSymbol = Symbol.for('key');
```

In this example, we can run a search on the **Symbol** key and store that reference in our new constant. The **Symbol** registry is a registry for all the symbols in our application. Here, you can store the symbols you created in a global registry so they can be retrieved later.

8. Retrieve the content of the **Symbol** property using its reference:

```
testObj[anotherSymbolKey] = 'another key';
console.log(testObj[copyOfAnotherSymbol]);
```

The following is the output of the preceding code:

node v10.16.0
>
another key
=> undefined
>

Figure 7.53: Result when we retrieve values using a symbol reference

When we run this, it will print out the result we wanted. When we create a symbol using **Symbol.for**, we will create a one-to-one relationship between the key and the reference so that when we use **Symbol.for** to get another reference, these two symbols will be equal.

In this exercise, we went over some of the properties of symbols. They are very useful if you need to use them as identifiers for an **object** property. Using the **Symbol** registry can also help us relocate the **Symbol** we created previously. In the next exercise, we will talk about the general usage of iterators and generators.

In the previous exercise, we went over Symbols. There is another type of **Symbol** in JavaScript known as **Symbol.iterator**, which is a specific symbol that's used to create iterators. In this exercise, we will make an iterrable object using generators.

Exercise 59: Iterators and Generators

There is a very useful function called **range()** in Python that generates numbers between a given range; now, let's try to recreate it with iterators:

1. Create a function called **range** that returns an object with the **iterator** property:

    ```
    function range(max) {
        return {
            *[Symbol.iterator]() {
                yield 1;
            }
        };
    }
    ```

2. Use the **for..in** loop on our **range** function:

    ```
    for (let value of range(10)) {
        console.log(value);
    }
    ```

    The following is the output of the preceding code:

Figure 7.54: Output using a for..in loop

When we run this, it only yields one value. To modify it to yield multiple results, we will be wrapping it with a loop.

3. Let's wrap the **yield** statement with a loop:

```
function range(max) {
    return {
        *[Symbol.iterator]() {
            for (let i = 0; i < max; i++) {
                yield i;
            }
        }
    };
}
```

Normally, this wouldn't work with **returns** as it can only be returned once. This is because the generator function is expected to be consumed multiple times using .**next()**. We can delay its execution until it is called again:

Figure 7.55: Output after wrapping the yield statement with a loop

To understand generator functions better, we can also define a simple generator function without implementing it in an iterator.

4. Create a generator function called **gen**:

```
function* gen() {
    yield 1;
}
```

This is a very simple definition of a generator function. When it is called, it will return a generator that can only be iterated through once. However, you can generate as many generators as you wish using the preceding function.

5. Generate a **generator** function:

```
const generator = gen();
```

6. Call the generator's **next** method to get its values:

```
console.log(generator.next());
console.log(generator.next());
console.log(generator.next());
```

When we call `.next()` on a generator, it will execute our code until it reaches the **yield** keyword. Then, it will return the value yielded by that statement. It also includes a **done** property to indicate whether this generator has finished iterating through all the possible values. Once the generator has reached the **done** status, there is no way to restart the iteration unless you are modifying the internal states:

```
node v10.15.2 linux/amd64
>
{ value: 1, done: false }
{ value: undefined, done: true }
{ value: undefined, done: true }
=> undefined
>
```

Figure 7.56: Value after yielding the statement

As you can see, the first time we call the next method, we will get the value 1. After that, the **done** property will be set to **true**. No matter how many times we call it, it will always return **undefined**, meaning the generator is done iterating.

In this exercise, we went over iterators and generators. They are very powerful in JavaScript and a lot of early async/await functionality, before it was officially supported, was created using generator functions. Next time you create custom classes or objects that can be iterated through, you can create generators. This makes the code cleaner as there is no need to manage a lot of internal states.

Proxies

When you need extra fine-grained control over your objects where you need to manage every fundamental operation, you can use proxies. You can consider the JavaScript proxy as a middleman between your operations and your objects. Every object manipulation can have proxies through it, meaning you can implement a very complex object. In the next exercise, we will go over creative ways we can use proxies to enable our objects.

Proxies act like a middleman between your object and the rest of the program. Any changes that are made to that object will be relayed by the proxy and the proxy will determine what to do with that change.

Creating proxies is very easy – all you need to do is call the **Proxy** constructor with the object, including our handlers and the object we are proxying. Once the proxy has been created, you can treat the proxy as the original value, and you can start modifying properties on the proxy.

The following is an example usage of a proxy:

```
const handlers = {
    set: (object, prop, value) => {
        console.log('setting ' + prop);
    }
}

const proxiesValue = new Proxy({}, handlers);

proxiesValue.prop1 = 'hi';
```

We've created a **proxiesValue** and given it a set handler. When we try to set the **prop1** property, we will get the following output:

```
node v10.16.0
>
setting prop1
=> 'hi'
>
```

Figure 7.57: Proxy value created

Exercise 60: Using Proxies to Build Complex Objects

In this exercise, we will be using proxies to show you how to build an object that is able to hide its values and enforce a data type on the properties. We will be expanding and customizing some fundamental operations here too. Let's get started:

1. Create a basic JavaScript object:

```
const simpleObject = {};
```

2. Create a **handlers** object:

```
const handlers = {
}
```

3. Create a proxy wrapping for our basic object:

```
const proxiesValue = new Proxy(simpleObject, handlers);
```

4. Now, add **handlers** to our proxy:

```
const handlers = {
    get: (object, prop) => {
        return 'values are private';
    }
}
```

Here, we added a **get** handler for our object, where we ignore the key it is requesting and just return a fixed string. When we do this, no matter what we do, the object will only return the value we have defined.

5. Let's test our handler in the proxy:

```
proxiedValue.key1 = 'value1';

console.log(proxiedValue.key1);
console.log(proxiedValue.keyDoesntExist);
```

The following is the output of the preceding code:

Figure 7.58: Testing the handler in the proxy

When we run this code, we assigned a value to **key1** in the object, but because of the way we defined our handlers when we tried to read back the values, it always gives us the string we defined earlier. When we try this on a value that doesn't exist, it also returns the same result.

6. Let's add a **set** handler for validation:

```
set: (object, prop, value) => {
        if (prop === 'id') {
            if (!Number.isInteger(value)) {
                throw new TypeError('The id needs to be an integer');
            }
        }
    }
```

We added a **set** handler; this handler will be called every time we try to perform a set operation on our proxy integer.

7. Try to set the **id** to a string:

```
proxiedValue.id = 'not an id'
```

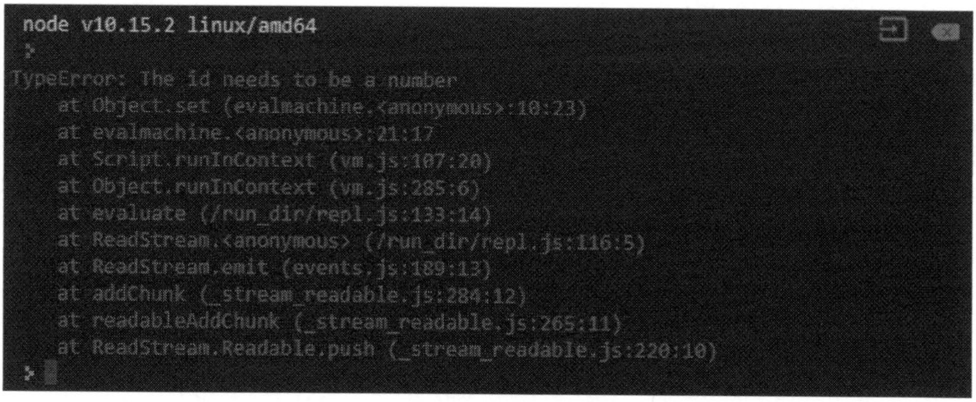

Figure 7.59: Screenshot showing TypeError when trying to set id to string

And just as you might have guessed, when we try to set this, it will give us a **TypeError** exception. This is very useful if you are building a library and you don't want the internal properties to be overwritten. You can do this using symbols, but using proxies is also an option. Another use for this is for implementing validation.

In this exercise, we talked about some of the creative methods we can use to make our objects. By using proxies, we can create very complex objects with built-in validation.

Refactoring in JavaScript

When using JavaScript in large-scale applications, we need to do refactoring from time to time. Refactoring means rewriting parts of the code while maintaining compatibility. Because JavaScript has gone through many phases and upgrades, refactoring also takes advantage of the new features that are offered and allows our application to run faster and be more reliable. An example of refactoring is as follows:

```javascript
function appendPrefix(prefix, input) {
    const result = [];
    for (var i = 0; i < input.length; i++) {
        result.push(prefix + input[i]);
    }
    return result;
}
```

This code simply appends a prefix to all the elements in the input array. Let's call it like this:

```javascript
appendPrefix('Hi! ', ['Miku', 'Rin', 'Len']);
```

We will get the following output:

```
node v10.16.0
>
=> [ 'Hi! Miku', 'Hi! Rin', 'Hi! Len' ]
>
```

Figure 7.60: Output after running an array code

During refactoring, we can write the preceding function with less code and still retain all the features:

```
function appendPrefix(prefix, input) {
    return input.map((inputItem) => {
        return prefix + inputItem;
    });
}
```

What happens when we call it again? Let's take a look:

```
appendPrefix('Hi! ', ['Miku', 'Rin', 'Len']);
```

We will still get the same output:

```
node v10.16.0
>
=> [ 'Hi! Miku', 'Hi! Rin', 'Hi! Len' ]
>
```

Figure 7.61: Getting the same output after refactoring the code

Activity 10: Refactoring Functions to Use Modern JavaScript Features

You have recently joined a company. The first task that's been assigned to you is to refactor a number of legacy modules. You opened the file and saw that the existing code has already been written using legacy JavaScript methods. You'll need to refactor all the functions in that file and make sure it can still pass the required test.

Perform the following steps to complete this activity:

1. Run **Activity10.js** using node.js to check that the tests have passed.

2. Refactor the **itemExist** function using the **includes** array.

3. Use **array push** to add a new item to the bottom of the **pushunique** function.

4. Use **array.fill** in **createFilledArray** to fill our array with an initial value.

5. Use **array.shift** in the **removeFirst** function to remove the first item.

6. Use **array.pop** in the **removeLast** function to remove the last item.

7. Use the spread operator in **cloneArray** to make a clone of our array.

8. Refactor the **Food** class using the **ES6** class.

9. After refactoring, run the code to observe that the same output is generated as it was by the legacy code.

> **Note**
>
> The solution for this activity can be found on page 611.

In this activity, we learned how to use modern JavaScript functions by using refactoring functions. We have successfully learned how to rewrite code while maintaining its compatibility.

Summary

In this chapter, we started by looking at the ways we can construct and manipulate arrays and objects in JavaScript. Then, we looked at ways we can concatenate arrays and objects using spread operators. Using spread operators saves us from having to write functions without a loop. Later, we looked at ways we can do OOP in JavaScript. By using these classes and class inheritance, we can build complex applications without having to write a lot of duplicate code. We also looked at built-in methods for Array, Map, Set, Regex, Date, and Math. These are very helpful when we need to deal with a large number of different types of data. Lastly, Symbols, Iterators, Generators, and Proxies opened up a huge range of possibilities when it comes to making our program dynamic and clean. This concludes our chapter on advanced JavaScript. In the next chapter, we will talk about asynchronous programming in JavaScript.

8

Asynchronous Programming

Learning Objectives

By the end of this chapter, you will be able to:

- Describe the workings of an asynchronous operation
- Use callback to handle async operations
- Demonstrate callbacks and event loops
- Implement promises to handle async operations
- Rewrite async code with callbacks using promises
- Refactor your legacy code using async and await functions

In this chapter, we will explore the asynchronous (later abbreviated as async) nature of JavaScript. The focus will be on how conventional languages handle operations that take time to complete, and how JavaScript handles these operations. Later, we will discuss various methods we can adopt to handle these situations in JavaScript.

Introduction

In the previous chapter, we learned how we can use arrays and objects and their helper functions. In this chapter, we will learn more about how JavaScript runs and how we can handle time-consuming operations.

When working on large-scale projects with JavaScript, often, we must deal with network requests, disk IO, and data processing. Many of these operations take time to complete, and for beginners who have just started using JavaScript, it is very difficult to understand how to retrieve the results of these time-consuming operations. This is because, unlike other languages, JavaScript has a special way of handling these operations. When coding programs, we are used to linear thinking; that is, the program executes line by line and only breaks that flow when we have loops or branches. For example, if you wanted to make a simple network request in Java, you would have to do something similar to what's shown in the following code:

```java
import java.net.*;

import java.io.*;

public class SynchronousFetch{


  public static void main(String[] args){
    StringBuilder content = new StringBuilder();
    try {
      URL url = new URL("https://www.packtpub.com");
      URLConnection urlConnection = url.openConnection();


      BufferedReader bufferedReader = new BufferedReader(new
InputStreamReader(urlConnection.getInputStream()));
      String line;


      while ((line = bufferedReader.readLine()) != null){
        content.append(line + "\n");
      }
```

```
        bufferedReader.close();
    } catch(Exception e) {
        e.printStackTrace();
    }
    System.out.println(content.toString());
    System.exit(0);
  }//end main
}//end class SynchronousFetch
```

It's simple to understand: you create an HTTP client and call a method within the client to request the contents of that URL. Once the request is made and a response is received, it will continue to run the next line of code that returns the body of the response. During this time, the whole function will halt and wait for the **fetch** and will only continue once the request is completed. This is the normal way these operations are handled in other languages. This way of handling time-consuming operations is called **synchronous handling** because it forces the program to pause and only resume once the operation is completed.

Because of this linear thinking, many developers (including me) get very confused when they first start coding in JavaScript. Most people will start writing code like this:

```
const request = require('request');
let response;
request('SOMEURL', (err, res) => {
    response = res.body;
});
console.log(response);
```

From the look of the code, it should behave just like our preceding code. It will make the request, set the response variable to the response body once it is completed, and then it will output the response. Most developers that have tried this will know that this is not how JavaScript works; the code will run, produce 'undefined' output, and exit.

How JavaScript Handles Time-Consuming Operations

In JavaScript, these operations are often handled using async programming. There are multiple ways to do that in JavaScript; the most widely used method, and the one you will see the most in legacy programs, is called a **callback**. A callback is just a fancy term for passing a function that includes the rest of your application logic to another function; they are actually very easy to understand. Consider the fact that traditional functions return their values once the logic is complete. In async programming, they often don't return a value; instead, they pass their result to the callback function provided by the caller. Consider the following code:

```
const request = require('request');

let response;

request('SOMEURL', (err, res) => {

    response = res.body;

});

console.log(response);
```

Let's look at why this is not going to produce the result we want. The **request** library that we have used can be considered as a function that performs some operation logic that is time-consuming. The **request** function expects you to pass it a parameter as a callback that includes everything you are about to do next. In the callback function, we accept two parameters, **err** and **res**; inside the function, we assign the response variable we declared earlier to the **res** body (the response body). Outside the **request** function, we have **console.log** to log out the response. Because the callback function will get called sometime in the future, we will log the value of the response before we set any value to it. Most developers get very frustrated when dealing with JavaScript because the preceding code is not linear. The order of the execution follows:

```
1const request = require('request');

2 let response;

3 request('SOMEURL', (err, res) => {

    5 response = res.body;

});

4 console.log(response);
```

As you can see from the order of execution in the preceding code, the first three lines work just as we expected. We import the **request** library and declare a variable response, and then call the **request** library with a URL with a callback. Because the callback is only invoked when the network request finishes, the program will continue executing the rest of the code, which outputs the response.

Lastly, when the network request is finished, it will invoke our callback function and run the line that assigns the body to our response. To make this code behave as we expected, we need to modify the code to the following:

```
const request = require('request');

let response;

request('SOMEURL', (err, res) => {
    response = res.body;

    console.log(response);
});
```

In the preceding code, we pulled `console.log` inside the callback so that it can be executed only when the assignment is complete. Now, when we run this code, it will output the actual response body.

Handling Async Operations Using Callbacks

In the introduction, we talked about how JavaScript treats async operations differently compared with other languages. In this chapter, we will explore how we can write complex JavaScript applications with many async operations using the callback method.

Exercise 61: Writing Your First Callback

In this exercise, we will first write a small function mimicking a function that takes a while to finish. Later, we will write another function that consumes our async function.

> ### Note
>
> The code files for this exercise can be found at https://github.com/TrainingByPackt/Professional-JavaScript/tree/master/Lesson08/Exercise61.

Perform the following steps to complete the exercise:

1. Create a **slowAPI** object to create a mock API library; its purpose is to return the results in a reasonable amount of time. We write this first to introduce you to how we can mimic an async function without the need to perform async operations:

    ```
    const slowAPI = {}
    ```

2. Create a **getUsers** function in the **slowAPI** object we just defined that returns nothing and expects a callback. Call the **setTimeout** function inside **getUsers**, which is used to add a 1-second delay to our code if needed:

```
slowAPI.getUsers = (callback) => {
        setTimeout(() => {
            callback(null, {
                status: 'OK',
                data: {
                    users: [
                        {
                            name: 'Miku'
                        },
                        {
                            name: 'Len'
                        }
                    ]
                }
            });
        }, 1000);
}
```

3. Create a **getCart** function in the **slowAPI** object and create an **if-else** loop inside the function to match the username and return an error if it doesn't:

```
slowAPI.getCart = (username, callback) => {
        setTimeout(() => {
            if (username === 'Miku') {
                callback(null, {
                    status: 'OK',
                    data: {
                        cart: ['Leek', 'Cake']
                    }
                })
            } else {
                callback(new Error('User not found'));
            }
        }, 500);
}
```

4. Create a **runRequests** function that calls **getUsers** to grab a user list. Inside the callback function, we are going to print out the response or error:

```
function runRequests() {
    slowAPI.getUsers((error, response) => {
        if (error) {
            console.error('Error occurred when running getUsers');
            throw new Error('Error occurred');
        }
        console.log(response);
    });
}
```

5. Call the **run Request** function:

```
runRequests();
```

The output should be as follows:

```
node v10.15.2 linux/amd64
>
=> undefined
{ status: 'OK',
  data: { users: [ [Object], [Object], [Object] ] } }
>
```

Figure 8.1: Output of runRequest

We can see that the **runRequest** function has finished running and our response is correctly printed out.

6. Modify the **runRequest** function to call **getCart** as well:

```
function runRequests() {
    slowAPI.getUsers((error, response) => {
        if (error) {
            console.error('Error occurred when running getUsers');
            throw new Error('Error occurred');
        }
        console.log(response);
    });
    slowAPI.getCart('Miku', (error, result) => {
            if (error) {
                console.error(error);
                throw new Error('Error occurred');
            }
```

```
            console.log(result);
        });
    }
```

Here, we put a similar call to **slowAPI** inside our **runRequest** function; nothing else is changed. When we run this, we get a very interesting output, as follows:

```
node v10.15.2 linux/amd64
>
=> undefined
{ status: 'OK', data: { cart: [ 'Leek', 'Cake' ] } }
{ status: 'OK',
  data: { users: [ [Object], [Object], [Object] ] } }
>
```

Figure 8.2: Output after modifying the runRequest function

It's very interesting because it first outputs the result from **getCart**, and then the result for **getUsers**. The program is behaving like this because of the async and non-blocking nature of JavaScript. In our operations, because the **getCart** function only takes 500 milliseconds to complete, it will be the first output.

7. Modify the preceding function to output the cart of the first user:

```
function runRequests() {
    slowAPI.getUsers((error, response) => {
        if (error) {
            console.error('Error occurred when running getUsers');
            throw new Error('Error occurred');
        }
        slowAPI.getCart(response.data.users[0].name,(error,result) => {
            if (error) {
                console.error(error);
                throw new Error('Error occurred');
            }
            console.log(result);
        });
    });
}
```

The output should be as follows:

```
node v10.16.0
>
=> undefined
{ status: 'OK', data: { cart: [ 'Leek', 'Cake' ] } }
>
```

Figure 8.3: Output of the cart for the first user

Because we will be using the data from the first request, we must write the logic for our next request inside the callback of the first request.

8. Trigger an error when accessing the cart of an unknown user:

```
function runRequests() {
    slowAPI.getUsers((error, response) => {
        if (error) {
            console.error('Error occurred when running getUsers');
            throw new Error('Error occurred');
        }
        slowAPI.getCart(response.data.users[1].name,(error,result) => {
            if (error) {
                console.error(error);
                throw new Error('Error occurred');
            }
            console.log(result);
        });
    });
}
```

What we do know about the data we are returning from **getCart** is that the last user does not match any **if** statements. Therefore, it will throw an error when called. When we run the code, we will see the following error:

```
node v10.15.2 linux/amd64
>
=> undefined
Error: User not found
    at Timeout.setTimeout [as _onTimeout] (evalmachine.<anonymous>:49:26)
    at ontimeout (timers.js:436:11)
    at tryOnTimeout (timers.js:300:5)
    at listOnTimeout (timers.js:263:5)
    at Timer.processTimers (timers.js:223:10)
Process crashed with: Error: Error occurred
    at slowAPI.getCart (evalmachine.<anonymous>:63:23)
    at Timeout.setTimeout [as _onTimeout] (evalmachine.<anonymous>:49:17)
    at ontimeout (timers.js:436:11)
    at tryOnTimeout (timers.js:300:5)
    at listOnTimeout (timers.js:263:5)
    at Timer.processTimers (timers.js:223:10)
>
```

Figure 8.4: Printing the error

The first error output we see in white is the error we are outputting through `console.error`. This can be customized to your preferred error message or output in a specific format using the logging framework. The second is from the process crashing because we are throwing a new error right after `console.log`.

In this exercise, we checked how we can mimic async functions with `setTimeout`. `setTimeout` is a very useful function. Although it's not really recommended for use in actual code, it is very useful if you need to mock a network request that takes time in tests or produces a race condition when debugging your software. Later, we went over ways to use async functions using callbacks and how error handling works in async functions.

Next, we are going to briefly talk about why callbacks are slowly becoming outdated and what can happen if you don't use callbacks properly.

Event Loops

You might have heard this term before, referring to how JavaScript handles time-consuming operations. It is also very important to know how event loops work under the hood.

When you consider what JavaScript is used most for, it is for making dynamic websites and it is used mostly in the browser. To the surprise of a lot of people, JavaScript code runs in a single thread, which simplifies a lot of things for developers, yet it opens challenges when dealing with multiple operations happening at the same time. In the JavaScript runtime, there is an infinite loop run in the background that manages messages for your code and handles events. The event loop is responsible for consuming callbacks in the callback queue, running functions in the stack, and calling web APIs. Most of the operations you can do in JavaScript are classified into two types: blocking and non-blocking. By blocking, we mean blocking the event loop (you can consider this as the normal UI thread for other languages). When the event loop is blocked, it cannot process any more events from other parts of the application, and the application will freeze until it is unblocked. Here is a list of sample operations and their classification:

Operation	Classification
Disk IO	Non-Blocking
Network Request	Non-Blocking
Timeouts	Non-Blocking
Arithmetic	Blocking
Infinite Loops	Blocking
Array/Object manipulation	Blocking

Figure 8.5: Table with sample operations and their classification

What you can see from the preceding list is that almost all I/O in JavaScript is non-blocking, meaning that even if it takes more time to complete than expected, it will not block the event loop. Blocking the event loop, as in any language, is a terrible thing to do because it makes the application unstable and unresponsive. This brings us to a question: How can we know if a non-blocking operation was completed.

How JavaScript Executes Code

When JavaScript is executing blocking code, it will block the loop and complete the operation before the program can continue with the rest of the code. If you run a loop that iterates 1 million times, the rest of your code must wait for that loop to finish before continuing. Therefore, it is not recommended to have a lot of blocking operations in your code because they affect performance, stability, and user experience. When JavaScript is executing non-blocking code, it initiates the process by handing it to web APIs to do the fetching, timeouts, and rests. Once the operation is complete, the callback is pushed to the callback queue so it can be consumed by the event loop later.

In modern browsers, this is implemented as follows, where we have the heap that stores most of our object allocations, and the stack for the function calls. During each event loop cycle, the event loop favors the stack first and executes those events by calling appropriate web APIs. Once the operation is complete, the callback for that operation will then be pushed to the callback queue, which will be consumed later by the event loop:

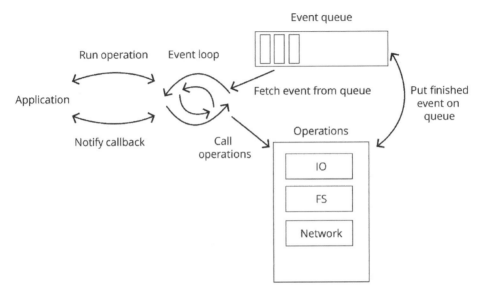

Figure 8.6: Event loop cycle

To see how everything works under the hood, let's consider the following code:

```
setTimeout(() => {console.log('hi')}, 2000)
while(true) {
    ;
}
```

From the look of it, the code does two things: it creates a timeout that prints out 'hi' after 2 seconds, and an infinite loop that does nothing at all. When you run the preceding code, it will behave a bit strangely – nothing gets printed out and the program just hangs. The reason it behaves like that is the event loop favors items on the stack more than items in the callback queue. Because we have an infinite **while** loop that keeps pushing to the call stack, the event loop is occupied with running the loop and ignores the completed **setTimeout** callback in the callback queue. Another interesting fact about the way **setTimeout** works is that we can use it to delay our function to the next cycle of the event loop. Consider the following code:

```
setTimeout(() => {console.log('hi again')}, 0)
console.log('hi');
```

Here, we have **setTimeout** followed by **console.log**, but here we are using **0** as the timeout, meaning we want this to be completed immediately. Once the timeout is complete and the callback is pushed to the callback queue, as our event loop favors call stacks, you can expect output like this:

```
node v10.15.2 linux/amd64
>
hi
hi again
=> undefined
>
```

Figure 8.7: Output after the timeout is complete

We see that **hi** is printed out before **hi again** because even when we set the timeout to zero, it will still be executed last because the event loop will execute items on the call stack before items in the callback queue.

Activity 11: Using Callbacks to Receive Results

In this activity, we will use callbacks to receive results. Suppose you are working as a software engineer for a local gas company and they want you to write a new feature for them:

- You are given a client API library that you can use to request a list of local users.

- You need to implement a feature that calculates the bill for those users and returns the result in the following format:

```
{
    id: 'XXXXX',
    address: '2323 sxsssssss',
    due: 236.6
}
```

- You need to implement a **calculateBill** function that takes **id** and calculates the gas bill for that user.

To accomplish this, you need to request the list of users and get the rates for those users and their usage. Lastly, calculate the final amount due and return the combined result.

> **Note**
>
> The code files for this activity can be found at https://github.com/TrainingByPackt/Professional-JavaScript/tree/master/Lesson08/Activity11.

Perform the following steps to complete the activity:

1. Create a **calculate** function that takes **id** and a callback as an argument.

2. Call **getUsers** to get all of the users, which will give us the address we need.

3. Call **getUsage** to get the usage of our user.

4. Finally, call **getRate** to get the rate of the user we are doing the calculation for.

5. Invoke the **calculate** function using an existing ID.

6. Invoke the **calculate** function using an ID that does not exist to check the resulting error.

   You should see the following output with the error returned:

```
node v10.15.2 linux/amd64
>
=> undefined
 Error: user not found
     at clientApi.getUsers (evalmachine.<anonymous>:62:45)
     at Timeout.setTimeout [as _onTimeout] (evalmachine.<anonymous>:21:13)
     at ontimeout (timers.js:436:11)
     at tryOnTimeout (timers.js:300:5)
     at listOnTimeout (timers.js:263:5)
     at Timer.processTimers (timers.js:223:10) undefined
>
```

Figure 8.8: Invoking a function using an ID that doesn't exist

> **Note**
>
> The solution for this activity can be found on page 613.

In this activity, the feature we implemented is very similar to what you might see in the real world. We worked with multiple async operations in one function. Next, we will talk about callback hell and how that can be a problem when we are dealing with multiple async operations.

Callback Hell

Callback hell refers to the obstacles faced by JavaScript developers when working on large-scale projects. The cause of callback hell is not entirely the fault of the developer; it's partially because of how JavaScript handles async operations. By using callbacks to handle multiple async operations, it's very easy for things to get out of control. The following code illustrates an example of callback hell:

```javascript
request('url', (error, response) => {
    // Do something here
    request('another url', (error, response) => {
        disk.write('filename', (result) => {
            if (result.this) {
                process(something, (result) => {
                    request('another url', (error, response) => {
                        if (response.this) {
                            request('this', (error, response) => {
                                // Do something for this
                            })
                        } else {
                            request('that', (error, response) => {
                                if (error) {
                                    request('error fallback', (error,
 response) => {

                                        // Error fallback
                                    })
                                }
                                if (response.this) {


                                }
                            })
                        }
                    });
                })
            } else {
```

```
        process(otherthing, (result) => {
            // Do something else
        })
    }
    })
  })
})
```

The preceding code example is a perfect example of callback hell. Although this code is shorter than actual callback hell code you will find in the real world, it is equally terrible. Callback hell is the condition where a block of code has so many callbacks nested inside it that it becomes hard for the developer to understand, maintain, and even debug the code. If the preceding code was being used to implement actual business logic, it would extend to more than 200 lines. With that many lines and that many levels of nesting, it would create the following issues:

- It would be difficult to figure out which callback you were currently in.

- It could cause variable name collision and overwrite.

- It would be almost impossible to debug and breakpoint the code.

- The code would be very hard to reuse.

- The code would not be testable.

These issues are just some of a list of issues that can be caused by callback hell. They are the reason why many companies even include questions about callback hell in their interview questions. There are many proposed ways to make code much more readable than the preceding code. One way is to pull almost every callback out as a separate function. Using this technique, the preceding code can be modified as follows:

```
function doAnotherUrl(error, response) {
    if (response.this) {
        request('this', (error, response) => {
            // Do something for this
        })
    } else {
        request('that', (error, response) => {
            if (error) {
                request('error fallback', (error, response) => {
```

```
                    // Error fallback
                })
            }
            if (response.this) {


            }
        })
    }
}


function process(result) {
    request('another url', doAnotherUrl);
}


function afterWrite(result) {
    if (result.this) {
        process(something, afterProcess)
    } else {
        process(otherthing, afterProcess)
    }
}


function doAnotherThing(error, response) {
    disk.write('filename', afterWrite)
}


function doFirstThing(error, response) {
    // Do something here
    request('another url', doAnotherThing)
}


request('url', doFirstThing)
```

When the code is rewritten like this, we can see that all our processing functions are separated out. Later, we can put them in a separate file and reference them using `require()` to import it. This does solve the problem of having all the code in one place and testability issues. It also makes the code base unnecessarily big and fragmented. In ES6, the promise was introduced. It opened up a brand new way to handle async operations. In the next section, we will go over how promises work and how we can use them to save us from callback hell.

Promises

In JavaScript, a promise is an object that represents some value in the future. Usually, it is a wrapper for an async operation. Promises can also be passed around in functions and used as returns for promises. Because a promise represents an async operation, it can have one of the following states:

- Pending, meaning the promise is pending, which means there might be an async operation still running and there is no way to determine its result.

- Fulfilled, meaning the async operation has completed without errors and the value is ready to be received.

- Rejected, meaning the async operation has finished with errors.

A promise can have only one of the preceding three states. When a promise is fulfilled, it will call the handler provided to the `.then` promise function, and when it is rejected, it will call the handler provided to the `.catch` promise function.

To create a promise, we use the **new** keyword in the **Promise** constructor. The constructor takes a function that will include the code for the async operation. It also passes two functions as a parameter, **resolve** and **reject**. **resolve** is called with the resulting value when the async operation is completed and the value is ready to be passed. **reject** is called when the async operation has failed and you want to return the failure reason, which is typically an error object:

```
const myPromise = new Promise((resolve, reject) => {


});
```

The following code uses Promise.resolve to return a promise:

```
const myPromiseValue = Promise.resolve(12);
```

Promise.resolve returns a promise that is resolved to the value you passed down as the parameter. It is very useful when you want to keep your code base consistent, or are unsure whether a value is a promise or not. Once you wrap the value using **Promise. resolve**, you can start work on the value of the promise using the **then** handler.

In the next exercise, we will look at how we can handle async operations with promises and how we can combine multiple async operations with promises without resulting in callback hell.

Exercise 62: Using Promises as Alternatives to Callbacks

In the last activity, we talked about how we can combine multiple async operations into one single result. It's very easy to understand, but it can also make the code very long and hard to manage. We went over callback hell and how to avoid it. One thing we can do is to utilize the **Promise** object introduced in ES6. In this exercise, we will go over ways in which we can use promises in our applications.

> **Note**
>
> The code files for this exercise can be found at https://github.com/TrainingByPackt/Professional-JavaScript/tree/master/Lesson08/Exercise62.

Perform the following steps to complete the exercise:

1. Create a promise:

```
const myPromise = new Promise(() => {

});
```

When creating a promise, we need to use the **new** keyword in the **Promise** constructor. The **Promise** constructor requires you to provide a resolver function to execute async operations. When a promise is created, it will automatically invoke the resolver function.

2. Add an operation to the resolver function:

```
const myPromise = new Promise(() => {
    console.log('hi');
});
```

The output should be as follows:

```
node v10.15.2 linux/amd64
>
hi
=> undefined
>
```

Figure 8.9: Adding an operation to the resolver function

Even though **console.log** is not an async operation, when we create a promise, it will automatically execute our resolver function and print out **hi**.

3. Resolve the promise using **resolve**:

```
const myPromise = new Promise((resolve) => {
    resolve(12);
});
myPromise
```

When the function is called, a **resolve** function is passed to our resolver function. When it is called, the promise will be resolved:

Figure 8.10: Resolved promise after the function is called

4. Retrieve the value using the **then()** function. By attaching a **then** handler, you are expected to read the resolved promise value from the callback:

```
const myPromise = new Promise((resolve) => {
    resolve(12);
}).then((value) => {
    console.log(value);
});
```

The output should be as follows:

Figure 8.11: Retrieving the value using the then function

Whenever you create a promise, you expect the async function to complete and return a value.

5. Create an immediately resolved promise:

```
const myPromiseValue = Promise.resolve(12);
```

6. Create an immediately rejected promise:

```
const myRejectedPromise = Promise.reject(new Error('rejected'));
```

The output should be as follows:

```
node v10.15.2 linux/amd64

(node:91) UnhandledPromiseRejectionWarning: Error: rejected
(node:91) UnhandledPromiseRejectionWarning: Unhandled promise rejection. This error
originated either by throwing inside of an async function without a catch block, or
by rejecting a promise which was not handled with .catch(). (rejection id: 1)
(node:91) [DEP0018] DeprecationWarning: Unhandled promise rejections are deprecated.
In the future, promise rejections that are not handled will terminate the Node.js
process with a non-zero exit code.
=> undefined
>
```

Figure 8.12: Immediately rejected promise creation

Just like **Promise.resolve**, creating a promise using **Promise.reject** will return a promise that is rejected with the reason you provided.

7. Handle **error** in the promise using **catch**:

```
myRejectedPromise.catch((error) => {
    console.log(error);
});
```

You can provide an error handler using **catch**. This adds a rejection callback to the promise. When you provide a catch handler, the error returned from the promise will be passed as the argument of the handler:

```
node v10.15.2 linux/amd64

Error: rejected
    at evalmachine.<anonymous>:1:42
    at Script.runInContext (vm.js:107:20)
    at Object.runInContext (vm.js:285:6)
    at evaluate (/run_dir/repl.js:133:14)
    at ReadStream.<anonymous> (/run_dir/repl.js:116:5)
    at ReadStream.emit (events.js:189:13)
    at addChunk (_stream_readable.js:284:12)
    at readableAddChunk (_stream_readable.js:265:11)
    at ReadStream.Readable.push (_stream_readable.js:220:10)
    at lazyFs.read (internal/fs/streams.js:181:12)
=> Promise { <pending> }
>
```

Figure 8.13: Handling an error in a promise using catch

8. Create a **wait** function that returns a promise:

```
function wait(seconds) {
    return new Promise((resolve) => {
        setTimeout(() => {
            resolve(seconds);
        }, seconds * 1000);
    })
}
```

9. Use an **async** function to delay our console log:

```
wait(2).then((seconds) => {
    console.log('i waited ' + seconds + ' seconds');
});
```

The output should be as follows:

```
node v10.15.2 linux/amd64
>
=> Promise { <pending> }
i waited 2 seconds
>
```

Figure 8.14: Delaying the console log using an async function

As you can see, using it is very simple. Our **wait** function returns a new promise every time we invoke it. To run our code once the operation is complete, pass it into the **then** handler.

10. Chain the promises using the **then** function:

```
wait(2)
    .then(() => wait(2))
    .then(() => {
        console.log('i waited 4 seconds');
    });
```

The output should be as follows:

```
node v10.15.2 linux/amd64
>
=> Promise { <pending> }
i waited 4 seconds
>
```

Figure 8.15: Promises chained using the then function

For example, when we want to chain two promises together, all we need to do is to pass them inside the **then** handler and make sure the result is also a promise. Here, we see that after we call **wait** for 2 seconds, we call another **wait** for 2 seconds and make sure the timer starts after the first one finishes.

In this exercise, we went over a couple of ways to create promises and how to create an async function that handles operations using promises instead of callbacks. Lastly, we chained promises using the **then** function. These are very simple ways to use promises. In the next chapter, we will talk about how to effectively chain them and how to handle errors from promises.

Chaining Promises

In the last exercise, we looked at a very simple way to chain promises. Promise chaining can be complex as well, and doing it properly can avoid a lot of potential issues in your code. When you are designing a complex application that requires you to do multiple async operations at once, it's easy to get into callback hell when using callbacks. Using promises solves some of the problems related to callback hell, but it is not a silver bullet. Often, you will see code written like this:

```
getUser('name').then((user) => {
    increaseLike(user.id).then((result) => {
        readUser(user.id).then((user) => {
            if (user.like !== result.like) {
                generateErrorLog(user, 'LIKE').then((result) => {
                    response.send(403);
                })
            } else {
                updateAvatar(user).then((result) => {
                    optimizeImage(result.image).then(() => {
                        response.send(200);
                    })
                })
            }
        });
    });
});
```

```
}).catch((error) => {
    response.send(403);
});
```

When you see code written like this, it's hard to tell whether switching to promises solved anything. The preceding code has the same problem as our callback-hell code; all the logic is fragmented and nested. We also have other issues, such as the potential for the value on the upper scope to be accidentally overwritten.

When we are writing code with promises, we should think about making the code as modular as possible and treat the collection of operations as a pipeline. For our preceding example, the pipeline would be like this:

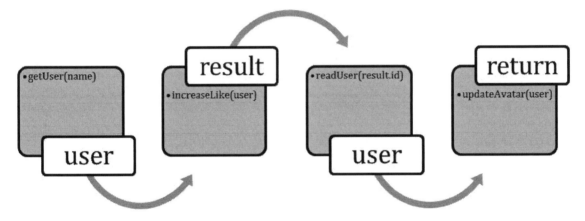

Figure 8.16: Example pipeline (a collection of operations)

You will see that we want to pipe our values from one process to the next. This helps us to chain promises and can make our code very clean and very easy to maintain. We can rewrite the preceding code as the following:

```
function increaseLike(user) {
    return new Promise((resolve) => {
        resolve({
            // Some result
        })
    });
};
function readUser(result) {
    return new Promise((resolve) => {
        resolve({
```

```
            // Return user
        })
    });
}
function updateAvatar(user) {
    return new Promise((resolve) => {
        resolve({
            // Return updated avatar
        })
    });
}
function optimizeImage(user) {
    return new Promise((resolve) => {
        resolve({
            // Return optimized images
        })
    });
}
function generateErrorLog(error) {
    // Handle some error
}
readUser('name')
    .then(increaseLike)
    .then(readUser)
    .then(updateAvatar)
    .then(optimizeImage)
    .catch(generateErrorLog)
```

As you can see, the rewritten code is much more readable, and anyone looking at this code will know exactly what is going to happen. When we chain promises in this way, we basically pass values from one process to another. By using this approach, we not only solve the problem of callback hell, but also make the code more testable as each of these helper functions is totally separate and they do not require anything more than the arguments passed to them. Not to mention that if there is any part of your application that wants to do a similar operation (for example, `optimizeImage`), you can reuse that part of the code easily. In the next exercise, we will go over how we can write complex functionality with multiple async operations using promise chaining.

Exercise 63: Advanced JavaScript Promises

In this exercise, we will write a simple program to run multiple async operations and chain their results together using promise chaining. Later, we will also use useful static methods from the `Promise` class to help us manage multiple promises at once.

> **Note**
>
> The code files for this activity can be found at https://github.com/TrainingByPackt/Professional-JavaScript/tree/master/Lesson08/Exercise63.

Perform the following steps to complete the exercise:

1. Create `getProfile` and `getCart` functions that return a promise. `getProfile` should take the `id` string as input and resolve different results based on the input:

```
function getProfile(id) {
    return new Promise((resolve, reject) => {
        switch(id) {
            case 'P6HB00':
                resolve({ id: 'P6HB00', name: 'Miku', age: 16, dob: '0831'
});
            break;
            case '2ADN23':
                resolve({ id: '2ADN23', name: 'Rin', age: 14, dob: '1227'
});
            break;
            case '6FFQTU':
                resolve({ id:'6FFQTU', name: 'Luka', age: 20, dob: '0130'
});
            break;
            default:
```

```
                reject(new Error('user not found'));
            }
        });
    }


    function getCart(user) {
        return new Promise((resolve, reject) => {
            switch(user.id) {
                case 'P6HB00':
                    resolve(['leek', 'cake', 'notebook']);
                break;
                case '2ADN23':
                    resolve(['ice cream', 'banana']);
                break;
                case '6FFQTU':
                    resolve(['tuna', 'tako']);
                break;
                default:
                    reject(new Error('user not found'));
            }
        });
    }
```

2. Create another async function, **getSubscription**, which takes an ID and resolves **true** and **false** values for that ID:

```
    function getSubscription(id) {
        return new Promise((resolve, reject) => {
            switch(id) {
                case 'P6HB00':
                    resolve(true);
                break;
                case '2ADN23':
                    resolve(false);
                break;
                case '6FFQTU':
                    resolve(false);
                break;
                default:
                    reject(new Error('user not found'));
            }
        });
    }
```

Here, the function only takes a string ID as input. If we want to chain this in our promise chain, we need to make sure the promise feeding this function resolves into a single string value.

3. Create **getFullRecord**, which returns a combined record for **id**:

```
function getFullRecord(id) {
    return {
        id: '',
        age: 0,
        dob: '',
        name: '',
        cart: [],
        subscription: true
    };
}
```

In the **getFullRecord** function, we want to call all the preceding functions and combine the record into the return shown in the preceding code.

4. Call the function we declared before, in **getFullRecord**, and return the combined result from **getProfile**, **getCart**, and **getSubscription**:

```
function getFullRecord(id) {
    return getProfile(id).then((user) => {
        return getCart(user).then((cart) => {
            return getSubscription(user.id).then((subscription) => {
                return {
                    ...user,
                    cart: cart,
                    subscription
                };
            });
        });
    });
}
```

This function also returns a promise. We can invoke the function and print out its value:

```
getFullRecord('P6HB00').then(console.log);
```

This returns the following output:

```
node v10.15.2 linux/amd64
>
{ id: 'P6HB0O',
  name: 'Miku',
  age: 16,
  dob: '0831',
  cart: [ 'leek', 'cake', 'notebook' ],
  subscription: true }
=> Promise { <pending> }
>
```

Figure 8.17: Calling the declared function in `getFullRecord`

But our code is very messy, and it didn't really utilize the promise chaining we mentioned earlier. To solve this, we need to make a modification to **getCart** and **getSubscription**.

5. Update the **getCart** function, which returns a new object, including every property of the **user** object and the **cart** items instead of just returning the **cart** items:

```
function getCart(user) {
    return new Promise((resolve, reject) => {
        switch(user.id) {
            case 'P6HB0O':
                resolve({ ...user, cart: ['leek', 'cake', 'notebook'] });
            break;
            case '2ADN23':
                resolve({ ...user, cart: ['ice cream', 'banana'] });
            break;
            case '6FFQTU':
                resolve({ ...user, cart: ['tuna', 'tako'] });
            break;
            default:
                reject(new Error('user not found'));
        }
    });
}
```

6. Update the **getSubscription** function, which takes the **user** object as an input and returns an object instead of a single value:

```
function getSubscription(user) {
    return new Promise((resolve, reject) => {
        switch (user.id) {
            case 'P6HB00':
                resolve({ ...user, subscription: true });
                break;
            case '2ADN23':
                resolve({ ...user, subscription: false });
                break;
            case '6FFQTU':
                resolve({ ...user, subscription: false });
                break;
            default:
                reject(new Error('user not found'));
        }
    });
}
```

7. Update the **getFullRecord** function:

```
function getFullRecord(id) {
    return getProfile(id)
        .then(getCart)
        .then(getSubscription);
}
```

Now, this is much more readable than all the nesting we had before. We just reduced **getFullRecord** a lot with minimal changes to the two functions we had previously. When we call this function again, it should produce the exact same result:

```
node v10.15.2 linux/amd64
>
{ id: 'P6HB00',
  name: 'Miku',
  age: 16,
  dob: '0831',
  cart: [ 'leek', 'cake', 'notebook' ],
  subscription: true }
=> Promise { <pending> }
>
```

Figure 8.18: Updated getFullRecord function

8. Create the **getFullRecords** function, which we will use to call multiple records and combine them into an array:

```
function getFullRecords() {
    // Return an array of all the combined user record in our system
    return [
        {
            // Record 1
        },
        {
            // Record 2
        }
    ]
}
```

9. Use **array.map** to generate a list of promises:

```
function getFullRecords() {
    const ids = ['P6HB0O', '2ADN23', '6FFQTU'];
    const promises = ids.map(getFullRecord);
}
```

Here, we utilized the **array.map** function to iterate through the array and return a new array. Because the array includes just the IDs, we can simply just pass the **getFullRecord** function in.

10. Use **Promise.all** to combine the results of a list of promises:

```
function getFullRecords() {
    const ids = ['P6HB0O', '2ADN23', '6FFQTU'];
    const promises = ids.map(getFullRecord);
    return Promise.all(promises);
}
```

Promise.all simply takes an array of promises and returns a promise that waits for all the promises to resolve. Once all the promises in the array are resolved, it will resolve with an array of the results from those promises. Because our objective is to return a list of full records, this does exactly what we want.

11. Test out **getFullRecords**:

```
getFullRecords().then(console.log);
```

The output should be as follows:

```
node v10.15.2 linux/amd64
>
[ { id: 'P6HB0O',
    name: 'Miku',
    age: 16,
    dob: '0831',
    cart: [ 'leek', 'cake', 'notebook' ],
    subscription: true },
  { id: '2ADN23',
    name: 'Rin',
    age: 14,
    dob: '1227',
    cart: [ 'ice cream', 'banana' ],
    subscription: false },
  { id: '6FFQTU',
    name: 'Luka',
    age: 20,
    dob: '0130',
    cart: [ 'tuna', 'tako' ],
    subscription: false } ]
=> Promise { <pending> }
>
```

Figure 8.19: Testing the getFullRecords function

In this exercise, we implemented complex logic using multiple async functions and their promise returns. We also tried to chain them and modified some of our functions to make chaining easy. Lastly, we used both **array.map** and **Promise.all** to create multiple promises using arrays and wait for all of them to resolve. This helps us to manage multiple promises and track their results. Next, we will talk about error handling in promises.

Error Handling in Promises

When we make requests to web servers or access files on disk, there is no guarantee that the operation we want to perform will be 100% successful. When it doesn't work the way we want, we will need to make sure that our application can handle these errors, so it doesn't quit unexpectedly or damage our data. When we were writing handlers for async functions before, we could simply get the error returned from the process in the error argument passed to our callback. When we are using promises, we can also get the error from the **catch** handler.

But when we are handling errors, we are not only trying to prevent something bad from happening to us or our users; we also need to make sure that our errors are meaningful enough for us to use that information and prevent that error from reoccurring. Generally, if we want to handle errors in promises, we can just do the following:

```
aFunctionReturnsPromise()
    .then(dosomething)
    .catch((error) => {
    // Handle some error here
});
```

When we want to handle a certain type of error, we can call the **catch** function and pass it an error handler. But what if we are dealing with multiple promises at once? What if we are using promise chaining? When dealing with multiple promises, you might think we need to do something like this:

```
aFunctionReturnsPromise().then((result) => {
    anotherFunctionReturnsPromise().then((anotherResult) => {

    }).catch((error) => {
        // Handle error here
    });
}).catch((error) => {
    // handle error
})
```

Here, we are handling any type of error from the promise returned by the **aFunctionReturnsPromise** function. Inside the **then** handler for that promise, we are calling **anotherFunctionReturnsPromise**, and inside the **then** handler for that, we are handling the error from that promise. This doesn't look too terrible because we are only using two nested promises, so chaining them is not strictly necessary, and we are handling each error separately. But usually, when you see people writing code like this, you will also see something like this:

```
aFunctionReturnsPromise().then((result) => {
    return anotherFunctionReturnsPromise().then((anotherResult) => {
        // Do operation here
    }).catch((error) => {
        // Handle error here
```

```
        logError(error);

        throw new Error ('something else');
    });
}).catch((error) => {
    // handle error
    logError(error);

    throw new Error ('something else');
});
```

I have even seen production-grade code written like this. While this looks like a great idea to a lot of developers, it is not an ideal way to handle errors in promises. There are some use cases for this way of handling errors. One is if you are certain of the type of error you are going to get and you want to do custom handling for each of the different types. When you have code like this, it is very easy for you to have duplication in your log files because, as you can see from the preceding code, the error is logged twice: once in the catch handler in the nested promise, and once in the parent promise. To reduce the duplication of error handling, you can simply remove any handler in the nested promise, so the preceding code would look like this:

```
aFunctionReturnsPromise().then((result) => {
    return anotherFunctionReturnsPromise().then((anotherResult) => {
        // Do operation here
    });
}).catch((error) => {
    // handle error
    logError(error);

    throw new Error ('something else');
});
```

You don't have to worry that the error in the nested promise is not handled – because we are returning the promise in the **then** handler, and we are passing the status over, not the value. So, when the nested promise encounters an error, it will eventually be caught by the **catch** handler in the parent error handler.

One thing we must keep in mind is that when we are using promises, the **then** handler is not called when there is an error. Consider the following example:

```
processSomeFile().then(() => {
    // Cleanup temp files
    console.log('cleaning up');
}).catch((error) => {
    console.log('oh no');
});
```

Suppose you are creating a file processing function and after it is finished processing, you run your cleanup logic in the **then** handler. This creates an issue when we have errors because the cleanup process will never be called when this promise is rejected. This can cause a lot of issues. We can run out of disk space because temp files are not being removed. We can also risk memory leak if we don't properly close connections. To solve this issue, some developers take the easy way and copy over the cleanup logic:

```
processSomeFile().then(() => {
    // Cleanup temp files
    console.log('cleaning up');
}).catch((error) => {
    // Cleanup temp files
    console.log('cleaning up');
    console.log('oh no');
})
```

While this solves our issue, it also creates a duplicated block, so eventually, when we want to change some logic in the cleanup process, we need to remember to make the change in both places. Luckily for us, the **Promise** class gives us a very useful handler we can set to make sure that the handler is always called regardless of the status:

```
processSomeFile().then(() => {
}).catch((error) => {

    console.log('oh no');
}).finally(() => {
    // Cleanup temp files
    console.log('cleaning up');
})
```

Here, we are appending a new type of handler to our promise. The `.finally` handler will always be called when the promise is **settled**, regardless of whether it is resolved or rejected. This is a very useful handler we can set on our promises to make sure that we properly clean up connections or remove files.

In the previous exercise, we managed to use **Promise.all** to grab a list of results from a list of promises. In our example, all the promises eventually resolved, and we got a very clean array returned to us. How would we handle cases where we are unsure about the result of the promises? Consider the **getFullRecords** function in the last exercise; when we run the function, it executes the following:

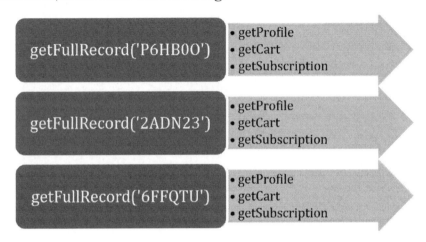

Figure 8.20: Executing the getFullRecords function

The function executes all three operations at the same time and will resolve when they are resolved. Let's modify the **getFullRecords** function to make it output an error:

```
function getFullRecords() {
    const ids = ['P6HB0O', '2ADN23', 'Not here'];
    const promises = ids.map(getFullRecord);
    return Promise.all(promises);
}
```

We know that the third ID we have provided doesn't exist in our **getProfile** function, so it will be rejected. When we run this function, we will get an output like this:

```
node v10.15.2 linux/amd64
>
Error: user not found
    at Promise (evalmachine.<anonymous>:14:24)
    at new Promise (<anonymous>)
    at getProfile (evalmachine.<anonymous>:2:12)
    at getFullRecord (evalmachine.<anonymous>:57:12)
    at Array.map (<anonymous>)
    at getFullRecords (evalmachine.<anonymous>:80:26)
    at evalmachine.<anonymous>:84:1
    at Script.runInContext (vm.js:107:20)
    at Object.runInContext (vm.js:285:6)
    at evaluate (/run_dir/repl.js:133:14)
=> Promise { <pending> }
>
```

Figure 8.21: Error when running the getProfile function

Promise.all waits for all the promises in the array to settle and will return a rejected promise if one of the requests is rejected. Keep this in mind when you are dealing with multiple promises using **Promise.all**; if a promise request is rejected, make sure you include as much info on the error message as you can so that you can tell which operation was rejected.

Exercise 64: Refactor the Bill Calculator Using Promises

In the last exercise, we wrote bill calculator logic using callbacks. Suppose the company you work for has now upgraded their Node.js runtime and they require you to rewrite that part of the logic with promises. Open the **promises.js** file and you will see the updated **clientApi** rewritten using promises:

> **Note**
>
> Promises.js is available at https://github.com/TrainingByPackt/Professional-JavaScript/tree/master/Lesson08/Exercise64.

- You are given **clientApi**, which supports promises.

- You need to implement a feature that calculates the bill for a user and returns the result in this format:

```
{
    id: 'XXXXX',
    address: '2323 sxssssss',
    due: 236.6
}
```

- You need to implement a **calculateBill** function that takes an ID and calculates the gas bill for that user.

- You need to implement a new **calculateAll** function to calculate the bill of all the users from **getUsers**.

We will open the file that includes **clientApi** and do our work there.

Perform the following steps to implement the exercise:

1. We will first create the **calculate** function. This time, we will only pass **id**:

```
function calculate(id) {}
```

2. In **calculate**, we will call **getUsers** first:

```
function calculate(id) {
return clientApi.getUsers().then((result) => {
    const currentUser = result.users.find((user) => user.id === id);
    if (!currentUser) { throw Error('user not found'); }
  }
}
```

Because we want to calculate and return a promise, and **getUsers** returns a promise, we will simply return promise when we call **getUsers**. Here, we will run the same **find** method to find the user we are currently calculating. Then, if the user doesn't exist, we can just throw an error inside the **then** handler.

3. Call **getUsage** inside the **then** handler of **getUsers**:

```
function calculate(id) {
return clientApi.getUsers().then((result) => {
    const currentUser = result.users.find((user) => user.id === id);
    if (!currentUser) { throw Error('user not found'); }
  return clientApi.getUsage(currentUser.id).then((usage) => {
  });

  }
}
```

Here, we are returning **clientApi** because we want to chain our promise and want the innermost promise to surface and be resolved.

4. Call **getRate** inside the **then** handler of **getUsage**:

```
function calculate(id) {
    return clientApi.getUsers().then((result) => {
        const currentUser = result.users.find((user) => user.id === id);
        if (!currentUser) { throw Error('user not found'); }
        return clientApi.getUsage(currentUser.id).then((usage) => {
            return clientApi.getRate(currentUser.id).then((rate) => {
    return {
        id,
        address: currentUser.address,
        due: (rate * usage.reduce((prev, curr) => curr + prev)).toFixed(2)
    };
});

});

}
}
```

This is the last function we need to call. We will also use **return** here. Inside our **then** handler, we will have all the information we need. Here, we can just run our calculation and return the value directly. That value will be the resolved value for the promise we are returning.

5. Create a **calculateAll** function:

```
function calculateAll() {}
```

6. Call **getUsers** to get the list of our users:

```
function calculateAll() {
    return clientApi.getUsers().then((result) => {});
}
```

7. Here, the result will be a list of the users in our system. Then, we will run **calculate** on each of them. Use **Promise.all** and a map array to call the **calculate** function on every user:

```
function calculateAll() {
    return clientApi.getUsers().then((result) => {
        return Promise.all(result.users.map((user) => calculate(user.
id)));

});
}
```

406 | Asynchronous Programming

We are using a map array to return a new array of promises. The array of promises will be the promise returned when we call our existing **calculate** function. When we feed that array to **Promise.all**, it will return a promise that will resolve into a list of results from the list of promises.

8. Call **calculate** on one of our users:

```
calculate('DDW2AU').then(console.log)
```

The output should be as follows:

```
node v10.15.2 linux/amd64
>
{ id: 'DDW2AU', address: '4560 Hickman Street', due: '22.51' }
=> Promise { <pending> }
>
```

Figure 8.22: Calling calculate on one of our users

9. Call the **calculateAll** function:

```
calculateAll().then(console.log)
```

The output should be as follows:

```
node v10.15.2 linux/amd64
>
[ { id: 'DDW2AU', address: '4560 Hickman Street', due: '22.51' },
  { id: 'DV50PD', address: '3445 Red Hawk Road', due: '18.81' },
  { id: 'WCGL6F',
    address: '2355 University Hill Road',
    due: '48.48' } ]
=> Promise { <pending> }
>
```

Figure 8.23: Calling the calculateAll function

In the previous exercises and the activity, we created functions that calculate results from multiple async functions using callbacks and later rewrote those functions using promises. Now, you know how to refactor old callback-style code using promises. This is very useful when you are working on refactoring big projects that require you to start using promises while keeping the same functionality. In the next chapter, we will go over a new method we can adopt to handle async functions.

Async and Await

It has always been the dream of JavaScript developers to handle async functions without the need to write wrappers around them. Then, a new feature was introduced, and that changed everything we know about JavaScript async operations. Consider the code we used in the last exercise:

```
function getFullRecord(id) {

    return getProfile(id)

        .then(getCart)

        .then(getSubscription);

}
```

It is simple enough because we used promise chaining, but it doesn't really tell us anything more than that, and it appears we are just calling a bunch of functions. What if we could have something like this:

```
function getFullRecord(id) {

    const profile = getProfile(id);

    const cart = getCart(id);

    const subscription = getSubscription(id);

    return {

        ...profile,

        cart,

        subscription

    };

}
```

Now, when you look at the preceding code, it makes much more sense and it looks like we are just calling some non-async functions to grab the data and later returning combined data. This is what async and await can achieve. By using async and await, we can write our code like this while maintaining full control of our async operations. Consider a simple **async** function that returns a promise:

```
function sayHello() {

    return Promise.resolve('hello world');

}
```

This is just a simple **async** function like the ones we used in the previous exercises and in the activity. Normally, if we wanted to call this function and get the value of the returned promise, we would need to execute the following command:

```
sayHello().then(console.log)
```

The output should be as follows:

```
node v10.15.2 linux/amd64
>
hello world
=> Promise { <pending> }
>
```

Figure 8.24: Getting the value of the returned promise

There is nothing new about this method; we are still calling the function to return a promise and later getting the resolved value via the **then** handler. If we want to use the new async and await feature, we first create a function that will run the operation:

```
async function printHello() {
    // Operation here
}
```

All we did is add **async** before the **function** keyword. We do this to mark this function as an **async** function so that we can use **await** on the **sayHello** function inside the **printHello()** function without the need to use the **then** handler:

```
async function printHello() {
    // Operation here
    const message = await sayHello();
    console.log(message);
}
```

In this **async** function, we are calling our **sayHello** function, which returns a promise. Because we used the **await** keyword before, it will try to resolve that promise and feed the resolved value into the constant we declared as a message. By using this, we just made our **async** function look like a synchronous function. Later, we can call the function just like a normal function:

```
printHello();
```

The output should be as follows:

```
node v10.15.2 linux/amd64
>
hello world
=> Promise { <pending> }
>
```

Figure 8.25: Calling the printHello function

Exercise 65: Async and Await Functions

In this exercise, we will go over creating async functions and calling them inside other async functions. Using async and await can really help us when dealing with a large amount of async operations within a single function. We will write our first **async** function together and explore some of the things you need keep in mind when dealing with async and await in your application.

> **Note**
>
> The code files for this activity can be found at https://github.com/TrainingByPackt/ Professional-JavaScript/tree/master/Lesson08/Exercise65.

Perform the following steps to complete the exercise:

1. Create a **getConcertList** function:

```
function getConcertList() {
    return Promise.resolve([
        'Magical Mirai 2018',
        'Magical Mirai 2019'
    ]);
}
```

2. Call the function and use **await**:

```
const concerts = await getConcertList();
```

When we run the preceding code, we will get an error like this:

```
node v10.15.2 linux/amd64
>
evalmachine.<anonymous>:8
const concerts = await getConcertList();
                 ^^^^^

SyntaxError: await is only valid in async function
    at new Script (vm.js:79:7)
    at createScript (vm.js:251:10)
    at Object.runInContext (vm.js:284:10)
    at evaluate (/run_dir/repl.js:133:14)
    at ReadStream.<anonymous> (/run_dir/repl.js:116:5)
    at ReadStream.emit (events.js:189:13)
    at addChunk (_stream_readable.js:284:12)
    at readableAddChunk (_stream_readable.js:265:11)
    at ReadStream.Readable.push (_stream_readable.js:220:10)
    at lazyFs.read (internal/fs/streams.js:181:12)
>
```

Figure 8.26: Calling the function using await

The reason we will get this error is that we can only use the **await** keyword inside an **async** function. If we want to use it, we must wrap the statement in an **async** function.

3. Modify the statement and wrap it in an **async** function:

```
async function printList() {
    const concerts = await getConcertList();
    console.log(concerts);
}

printList();
```

The output should be as follows:

```
node v10.15.2 linux/amd64
>
[ 'Magical Mirai 2018', 'Magical Mirai 2019' ]
=> Promise { <pending> }
>
```

Figure 8.27: Modifying the statement and wrapping it in an async function

When we run this function, we will see the list printed out and everything has worked out. We can also treat the **async** function as a function that returns a promise, so if we want to run code after the operation is over, we can use the **then** handler.

4. Call the **then()** function with a handler of the **async** function:

```
printList().then(() => {
    console.log('I am going to both of them.')
});
```

The output should be as follows:

```
node v10.15.2 linux/amd64
>
=> Promise { <pending> }
[ 'Magical Mirai 2018', 'Magical Mirai 2019' ]
I am going to both of them.
>
```

Figure 8.28: Calling the then function with a handler of the async function

Now, we know that the **async** function behaves just like a normal function that returns a promise.

5. Create a **getPrice** function to retrieve the price of a concert:

```
function getPrice(i) {
    const prices = [9900, 9000];
    return Promise.resolve(prices[i]);
}
```

6. Modify **printList** to include the price from **getPrice**:

```
async function printList() {
    const concerts = await getConcertList();
    const prices = await Promise.all(concerts.map((c, i) => getPrice(i)));
    return {
        concerts,
        prices
    };
}
printList().then(console.log);
```

In this function, we are simply trying to get all the prices using the **getPrice** function. In the last section, we mentioned how to use **Promise.all** to wrap an array of promises in a promise that will only resolve once every promise in the array is resolved. Because the **await** keyword can be used on any function that returns a promise and will resolve its value, we can use this to get a price array. When we run the preceding code, we will see that this function resolves into the following:

```
node v10.15.2 linux/amd64
>
{ concerts: [ 'Magical Mirai 2018', 'Magical Mirai 2019' ],
  prices: [ 9900, 9000 ] }
=> Promise { <pending> }
>
```

Figure 8.29: Modifying printList to include the price from getPrice

This means that if we have a promise-returning function, we don't need to use the **then** handler anymore. In an **async** function, we can simply use the **await** keyword to get the resolved value. However, handling errors in **async** functions work a bit differently.

7. Create a **buggyCode** function that returns a rejected promise:

```
function buggyCode() {
    return Promise.reject(new Error('computer: dont feel like working
today'));
}
```

8. Call **buggyCode** in **printList**:

```
async function printList() {
    const concerts = await getConcertList();
    const prices = await Promise.all(concerts.map((c, i) => getPrice(i)));
    await buggyCode();
    return {
        concerts,
        prices
    };
}
printList().then(console.log);
```

The output should be as follows:

```
node v10.15.2 linux/amd64
>
(node:93) UnhandledPromiseRejectionWarning: Error: computer: dont feel like working
today
=> Promise { <pending> }
(node:93) UnhandledPromiseRejectionWarning: Unhandled promise rejection. This error
originated either by throwing inside of an async function without a catch block, or
by rejecting a promise which was not handled with .catch(). (rejection id: 2)
(node:93) [DEP0018] DeprecationWarning: Unhandled promise rejections are deprecated.
In the future, promise rejections that are not handled will terminate the Node.js
process with a non-zero exit code.
>
```

Figure 8.30: Calling buggyCode in printList

Because **buggyCode** throws an error, this stops the execution of our function and, in the future, it might even terminate our process. To handle this type of error, we will need to catch it.

9. Use a **catch** handler on **buggyCode**:

```
async function printList() {
    const concerts = await getConcertList();
    const prices = await Promise.all(concerts.map((c, i) => getPrice(i)));
    await buggyCode().catch((error) => {
        console.log('computer produced error');
        console.log(error);
    });
    return {
        concerts,
        prices
    };
}
printList().then(console.log);
```

We can handle the error of **buggyCode** just like a regular promise and pass it a **catch** handler. This way, the promise rejection will be marked as handled and will not return **UnhandledPromiseRejectionWarning**:

```
node v10.15.2 linux/amd64
>
computer produced error
=> Promise { <pending> }
 Error: computer: dont feel like working today
     at buggyCode (evalmachine.<anonymous>:14:27)
     at printList (evalmachine.<anonymous>:20:11)
     at process._tickCallback (internal/process/next_tick.js:68:7)
 { concerts: [ 'Magical Mirai 2018', 'Magical Mirai 2019' ],
   prices: [ 9900, 9000 ] }
>
```

Figure 8.31: Using the catch handler on buggyCode

This is one way to handle promise rejection in **async** functions. There is also a more familiar way to do it.

10. Modify error handling using **try...catch**:

```
async function printList() {
    const concerts = await getConcertList();
    const prices = await Promise.all(concerts.map((c, i) => getPrice(i)));
    try {
        await buggyCode();
    } catch (error) {
        console.log('computer produced error');
        console.log(error);
    }
    return {
        concerts,
        prices
    };
}
printList().then(console.log);
```

The output should be as follows:

```
node v10.15.2 linux/amd64
>
computer produced error
=> Promise { <pending> }
 Error: computer: dont feel like working today
    at buggyCode (evalmachine.<anonymous>:14:27)
    at printList (evalmachine.<anonymous>:20:11)
    at process._tickCallback (internal/process/next_tick.js:68:7)
 { concerts: [ 'Magical Mirai 2018', 'Magical Mirai 2019' ],
   prices: [ 9900, 9000 ] }
>
```

Figure 8.32: Modifying error handling using try...catch

Using **try...catch** is what many developers are familiar with when dealing with functions that might throw errors. To handle the error from our **buggyCode**, using a **try...catch** block will make the code much more readable and achieve the goal of async, that is, eliminating passing promise handlers. Next, we will talk about how to properly handle multiple promises and concurrency.

Async Await Concurrency

When dealing with multiple async operations in JavaScript, it's crucial to know the order of the operations you want to run. The way you write this code can alter the behavior of your application a lot. Let's look at this example:

```
function wait(seconds) {
    return new Promise((resolve) => {
        setTimeout(() => {
            resolve();
        }, seconds * 1000);
    });
}
```

This is a very simple function that returns a promise that only resolves after **n** seconds has passed. To visualize concurrency, we declare the **runAsync** function:

```
async function runAsync() {
    console.log('starting', new Date());
    await wait(1);
    console.log('i waited 1 second', new Date());
    await wait(2);
    console.log('i waited another 2 seconds', new Date());
}
```

When we run this function, we will see that our program will wait 1 second and print out the first statement, and another one after 2 seconds. The total wait time will be 3 seconds:

```
node v10.15.2 linux/amd64
>
starting 2019-06-18T20:08:44.259Z
=> Promise { <pending> }
 i waited 1 second 2019-06-18T20:08:45.270Z
 i waited another 2 seconds 2019-06-18T20:08:47.275Z
>
```

Figure 8.33: Function returning a promise that resolves after n seconds

What if we want to run both **wait** functions together? Here, we can use **Promise.all**:

```
async function runAsync() {
    console.log('starting', new Date());
    await Promise.all([wait(1), wait(2)]);
    console.log('i waited total 2 seconds', new Date());
}
```

The output should be as follows:

```
node v10.16.0
>
starting 2019-09-07T05:57:33.141Z
=> Promise { <pending> }
 i waited total 2 seconds 2019-09-07T05:57:35.164Z
>
```

Figure 8.34: Running both wait functions using Promise.all

What we did here is we removed **await** and put the two promises returned by the **wait** function in the array, and then fed it to **Promise.all**. When we remove the **await** keyword and use **Promise.all**, we can make sure that the code is not out of control and will continue to execute. What if you are dealing with promises in a loop, as in the following code:

```
async function runAsync() {
    console.log('starting', new Date());
    for (let i = 0; i < 2; i++) {
        await wait(1);
    }
    console.log('i waited another 2 seconds', new Date());
}
```

This offers no concurrency. Imagine that, instead of waiting, we are getting user information from a database:

```
async function runAsync() {
    const userProfiles = [];
    for (let i = 0; i < 2; i++) {
        const profile = await getProfile(i);
        userProfiles.push(profile);
    }
    return userProfiles;
}
```

Here, our use case is fetching multiple user profiles from the database. While the preceding code will work, it is not the most performant implementation. Just as we have mentioned previously, this code will wait until the last request has finished before fetching the next one. To optimize this code, we can simply use **array.map** and **Promise. all** together:

```
async function runAsync() {
    return await Promise.all([0, 1].map(getProfile));
}
```

This way, we aren't waiting for each operation to finish; we are only waiting for the wrapper promise to be resolved. In map array, we are only generating the promises and, once they are created, it will execute our operation. Compared to the **for** loop method, we don't need to wait for the previous promise to settle before executing the next promise. We will talk about their differences in the next chapter.

When to Use await

In the previous examples, we went over using the **await** keyword inside our **async** functions. But when should we use **await**, and when should we avoid it? In the last section, we discussed avoiding using **await** when we want to enable concurrency and make sure operations are not waiting for one another. Consider the following code example:

```
async function example() {
    const result1 = await operation1();
    const result2 = await operation2(result1.something);
    return result2;
}
```

In this example, the **operation2** function will only be executed once **operation1** is complete. This is useful when you have dependencies and **result2** depends on something from **result1**, as shown in the example. If they don't have dependencies on one another, you could leverage **Promise.all** to ensure concurrency:

```
async function example() {
    const result1 = operation1();
    const result2 = operation2();
    return await Promise.all([result1, result2]);
}
```

Without the **await** keyword, the code simply assigns the promise returned from both operations in the constant we declared. This ensures that **operations2** is fired right after **operation1** and that there is no **wait**. Another point that we need to be careful of is error handling. Consider the **buggyCode** we used in the last exercise:

```
function buggyCode() {
    return Promise.reject(new Error('computer: dont feel like working
today'));
}
```

This function simply returns a promise that is rejected. When using it, we should use **catch** to handle the error from the promise:

```
async function printList() {
    try {
        await buggyCode();
    } catch (error) {
        console.log('computer produced error');
        console.log(error);
    }
}
```

When we run this code, we will see that our error is handled beautifully, and the error message is logged. Here, we used **await** when we ran the **buggyCode** function, but when we remove the **await** keyword, here is what we will see:

```
node v10.15.2 linux/amd64

(node:105) UnhandledPromiseRejectionWarning: Error: computer: dont feel like working
today
(node:105) UnhandledPromiseRejectionWarning: Unhandled promise rejection. This error
originated either by throwing inside of an async function without a catch block, or
by rejecting a promise which was not handled with .catch(). (rejection id: 1)
(node:105) [DEP0018] DeprecationWarning: Unhandled promise rejections are
deprecated. In the future, promise rejections that are not handled will terminate
the Node.js process with a non-zero exit code.
=> Promise { <pending> }
```

Figure 8.35: Running the buggyCode function after removing the await keyword

You will see that we have an unhandled promise rejection; it just appeared as our **try...catch** didn't do anything. The reason for this is that without the **await** keyword, JavaScript will not try to wait for the promise to resolve; therefore, it has no idea that an error is going to be thrown in the future. What this **try...catch** block will catch is if there is an error thrown when executing the function. This is something we need to keep in mind when writing code using **async** and **await**. In the next exercise, we will write a complex function calling multiple **async** functions and that is able to recover from an error.

Exercise 66: Complex Async Implementation

In this exercise, we will build a very complex **async** function and use everything we have learned previously to make sure the function is high-performance and resilient to errors.

> **Note**
>
> The code files for this activity can be found at https://github.com/TrainingByPackt/
> Professional-JavaScript/tree/master/Lesson08/Exercise66.

Perform the following steps to complete the exercise:

1. Create a **getPlaylists** function that returns an array of IDs given a playlist name:

```
function getPlaylist(id) {
    const playLists = {
        'On the road': [0, 6, 5, 2],
        'Favorites' : [1, 4, 2],
        'Corrupted': [2, 4, 7, 1]
    };
    const playList = playLists[id];
    if (!playList) {
        throw new Error('Playlist does not exist');
    }
    return Promise.resolve(playLists[id]);
}
```

This function will return an array of song IDs as a playlist. If not found, it will simply return **null**.

2. Create a **getSongUrl** function that returns a song URL given a number **id**:

```
function getSongUrl(id) {
    const songUrls = [
        'http://example.com/1.mp3',
        'http://example.com/2.mp3',
        'http://example.com/3.mp3',
        'http://example.com/4.mp3',
        'http://example.com/5.mp3',
```

```
        'http://example.com/6.mp3',
        'http://example.com/7.mp3',
    ];
    const url = songUrls[id];
    if (!url) {
        throw new Error('Song does not exist');
    }
    return Promise.resolve(url); // Promise.resolve returns a promise that
is resolved with the value given
}
```

3. Create a **playSong** async function that takes the ID of a song and generates two outputs – one displaying the song that is being played, and another that informs the user that the song is finished:

```
async function playSong(id) {
    const url = await getSongUrl(id);
    console.log(`playing song #${id} from ${url}`);
    return new Promise((resolve) => {
        setTimeout(() => {
            console.log(`song #${id} finished playing`);
            resolve();
        }, Math.random() * 3 * 1000);
    });
}
```

4. Create a **playPlaylist** function that takes a playlist ID and calls **playSong** on each song in the playlist:

```
async function playPlaylist(id) {
    const playList = await getPlayLlist(id);
    await Promise.all(playList.map(playSong));
}
```

This is a simple implementation that doesn't perform error handling.

5. Run the **playPlaylist** function:

```
playPlaylist('On the road').then(() => {
    console.log('finished playing playlist');
});
```

The output should be as follows:

```
node v10.15.2 linux/amd64
>
playing song #0 from http://example.com/1.mp3
playing song #6 from http://example.com/7.mp3
playing song #5 from http://example.com/6.mp3
playing song #2 from http://example.com/3.mp3
=> Promise { <pending> }
song #0 finished playing
song #5 finished playing
song #2 finished playing
song #6 finished playing
finished playing playlist
>
```

Figure 8.36: Running the playPlaylist function

We get a very interesting output; it is playing all the songs at the same time. Also, it doesn't handle errors gracefully.

6. Call **playPlaylist** with no argument:

```
playPlaylist().then(() => {
    console.log('finished playing playlist');
});
```

The output should be as follows:

```
node v10.15.2 linux/amd64
>
(node:403) UnhandledPromiseRejectionWarning: Error: Playlist does not exist
(node:403) UnhandledPromiseRejectionWarning: Unhandled promise rejection. This error
originated either by throwing inside of an async function without a catch block, or
by rejecting a promise which was not handled with .catch(). (rejection id: 2)
(node:403) [DEP0018] DeprecationWarning: Unhandled promise rejections are
deprecated. In the future, promise rejections that are not handled will terminate
the Node.js process with a non-zero exit code.
=> Promise { <pending> }
>
```

Figure 8.37: Calling playPlaylist with no argument

The reason we are getting this error is that we are not handling errors when **getPlaylist** throws an error.

7. Modify **playPlaylist** to handle errors:

```
async function playPlaylist(id) {
    try {
        const playList = await getPlaylist(id);
        return await Promise.all(playList.map(playSong));
    } catch (error) {
        console.log(error);
    }
}
```

We aren't doing anything special here; we simply added a **try...catch** block around the **getPlaylist** so that when the promise does get rejected, it will be properly handled. After the update, when we run our code again, we will receive the following output:

```
node v10.15.2 linux/amd64
>
Error: Playlist does not exist
    at getPlayList (evalmachine.<anonymous>:9:15)
    at playPlayList (evalmachine.<anonymous>:44:32)
    at evalmachine.<anonymous>:52:1
    at Script.runInContext (vm.js:107:20)
    at Object.runInContext (vm.js:285:6)
    at evaluate (/run_dir/repl.js:133:14)
    at ReadStream.<anonymous> (/run_dir/repl.js:116:5)
    at ReadStream.emit (events.js:189:13)
    at addChunk (_stream_readable.js:284:12)
    at readableAddChunk (_stream_readable.js:265:11)
finished playing playlist
=> Promise { <pending> }
>
```

Figure 8.38: Modifying **playPlaylist** for error handling

We see that the error is properly handled, but we still get the **finished** message at the end. This is something we do not want because when an error has occurred, we do not want the promise chain to continue.

8. Modify the **playPlaylist** function and the caller:

```
async function playPlaylist(id) {
    const playList = await getPlaylist(id);
    return await Promise.all(playList.map(playSong));
}
playPlaylist().then(() => {
    console.log('finished playing playlist');
}).catch((error) => {
    console.log(error);
});
```

When writing **async** code, it is a good idea to keep the promise handling in the parent and let the error bubble up. This way, we can have only one error handler for this operation and be able to handle multiple errors at once.

9. Try to call a corrupted playlist:

```
playPlaylist('Corrupted').then(() => {
    console.log('finished playing playlist');
}).catch((error) => {
    console.log(error);
});
```

The output should be as follows:

```
node v10.15.2 linux/amd64
>
playing song #2 from http://example.com/3.mp3
playing song #4 from http://example.com/5.mp3
playing song #1 from http://example.com/2.mp3
Error: Song does not exist
    at getSongUrl (evalmachine.<anonymous>:26:15)
    at playSong (evalmachine.<anonymous>:32:23)
    at Array.map (<anonymous>)
    at playPlayList (evalmachine.<anonymous>:44:39)
    at process._tickCallback (internal/process/next_tick.js:68:7)
=> Promise { <pending> }
song #4 finished playing
song #2 finished playing
song #1 finished playing
>
```

Figure 8.39: Calling a corrupted playlist

This code runs fine, and the error is handled, but it is still playing everything together. We wanted to show the **finished** message because the **song does not exist** error is a minor one and we want to suppress it.

10. Modify **playPlaylist** to play songs sequentially:

```
async function playPlaylist(id) {
    const playList = await getPlaylist(id);
    for (const songId of playList) {
        await playSong(songId);
    }
}
```

The output should be as follows:

```
node v10.15.2 linux/amd64
>
=> Promise { <pending> }
playing song #0 from http://example.com/1.mp3
song #0 finished playing
playing song #6 from http://example.com/7.mp3
song #6 finished playing
playing song #5 from http://example.com/6.mp3
song #5 finished playing
playing song #2 from http://example.com/3.mp3
song #2 finished playing
finished playing playlist
>
```

Figure 8.40: Modifying **playPlaylist** to play songs sequentially

In the modification, we removed **Promise.all** and replaced it with a **for** loop with **await** for each song. This makes sure that we wait for each song to complete before we go on to the next song.

11. Modify **playSong** to suppress the **not found** error:

```
async function playSong(id) {
    try {
        const url = await getSongUrl(id);
        console.log('playing song #${id} from ${url}');
        return new Promise((resolve) => {
            setTimeout(() => {
                console.log('song #${id} finished playing');
                resolve();
            }, Math.random() * 3 * 1000);
        });
    } catch (error) {
        console.log('song not found');
    }
}
```

The output should be as follows:

```
node v10.16.0
»
playing song #2 from http://example.com/3.mp3
=> Promise { <pending> }
song #2 finished playing
playing song #4 from http://example.com/5.mp3
song #4 finished playing
song not found
playing song #1 from http://example.com/2.mp3
song #1 finished playing
finished playing playlist
»
```

Figure 8.41: Modifying **playSong** to suppress the not found error

What we did here is wrapped our logic with a **try...catch** block. This allows us to suppress any error generated by the code. When **getSongUrl** does throw an error, it will not be bubbled up to the parent; it will be caught by the **catch** block.

In this exercise, we implemented a playlist player using **async** and **await**, and used our knowledge about **Promise.all** and **async** concurrency to optimize our playlist player to only play one song at a time. This enabled us to have a deeper understanding of async and await and implement our own **async** function in the future. In the next section, we will go over how we can migrate our existing promise- or callback-based code to async and await.

Activity 12: Refactor the Bill Calculator Using Async and Await

Your company has updated its Node.js runtime again. In this activity, we will refactor the bill calculator we created previously using async and await:

- You are given **clientApi**, implemented using promises.
- You need to update **calculate()** to an **async** function.
- You need to update **calculateAll()** to an **async** function.
- **calculateAll()** needs to get all the results at once using **Promise.all**.

Open the **async.js** file to implement the **calculate** and **calculateAll** function using **async** and **await**.

> **Note**
>
> The code files for this activity can be found at https://github.com/TrainingByPackt/ Professional-JavaScript/blob/master/Lesson08/Activity12/Activity12.js.

Perform the following steps to complete the activity:

1. Create a **calculate** function that takes an ID as input.

2. Inside **calculate**, use **await** to call **clientApi.getUsers()** to retrieve all of the users.

3. Use **array.find()** to find **currentUser** using the **id** argument.

4. Use **await** to call **getUsage()** to get the usage for that user.

5. Use **await** to call **getRate** to get the rate for at user.

6. Return a new object with **id**, **address**, and the total due amount.

7. Write the **calculateAll** function as an **async** function.

8. Use **await** to call **getUsers** to retrieve all of the users.

9. Use an array map to create a list of promises and use **Promise.all** to wrap them. Then, use await on the promise returned by **Promise.all** and return its value.

10. Call **calculate** on one of the users.

11. Call **calculateAll**.

    The output should be as follows:

```
node v10.15.2 linux/amd64
>
[ { id: 'DDW2AU', address: '4560 Hickman Street', due: '22.51' },
  { id: 'DV50PD', address: '3445 Red Hawk Road', due: '18.81' },
  { id: 'WCGL6F',
    address: '2355 University Hill Road',
    due: '48.48' } ]
=> Promise { <pending> }
>
```

Figure 8.42: Calling the calculateAll function

> **Note**
>
> The solution for this activity can be found on page 615.

Migrating Callback- and Promise-Based Code to Async and Await

When working on large-sized projects, it's very common to have to refactor existing code using async and await. When we are doing these refactors, we need to keep in mind that we should keep the same functionality and type of error handling. In this section, we will learn how we can migrate existing callback and promise-based code to async and await.

Migrating Callback-Based Code to Async and Await

When we are migrating callback-based code, we need to rewrite the function and make sure it returns a promise instead of taking a callback. Consider the following code:

```
function makeRequest(param, callback) {
    request(param, (err, data) => {
        if (err) {
            return callback(err);
        }
        const users = data.users;
        callback(null, users.map((u) => u.id));
    });
}
```

The preceding code takes a parameter and calls a **request** module, which we do not have access to modify, and returns a list of the user IDs. Once it is finished, if there is an error, it is simply returned through the callback. When we want to refactor this code using async and await, we can first make sure it returns a promise. When we do that, we also want to remove the **callback** parameter:

```
function makeRequest(param) {
    return new Promise((resolve, reject) => {
        // Logic here
    });
}
```

Then, we need to copy our logic in:

```
function makeRequest(param) {
    return new Promise((resolve, reject) => {
        request(param, (err, data) => {
            if (err) {
```

```
            return callback(err);
        }
        const users = data.users;
        callback(null, users.map((u) => u.id));
    });
});
}
```

Here, we need to make modifications. We need to remove all the references to **callback** and change them to use **reject** and **resolve**:

```
function makeRequest(param) {
    return new Promise((resolve, reject) => {
        request(param, (err, data) => {
            if (err) {
                return reject(err);
            }
            const users = data.users;
            resolve(users.map((u) => u.id));
        });
    });
}
```

You can see here that we are still using the callback style when calling **request**. That is because we have no control over that external library. What we can do is make sure that each time we call it, we return a promise. Now, we have fully converted our legacy code to modern standards. You can now use it in the **async** function like this:

```
async function use() {
    const userIds = await makeRequest({});
}
```

Usually, code is much more difficult to refactor. It is recommended to start from the most basic level and work your way up as you refactor. When you are dealing with nested callbacks, make sure you use **await** to ensure you preserve dependencies.

Summary

In this chapter, we went over how we can use promises and async and await to better manage our async operations in our code. We also talked about the various ways in which we can refactor our existing callback code to async and await. Using async and await in our applications will not only help to make our code more readable, but will also help us to do future testing on our implementation. In the next chapter, we will go over how we can use event-based programming in our applications.

Event-Driven Programming and Built-In Modules

Learning Objectives

By the end of this chapter, you will be able to:

- Use event modules in Node.js
- Create an event emitter to enhance the functionality of existing code
- Build custom event emitters
- Use built-in modules and utilities
- Implement a timer module to get an API to schedule timer functions

In this chapter, we will use event emitters and built-in modules to avoid creating projects with deeply coupled dependencies.

Introduction

In the previous chapter, we talked about how event-driven programming is used in Node.js and how we can modify normal callback-based async operations to use async-await and promises. We know that the Node.js core API is built on async-driven architecture. Node.js has one event loop that does the processing for most async and event-based operations.

In JavaScript, the event loops run constantly and digest messages from the callback queue to make sure it is executing the right functions. Without events, we can see that the code is very deeply coupled. For a simple chatroom application, we would need to write something like this:

```
class Room {
    constructor() {
        this.users = [];
    }
    addUser(user) {
        this.users.push(user);
    }
    sendMessage(message) {
        this.users.forEach(user => user.sendMessage(message));
    }
}
```

As you can see, because we are not using events, we need to keep a list of all the users in the room. When we add a user to the room, we also need to add the user to the list we created. When sending messages, we also need to iterate through all the users in our list and call the **sendMessage** method. Our user class would be defined like this:

```
class User {
    constructor() {
        this.rooms = {}
    }
    joinRoom(roomName, room) {
        this.rooms[roomName] = room;
        room.addUser(this);
    }
    sendMessage(roomName, message) {
```

```
        this.rooms[roomName].sendMessage(message);
    }
}
```

You can see how this is getting far too complicated; in order to join a chatroom, we need to add both the room and the current user to the room. When our application eventually gets very complicated, we will see that this raises an issue with the traditional approach. If this application ever requires network requests (async operations), it will get very complex because we would need to wrap all the code we wish to execute with the async operation. We might be able to pull that logic out but when we are dealing with applications that are being driven by an unknown number of random events, using event-driven programming has the benefit of making our code much easier to maintain.

The Traditional Approach versus Event-Driven Programming

As we mentioned in the introduction, in traditional programming patterns, we like to have a direct link between our components when we want them to communicate. This is shown in the following diagram:

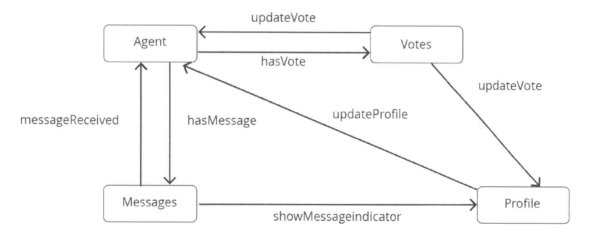

Figure 9.1: Traditional programming approach

For a simple application that allows the user to update their profile and receive messages, we can see that we have four components:

- Agent
- Profile
- Votes
- Messages

The way these components interact with each other is by calling the appropriate methods in the component that wishes to communicate. By doing this, it makes the code very easy to understand, but we might have to pass the component reference over. Take our **Agent** class, for example:

```
class Agent {
    constructor(id, agentInfo, voteObj, messageObj) {
        this.voteObj = voteObj;
        this.messageObj = messageObj;
    }
    checkMessage() {
        if (this.messageObj.hasMessage()) {
            const message = this.messageObj.nextMessate();
            return message;
        }
        return undefined;
    }
    checkVote() {
        if (this.voteObj.hasNewVote()) {
            return true;
        }
        return false;
    }
}
```

The **Agent** class must store the reference to the component it wants to communicate with in the future. Without it, there is no way for our component to communicate with other components. In the preceding example, the **Agent** object we created is very deeply coupled with everything else. It needs all the references for these objects when it is created, which makes our code very hard to decouple if we want to change something in the future. Consider the preceding **Agent** code. If we are going to add more features to it, we want the agent class to communicate with new features such as a social page, a live stream page, and so on. It is technically doable as long we add the reference to these objects in our **constructor**. By doing this, we risk having our code look like this in the future:

```
class Agent {
    constructor(id, agentInfo, voteObj, messageObj, socialPage, gamePage,
```

```
liveStreamPage, managerPage, paymentPage...) {
        this.voteObj = voteObj;
        this.messageObj = messageObj;
        this.socialPage = socialPage;
        this.gamePage = gamePage;
        this.liveStreamPage = liveStreamPage;
        this.managerPage = managerPage;
        this.paymentPage = paymentPage;
        ...


    }
    ...
}
```

When our application gets more and more complex, so does our **Agent** class. Since it has all the references in **constructor**, we are open to issues that can be caused by mistakenly passing the wrong type for a parameter. This is a common problem when we are trying to communicate between multiple components at once.

Eventing

Our previous approach – that is, dealing with component communication – was direct and really static. We need to store the component reference we want to communicate with and write very component-specific code when we want to send a message to it. In JavaScript, there is a new way of communicating, and it's called **eventing**.

Let's consider this example; the light that's passed to you by your friend is a way for you to receive events from your friend. In JavaScript, we can have objects that have the ability to emit events. By emitting events, we can create a new way of communicating between our objects. This is also called the observer pattern. The following diagram depicts the observer pattern:

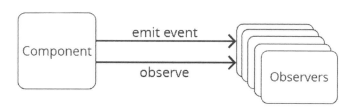

Figure 9.2: The observer pattern

In this pattern, instead of calling specific methods in our component, the component that wants to initiate communication will simply emit an event. We can have multiple observers that observe events from the components. This way, we put the responsibility of consuming the message purely on the consumer. When the observer decides to observe the event, it will receive the event every time the component emits it. If the preceding complex example is implemented using events, it will look like this:

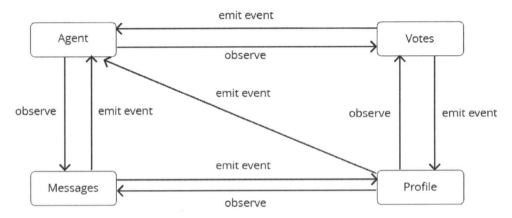

Figure 9.3: Observer patterns using events

Here, we can see that each component follows our observer pattern, and when we convert this into code, it will look something like this:

```
class Agent {
    constructor(id, agentInfo, emitter) {
        this.messages = [];
        this.vote = 0;
        emitter.on('message', (message) => {
            this.messages.push(message);
        });
        emitter.on('vote', () => {
            this.vote += 1;
        })
    }
}
```

Now, instead of taking all the references of all the components we want to communicate with, we are only passing one event emitter over, which handles all the messaging. This makes our code much more decoupled from the other components. This is basically how we implement an event observer pattern in our code. In real life, this can get more complicated. In the next exercise, we will go over a simple example to demonstrate how we can use the built-in event system in Node.js to emit events.

Exercise 67: A Simple Event Emitter

In the introduction, we talked about how we can use the event observer pattern to remove the references of all the components we want to communicate within our code. In this exercise, we will go over the built-in event module in Node.js, how we can create an **EventEmitter**, and how we can use it.

Perform the following steps to complete this exercise:

1. Import the **events** module:

   ```
   const EventEmitter = require('events');
   ```

   We will be importing the **events** module built-in in Node.js. It provides a constructor that we can use to create our custom event emitters or create a class that inherits from it. Because this is a built-in module, there is no need to install it.

2. Create a new **EventEmitter**:

   ```
   const emitter = new EventEmitter();
   ```

3. Try to emit an event:

   ```
   emitter.emit('my-event', { value: 'event value' });
   ```

4. Attach an event listener:

   ```
   emitter.on('my-event', (value) => {
       console.log(value);
   });
   ```

   To add an event listener to our emitter, we need to call the **on** method on our emitter with the event name and the function to be called when an event is emitted. When we add the event listener after we emit an event, we will see that the event listener is not called. The reason for this is that when we emitted our event before, there was no event listener attached for that event, and so it wasn't called.

5. Emit another event:

```
emitter.emit('my-event', { value: 'another value' });
```

When we emit an event this time, we will see that our event listener is correctly called, and our event value is correctly printed out, like so:

```
node v10.15.2 linux/amd64
>
{ value: 'another value' }
=> true
>
```

Figure 9.4: Emitted event with the correct event value

6. Attach another event listener for **my-event**:

```
emitter.on('my-event', (value) => {
    console.log('i am handling it again');
});
```

We are not limited to only one listener per event – we can attach as many event listeners as possible. When an event is emitted, it will invoke all the listeners.

7. Emit another event:

```
emitter.emit('my-event', { value: 'new value' });
```

The following is the output of the preceding code:

```
node v10.15.2 linux/amd64
>
{ value: 'another value' }
{ value: 'new value' }
i am handling it again
=> true
>
```

Figure 9.5: Output after emitting an event multiple times

When we emit the events again, we will see the first event we emitted. We will also see that it successfully printed out our messages. Notice that it kept the same order as when we attached the listener. When we emit an error, the emitter iterates through the array and invokes each listener, one by one.

8. Create the **handleEvent** function:

```
function handleEvent(event) {
    console.log('i am handling event type: ', event.type);
}
```

When we set our event listeners, we used anonymous functions. While this is easy and simple, it doesn't offer us all of the capability that **EventEmitters** offers:

9. Attach the new **handleEvent** to a new type of event:

```
emitter.on('event-with-type', handleEvent);
```

10. Emit the new event type:

```
emitter.emit('event-with-type', { type: 'sync' });
```

The following is the output of the preceding code:

```
node v10.15.2 linux/amd64
>
i am handling event type:  sync
=> true
>
```

Figure 9.6: Emitting the new event type

11. Remove the event listener:

```
emitter.removeListener('event-with-type', handleEvent);
```

Because we are using a named function, we can use this function reference to remove listeners once we no longer need events to be passed to that listener.

12. Emit the event after the listener has been removed:

```
emitter.emit('event-with-type', { type: 'sync2' });
```

The following is the output of the preceding code:

```
node v10.15.2 linux/amd64
>
=> false
>
```

Figure 9.7: Output of the emit event after the listener has been removed

Because we just removed the listener to **event-with-type**, when we emit the event again, it will not be invoked.

In this exercise, we built a very simple event emitter and tested adding and removing listeners. Now, we know how to use events to pass messages from one component to another. Next, we will dig deeply into event listener methods and see what we can accomplish by calling them.

EventEmitter Methods

In the previous exercise, we went over a couple of methods we can call to emit events and attach listeners. We also used **removeListener** to remove the listener we had attached. Now, we will go over the various methods we can call on the event listeners. This will help us manage event emitters much more easily.

Removing Listeners

There are cases where we want to remove listeners from our emitter. Like we did in the previous exercise, we can remove a listener simply by calling **removeListener**:

```
emitter.removeListener('event-with-type', handleEvent);
```

When we call the **removeListener** method, we must provide it with an event name and function reference. When we are calling the method, it doesn't matter if the event listener is set or not; if the listener is not set to begin with, nothing will happen. If it is set, it will iterate through the array of the listener in our event emitter and remove the first occurrence of that listener, like so:

```
const emitter = new EventEmitter();

function handleEvent(event) {
    console.log('i am handling event type: ', event.type);
}
emitter.on('event-with-type', handleEvent);
emitter.on('event-with-type', handleEvent);
emitter.on('event-with-type', handleEvent);
emitter.emit('event-with-type', { type: 'sync' });
emitter.removeListener('event-with-type', handleEvent);
```

In this code, we attached the same listener three times. This is allowed in event emitters when we are attaching event listeners; it is simply appended to the event listener array for that event. When we emit our event before **removeListener**, we will see that our listener is invoked three times:

```
node v10.15.2 linux/amd64
>
i am handling event type:  sync
i am handling event type:  sync
i am handling event type:  sync
=> EventEmitter {
  _events:
   [Object: null prototype] {
     'event-with-type': [ [Function: handleEvent], [Function: handleEvent] ] },
  _eventsCount: 1,
  _maxListeners: undefined }
>
```

Figure 9.8: Listener invoked three times with the emit event before removing the listener

In this case, because we have three of the same listeners attached to our event, when we call **removeListener**, it will only remove the first listener in our **listener** array. When we emit the same event again, we will see that it will only runs two times:

```
node v10.15.2 linux/amd64
>
i am handling event type:  sync
i am handling event type:  sync
=> true
>
```

Figure 9.9: After using removeListener, the first listener is removed

Removing all Listeners

We can remove a specific listener from our event emitter. But often, when we are dealing with several listeners on our emitter, there are cases where we want to remove all listeners. The **EventEmitter** class provides us with a method that we can use to remove all the listeners for a specific event. Consider the same example we used previously:

```
const emitter = new EventEmitter();

function handleEvent(event) {
    console.log('i am handling event type: ', event.type);
}

emitter.on('event-with-type', handleEvent);

emitter.on('event-with-type', handleEvent);

emitter.on('event-with-type', handleEvent);
```

If we wanted to remove all the listeners for the **event-with-type** event, we would have to call **removeListener** multiple times. Sometimes, when we are sure that all the event listeners have been added by us and no other component or module, we can use a single method call to remove all the listeners for that event:

```
emitter.removeAllListeners('event-with-type');
```

When we are calling **removeAllListeners**, all we need to provide is the event name. This removes all the listeners attached to the event. After it is called, the event will have no handlers. Make sure you are not removing listeners that have been attached by another component if you are using this:

```
emitter.emit('event-with-type', { type: 'sync' });
```

When we emit the same event again after calling **removeAllListeners**, we will see that our program will output nothing:

Figure 9.10: Using removeAllListeners will output nothing

Attaching a One-Time Listener

There are times when we want our component to receive a certain event only once. We can accomplish this by using **removeListener** to make sure we remove the listener after it is called:

```
const EventEmitter = require('events');


const emitter = new EventEmitter();


function handleEvent(event) {
    console.log('i am handling event type once : ', event.type);
    emitter.removeListener('event-with-type', handleEvent);
}
```

```
emitter.on('event-with-type', handleEvent);
emitter.emit('event-with-type', { type: 'sync' });
emitter.emit('event-with-type', { type: 'sync' });
emitter.emit('event-with-type', { type: 'sync' });
```

Here, we can see that, in our **handleEvent** listener, we are also removing the listener after it has been executed. This way, we can make sure that our event listener will only be called once. When we run the preceding code, we will see this output:

```
node v10.15.2 linux/amd64
>
i am handling event type once :  sync
=> false
>
```

Figure 9.11: Output after using the handleEvent listener

This does what we want, but it is not good enough. It requires us to keep a reference of the emitter inside the event listener. Also, it is not robust enough because there is no way for us to separate the listener logic into a different file. The **EventEmitter** class provided us with a very simple method that can be used to attach a one-time listener:

. . .

```
emitter.once('event-with-type', handleEvent);
emitter.emit('event-with-type', { type: 'sync' });
emitter.emit('event-with-type', { type: 'sync' });
emitter.emit('event-with-type', { type: 'sync' });
```

Here, we used the **.once** method when we were attaching our event listener. This tells our emitter that the function we are passing should only be invoked once and will be removed from the list of event listeners after it is invoked. When we run it, it will provide us with the same output as before:

```
node v10.15.2 linux/amd64
>
i am handling event type once :  sync
=> false
>
```

Figure 9.12: Getting a one-time listener using the .once method

This way, we do not need to keep a reference to our event emitter in our listener. This makes our code more flexible and easily modularized.

Reading from Event Emitters

Until now, we have been setting and removing listeners from our event emitter. The `EventEmitter` class also provides us with several read methods where we can get more information about our event emitter. Consider the following example:

```
const EventEmitter = require('events');
const emitter = new EventEmitter();


emitter.on('event 1', () => {});
emitter.on('event 2', () => {});
emitter.on('event 2', () => {});
emitter.on('event 3', () => {});
```

Here, we added three types of event listeners to our emitter. For **event 2**, we set two listeners to it. To get the number of event listeners for a certain event in our emitter, we can call **listenerCount**. For the preceding example, if we want to know the number of event listeners that are attached to **event 1**, we can execute the following command:

```
emitter.listenerCount('event 1');
```

The following is the output of the preceding code:

Figure 9.13: Output showing the number of events attached to event 1

Similarly, we can check the number of event listeners attached to **event 2** by executing the following command:

```
emitter.listenerCount('event 2');
```

The following is the output of the preceding code:

```
node v10.15.2 linux/amd64
>
=> 2
>
```

Figure 9.14: Output showing the number of events attached to event 2

There are times when we want to know about a list of event listeners that are attached to an event so that we can determine whether a certain handler is already attached, like so:

```
function anotherHandler() {}

emitter.on('event 4', () => {});

emitter.on('event 4', anotherHandler);
```

Here, we have attached one anonymous function to **event 4** and another listener using a named function. If we want to know whether **anotherHandler** is already attached to **event 4**, we can attach a list of listeners to that event. The **EventEmitter** class provides us with a very easy method to invoke this:

```
const event4Listeners = emitter.listeners('event 4');
```

The following is the output of the preceding code:

```
node v10.15.2 linux/amd64
>
=> [ [Function], [Function: anotherHandler] ]
>
```

Figure 9.15: Getting a list of listeners attached to the event using the EventEmitter class

Here, we can see the two listeners we have already attached to our emitter: one is our anonymous function, while the other is our named function, **anotherHandler**. To check whether our handler is already attached to the emitter, we can check to see if **anotherHandler** is in the **event4Listeners** array:

```
event4Listeners.includes(anotherHandler);
```

The following is the output of the preceding code:

```
node v10.15.2 linux/amd64
>
=> true
>
```

Figure 9.16: Checking whether the handler is attached to the emitter

By using this method with the array includes a method, we can determine whether a function is already attached to our event.

Getting a List of Events That Have Listeners Registered

There are also times when we need to get a list of events that have listeners registered to them. This could be used to determine whether we have already attached listeners to an event or to see if an event name is already taken. Continuing from the preceding example, we can get that information by calling another internal method in the **EventEmitter** class:

```
emitter.eventNames();
```

The following is the output of the preceding code:

```
node v10.15.2 linux/amd64
>
=> [ 'event 1', 'event 2', 'event 3', 'event 4' ]
>
```

Figure 9.17: Getting information on event names using the EventEmitter class

Here, we can see that our event emitter has listeners attached to four different event types; that is, events 1-4.

Max Listeners

By default, each event emitter can only register a maximum of 10 listeners for any single event. When we attach more than the maximum, we will get a warning like this:

```
node v10.15.2 linux/amd64
>
(node:71) MaxListenersExceededWarning: Possible EventEmitter memory leak detected. 11 event 1
listeners added. Use emitter.setMaxListeners() to increase limit
```

Figure 9.18: Warning when attaching more than 10 listeners for a single event

This is set as a preventive measure to make sure that we aren't leaking memory, but there are also times where we need to set more than 10 listeners for an event. If we are sure of that, we can update the default maximum by calling **setMaxListeners**:

```
emitter.setMaxListeners(20)
```

Here, we set the max listener default to **20**. We can also set it to **0** or Infinity to allow an unlimited number of listeners.

Prepend Listeners

When we add listeners, they are appended to the end of the listener array. When an event is emitted, the emitter will call each of the assigned listeners in the order they were assigned. In some cases, where we need our listener to be invoked first, we can use a built-in method provided by the event emitter to accomplish this:

```
const EventEmitter = require('events');
const emitter = new EventEmitter();


function handleEventSecond() {
    console.log('I should be called second');
}
function handleEventFirst() {
    console.log('I should be called first');
}


emitter.on('event', handleEventSecond);
emitter.on('event', handleEventFirst);


emitter.emit('event');
```

Here, we attached **handleEventSecond** before **handleEventFirst**. When we emit the event, we will see the following output:

```
node v10.15.2 linux/amd64
>
I should be called second
I should be called first
=> true
>
```

Figure 9.19: Emitting the event after attaching the second event before the first one

Because the event listeners are invoked in the order in which they are attached, we can see that when we emit the event, **handleEventSecond** is called first and **handleEventFirst** is called after. If we want **handleEventFirst** to be called first without modifying the order when they are attached using **emitter.on()**, we can call **prependListener**:

```
. . .
emitter.on('event', handleEventSecond);
emitter.prependListener('event', handleEventFirst);


emitter.emit('event');
```

The preceding code will yield the following output:

Figure 9.20: Ordering the event using prependListener

This can help us keep the order of our listeners and make sure the higher-priority listener is always called first. We will talk about concurrency in listeners next.

Concurrency in Listeners

In the previous chapters, we mentioned how we can attach multiple listeners to our emitter and how these work when an event is emitted. Later, we also talked about how to prepend listeners so that they are called first when an event is emitted. The reason we might want to prepend listeners is that when listeners are called, they are called one by one synchronously. Consider the following example:

```
const EventEmitter = require('events');
const emitter = new EventEmitter();


function slowHandle() {
    console.log('doing calculation');
    for(let i = 0; i < 10000000; i++) {
        Math.random();
    }
}
```

```
function quickHandle() {
    console.log('i am called finally.');
}


emitter.on('event', slowHandle);
emitter.on('event', quickHandle);


emitter.emit('event');
```

Here, we have two listeners attached to the **event** type. When the event is emitted, it will call **slowHandle** first and **quickHandle** second. In **slowHandle**, we have a very large loop simulating a very time-consuming operation you can perform in the event listener. When we run the preceding code, we will first see **doing calculation** printed out, and then there will be a long wait until **I am called finally** is called. We can see that when the emitter invokes the event listeners, it does so synchronously. This might create issues for us because, in most cases, we do not want to wait for one listener to finish before we fire another one. There is an easy way to solve this, though: we can wrap our costly logic with the **setImmediate** function. The **setImmediate** function will wrap our logic into an immediately executed async block, meaning that the time-consuming loop is then non-blocking. We will cover the **setImmediate** function later in this book:

```
...

function slowHandle() {
    console.log('doing calculation');
    setImmediate(() => {
        for(let i = 0; i < 10000000; i++) {
            Math.random();
        }
    });
}
```

When we wrap our costly logic with **setImmediate()**, the code outputs **doing calculation** and **I am called finally** at almost the same time. By wrapping all the logic with **setImmediate**, we can make sure that it is invoked asynchronously.

Building Custom Event Emitters

There are cases where we want to build event emitting functionality into our own custom classes. We can do that by using **JavaScript ES6** inheritance. This allows us to create a custom class while extending all the functionality of event emitters. For example, let's say we are building a class for fire alarms:

```
class FireAlarm {
    constructor(modelNumber, type, cost) {
        this.modelNumber = modelNumber;
        this.type = type;
        this.cost = cost;
        this.batteryLevel = 10;
    }
    getDetail() {
        return '${this.modelNumber}:[${this.type}] - $${this.cost}';
    }
    test() {
        if (this.batteryLevel > 0) {
            this.batteryLevel -= 0.1;
            return true;
        }
        return false;
    }
}
```

Here, we have a **FireAlarm** class with a constructor storing information about this fire alarm. It also has a couple of custom methods for testing the alarm, such as checking the battery level, and a **getDetail** method to return a string representing information about the alarm. After defining this class, we can use the **FireAlarm** class like this:

```
const livingRoomAlarm = new FireAlarm('AX-00101', 'BATT', '20');

console.log(livingRoomAlarm.getDetail());
```

The following is the output of the preceding code:

```
node v10.15.2 linux/amd64
>
AX-00101:[BATT] - $20
=> undefined
>
```

Figure 9.21: Defining the fire alarm class

Now, we want to set up events on the fire alarm we just created. One way we can do this is by creating a generic event emitter and storing that inside our **FireAlarm** object:

```
class FireAlarm {

    constructor(modelNumber, type, cost) {

        this.modelNumber = modelNumber;

        this.type = type;

        this.cost = cost;

        this.batteryLevel = 10;

        this.emitter = new EventEmitter();

    }

    ...

}
```

And when we want to watch the events on the alarm, we must do something like this:

```
livingRoomAlarm.emitter.on('low-battery', () => {

    console.log('battery low');

});
```

While this is perfectly fine and will work for our use cases, this is certainly not the most robust solution. Because our fire alarm is the one emitting the event, we want something like this:

```
livingRoomAlarm.on('low-battery', () => {

    console.log('battery low');

});
```

By using `.on` directly on the fire alarm, we tell the future developer who's going to be working on this that our fire alarm is also an event emitter. But right now, our class definition does not allow one to be used. We can fix this by using class inheritance, where we can make our **FireAlarm** class extend the **EventEmitter** class. By doing that, it will have all the functionality of **EventEmitter**. We can modify our class like this:

```
class FireAlarm extends EventEmitter {

    constructor(modelNumber, type, cost) {

        this.modelNumber = modelNumber;

        this.type = type;

        this.cost = cost;

        this.batteryLevel = 10;

    }

    ...

}
```

By using the **extends** keyword followed by **EventEmitter**, we tell JavaScript that the **FireAlarm** class is a child class of **EventEmitter**. Therefore, it will inherit all the properties and methods from the parent. But this alone doesn't solve everything. When we run our code with the updated **FireAlarm**, we will see that an error is thrown:

Figure 9.22: An error is thrown when we run the code with the updated FireAlarm

This is happening because we are using a very customized class with a custom constructor and accessing **this** (this is used as a reference to the current object). We will need to make sure we call the parent constructor before that. To make this error disappear, we simply add a call to our parent constructor in our own constructor:

```
class FireAlarm extends EventEmitter {

    constructor(modelNumber, type, cost) {

        super();

        this.modelNumber = modelNumber;

        this.type = type;

        this.cost = cost;

        this.batteryLevel = 10;

    }

    ...

}
```

Now, let's test our own custom **EventEmitter**:

```
livingRoomAlarm.on('low-battery', () => {

    console.log('battery low');

});

livingRoomAlarm.emit('low-battery');
```

The following is the output of the preceding code:

```
node v10.15.2 linux/amd64
>
battery low
=> true
>
```

Figure 9.23: Event listener for the 'low-battery' event triggered correctly

Here, we can see that we are treating **livingRoomAlarm** just like a regular **EventEmitter**, and when we emit the *low-battery* event, we see that the event listener for that event is triggered correctly. In the next exercise, we will make a very simple chatroom application with everything we have learned about **EventEmitters**.

Exercise 68: Building A Chatroom Application

Previously, we talked about how to attach event listeners and emit events on our event emitter. In this exercise, we will build a simple piece of chatroom managing software that communicates with events. We will create multiple components and see how we can make them communicate with each other.

> **Note:**
>
> The code files for this exercise can be found at https://github.com/TrainingByPackt/ Professional-JavaScript/tree/master/Lesson09/Exercise68.

Perform the following steps to complete this exercise:

1. Create a **User** class:

```
class User {
    constructor(name) {
        this.name = name;
        this.messages = [];
        this.rooms = {};
    }
    joinRoom(room) {
        room.on('newMessage', (message) => {
            this.messages.push(message);
        });
        this.rooms[room.name] = room;
    }
    getMesssages(roomName) {
        return this.messages.filter((message) => {
            return message.roomName === roomName;
        })
    }
    printMessages(roomName) {
        this.getMesssages(roomName).forEach((message) => {
            console.log(`>> [${message.roomName}]:(${message.from}):
${message.message}`);
        });
    }
    sendMessage(roomName, message) {
        this.rooms[roomName].emit('newMessage', {
            message,
```

```
            roomName,
            from: this.name
        });
    }
}
```

Here, we created a **User** class for our user. It has a **joinRoom** method that we can call to join that user to a room. It also has a **sendMessage** method, which will send the message to everyone in the room. When we join a room, we also listen to all the new message events from that room and append messages when we receive them.

2. Create a **Room** class that extends the **EventEmitter** class:

```
class Room extends EventEmitter {
    constructor(name) {
        super();
        this.name = name;
    }
}
```

Here, we created a new **Room** class by extending the existing **EventEmitter** class. The reason we are doing this is that we want to have our own custom properties on our **room** object, and this creates more flexibility in our code.

3. Create two users, **bob** and **kevin**:

```
const bob = new User('Bob');
const kevin = new User('Kevin');
```

4. Create a room using our **Room** class:

```
const lobby = new Room('Lobby');
```

5. Join **bob** and **kevin** to **lobby**:

```
bob.joinRoom(lobby);
kevin.joinRoom(lobby);
```

6. Send a couple of messages from **bob**:

```
bob.sendMessage('Lobby', 'Hi all');
bob.sendMessage('Lobby', 'I am new to this room.');
```

7. Print the message log for **bob**:

    ```
    bob.printMessages('Lobby');
    ```

    The following is the output of the preceding code:

```
node v10.15.2 linux/amd64
.'.
>> [Lobby]:(Bob): Hi all
>> [Lobby]:(Bob): I am new to this room.
=> undefined
.'.
```

Figure 9.24: Printing the message log for bob

Here, you can see that all of our messages are added correctly to the log of **bob**. Next, we will check the log of **kevin**.

8. Print the message log for **kevin**:

    ```
    kevin.printMessage('Lobby');
    ```

    The following is the output of the preceding code:

```
node v10.15.2 linux/amd64
.'.
>> [Lobby]:(Bob): Hi all
>> [Lobby]:(Bob): I am new to this room.
=> undefined
.'.
```

Figure 9.25: Printing the message log for kevin

Even though we never explicitly did anything with **kevin**, he is receiving all the messages because he is listening to a new message event in the room.

9. Send messages from **kevin** and **bob**:

    ```
    kevin.sendMessage('Lobby', 'Hi bob');
    bob.sendMessage('Lobby', 'Hey kevin');
    kevin.sendMessage('Lobby', 'Welcome!');
    ```

10. Check the message log for **kevin**:

    ```
    kevin.printMessages('Lobby');
    ```

The following is the output of the preceding code:

```
node v10.15.2 linux/amd64
>
>> [Lobby]:(Bob): Hi all
>> [Lobby]:(Bob): I am new to this room.
>> [Lobby]:(Kevin): Hi bob
>> [Lobby]:(Bob): Hey kevin
>> [Lobby]:(Kevin): Welcome!
=> undefined
>
```

Figure 9.26: Checking the message log for kevin

Here, we can see that all our messages are added correctly to our **user** objects. Because we are using event emitters, we avoided passing references of our receiver around. Also, because we are emitting the message event on our room and our users just listen to that event, we do not need to manually iterate through all the users in the room and pass the message on.

11. Let's modify **joinRoom** and **constructor** so that we can remove the listener later:

```
class User {
    constructor(name) {
        this.name = name;
        this.messages = [];
        this.rooms = {};
        this.messageListener = (message) => {
            this.messages.push(message);
        }
    }
    joinRoom(room) {
        this.messageListener = (message) => {
            this.messages.push(message);
        }
        room.on('newMessage', this.messageListener);
        this.rooms[room.name] = room;
    }
    ...
}
```

When we remove our listener, we need to pass a reference of that listener function, Because of this, we need to store that reference in the object so that we can use it to remove our listener later.

12. Add **leaveRoom**:

```
class User {
    ...
    leaveRoom(roomName) {
        this.rooms[roomName].removeListener('newMessage', this.
messageListener);
        delete this.rooms[roomName];
    }
}
```

Here, we are using the function reference we set in our constructor and passing it to the **removeListener** for our room. We also removed the reference in our object so that it can be released in memory later.

13. Remove **bob** from **room**:

```
bob.leaveRoom('Lobby');
```

14. Send a message from **kevin**:

```
kevin.sendMessage('Lobby', 'I got a good news for you guys');
```

15. Check the message list for **bob**:

```
bob.printMessages('Lobby');
```

The following is the output of the preceding code:

```
node v10.15.2 linux/amd64
>
>> [Lobby]:(Bob): Hi all
>> [Lobby]:(Bob): I am new to this room.
>> [Lobby]:(Kevin): Hi bob
>> [Lobby]:(Bob): Hey kevin
>> [Lobby]:(Kevin): Welcome!
=> undefined
>
```

Figure 9.27: Checking the message list for bob

Because **bob** left the room, and we removed the message listener, the **newMessage** event handler is not invoked again when a new message event is emitted.

16. Check the message list for **kevin**:

```
kevin.printMessages('Lobby');
```

The following is the output of the preceding code:

```
node v10.15.2 linux/amd64
>
>> [Lobby]:(Bob): Hi all
>> [Lobby]:(Bob): I am new to this room.
>> [Lobby]:(Kevin): Hi bob
>> [Lobby]:(Bob): Hey kevin
>> [Lobby]:(Kevin): Welcome!
>> [Lobby]:(Kevin): I got a good news for you guys
=> undefined
>
```

Figure 9.28: Checking the message list for kevin again

When we check the message list for **kevin**, we should still able to see that he is still getting new messages from the room. If this was done using the traditional approach, we would need to write way more code to accomplish the same thing, which would be very error-prone.

In this exercise, we built a mock chat application with events in Node.js. We can see how easy passing events is in Node.js and how we can use it properly. Event-driven programming is not for every application, but when we need to connect multiple components together, it is much easier to implement that logic with events. The preceding code can still be improved – we can add notifications to the room when a user leaves a room and we can add checks while adding and removing rooms to make sure we aren't adding a duplicate room and make sure we are only removing rooms that we are in. Please feel free to extend this functionality on your own.

During this chapter we went over ways we can use events to manage the communication between components in our applications. In the next activity, we will build an event-driven module.

Activity 13: Building an Event-Driven Module

Suppose you are working for a software company that builds simulators for smoke detectors. You need to build a smoke detector simulator that raises an alarm when the detector's battery drops below a certain level. Here are the requirements:

- The detector needs to emit an **alarm event**.

- The smoke detector needs to emit a *low battery* event when the battery is below 0.5 units.

- Each smoke detector has 10 units of battery level when it's initially created.

- The test function on the smoke detector will return true if the battery level is above 0 and false if it's below 0. Each time a test function is run, it will decrease the battery by 0.1 units.

- You need to modify the provided **House** class to add the **addDetector** and **demoveDetector** methods.

- **addDetector** will take a detector object and attach a listener for the alarm event before printing out both *low battery* and an *alarm event* when they are emitted.

- The **removeDetector** method will take a **detector** object and remove the listeners.

Perform the following steps to complete this activity:

1. Open the **event.js** file and find the existing code. Then, modify and add your own changes to it.

2. Import the **events** module.

3. Create the **SmokeDetector** class that extends **EventEmitter** and set **batteryLevel** to **10**.

4. Create a **test** method inside the **SmokeDetector** class to emit the *low battery* message.

5. Create the **House** class, which will store the instances of our alarms.

6. Create an **addDetector** method in the **House** class, which will attach the event listeners.

7. Create a **removeDetector** method, which will help us remove the *alarm event* listeners we attached previously.

8. Create a **House** instance called **myHouse**.

9. Create a `SmokeDetector` instance called `detector`.

10. Add the detector to `myHouse`.

11. Create a loop to call the test function 96 times.

12. Emit an alarm on the `detector` object.

13. Remove the detector from the `myHouse` object.

14. Test it to emit alarms on the detector.

> **Note**
>
> The solution for this activity can be found on page 617.

In this activity, we learned how we can model a smoke detector using event-driven programming. By using this approach, we eliminated the need to store multiple instances in our `House` object and avoided using many lines of code for their interactions.

In the section, we went over ways we can use the event system fully to help us manage complex communications in our application. In the next section, we will go over some of the best practices for working with event emitters.

Event-Driven Programming Best Practices

In the previous chapter, we mentioned ways we can create event-driven components using the event emitter and event emitter inheritance. But often, your code needs to be more than just able to work correctly. Having a better-managed code structure will not only make our code look less messy, it can also help us avoid making some avoidable mistakes in the future. In this section, we will go over some of the best practices when dealing with events in our code.

Recalling what we went over at the beginning of this chapter, we can pass events using the `EventEmitter` object:

```
const EventEmitter = require('events');
const emitter = new EventEmitter();
emitter.emit('event');
```

When we want to use the event emitter we have created, we will need to have its reference so that we can attach listeners and call the **emit** function on the emitter when we want to emit events later. This might cause our source code to be incredibly large, which will make future maintenance very difficult:

```
const EventEmitter = require('events');

const userEmitter = new EventEmitter();

const registrationEmitter = new EventEmitter();

const votingEmitter = new EventEmitter();

const postEmitter = new EventEmitter();

const commentEmitter = new EventEmitter();


userEmitter.on('update', (diff) => {
    userProfile.update(diff);
});


registrationEmitter.on('user registered:activated', (user) => {
    database.add(user, true);
});


registrationEmitter.on('user registered: not activated', (user) => {
    database.add(user, false);
});


votingEmitter.on('upvote', () => {
    userProfile.addVote();
});


votingEmitter.on('downvote', () => {
    userProfile.removeVote();
});


postEmitter.on('new post', (post) => {
```

```
        database.addPost(post);
    });


    postEmitter.on('edit post', (post) => {
        database.upsertPost(post);
    });


    commentEmitter.on('new comment', (comment) => {
        database.addComment(comment.post, comment);
    });
```

To be able to use our emitters, we need to make sure that our emitter is accessible in the current scope. One way to do this is to create a file to keep all our emitters and the logic for attaching the event listeners. While this simplifies our code a lot, we will create very large source code that will confuse future developers, and maybe even us. To make our code more modularized, we can start by pulling all the listener functions into their respective files. Consider the following huge source code:

```
// index.js
const EventEmitter = require('events');
const userEmitter = new EventEmitter();
const registrationEmitter = new EventEmitter();
const votingEmitter = new EventEmitter();
const postEmitter = new EventEmitter();
const commentEmitter = new EventEmitter();


// Listeners
const updateListener = () => {};
const activationListener = () => {};
const noActivationListener = () => {};
const upvoteListener = () => {};
const downVoteListener = () => {};
const newPostListener = () => {};
const editPostListener = () => {};
```

```
const newCommentListener = () => {};


userEmitter.on('update', updateListener);


registrationEmitter.on('user registered:activated', activationListener);


registrationEmitter.on('user registered: not activated',
noActivationListener);


votingEmitter.on('upvote', upvoteListener);


votingEmitter.on('downvote', downVoteListener);


postEmitter.on('new post', newPostListener);


postEmitter.on('edit post', editPostListener);


commentEmitter.on('new comment', newCommentListener);
```

Just by doing this, we have considerably reduced the file size of our code. But we can do more. One way to keep our code organized is to put all the emitters in one file and then import it when we need them. We can do that by creating a file called **emitters.js** and storing all the emitters in that file:

```
// emitters.js
const EventEmitter = require('events');


const userEmitter = new EventEmitter();
const registrationEmitter = new EventEmitter();
const votingEmitter = new EventEmitter();
const postEmitter = new EventEmitter();
const commentEmitter = new EventEmitter();


module.exports = {
    userEmitter,
```

```
    registrationEmitter,

    votingEmitter,

    postEmitter,

    commentEmitter

};
```

What we did here is to create all our emitters in one file and set that **emitter** file to the exports module. By doing this, we can have all the emitters in one place and then, when we use the emitters, we can just import the file. This changes our code to the following:

```
// index.js

// Emitters

const {

    userEmitter,

    registrationEmitter,

    votingEmitter,

    postEmitter,

    commentEmitter

} = require('./emitters.js');

... rest of index.js
```

Now, when we import **emitter.js**, we can use object restructuring to only pick the emitter we want. We can have multiple emitters in one file, and we can just pick the one we want when we require it. When we want to emit an event on the **userEmitter**, all we need to do is import the emitter into our code and send that event over:

```
const { userEmitter } = require('./emitters.js');


function userAPIHandler(request, response) {

    const payload = request.payload;


    const event = {

        diff: payload.diff

    };


    userEmitter.emit('update', event);

}
```

We can see that whenever we want to use **userEmitter**, we can just import our **emitter** file over. This also applies when we want to attach listeners:

```
const { userEmitter } = require('./emitters.js');


userEmitter.on('update', (diff) => {
    database.update(diff);
})
```

When we separate our emitters into different files, we not only make our code smaller but also make it more modular. By pulling our emitters into a separate file, it makes it very easy for us to reuse that file if we want to access our emitters in the future. By doing this, we do not need to pass our emitters around in functions, thus ensuring that our function declaration isn't cluttered.

Node.js Built-In Modules

In the previous section, we extensively went over the **events** module and learned everything about using events to achieve easy communication within our applications. The **events** module is a built-in module offered by Node.js, meaning that we do not need to use **npm** to install it. In this module, we will discuss how to use the **fs**, **path**, and **util** modules.

path

The **path** module is a built-in module that provides utilities that can help us work with file paths and filenames.

path.join(...paths)

Path.join() is a very useful function when we are working with directories and files in our applications. It allows us to join paths together and output a path string that we can use in the **fs** module. To use **join** paths, we can call the **join** method and provide it with a list of paths. Let's look at the following example:

```
const currentDir = '/usr/home/me/Documents/project';
const dataDir = './data';
const assetDir = './assets';
```

If we want to access the data directory in our current directory, we can use the **path. join** function to combine different paths into one string:

```
const absoluteDataDir = path.join(currentDir, dataDir);
```

The following is the output of the preceding code:

```
node v10.16.0
>
=> '/usr/home/me/Documents/project/data'
>
```

Figure 9.29: Using the path.join function to combine different paths

It also works with `..` and `.`, if you are familiar with how the POSIX system signifies the current directory and parent directories. `..` represents the parent directory while `.` represents the current directory. For example, the following code can give us the path of the parent directory of our current directory:

```
const parentOfProject = path.join(currentDir, '..');
```

The following is the output of the preceding code:

```
node v10.16.0
>
=> '/usr/home/me/Documents'
>
```

Figure 9.30: Showing the parent directory of our current directory

path.parse(path)

When we want to get information about a file path, we can use the `path.parse()` function to get its root directory, base directory, filename, and extension. Let's look at the following example:

```
const myData = '/usr/home/me/Documents/project/data/data.json';
```

If we want to parse this file path, we can call **path.parse** with the **myData** string to get the different path elements:

```
path.parse(myData);
```

This will generate the following output:

```
node v10.16.0
>
=> { root: '/',
  dir: '/usr/home/me/Documents/project/data',
  base: 'data.json',
  ext: '.json',
  name: 'data' }
>
```

Figure 9.31: File path parsed using the path.parse function

Here, we can see that our file path includes a filename with a base name of **data.json**. The extension is **.json** and the filename is **data**. It also parsed out the directory in which the file is present.

path.format(path)

In the previous **parse** function, we managed to parse out our file path into its respected components. We can use **path.format** to combine that information into a single string path. Let's have a look at it:

```
path.format({
    dir: '/usr/home/me/Pictures',
    name: 'me',
    ext: '.jpeg'
});
```

The following is the output of the preceding code:

```
node v10.16.0
>
=> '/usr/home/me/Pictures/me.jpeg'
>
```

Figure 9.32: Combining information into a single string path using path.format

This gives us the file path from the components we supplied to it.

fs

The **fs** module is a built-in module that provides APIs for you so that you can interact with the host filesystem. It is very useful when we need to work with files in our application. In this section, we will talk about how we can use the **fs** module in our application with **async** and **await**. Later, we will go over the recently added **fs.promises** API, which provides the same functionality but returns a promise rather than using callbacks.

> **Note**
>
> In this section, we will be using a POSIX system. If you are using a Windows system, make sure that you update the file path to the Windows equivalent. To import the fs module into your code, execute the following command:

```
const fs = require('fs');
```

fs.createReadStream(path, options)

When we are dealing with large files in Node.js, it is advised to always use `stream`. To create a read stream, we can call the `fs.createReadStream` method. It will return a stream object that we can attach to event handlers so that they get the content of the file:

```
const stream = fs.createReadStream('file.txt', 'utf-8');
```

fs.createWriteStream(path, options)

This works similar to `createReadStream`, but instead creates a writable stream that we can use to stream contents to it:

```
const stream = fs.createWriteStream('output', 'utf-8');
```

fs.stat(path, callback)

The `fs.stat` method is very useful when we need detailed information about the file we are accessing. We also see many developers use `fs.stat` to check for the existence of the file before calling, opening, reading, or writing data to it. While checking the file's existence using `stat` doesn't create any new issues, it is not recommended to do this. We should just use the error that's returned from the function we are using; this will eliminate any extra layers of logic and can reduce the number of API calls.

Consider the following example:

```
const fs = require('fs');


fs.stat('index.js', (error, stat) => {
    console.log(stat);
});
```

This will give us output similar to the following:

```
node v10.15.2 linux/amd64
>
Stats {
  dev: 1006,
  mode: 33188,
  nlink: 1,
  uid: 1000,
  gid: 1000,
  rdev: 0,
  blksize: 4096,
  ino: 1614411,
  size: 92,
  blocks: 8,
  atimeMs: 1562617590045.512,
  mtimeMs: 1562617589825.4946,
  ctimeMs: 1562617589825.4946,
  birthtimeMs: 1562616740050.4658,
  atime: 2019-07-08T20:26:30.046Z,
  mtime: 2019-07-08T20:26:29.825Z,
  ctime: 2019-07-08T20:26:29.825Z,
  birthtime: 2019-07-08T20:12:20.050Z }
=> undefined
>
```

Figure 9.33: Output after using the fs.stat method

fs.readFile(path, options, callback)

This is the function that most people will be familiar with. When supplied with a file path, the method will attempt to read the entire content of a file. It will do so in an async fashion, and the callback will be called with the entire content of the file. When the file doesn't exist, the callback will be called with an error.

Consider the following example:

```
const fs = require('fs');


fs.readFile('index.js', (error, data) => {
    console.log(data);
});
```

This will give us the following output:

```
node v10.15.2 linux/amd64
>
<Buffer 63 6f 6e 73 74 20 66 73 20 3d 20 72 65 71 75 69 72 65 28 27 66 73 27 29 3b 0a 0a 66
73 2e 72 65 61 64 46 69 6c 65 28 27 69 6e 64 65 78 2e 6a 73 27 2c ... >
=> undefined
>
```

Figure 9.34: Reading the entire content of a file using the fs.readFile function

This didn't output the result we wanted. This is because we didn't supply the encoding in our options; to read the contents into a string, we will need to supply encoding options. This changes our code into the following:

```
fs.readFile('index.js', 'utf-8', (error, data) => {

    console.log(data);

});
```

Now, when we run the preceding code, it will give us the following output:

```
node v10.15.2 linux/amd64
>
const fs = require('fs');

fs.readFile('index.js', 'utf-8', (error, data) => {
    console.log(data);
});
=> undefined
>
```

Figure 9.35: Reading the entire content of a file using the fs.readFile function after encoding

We just made a program that output itself.

fs.readFileSync(path, options)

This function does the same thing as the **readFile** method, but executes the **read** function synchronously, meaning it will block execution. During program startup, it is recommended – and is expected – to be called only once. The synchronous function is not recommended when it needs to be invoked more than once.

fs.writeFile(file, data, options, callback)

The **writeFile** function writes data to the file we specified. It will also replace the existing file unless you pass an append as **flag** to options.

fs.writeFileSync()

Just like **readFileSync**, it does the same as its non-sync counterpart. The difference between them is that this does the operation synchronously.

Exercise 69: Basic Usage of the Fs Module

In this exercise, we will be using the **fs** module to read and write files in our application. We will be using the methods we covered in the preceding section and will use them with callbacks. Then, we will **promisify** them so that we can use them with **async** and **await**.

Perform the following steps to complete this exercise:

1. Create a new file called **test.txt**:

```
fs.writeFile('test.txt', 'Hello world', (error) => {
    if (error) {
        console.error(error);
        return;
    }
    console.log('Write complete');
});
```

If you did this correctly, you will see the following output:

Figure 9.36: New test.txt file created

You should be able to see the new file in the same directory as your source code:

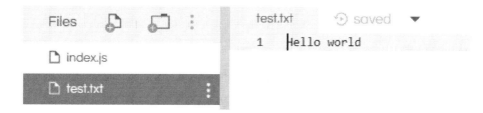

Figure 9.37: New file created in the same directory as your source code

2. Read its contents and output it in the console:

```
fs.readFile('test.txt', 'utf-8', (error, data) => {
    if (error) {
        console.error(error);
    }
    console.log(data);
});
```

This simply reads our file back; we are supplying an encoding because we want the output to be a string instead of a buffer. This will give us the following output:

Figure 9.38: Reading the file's content using fs.readFile

3. Try to read from a file that doesn't exist:

```
fs.readFile('nofile.txt', 'utf-8', (error, data) => {
    if (error) {
        console.error(error);
    }
    console.log(data);
});
```

When we try to open a file that doesn't exist, our callback will be called with an error. It is recommended that we handle any file-related errors inside the handler instead of creating a separate function to check it. When we run the preceding code, we will get the following error:

Figure 9.39: Error thrown when we try to read a file that doesn't exist

4. Let's create our own version of **readFile** with promises:

```
function readFile(file, options) {
    return new Promise((resolve, reject) => {
        fs.readFile(file, options, (error, data) => {
            if (error) {
                return reject(error);
            }
            resolve(data);
        })
    })
}
```

This is the same thing we could have done with any callback-based methods, as follows:

```
readFile('test.txt', 'utf-8').then(console.log);
```

This will generate the following output:

```
node v10.15.2 linux/amd64
>
Hello world
=> undefined
>
```

Figure 9.40: Creating a readFile using callback-based methods

5. Let's use file **stat** to get information about our file. After Node.js 10.0.0, **fsPromises** was introduced, so instead of converting them into promises and returning functions manually, we can simply import **fsPromise** and call the promised counterpart:

```
const fsPromises = require('fs').promises;
fsPromises.stat('test.txt').then(console.log);
```

This will generate the following output:

```
node v10.16.0
>
=> Promise { <pending> }
(node:27) ExperimentalWarning: The fs.promises API is experimental
Stats {
  dev: 1322,
  mode: 33188,
  nlink: 1,
  uid: 1000,
  gid: 1000,
  rdev: 0,
  blksize: 4096,
  ino: 1589614,
  size: 11,
  blocks: 8,
  atimeMs: 1562873635180.9255,
  mtimeMs: 1562873635168.9246,
  ctimeMs: 1562873635168.9246,
  birthtimeMs: 1562873635168.9246,
  atime: 2019-07-11T19:33:55.181Z,
  mtime: 2019-07-11T19:33:55.169Z,
  ctime: 2019-07-11T19:33:55.169Z,
  birthtime: 2019-07-11T19:33:55.169Z }
>
```

Figure 9.41: Calling the promise counterpart by importing fspromise

Here, you can get the size, creation time, modification time, and permission information about our file.

In this exercise, we went over some of the basic usages of the **fs** module. It is a very useful module in Node.js. Next, we will talk about how we should handle large files in Node.js.

Handling Large Files in Node.js

In the previous exercise, we went over how we can use the **fs** module to read file contents in Node.js. This works well when we are dealing with small files that are smaller than 100 MB. When we are dealing with large files (> 2 GB), sometimes, it is not possible to read the entire file using **fs.readFile**. Consider the following scenario.

You are given a 20 GB text file and you need to process the data in the file line by line and write the output into an output file. Your computer only has 8 GB of memory.

When you are using **fs.readFile**, it will attempt to read the entire content of the file into the computer's memory. In our case, this won't be possible because our computer does not have enough memory installed to fit the entire content of the file we are processing. Here, we need a separate approach to this problem. To process large files, we need to use streams.

The stream is an interesting concept in programming. It treats data not as a single block of memory but a stream of data that comes from the source one chunk at a time. This way, we do not need to fit all the data inside the memory. To create a file stream, we simply use the provided method in the **fs** module:

```
const fs = require('fs');
const stream = fs.createReadStream('file.txt', 'utf-8');
```

By using **fs.createReadStream**, we create a file stream that we can use later to get the contents of the file. We call this function just like **fs.readFile**, with the file path and encoding. The difference with this is that this doesn't require a callback to be supplied because it simply returns a **stream** object. To get the file content from the stream, we need to attach the event handlers to the **stream** object:

```
stream.on('data', data => {
    // Data will be the content of our file
    Console.log(data);
    // Or
    Data = data + data;
});
```

Inside the event handler for the **data** event, we will get the content of the file, and this handler will be called multiple times when the file is read by the stream. When we finish reading the file, we will also get an event emitted on the stream object to handle this event:

```
stream.on('close', () => {
    // Process clean up process
});
```

Util

Util is a module that includes a lot of functions that help with the Node.js internal APIs. These can also be useful in our own development.

util.callbackify(function)

This is very useful when we are working on **async** and **await** code with existing legacy callback-based code. To use our **async** function as a callback-based function, we can call **util.callbackify** function. Let's consider the following example:

```
async function outputSomething() {
    return 'Something';
}


outputSomething().then(console.log);
```

The following is the output of the preceding code:

```
node v10.16.0
>
Something
=> Promise { <pending> }
>
```

Figure 9.42: Using the async function as a callback-based function

To use this **async** function with callbacks, simple call **callbackify**:

```
const callbackOutputSomething = util.callbackify(outputSomething);
```

Then, we can use it like this:

```
callbackOutputSomething((err, result) => {
    if (err) throw err;
    console.log('got result', result);
})
```

This will generate the following output:

Figure 9.43: Using the async function by calling the callbackify function

We have successfully converted an **async** function into a legacy function that uses callbacks. This is very useful when we need to keep backward compatibility.

util.promisify(function)

There is also a very useful method in the **util** module to help us **promisify** callback-based functions. This method takes a function as its parameter and will return a new function that returns a promise, like so:

```
function callbackFunction(param, callback) {
    callback(null, 'I am calling back with: ${param}');
}
```

callbackFunction takes a parameter and will call the callback function we supplied with a new string. To convert this function to use promises, we can use the **promisify** function:

```
const promisifiedFunction = util.promisify(callbackFunction);
```

This returns a new function. Later, we can use it as a function that returns a promise:

```
promisifiedFunction('hello world').then(console.log);
```

The following is the output of the preceding code:

```
node v10.16.0
>
I am calling back with: hello world
=> Promise { <pending> }
>
```

Figure 9.44: The promisify function is used for callbacks

There are also a number of type checking methods in the **util** module, which are very useful when we are trying to figure out the types of variables in our application.

Timer

The timer module gives us an API for scheduling timer functions. We can use it to set delays on parts of our code or to execute our code at desired intervals. Unlike the previous modules, the **timer** module does not need to be imported before we use it. Let's have a look at all the timer functions that are provided in Node.js and how we can use them in our application.

setInterval(callback, delay)

When we want to set up a function that is repeatedly executed by Node.js, we can use the **setInterval** function while providing a callback and a delay. To use it, we call the **setInterval** function with a function we want to run and a delay in milliseconds. For example, if we want to print the same message every second, we can achieve this like this:

```
setInterval(() => {
    console.log('I am running every second');
}, 1000);
```

When we run the preceding code, we will see the following output:

```
node v10.16.0
>
=> Timeout {
  _called: false,
  _idleTimeout: 1000,
  _idlePrev: [TimersList],
  _idleNext: [TimersList],
  _idleStart: 970,
  _onTimeout: [Function],
  _timerArgs: undefined,
  _repeat: 1000,
  _destroyed: false,
  [Symbol(unrefed)]: false,
  [Symbol(asyncId)]: 8,
  [Symbol(triggerId)]: 7 }
I am running every second
I am running every second
I am running every second
I am running every second
I am running every second
I am running every second
I am running every second
>
```

Figure 9.45: Setting up a repeatedly executing function using the setInterval function

Here, we can see that the message is printed out every second.

setTimeout(callback, delay)

Using this function, we can set a one-time delayed invocation of a function. When we want to wait a certain amount of time before we run the function, we can use **setTimeout** to achieve this. In the previous sections, we also used **setTimeout** to simulate network and disk requests in our tests. To use it, we need to pass a function we want to run and a delay integer in milliseconds. If we want to print a message after 3 seconds, we can use the following code:

```
setTimeout(() => {
    console.log('I waited 3 seconds to run');
}, 3000);
```

This will generate the following output:

```
node v10.16.0
>
=> Timeout {
  _called: false,
  _idleTimeout: 3000,
  _idlePrev: [TimersList],
  _idleNext: [TimersList],
  _idleStart: 198,
  _onTimeout: [Function],
  _timerArgs: undefined,
  _repeat: null,
  _destroyed: false,
  [Symbol(unrefed)]: false,
  [Symbol(asyncId)]: 8,
  [Symbol(triggerId)]: 7 }
I waited 3 seconds to run
>
```

Figure 9.46: Setting a one-time delayed invocation of a function using the setTimeout function

You will see that the message is printed out after 3 seconds. This is very useful when we need delayed invocation of a function or just want to use it to mock API calls in our tests.

setImmediate(callback)

By using this method, we can push a function to be executed at the end of the event loop. If you want to invoke a certain piece of code after everything has completed running in the current event loop, you can use **setImmediate** to achieve this. Have a look at the following example:

```
setImmediate(() => {
    console.log('I will be printed out second');
});
console.log('I am printed out first');
```

Here, we made a function that prints out **I will be printed out second**, which will be executed at the end of the event loop. When we execute this, we will see the following output:

```
node v10.16.0
>
I am printed out first
I will be printed out second
=> undefined
>
```

Figure 9.47: Function to be executed at the end of the event loop pushed using setimmediate

We can also achieve the same by using **setTimeout** and using **0** as the delay parameter:

```
setTimeout(() => {
    console.log('I will be printed out second');
}, 0);
console.log('I am printed out first');
```

clearInterval(timeout)

When we use **setInterval** to create a recurring function, the function also returns an object representing the timer. When we want to stop the interval from running, we can use **clearInterval** to clear the timer:

```
const myInterval = setInterval(() => {
    console.log('I am being printed out');
}, 1000);


clearInterval(myInterval);
```

When we run the preceding code, we will see no output being produced because we cleared the interval we just created and it never got the chance to run:

```
node v10.16.0
>
=> undefined
>
```

Figure 9.48: Stopping the interval from running using the clearInterval function

If we want to run this interval for 3 seconds, we can wrap **clearInterval** inside **setTimeout** so that it will clear our interval after **3.1** seconds. We are giving 100 ms extra because we want the third invocation to happen before we clear the interval:

```
setTimeout(() => {

    clearInterval(myInterval);

}, 3100);
```

When we run the preceding code, we will see our output printed out 3 times:

```
node v10.16.0

=> Timeout {
  _called: false,
  _idleTimeout: 3100,
  _idlePrev: [TimersList],
  _idleNext: [TimersList],
  _idleStart: 1123,
  _onTimeout: [Function],
  _timerArgs: undefined,
  _repeat: null,
  _destroyed: false,
  [Symbol(unrefed)]: false,
  [Symbol(asyncId)]: 10,
  [Symbol(triggerId)]: 7 }
I am being printed out
I am being printed out
I am being printed out
>
```

Figure 9.49: Using setTimeout to wrap clearInterval within the specified seconds

This is very useful when we are dealing with multiple scheduled timers. By clearing them, we can avoid issues such as memory leaks and unexpected issues in our application.

Activity 14: Building a File Watcher

In this activity, we will create a file watcher using timer functions that will indicate any modifications in the file. These timer functions will set up a watch on the file and will generate output every time there is a change in the file. Let's get started:

- We will need to create a **fileWatcher** class.

- A file watcher will be created with a file to watch. If no file exists, it will throw an exception.

- The file watcher will take another parameter to store the time between checks.

- The file watcher needs to allow us to remove the watch on the file.

- The file watcher needs to emit the file change event when the file is changed.

- When the file is changed, the file watcher will emit the event with the new content of the file.

Open the **filewatcher.js** file and do your work in that file. Perform the following steps to complete this activity:

1. Import our libraries; that is, **fs** and **events**.

2. Create a file watcher class that extends the **EventEmitter** class. Use a **modify** timestamp to keep track of the file change.

3. Create the **startWatch** method to start watching the changes on the file.

4. Create the **stopWatch** method to stop watching the changes on the file.

5. Create a **test.txt** file in the same directory as **filewatch.js**.

6. Create a **FileWatcher** instance and start watching the file.

7. Modify some content in **test.txt** and save it.

8. Modify **startWatch** so that it also retrieves the new content.

9. Modify **startWatch** so that it emits events when the file is modified and an error when it encounters an error.

10. Attach event handlers to the error and change it in **fileWatcher**.

11. Run the code and modify **test.txt** to see the result.

> **Note**
>
> The solution for this activity can be found on page 620.

If you see the preceding output, this means your event system and file reading is working perfectly. Please feel free to extend this functionality on your own. You can also try to enable watching the entire folder or multiple files. In this activity, we just created a simple `fileWatcher` class using the filesystem module and event-driven programming. Using this helped us create a much smaller code base and gave us more clarity when we read the code directly.

Summary

In this chapter, we talked about the event system in JavaScript and how we can use the built-in `events` module to create our own event emitters. Later, we went over a few useful built-in modules and their sample usage. Using event-driven programming can help us avoid interlaced logic when we are writing a program that requires multiple components to communicate with each other. Also, by using built-in modules, we can avoid adding modules that provide the same functionality and avoid creating projects with huge dependencies. We also mentioned how we can use timers to control program execution, `fs` to manipulate files, and `path` to combine and get useful information about our file path. These are all very useful modules that can help us later when building applications. In the next chapter, we will go over how we can use functional programming in JavaScript.

10

Functional Programming with JavaScript

Learning Objectives

By the end of this chapter, you will be able to:

- Use pure functions in Redux reducers and selectors

- Solve advanced function testing situations

- Apply currying, partial application, and closures in modern JavaScript applications

- Implement a compose function for use in a backend for frontend (BFF) built with micro

- Apply JavaScript built-ins to write in an immutable style specifically in a Redux application

- Implement a query and a mutation in the context of a BFF using GraphQL

- Select from three approaches to handle side effects in a React/Redux application

In this chapter, you will learn about the concepts of functional programming, how to apply them in JavaScript, and identify them "in the wild" in popular libraries such as React, Redux, and systems such as the GraphQL query language.

Introduction

Functional programming leans heavily on the mathematical definition of functions. Mathematical functions are defined through a declaration expression. The functional programming style is also declarative (as opposed to imperative programming) and promotes expressions over statements.

JavaScript has functional programming constructs built into it. Unlocking the functional programming style in JavaScript is crucial to reaching a deeper understanding of the language and its ecosystem.

As part of each section, React, Redux, and DOM access and testing patterns in JavaScript will be used to illustrate pragmatic functional programming in JavaScript. More recent developments such as GraphQL and **backend for frontends** (**BFFs**) will also be included to show how functional programming permeates both the present and the future of the JavaScript programming language.

Functional programming concepts can explain why Redux reducers and React render functions can't contain API calls. A lot of JavaScript patterns and best practices are enabled by functional constructs in the language; leveraging functional programming leads to more expressive, concise JavaScript programs that are easier to reason about, modify, and extend.

Functions – First-Class Citizens

Functions being **first-class** means they are considered by the language to be like any other "value" type. This means that, in JavaScript, a function can be used just like a number, a string, a Boolean, an array, an object, and so on.

> **Note**
>
> Now would probably be a good time to see how well-versed in JavaScript data types everyone is. The primitives are Boolean, Null, Undefined, Number, (BigInt), String, Symbol, Object → Array/Set/Map. They can be found under the Object data type.

First-Class Functions – Idiomatic JavaScript Building Blocks

Another way to define first-class support is as "functions are first-class if they are regular values." That means that a function can be assigned (as a value) to a variable, passed into other functions as a parameter, and be the return value of another function. Let's try and understand the preceding concept with code examples.

A function can be assigned to a variable in JavaScript and applied to function expressions (as follows) and arrow functions. A variable can hold a reference to an already defined function or a function that's been declared inline. The function can be named or anonymous:

```
const fn = function run() {

  return 'Running...';

};



function fnExpression() {}



const otherFn = fnExpression;



const anonymousArrow = () => {};
```

A function can be set as a value in an Array:

```
const fn = () => {};

const operations = [

  fn,

  function() {

    console.log('Regular functions work');

  },

  () => console.log('Arrows work too')

];
```

A function can be set as a value in an object. This example uses ECMAScript 6/2015 shorthand properties and methods. We also assert that the output of **Module.fn** is the same as the output of **fn**:

```
const fn = () => 'Running...';

const Module = {

  fn,

  method1() {},

  arrow: () => console.log('works too')

};

console.assert(Module.fn() === 'Running...');
```

A function can be passed as an argument to another function:

```
const fn = () => 'Running...';
function runner(fn) {
  return fn();
}
console.assert(runner(fn) === 'Running...');
```

Inversion of Control Using First-Class Functions

Having first-class functions in JavaScript means that injecting a dependency can be as small as passing a function.

In languages where functions are not first-class, we might have to pass an object (instance of a class) into a constructor to be able to inject a dependency into the consumer of said dependency. In JavaScript, we can leverage the fact that functions are first-class citizens and simply inject a function implementation. The simplest example of this comes from the preceding **runner** function. It calls whatever function is passed into it as a parameter.

This type of dependency is very useful in JavaScript. Types are dynamic and tend to go unchecked. The benefit of class and class types such as checked errors and method overloading don't exist in JavaScript.

JavaScript functions have a simple interface. They are called with zero or more parameters and cause side effects (network requests, file I/O) and/or output some data.

In a dependency injection scenario without types or type checks, passing a single function instead of a whole instance is very beneficial for the dependency's consumer (the code where the dependency is injected into).

The following example illustrates a scenario where a JavaScript application can be run both on the client and the server. This is called a universal JavaScript application, that is, a JavaScript program that runs both in Node.js and in browsers. Universal JavaScript is usually achieved through a combination of build tools and patterns such as dependency injection.

In this case, when an HTTP call is made server-side, a header-based authorization mechanism is used. When the HTTP call is made from the client, a cookie-based authorization mechanism is used.

See the following function definition:

```
function getData(transport) {
  return transport('https://hello-world-micro.glitch.me').then(res => res.
text())
}
```

Server-side code that consumes **getData** would look like the following, where an **axios** function instance is created to default the authorization header. This function instance is then passed as **transport** to **getData**:

```
const axios = require('axios');
const axiosWithServerHeaders = axios.create({
  headers: { Authorization: 'Server-side allowed' }
});
getData(axiosWithServerHeaders);
```

Client-side code that consumes **getData** would look like the following. Again, an **axios** function instance is created, this time with the **withCredentials** option (which enables the sending/receiving of cookies) enabled:

```
import axios from 'axios';
const axiosWithCookies = axios.create({
  withCredentials: true
})
getData(axiosWithCookies);
```

The preceding example shows how we can leverage first-class function support to share code between applications running in different JavaScript environments by delegating the implementation of the transport mechanism for the HTTP request. Passing a function as a parameter is the idiomatic JavaScript way to do dependency injection.

Functions that Enable Asynchronous I/O and Event-Driven Programming in JavaScript

I/O, that is, non-blocking, and the JavaScript event loop are at the core of JavaScript's popularity both for browser-based applications and more recently server-side applications with Node.js. JavaScript is single-threaded, which means it is easy to reason about. Race conditions and deadlocks are nearly impossible to find in a JavaScript program.

JavaScript's asynchronous programming model of non-blocking interactions with input and output mechanisms means that if a program is I/O-bound, JavaScript is a very efficient way to handle it. JavaScript doesn't wait for the I/O to finish; instead, it schedules for the code to resume execution when the I/O has completed using the event loop.

For event-driven programming, the function is a lightweight container for logic that needs to be executed at a later point in time. Functions and event-driven programming in JavaScript have led to patterns such as the **addEventListener** Web API, the Node.js error-first callback, and the subsequent move to an A+ Promise-compliant specification in ECMAScript 6/ECMAScript 2015.

All the patterns here expose a function that accepts a function as one of its parameters.

The **addEventListener** Web API allows JavaScript programs running in the browser to execute a function when an event occurs on a DOM element; for example, we can listen to **scroll**, **click**, or keyboard events. The following example will print **Scrolling...** if you scroll. It should be run in a browser JavaScript environment:

```
document.addEventListener('scroll', () => {

  console.log('Scrolling...');

});
```

Node.js error-first callbacks are used in any I/O API it exposes. The following example shows how to handle errors from the Node.js filesystem module, **fs**. The callback that's passed always has an error property as its first parameter. This error is **null** or **undefined** when there is no error and has an **Error** value if an error occurs:

```
const fs = require('fs');

fs.readdir('.', (err, data) => {

  // Shouldn't error

  console.assert(Boolean(data));

  console.assert(!err);

});

fs.readdir('/tmp/nonexistent', (err, data) => {

  // Should error

  console.assert(!data);

  console.assert(Boolean(err));

});
```

The Web Fetch API exposes an A+ Promise implementation. An A+ Promise is an object that encapsulates asynchronous logic and has .**then** and .**catch** functions, which accept a function as a parameter. Promises are a more recent and advanced way to abstract I/O in JavaScript compared to the error-first Node.js callback approach. The Fetch API is not available natively in Node.js; however, it is available as an npm module for use in Node.js. This means that the following code works in Node.js:

```
const fetch = require('node-fetch');


fetch('https://google.com')
  .then(response => {
    console.assert(response.ok);
  })
  .catch(error => {
    // Shouldn't error
    console.assert(false);
    console.error(error.stack);
  });
```

More recent versions of Node.js (10+) expose a Promise interface for some of its APIs. The following is equivalent to the earlier filesystem access and error handling but using the Promise interface instead of error-first callbacks:

```
const fs = require('fs').promises;


fs.readdir('.')
  .then(data => {
    console.assert(Boolean(data));
  })
  .catch(() => {
    // Shouldn't error
    console.assert(false);
  });


fs.readdir('/tmp/nonexistent')
  .then(() => {
```

```
    // Should error
    console.assert(false);
  })
  .catch(error => {
    // Should error
    console.assert(Boolean(error));
  });
```

JavaScript Built-In Array Methods that Showcase First-Class Function Support

JavaScript comes with several built-in methods on the Array object. A lot of these methods showcase first-class function support.

The **Array#map** function returns the array of the output of the function that's passed and is applied to each element. The following example shows a common use case, which is to convert an array of objects into an array of primitive values by extracting a certain object key for each element. In this case, the **id** property of the objects is returned in a new array:

```
const assert = require('assert').strict


assert.deepStrictEqual(
  [{id: '1'}, {id: '2'}].map(el => el.id),
  ['1', '2']
);
```

The **Array#filter** function returns elements of the array for which the function passed as a parameter returns a truthy value. In the following case, we filter out any element that is less than or equal to 2:

```
const assert = require('assert').strict


assert.deepStrictEqual(
  [1, 2, 3, 4, 5].filter(el => el > 2),
  [3, 4, 5]
);
```

The **Array#reduce** function takes a function parameter is called for each element with an accumulator and the current element value. **Reduce** returns the last output of the passed function parameter. It is used to change the shape of the array, for example, summing over each element in the array:

```
console.assert([2, 4].reduce((acc, curr) => acc + curr) === 6);
```

The **Array#flatMap** function returns the flattened output of the function that's passed as a parameter and is applied to each of the elements in the array. The following example is a case where the new array is double the length of the initial one since we return a pair of values for **flatMap** to flatten into an array:

```
const assert = require('assert').strict


assert.deepStrictEqual(
  [1, 2, 3, 4, 5, 6].flatMap(el => [el, el + 1]),
  [ 1, 2, 2, 3, 3, 4, 4, 5, 5, 6, 6, 7 ]
);
```

> **Note**
>
> **flatMap** is a stage 4 feature that's works in Node.js 11+ and is supported natively in Chrome 69+, Firefox 62+, and Safari 12+.

The **Array#forEach** function calls the function that's passed as a parameter on each element of the array. It is equivalent to a for loop, except it can't be broken. The function that's passed will always be called on each element:

```
let sum = 0;
[1, 2, 3].forEach(n => {
  sum += n;
});
console.assert(sum === 6);
```

The **Array#find** function calls the function that's passed as a parameter on each element of the array until the function returns a truthy value, at which point it returns that value or there are no more elements to call it against, at which point it returns **undefined**:

```
console.assert(['a', 'b'].find(el => el === 'c') === undefined);
```

The `Array#findIndex` function calls the function that's passed as a parameter on each element of the array until the function returns a truthy value, at which point it returns the index or there are no more elements to call it against, at which point it returns -1:

```
console.assert(['a', 'b'].findIndex(el => el === 'b') === 1);
```

The `Array#every` function calls the function that's passed as a parameter on each element of the array. At each iteration, if the passed function returns a **false** value, `.every` breaks and returns **false**. If `.every` gets to the end of the array without the function that's being passed as the parameter returning a **false** value, it returns **true**:

```
console.assert([5, 6, 7, 8].every(el => el > 4));
```

The `Array#some` function calls the function that's passed as a parameter on each element of the array. At each iteration, if the passed function returns a truthy value, `.some` breaks and returns **true**. If `.some` gets to the end of the array without the function that's being passed as the parameter returning a truthy value, it returns **false**:

```
console.assert([0, 1, 2, 5, 6, 7, 8].some(el => el < 4));
```

The `Array#sort` function calls the function that's passed as a parameter to sort the array. The passed function is called with two elements of the array (which we will call **a** and **b**). If it returns a value greater than 0, **a** will appear before **b** in the sorted array. If the comparison function returns a value less than 0, **b** will appear before **a** in the sorted array. If the comparison function returns a value equal to 0, **a** and **b** will appear in the same order as in the original array, that is, relative to each other:

```
const assert = require('assert').strict


assert.deepStrictEqual(
  [3, 5, 1, 4].sort((a, b) => (a > b ? 1 : -1)),
  [1, 3, 4, 5]
);
```

There are other Array methods, specifically ones that operate on non-function arguments. This is a good way to show how much more powerful the methods that support passing a function are.

Exercise 70: Re-Implementing includes, indexOf, and join with some, findIndex, and reduce

In this exercise, you will reimplement `Array#includes`, `Array#indexOf`, and `Array#join` using the array methods `Array#some`, `Array#findIndex`, and `Array#reduce` by leveraging first-class function support. They are more powerful versions of their primitive-only counterparts.

The final output of `npm run Exercise70` should have all the assertions passing. This means that we have now got `includes`, `indexOf`, and `join` functions that are compliant with the following assertions:

- `includes` should return true if the value is in array.

- `includes` should return false if the value is in array.

- `indexOf` should return the index if the value in the array.

- `indexOf` should return -1 if value not in the array.

- `join` should work with no delimiter passed.

- `join` should work with a comma delimiter.

> **Note**
>
> In this exercise, we will have tests and a skeleton for the methods in the starter file, `exercise-re-implement-array-methods-start.js`. The file can be run with **node exercise-re-implement-array-methods-start.js**. This command has been aliased with npm scripts to **npm run Exercise70**.

Perform the following steps to complete this exercise:

1. Change the current directory to **Lesson10**. This allows us to use pre-mapped commands to run our code. Now, run the **npm run Exercise70** command (or **node exercise-re-implement-array-methods-start.js**):

```
> node exercise-re-implement-array-methods-start.js

Assertion failed: includes should return true if value is in array
Assertion failed: includes should return false if value is in array
Assertion failed: indexOf should return the index if value in array
Assertion failed: indexOf should return -1 if value not in array
Assertion failed: join should work with no delimiter passed
Assertion failed: join should work with comma delimiter
```

Figure 10.1: Initial output of npm run Exercise70

These errors show that the tests that have been provided are currently failing because the implementations don't work as expected (since they currently do nothing).

2. Implement **includes** in **exercise-re-implement-array-methods-start.js**:

```
function includes(array, needle) {
    return array.some(el => el === needle);
}
```

There is an **includes** skeleton that we will replace. The function we can use to implement includes is **.some**. What we will do is check that any/some element of the array is equal to the **needle** parameter.

3. Run **npm run Exercise70**. This should give the following output, which means that **includes** works as expected according to our two assertions (the assertion errors for **includes** are gone):

```
> node exercise-re-implement-array-methods-start.js

Assertion failed: indexOf should return the index if value in array
Assertion failed: indexOf should return -1 if value not in array
Assertion failed: join should work with no delimiter passed
Assertion failed: join should work with comma delimiter
```

Figure 10.2: Output after implementing includes

The **needle** is a primitive type, so doing **el === needle** is good enough if we need to compare something.

4. Use **.findIndex** to implement **indexOf**:

```
function indexOf(array, needle) {
  return array.findIndex(el => el === needle);
}
```

After this step, running **npm run Exercise70** should give the following output, which means that **indexOf** works as expected according to our two assertions (the assertion errors for **indexOf** are gone):

```
> node exercise-re-implement-array-methods-start.js

Assertion failed: join should work with no delimiter passed
Assertion failed: join should work with comma delimiter
```

Figure 10.3: Output after implementing includes and indexOf

Finally, we will implement **join** using **.reduce**. This function is trickier to implement since **reduce** is a very generic traversal/accumulation operator.

5. Start by concatenating the accumulator with the current element:

```
function join(array, delimiter = '') {
  return array.reduce((acc, curr) => acc + curr);
}
```

6. Run **npm run Exercise70**. You will see that "should work with no delimiter passed" now passes:

```
> node exercise-re-implement-array-methods-start.js

Assertion failed: join should work with comma delimiter
```

Figure 10.4: Implementing includes, indexOf, and a naïve join

7. In addition to concatenating the accumulator with the current element, add the delimiter in between them:

```
function join(array, delimiter = '') {
    return array.reduce((acc, curr) => acc + delimiter + curr);
}
```

Following is the output of the preceding code:

```
> node exercise-re-implement-array-methods-start.js
```

Figure 10.5: Final output of npm after running the exercise

This exercise shows how functions that support passing another function into them are more powerful than their equivalents, which only receive primitive parameters. We have shown this by reimplementing the primitive parameter functions using their function-parameter counterparts.

In the next exercise, we will show you another JavaScript use case for Array functions that support function parameters.

Exercise 71: Computing the Price of a Basket Using Map and Reduce

In this exercise, you will use the array's **map**, **filter**, and **reduce** functions to complete a simple transformation from a list of line items to a basket's total cost.

> **Note**
>
> In this exercise, you will have tests and a skeleton for the methods in the starter file, **exercise-price-of-basket-start.js**. The file can be run with **node exercise-price-of-basket-start.js**. This command has been aliased with npm scripts to **npm run Exercise71**. The working solution for this exercise can be run using the **npm run Exercise71** file on GitHub.

1. Change the current directory to **Lesson10**. This allows us to use pre-mapped commands to run our code. Run **npm run Exercise71** (or **node exercise-price-of-basket-start.js**). You will see the following:

```
> node exercise-price-of-basket-start.js

Assertion failed: basket1 should tally up to 5197
Assertion failed: basket2 should tally up to 897
```

Figure 10.6: Initial output of npm run

The failing assertions show that our skeleton implementation doesn't output what it is supposed to since the contents of **basket1** should tally to **5197** and the contents of **basket2** should tally to **897**. We can run this calculation manually: 1 * 199 + 2 * 2499 is 5197 and 2 * 199 + 1 * 499 is 897.

2. First, get the line item price, which is done by mapping over each item in **totalBasket** and multiplying **item.price** by **item.quantity**:

```
function totalBasket(basket) {
  return basket.map(item => item.price * item.quantity);
}
console.log(totalBasket(basket1))
console.log(totalBasket(basket2))
```

Running **npm run Exercise71** should give you the following output:

```
> node exercise-price-of-basket-start.js

[ 199, 4998 ]
[ 398, 499 ]
Assertion failed: basket1 should tally up to 5197
Assertion failed: basket2 should tally up to 897
```

Figure 10.7: Output of npm run and totalBasket with line item calculation in a .map

Note how the assertions are still failing since we're not adding the line item prices up; we're just returning an array of the line item price.

3. Next, use **reduce** to sum the accumulator and current line item price, and remove the **console.log**:

```
function totalBasket(basket) {
  return basket
    .map(item => item.price * item.quantity)
    .reduce((acc, curr) => acc + curr);
}
```

The final output of **npm run Exercise71** should not have assertion errors:

```
> node exercise-price-of-basket-start.js
```

Figure 10.8: Final output with totalBasket implemented

Adding the **reduce** step sums over the line item prices that we calculated with the initial **map**. Now **totalBasket** returns the correct total price for both **basket1** and **basket2**, which is **5197** and **897**, respectively. Hence, the following assertions are now true:

- **basket1** should tally up to **5197**.

- **basket2** should tally up to **897**.

This exercise shows how to use map and reduce to first transform an array of objects into an array of primitive values and then aggregate data from that intermediate array.

Child-Parent Component Communication in React

The popular JavaScript user interface library React leverages the first-class nature of functions in JavaScript for its Component API interface.

A Component only explicitly receives props from the component that is consuming it. This consumption of one Component by another in React is usually referred to as rendering since its own rendering is the only place where one component can use another.

In this situation, the parent component (the one that renders) can pass props to the child component (the one that is being rendered), like so:

```
import React from 'react';


class Child extends React.Component {
  render() {
    return <div>Hello {this.props.who}</div>;
  }
}
```

```
}

class Parent extends React.Component {
  render() {
    return (
      <div>
        <Child who="JavaScript" />
      </div>
    );
  }
}
```

In contrast to other popular user interface libraries such as Vue.js and Angular where there are two concepts for parent-child communication, in Vue.js, props are passed from parent to child and events are emitted from the child to the parent. In Angular, input binding is used for passing data from the parent to child. The parents listen to events that are emitted by the child and react to them.

React does not expose a construct that allows data to be passed back to the parent; there are only props. To achieve child-parent communication, React champions a pattern whereby a function is passed as a prop to the child. The passed function is defined in the parent's context and therefore can do what it wishes in that parent component, such as updating the state, triggering a Redux action, and so on:

```
import React from 'react';

class Child extends React.Component {
  render() {
    return (
      <div>
        <button onClick={this.props.onDecrement}>-</button>
        <button onClick={this.props.onIncrement}>+</button>
      </div>
    );
  }
}
```

```javascript
class Parent extends React.Component {
  constructor() {
    super();
    this.state = {
      count: 0
    };
  }

  increment() {
    this.setState({
      count: this.state.count + 1
    });
  }

  decrement() {
    this.setState({
      count: this.state.count - 1
    });
  }

  render() {
    return (
      <div>
        <p>{this.state.count}</p>
        <Child
          onIncrement={this.increment.bind(this)}
          onDecrement={this.decrement.bind(this)}
        />
      </div>
    );
  }
}
```

This pattern also exposes one of the big problems of first-class functions in JavaScript. When mixing classes/instances and first-class functions, by default, the function on a class instance object is not automatically bound to it. In other words, we have the following:

```
import React from 'react';


class Child extends React.Component {
  render() {
    return <div>
      <p><button onClick={() => this.props.withInlineBind('inline-
bind')}>inline bind</button></p>
      <p><button onClick={() => this.props.withConstructorBind('constructor-
bind')}>constructor bind</button></p>
      <p><button onClick={() => this.props.withArrowProperty('arrow-
property')}>arrow property</button></p>
    </div>;
  }
}


class Parent extends React.Component {
  constructor() {
    super();

    this.state = {
      display: 'default'
    };

    this.withConstructorBind = this.withConstructorBind.bind(this);
  }

  // check the render() function
  // for the .bind()
  withInlineBind(value) {
```

```javascript
    this.setState({
      display: value
    })
  }


  // check the constructor() function
  // for the .bind()
  withConstructorBind(value) {
    this.setState({
      display: value
    })
  }


  // works as is but needs an
  // experimental JavaScript feature
  withArrowProperty = (value) => {
    this.setState({
      display: value
    })
  }


  render() {
    return (
      <div>
        <p>{this.state.display}</p>
        <Child
          withInlineBind={this.withInlineBind.bind(this)}
          withConstructorBind={this.withConstructorBind}
          withArrowProperty={this.withArrowProperty}
          />
```

```
        </div>
    );
  }
}
```

Callback props are core to any sort of child-parent communication in React since their props are the only way to communicate from parent to child and child to parent. The next activity aims to implement an **onCheckout** prop that the consumer of the **Basket** component can use to react when the Basket's checkout button is clicked.

Activity 15: onCheckout Callback Prop

In this activity, we will implement an **onCheckout** prop to display the number of items in the shopping cart during checkout.

> **Note**
>
> Activity 15 comes with a preconfigured development server and a skeleton for the methods in the starter files, that is, **activity-on-checkout-prop-start.js** and **activity-on-checkout-prop-start.html**. The development server can be run with **npm run Activity15**. The working solution for this activity can be run using the npm run **Activity15** file on GitHub.

1. Change the current directory to **Lesson10** and run **npm install** if you haven't done so in this directory before. **npm install** downloads the dependencies that are required in order to run this activity (React and Parcel). This command is an alias of **npx parcel serve activity-on-checkout-prop-start.html**.

2. Go to **http://localhost:1234** (or whichever URL the start script output) to see the HTML page.

3. Click on the **Proceed to checkout** button. You will notice that nothing happens.

> **Note**
>
> The solution for this activity can be found on page 625.

The next exercise will show you how to leverage state and props to add a product to our basket. This exercise's starting code isn't strictly the same as what we finished with after the activity. For example, the state was hoisted from the Basket component to the **App** component.

Exercise 72: Adding a Product to the Basket

In this exercise, we will modify the **addProduct** method to update the number of items in the basket when the **Add to basket** option is clicked.

> **Note**
>
> Exercise 72 comes with a preconfigured development server and a skeleton for the methods in the starter files, that is, **exercise-add-product-start.js** and **exercise-add-product-start.html**. The development server can be run with **npm run Exercise72**. This command is an alias of **npx parcel serve exercise-add-product-start.html**. The working solution for this exercise can be run using the **npm run Exercise72** file on GitHub.

1. Change the current directory to **Lesson10**. Run **npm install** if you haven't done so in this directory before. Now, run **npm run Exercise 72**. You will see the application starting up, as follows:

```
> parcel serve exercise-add-product-start.html

Server running at http://localhost:1234
'+   Built in 7.85s.
```

Figure 10.9: Output of npm run Exercise 72

For the development server to live-reload our changes and to avoid configuration issues, edit the **exercise-add-product-start.js** file directly.

2. Go to **http://localhost:1234** (or whichever URL the start script output). You should see the following HTML page:

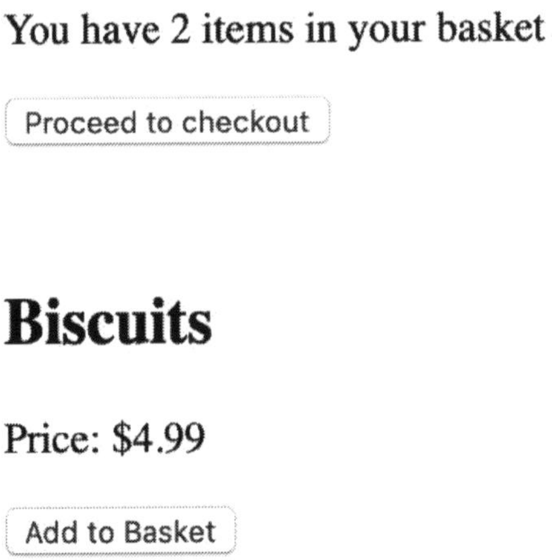

You have 2 items in your basket

Proceed to checkout

Biscuits

Price: $4.99

Add to Basket

Figure 10.10: Initial application in the browser

When clicking of **Add to Basket**, the application crashes and shows a blank HTML page.

3. Update `App#addProduct` to fix the crashes.

```
addProduct(product) {
    this.setState({
      basket: {
        items: this.state.basket.items.concat({
          name: product.name,
          price: product.price,
          quantity: 1
        })
      }
    });
  }
```

Instead of setting the basket value to `{}`, we use the JavaScript Array's `concatenate` method to take the current items in the basket (`this.state.basket.items`) and add the passed-in `product` parameter with `quantity: 1`.

4. To find out what happens when we click **Add to Basket**, we need to find the `onClick` handler for the **Add to Basket** button and then diagnose the issue with the `this.addProduct()` call (basket being set to `{}`):

```
<button onClick={() => this.addProduct(this.state.product)}>
  Add to Basket
</button>
```

When we click the **Add to Basket** button, we will see the following:

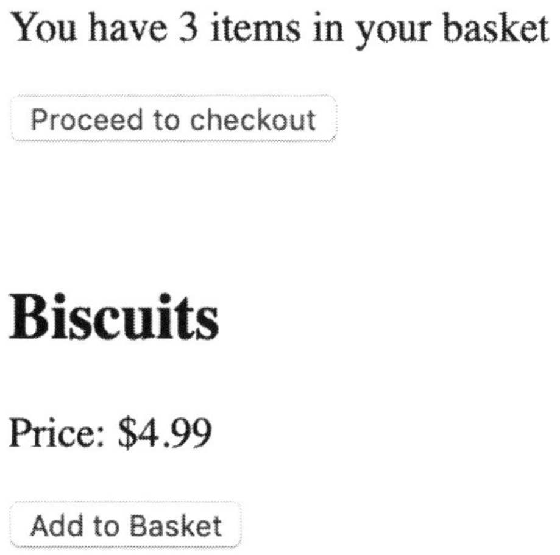

You have 3 items in your basket

Proceed to checkout

Biscuits

Price: $4.99

Add to Basket

Figure 10.11: Implemented Add to Basket after one click

When we click **Add to Basket** again, we will see the following:

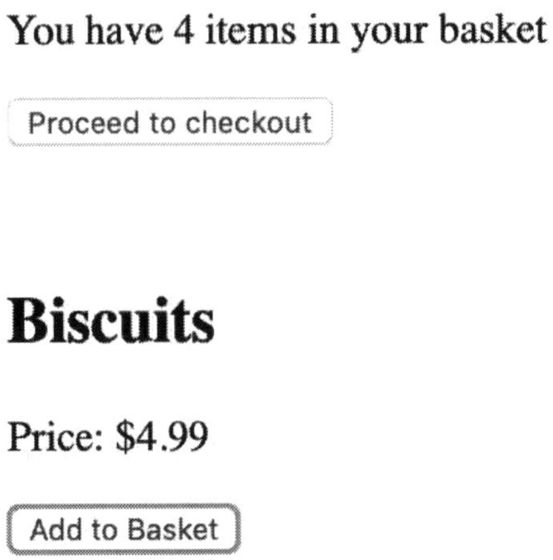

You have 4 items in your basket

Proceed to checkout

Biscuits

Price: $4.99

Add to Basket

Figure 10.12: Implemented Add to Basket after two clicks

First-Class Functions in React Render Props

Render props are a React component pattern where a component delegates the rendering of a whole area to its parent.

A render prop is a function that returns JSX (since it needs to be renderable). It tends to be called with child-specific data. That data is then used by the implementation of the prop to render JSX. This pattern is very popular with library authors since it means they can focus on implementing the logic of the component without having to worry about how to allow the user to override the rendered output (since it is all delegated back to the user).

A very simple example of a render prop is to delegate the rendering to the parent component, but the action or data comes from the component that exposes a render prop. `ExitComponent` wraps the `window.close()` functionality but delegates render to its `renderExit` prop:

```
class ExitComponent extends React.Component {
  exitPage() {
    window.close();
  }

  render() {
```

```
> parcel serve exercise-render-prop-start.html

Server running at http://localhost:1234
+  Built in 3.08s.
```

Figure 10.13: Output after running the start file

For the development server to live-reload our changes and to avoid configuration issues, edit the **exercise-render-prop-start.js** file directly.

2. Go to **http://localhost:1234** (or whichever URL the starting script output). You should see the following HTML page:

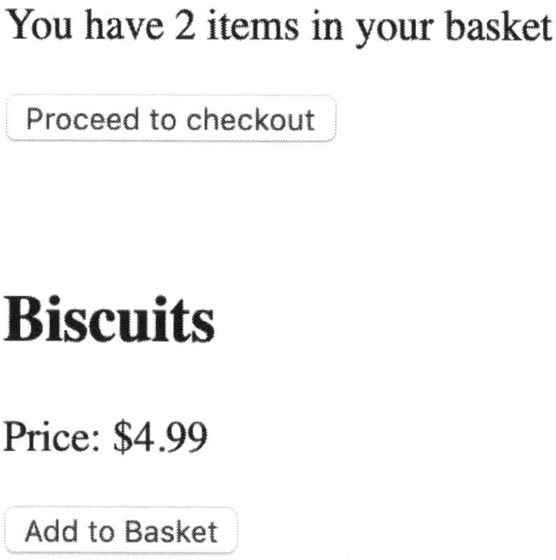

You have 2 items in your basket

Proceed to checkout

Biscuits

Price: $4.99

Add to Basket

Figure 10.14: Initial application in the browser

3. Find where **Basket** is being rendered and add a **renderItem** prop, which is a function from the item to JSX. This is the implementation of the render prop that **Basket** will use to render each basket item:

```
{this.state.status === 'SHOPPING' && (
  <Basket
    items={this.state.basket.items}
    renderItem={item => (
      <div>
        x{item.quantity} - {item.name} - $
        {(item.price / 100).toFixed(2)} each{' '}
      </div>
```

```
      )}
      onCheckout={this.handleCheckout}
    />
  )}
```

4. Go to the **Basket#render** method and map over each **this.props.items**, using **this.props.renderItem** to render the item:

```
render() {
  return (
    <div>
      <p>You have {this.props.items.length} items in your basket</p>
      <div>{this.props.items.map(item => this.props.renderItem(item))}</
div>
      <button onClick={() => this.props.onCheckout(this.props.items)}>
        Proceed to checkout
      </button>
    </div>
  );
}
```

To see our changes, we can go to the browser and see how the basket items are rendered:

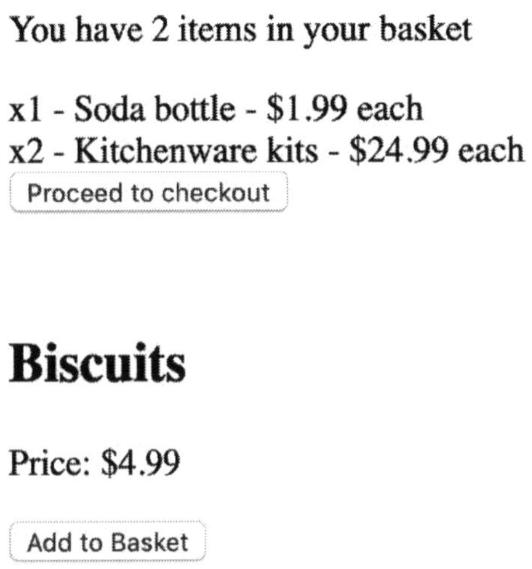

You have 2 items in your basket

x1 - Soda bottle - $1.99 each
x2 - Kitchenware kits - $24.99 each

[Proceed to checkout]

Biscuits

Price: $4.99

[Add to Basket]

Figure 10.15: Rendering the basket items

Our **Basket** component now renders the items according to the function that's defined by the component rendering it. This makes **Basket** more powerful (it can render items) but still highly reusable. In different instances, we could use **Basket** with a `renderItem` prop that renders nothing, the breakdown of the item, or the line item price for the basket item, for example.

First-class functions and the patterns we have covered are crucial to writing idiomatic JavaScript. Another way we can leverage functional programming in JavaScript is by using pure functions.

Pure Functions

Pure functions are functions that don't have side effects and for the same input, arguments will return the same output value(s). A side effect can be anything from mutating the value of an argument passed by reference (which in JavaScript mutates the original) to mutating the value of a local variable, or doing any sort of I/O.

A pure function can be thought of as a mathematical function. It only operates using input and only affects its own output.

Here is a simple pure function, the `identity` function, which returns whatever is passed to it as a parameter:

```
const identity = i => i;
```

Notice how there are no side effects and no mutation of parameters or creation of new variables. This function doesn't even have a body.

Pure functions have the advantage of being simple to reason about. They're also easy to test; there is usually no need to mock any dependencies out since any and all dependencies should be passed as arguments. Pure functions tend to operate on data since they're not allowed to have side effects if data is their only dependency. This reduces the testing surface area.

The cons of pure functions are that pure functions technically can't do anything interesting such as I/O, which means no sending of HTTP requests and no database calls.

> **Note**
>
> An interesting gap in the definition of pure functions is JavaScript async functions. Technically they can still be pure if they don't contain side effects. In practice, an async function is likely to be used to run asynchronous operations with **await** such as accessing the filesystem, HTTP, or database requests. A good rule of thumb is that if a function is async, it likely uses **await** to do some sort of I/O and therefore it is not pure.

Redux Reducers and Actions

Redux is a state management library. It imposes a few constraints on the user to improve the predictability of state updates and the long-term scalability of the codebase.

Let's look at a simple Redux counter implementation to highlight some features:

```
const {createStore} = require('redux');


const counterReducer = (state = 0, action) => {
  switch (action.type) {
    case 'INCREMENT':
      return state + 1;
    case 'DECREMENT':
      return state - 1;
    default:
      return state;
  }
};


const store = createStore(counterReducer);
```

The store initializes its state to 0:

```
console.assert(store.getState() === 0, 'initalises to 0');
```

The store's internal state is only exposed through the read-only interface of **getState**. To update the state, an action needs to be dispatched. Calling **dispatch** with the **INCREMENT** and **DECREMENT** types show that the **counterReducer** works as expected and reduces the actions in the store:

```
store.dispatch({type: 'INCREMENT'});
console.assert(store.getState() === 1, 'incrementing works');


store.dispatch({type: 'DECREMENT'});
console.assert(store.getState() === 0, 'decrementing works');
```

> **Note**
>
> There are three pillars of Redux, as per the Redux documentation: https://redux.
> js.org/introduction/three-principles.

The three pillars of Redux are illustrated in the preceding example. We have a system with a single store, the state is read-only (and accessed through **getState**), and changes are made by our reducer, which is a pure function. **counterReducer** takes state and an action and returns a new value without mutating **state** or **action**.

In exchange for following these rules, we get a predictable and performant state container for our JavaScript applications. A single store means there is no question as to where the state is stored; the read-only state forces updates to be done through dispatching actions and reducing them. Since reducers are pure functions, they're both easy to test and reason about since they will give the same output for the same input and will not cause side effects or unwanted mutations.

Redux is used to manage the state. Up until now, we have been storing our data in a React state.

Exercise 74: Redux Dispatching Actions and Reducing Them into State

In this exercise, we will move the state of our data into Redux in order to separate data manipulation and state updates from code that renders data to the page.

> **Note**
>
> Exercise 74 comes with a preconfigured development server and a skeleton for the methods in the starter files, that is, **exercise-redux-dispatch-start.js** and **exercise-redux-dispatch-start.html**. The development server can be run with **npm run Exercise74**. The working solution for this exercise can be run using the **npm run Exercise74** file on GitHub.

Perform the following steps to complete this exercise:

1. Change the current directory to **Lesson10** and run **npm install** if you haven't done so in this directory before. This command is an alias of **npx parcel serve exercise-redux-dispatch-start.html**. Now, run **npm run Exercise74**. You will see the application starting up, as follows:

```
> parcel serve exercise-redux-dispatch-start.html

Server running at http://localhost:1234
'+  Built in 3.21s.
```

Figure 10.16: Output of npm run Exercise74

2. Go to **http://localhost:1234** (or whichever URL the starting script output). You should see the following HTML page:

You have 2 items in your basket

x1 - Soda bottle - $1.99 each
x2 - Kitchenware kits - $24.99 each
Proceed to checkout

Biscuits

Price: $4.99

Add to Basket

Figure 10.17: Initial Exercise74 application in the browser

Notice how clicking the buttons doesn't work.

3. Implement **App#continueShopping** by dispatching an action of the CONTINUE_
SHOPPING type:

```
continueShopping() {
  this.props.dispatch({
    type: 'CONTINUE_SHOPPING'
  });
}
```

4. In **appReducer**, implement the corresponding state reduction. For CONTINUE_
SHOPPING, we only need to change the **status** in the state since it is what we use to
display the checkout view or the main product and basket view:

```
switch(action.type) {
  // other cases
  case 'CONTINUE_SHOPPING':
    return {
      ...state,
      status: 'SHOPPING'
    };
  // other cases
}
```

5. Implement **App#finish** by dispatching an action of the DONE type:

```
finish() {
  this.props.dispatch({
    type: 'DONE'
  });
}
```

6. In **appReducer**, implement the corresponding state reduction. We only need to
change the **status** in state since it is what we use to display the **Done** view:

```
switch(action.type) {
  // other cases
  case 'DONE':
    return {
      ...state,
      status: 'DONE'
    };
  // other cases
}
```

7. Implement **handleCheckout** by dispatching an action of the **START_CHECKOUT** type:

```
handleCheckout(items) {
  this.props.dispatch({
    type: 'START_CHECKOUT',
    basket: {
      items
    }
  });
}
```

8. In **appReducer**, implement the corresponding state reduction. For **START_CHECKOUT**, we only need to change the **status** in the state since it is what we use to display the checkout view or the main product and basket view:

```
switch(action.type) {
  // other cases
  case 'START_CHECKOUT':
    return {
      ...state,
      status: 'CHECKING_OUT'
    };
  // other cases
}
```

> **Note**
>
> The **basket** object is not being reduced, so it can be omitted from the action at dispatch.

9. Implement **addProduct** by dispatching an action as follows. For **ADD_PRODUCT**, we need the **newProduct**, as well as the action type:

```
addProduct(product) {
  this.props.dispatch({
    type: 'ADD_PRODUCT',
    newProduct: {
      name: product.name,
      price: product.price,
      quantity: 1
    }
  });
}
```

10. In **appReducer**, implement the corresponding state reduction, which takes the new product and adds it to the current basket of items:

```
switch(action.type) {
  // other cases
  case 'ADD_PRODUCT':
    return {
      ...state,
      basket: {
        items: state.basket.items.concat(action.newProduct)
      }
    };
  // other cases
}
```

The **appReducer**, in full, should now look as follows:

```
const appReducer = (state = defaultState, action) => {
  switch (action.type) {
    case 'START_CHECKOUT':
      return {
        ...state,
        status: 'CHECKING_OUT'
      };
    case 'CONTINUE_SHOPPING':
      return {
        ...state,
        status: 'SHOPPING'
      };
    case 'DONE':
      return {
        ...state,
        status: 'DONE'
      };
    case 'ADD_PRODUCT':
      return {
        ...state,
        basket: {
          items: state.basket.items.concat(action.newProduct)
        }
      };
```

```
        default:
          return state;
    }
  };
```

11. Go to **http://localhost:1234** (or whichever URL the starting script output). The application should now respond to clicks, as expected:

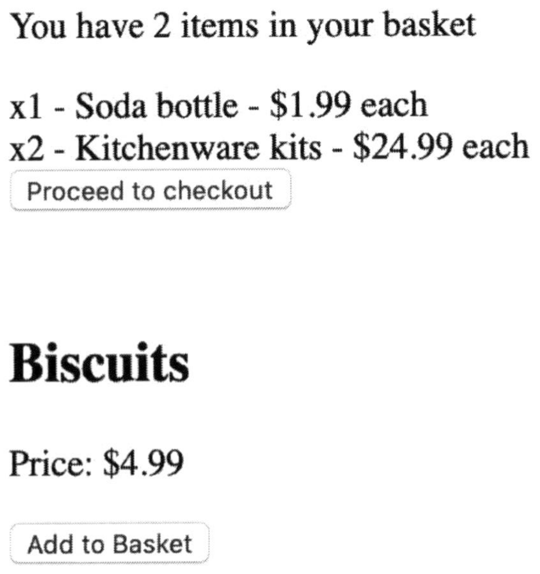

You have 2 items in your basket

x1 - Soda bottle - $1.99 each
x2 - Kitchenware kits - $24.99 each

Proceed to checkout

Biscuits

Price: $4.99

Add to Basket

Figure 10.18: Application with clicks responding

Adding items to baskets and navigating through the application (proceed to checkout, done, continue shopping) should behave as it did prior to the Redux store implementation.

Testing Pure Functions

Pure functions are easy to test since they are fully encapsulated. The only thing that can change is the output, that is, the return value. The only thing that can affect the output is the parameter/argument values. What's more, for the same set of inputs, the output of a pure function needs to be the same.

Testing pure functions is as simple as calling them with different inputs and asserting on the outputs:

```
const double = x => x * 2;


function test() {
```

```
console.assert(double(1) === 2, '1 doubled should be 2');
console.assert(double(-1) === -2, '-1 doubled should be -1');
console.assert(double(0) === 0, '0 doubled should be 0');
console.assert(double(500) === 1000, '500 doubled should be 1000');
}


test();
```

Redux reducers are pure functions, which means to test them, we can use the approach we just looked at in the previous example.

Exercise 75: Testing a Reducer

In this exercise, we will write tests for part of the reducer we used in the previous exercise, that is, the **ADD_PRODUCT** case of the **appReducer**.

> **Note**
>
> Exercise 75 comes with tests and a skeleton for the methods in the starter file, **exercise-reducer-test-start.js**. The file can be run with **node exercise-reducer-test-start.js**. This command has been aliased with npm scripts to **npm run Exercise75**. The working solution for this exercise can be run using the npm run exercise6 file on GitHub.

Perform the following steps to complete this exercise:

1. Change the current directory to **Lesson10**. This allows us to use pre-mapped commands to run our code.

2. Now, run **npm run Exercise75** (or **node exercise-reducer-test-start.js**). You will see the following output:

```
> node exercise-reducer-test-start.js
```

Figure 10.19: Empty tests passing after running the start file

A simplified **appReducer** that only contains the **ADD_PRODUCT** action reduction is present in this starter file, along with a **test** function, which is where the new tests are going to be added. The output doesn't contain errors because we haven't created any tests yet.

> **Note**
>
> To get the output of **appReducer**, it should be called with a **state** object and the relevant **action**. In this case, the type should be **'ADD_PRODUCT'**.

3. As in the previous examples, we will use **assert.deepStrictEqual**, which checks for the deep equality of two objects. We can write a failing test like so. We're calling **appReducer** with **state** and the relevant **action**:

```javascript
function test() {
  assert.deepStrictEqual(
    appReducer(
      {
        basket: {items: []}
      },
      {
        type: 'ADD_PRODUCT',
        newProduct: {
          price: 499,
          name: 'Biscuits',
          quantity: 1
        }
      }
    ),
    {}
  );
}
```

If we run **npm run Exercise75**, we will see the following error. This is expected since **appReducer** doesn't return an empty object as the state:

```
> node exercise-reducer-test-start.js

assert.js:86
  throw new AssertionError(obj);
  ^

AssertionError [ERR_ASSERTION]: Expected values to be strictly deep-equal:
+ actual - expected

+ {
+   basket: {
+     items: [
+       {
+         name: 'Biscuits',
+         price: 499,
+         quantity: 1
+       }
+     ]
+   }
+ }
- {}
```

Figure 10.20: Errors shown after executing the start file

4. We should use **assert.deepStrictEqual** to ensure that **appReducer** adds the new product as expected. We will assign the expected value to an **expected** variable and the actual value to an **actual** variable. This will help keep the test more readable:

```
function test() {
  const expected = {
    basket: {
      items: [
        {
          price: 499,
          name: 'Biscuits',
          quantity: 1
        }
      ]
    }
  };
  const actual = appReducer(
    {
```

```
          basket: {items: []}
        },
        {
          type: 'ADD_PRODUCT',
          newProduct: {
            price: 499,
            name: 'Biscuits',
            quantity: 1
          }
        }
    );
    assert.deepStrictEqual(actual, expected);
}
```

The output should now not be throwing any errors:

```
> node exercise-reducer-test-start.js
```

Figure 10.21: Test passed as no errors were found

The following is the output after we run the **node exercise-reducer-test.js** command:

```
> node exercise-reducer-test.js

assert.js:86
  throw new AssertionError(obj);
  ^

AssertionError [ERR_ASSERTION]: Expected values to be strictly deep-equal:
+ actual - expected ... Lines skipped


  {
    basket: {
  ...
          name: 'Biscuits',
+         price: 499,
-         price: 4999,
          quantity: 1
  ...
    }
  }
```

Figure 10.22: Output showing assertion failing

Redux Selectors

Selectors are an additional Redux concept that means we can encapsulate internal store state shape with selectors. The consumer of a selector asks for what it wants; the selector is left to implement that with store state shape-specific knowledge. Selectors are pure functions; they take store state and return one or more sections of it.

Since selectors are pure functions, they are simple to implement. The following exercise shows us how to use selectors so that instead of putting messaging data in the render function or when passing props, we do it in a pure function.

Exercise 76: Implementing a Selector

In this exercise, we will use selectors and take advantage of their simplicity to render items to the shopping basket.

> **Note**
>
> Exercise 76 comes with a preconfigured development server and a skeleton for the methods in the starter files that is, **exercise-items-selector-start.js** and **exercise-items-selector-start.html**. The development server can be run with **npm run Exercise76**. The working solution for this exercise can be run using the npm run Exercise76 file on GitHub.

1. Change the current directory to **Lesson10** and run **npm install** if you haven't done so in this directory before.

2. Run **npx parcel serve exercise-items-selector-start.html** and execute **npm run Exercise76**. You will see the application starting up, as follows:

```
> parcel serve exercise-items-selector-start.html

Server running at http://localhost:1234
+  Built in 3.71s.
```

Figure 10.23: Output after running the start html file

For the development server to live-reload our changes and to avoid configuration issues, edit the **exercise-items-selector-start.js** file directly.

3. Go to **http://localhost:1234** (or whichever URL the starting script output). You should see the following HTML page:

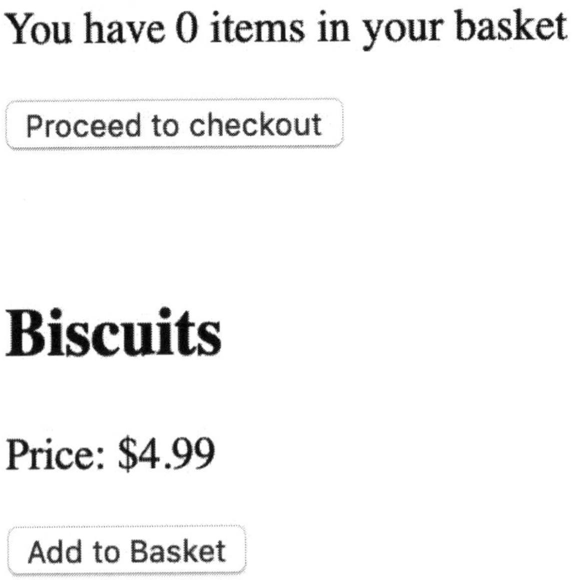

You have 0 items in your basket

Proceed to checkout

Biscuits

Price: $4.99

Add to Basket

Figure 10.24: Initial application in the browser

Note how no basket items are being rendered. This is because of the initial implementation of **selectBasketItems**. It returns an empty array:

```
const selectBasketItems = state => [];
```

4. Implement **selectBasketItems** by drilling down into the state with dot notation and short-circuiting. Default to **[]** if there is any issue with the state:

```
const selectBasketItems = state =>
    (state && state.basket && state.basket.items) || [];
```

The application should now work as expected again; the items will be displayed:

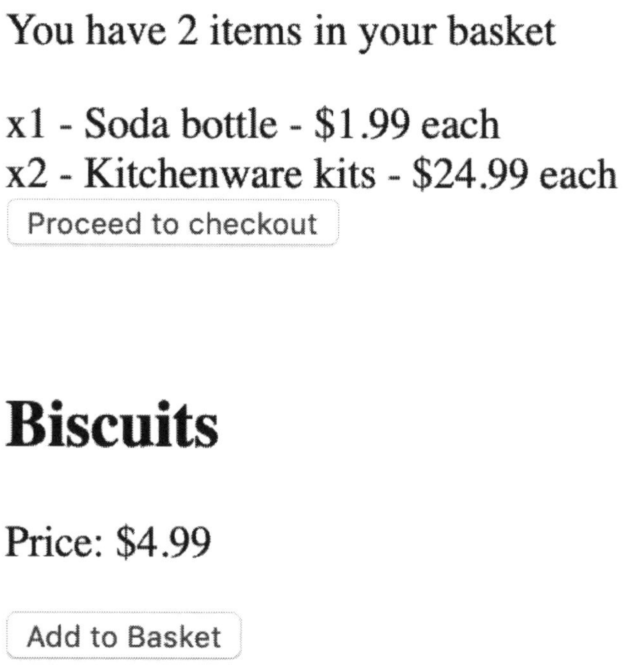

You have 2 items in your basket

x1 - Soda bottle - $1.99 each
x2 - Kitchenware kits - $24.99 each

Proceed to checkout

Biscuits

Price: $4.99

Add to Basket

Figure 10.25: Application after implementing selectBasketItems

The **selectBasketItems** selector takes the full state and returns a slice of it (the items). Selectors allow us to further abstract the internal shape of state inside the Redux store from how it is used in the React components.

Selectors are a crucial part of a React/Redux application. As we have seen, they allow the React components to be decoupled from Redux's internal state shape. The following activity aims to give us the ability to write tests for selectors. This is a similar scenario to testing a reducer, which we did in a previous exercise.

Activity 16: Testing a Selector

In this activity, we will test the selector for various states of the items array and ensure that the selector returns an array corresponding to the items in the basket. Let's get started:

1. Change the current directory to **Lesson10**. This allows us to use pre-mapped commands to run our code.

> **Note**
>
> Activity 16 comes with tests and a skeleton for the methods in the starter file, `activity-items-selector-test-start.js`. This file can be run with **node** `activity-items-selector-test-start.js`. This command has been aliased with npm scripts to **npm run Activity16**. The working solution for this exercise can be run using the npm run Activity16 file on GitHub.

Inside the test function, using `assert.deepStrictEqual`, do the following:

2. Test that, for empty state(s), the selector returns `[]`.

3. Test that, for an empty basket object, the selector returns `[]`.

4. Test that, if the **items** array is set but empty, the selector returns `[]`.

5. Test that, if the items array is not empty and set, the selector returns it.

> **Note**
>
> The solution for this activity can be found on page 626.

Pure functions are predictable, easy to test, and easy to reason about. Both first-class functions and pure functions tie into the next JavaScript functional programming concept: higher-order functions.

Higher-Order Functions

A higher-order function is a function that either takes a function as a parameter or returns a function as a value.

This builds on top of JavaScript's first-class function support. In a language that doesn't support first-class functions, it is difficult to implement higher-order functions.

Higher-order functions enable function composition patterns. In most instances, we use higher-order functions to augment an existing function.

bind, apply, and call

There are a few JavaScript built-in methods on the `Function` object: `bind`, `apply` and `call`.

`Function#bind` allows you to set the execution context for a function. When called, bind returns a new function with the first parameter to the call bound as the `this` context of the function. The following arguments to bind are used when the returned function is called. When the bound function is called, parameters can be supplied. These will appear in the argument list, after the parameters are set during the call to bind.

bind is used extensively in React code when passing functions as props that still need to access the current component's `this` to do operations such as `setState` or to call other component methods:

```
import React from 'react';


class Parent extends React.Component {
  constructor() {
    super();

    this.state = {
      display: 'default'
    };


    this.withConstructorBind = this.withConstructorBind.bind(this);
  }


  // Check the render() function
  // for the .bind()
  withInlineBind(value) {
    this.setState({
      display: value
    });
  }
```

```
// Check the constructor() function
// for the .bind()
withConstructorBind(value) {
  this.setState({
    display: value
  });
}


render() {
  return (
    <div>
      <p>{this.state.display}</p>
      <Child
        withInlineBind={this.withInlineBind.bind(this)}
        withConstructorBind={this.withConstructorBind}
      />
    </div>
  );
}
}
```

The **Function#bind** method can also be used when testing that a function is thrown in tests. For example, running the function would mean having to write a try/catch that somehow fails the test if the catch is not triggered. With bind and the **assert** module, this can be written in a much shorter form:

```
// Node.js built-in
const assert = require('assert').strict;


function mightThrow(shouldBeSet) {
  if (!shouldBeSet) {
    throw new Error("Doesn't work without shouldBeSet parameter");
  }
}
```

```
    return shouldBeSet;
}


function test() {
  assert.throws(mightThrow.bind(null), 'should throw on empty parameter');
  assert.doesNotThrow(
    mightThrow.bind(null, 'some-value'),
    'should not throw if not empty'
  );
  assert.deepStrictEqual(
    mightThrow('some-value'),
    'some-value',
    'should return input if set'
  );
}


test();
```

Function#apply and **Function#call** allow you to call a function without using the
fn(param1, param2, [paramX]) syntax, as well as setting the **this** context in a similar
way to **Function#bind**. The first parameter to **Function#apply** is the **this** context,
while the second parameter is an array or array-like and contains the parameters the
function expects. Similarly, the first parameter to **Function#call** is the **this** context;
the difference in regards to **Function#apply** lies in the definition of parameters. In
Function#call, they're an argument list, just like when using **Function#bind**, as opposed
to the array that **Function#apply** expects.

> **Note**
>
> Array-like objects, also known as indexed collections, the most used of which
> are the arguments object in functions, and the NodeList Web API, are objects
> that follow part of the Array API (for example, implementing .**length**) without
> implementing it fully. Array functions can still be used on them with JavaScript's
> apply/call.

Function#apply and **Function#call** don't strictly meet the higher-order function criteria. At a stretch, since they're methods on function objects, we could say that they're implicitly higher-order functions. The function object they're called on is an implicit parameter to the apply/call method call. By reading from the function prototype, we can even use them like so:

```
function identity(x) {

  return x;

}


const identityApplyBound = Function.prototype.bind.apply(identity, [

  null,

  'applyBound'

]);


const identityCallBound = Function.prototype.bind.call(

  identity,

  null,

  'callBound'

);


console.assert(

  identityApplyBound() === 'applyBound',

  'bind.apply should set parameter correctly'

);

console.assert(

  identityCallBound() === 'callBound',

  'bind.call should set parameter correctly'

);
```

In this example, we show that apply and call are higher-order functions, but only in as far as they can be used with functions on other functions.

Function#apply and **Function#call** have historically converted array-like objects into Arrays. In ECMAScript 2015+ compliant environments, the **spread** operator can be used in a similar fashion.

The three following functions allow you to convert Array-likes into Arrays using **Function#apply**, **Function#call**, and array spread, respectively:

```
function toArrayApply(arrayLike) {

  return Array.prototype.slice.apply(arrayLike);

}
```

```
function toArrayCall(arrayLike) {

  return Array.prototype.slice.call(arrayLike);

}
```

```
function toArraySpread(arrayLike) {

  return [...arrayLike];

}
```

Currying and Partial Application

A curried function is a function that, instead of taking the number of parameters it needs in one go, will accept one parameter at a time.

For example, if a function takes two parameters, its curried equivalent will be called twice, with one parameter each time.

Currying can, therefore, be expressed as taking an n-parameter function and turning it into a function that can be called n times with one parameter each time. The classic denomination for an n-parameter function is to call it n-ary. With that in mind, currying is the transformation from an n-ary function to an n-length set of unary function calls:

```
const sum = (x, y) => x + y;
const sumCurried = x => y => x + y;


console.assert(
  sum(1, 2) === sumCurried(1)(2),
  'curried version works the same for positive numbers'
);
console.assert(
```

```
  sum(10, -5) === sumCurried(10)(-5),

  'curried version works the same with a negative operand'
);
```

Partial application and currying are often introduced together and conceptually, they go hand in hand.

With a two-parameter function that is curried, it takes two calls with one parameter, with each doing the same work as the two-parameter un-curried function. When it is called once, it has half the necessary parameters fully applied. The function resulting from that first call is a partial application of the overall function:

```
const sum = (x, y) => x + y;

const sumCurried = x => y => x + y;


const add1Bind = sum.bind(null, 1);

const add1Curried = sumCurried(1);


console.assert(

  add1Bind(2) === add1Curried(2),

  'curried and bound versions behave the same'
);


console.assert(add1Bind(2) === 3, 'bound version behaves correctly');


console.assert(add1Curried(2) === 3, 'curried version behaves correctly');
```

In other words, a partial application is a way of expressing the transformation from the function that takes n parameters to a function that takes $n - m$ parameters, where m is the number of parameters that have been partially applied.

Currying and partial application are useful if we want to be able to reuse generic functionality. The partial application doesn't require currying; currying is the case of turning a function into one that can be partially applied. The partial application can also be done using bind.

Currying and partial application allow you to start with a very generic function and turn it into a more specialized function with every application.

Currying standardizes the number of parameters at each call. The partial application does not have such limitations. You can partially apply with more than one parameter at a time.

A unary function is simpler than a binary function, which is simpler than an N-ary (with N > 2) function.

Also, currying is simpler if we only allow one parameter to be applied at any time. We can see the arbitrary n-parameter partial application with more runtime complexity since each function needs to run some logic on whether this call is the final call or not.

A generic n-ary curry can be defined as follows in ES2015:

```
const curry = fn => {
  return function curried(...args) {
    if (fn.length === args.length) {
      return fn.apply(this, args);
    }


    return (...args2) => curried.apply(this, args.concat(args2));
  };
};
```

Leveraging Closures React Function Components

When defining a function, anything that's in scope of the function at definition time will remain in scope at call/execution time. Historically, closures were used to create private variable scopes. The closure is this function and its remembered definition-time scope:

```
const counter = (function(startCount = 0) {
  let count = startCount;
  return {
    add(x) {
      count += x;
    },
    substract(x) {
      count -= x;
    },
    current() {
```

```
      return count;
    }
  };
})(0);
```

We leverage this within React render functions to cache props and state in the local render scope.

React function components also leverage closures, especially with hooks:

```javascript
import React from 'react';


function Hello({who}) {
  return <p>Hello {who}</p>;
}


const App = () => (
  <>
    <Hello who="Function Components!" />
  </>
);
```

Function components are quite powerful since they're a bit simpler than class components.

When using a state management solution such as Redux, most of the important state is in the Redux store. This means that we can write mainly stateless functional components since the store manages any stateful part of our application.

Higher-order functions allow us to effectively deal with functions and augment them. Higher-order functions build on top of first-class function support and pure functions. Much in the same way, function composition builds on higher-order functions.

Function Composition

Function composition is another concept that leaks over from mathematics.

Given two functions, a and b, compose returns a new function that applies a to the output of b, which is then applied to a given set of parameters.

Function composition is a way to create a complex function from a set of smaller ones.

This will mean you might end up with a bunch of simple functions that do one thing well. Functions with a single purpose are better at encapsulating their functionality and therefore help with separation of concerns.

Composing functions ties in with currying and the partial application of functions since currying/partial application is a technique that allows you to have specialized versions of generic functions, like so:

```
const sum = x => y => x + y;
const multiply = x => y => x * y;


const compose = (f, g) => x => f(g(x));


const add1 = sum(1);
const add2 = sum(2);
const double = multiply(2);
```

To explain the following code, it stands to reason that we have the following:

- Doubling 2 and then adding 1 is 5 (4 + 1).
- Adding 1 to 2 and then doubling is 6 (3 * 2).
- Adding 2 to 2 and then doubling is 8 (4 * 2).
- Doubling 2 and then adding 2 is 6 (4 + 2).

The following uses our already defined functions, **add1**, **add2**, and **double**, and shows how we would use **compose** to implement the preceding cases. Note that compose applies the rightmost parameter first:

```
console.assert(
  compose(add1, double)(2) === 5
);
console.assert(
  compose(double, add1)(2) === 6
);
console.assert(
  compose(double, add2)(2) === 8
);
```

```
console.assert(
    compose(add2, double)(2) === 6
);
```

An alternative way to define **compose** is using a left-to-right traversal (with **reduce**). This has the benefit of allowing us to pass an arbitrary number of arguments when calling the output of composing. To this effect, we reduce from the first parameter to the last parameter, but the output of **reducing** is a function that supports any number of arguments and calls the previous output after the current function when called.

The following code uses parameter rest to allow for an arbitrary number of functions to be composed:

```
const composeManyUnary = (...fns) => x =>
    fns.reduceRight((acc, curr) => curr(acc), x);
```

Then, it returns a function that takes a single parameter, **x** (hence, it's unary). When this second function is called, it will call all the functions that were passed as parameters to **composeManyUnary** from right to left (the function that was the last parameter will be called first). The first iteration of **reduceRight** will call the rightmost function with **x** as its parameter. Subsequent functions are called on the output of the previous function call. The second-to-last function in the parameter list is called with the output of the last function in the parameter list that's applied to **x**. The third-to-last function in the parameter list is called with the output of the second-to-last function and so on until there are no more functions to call.

Exercise 77: A Binary to n-ary Compose Function

In this exercise, we will implement an n-ary **compose** function can be used to compose an arbitrary number of functions.

> **Note**
>
> Exercise 77 comes with tests and a skeleton for the methods in the starter file, **exercise-2-to-n-compose-start.js**. The file can be run with **node exercise-2-to-n-compose-start.js**. This command has been aliased with npm scripts to **npm run Exercise77**. The working solution for this exercise can be run using the npm run Exercise77 file on GitHub.

1. Change the current directory to **Lesson10**. This allows us to use pre-mapped commands to run our code.

2. Now, run **npm run Exercise77** (or **node exercise-to-n-compose-start.js**). You will see the following output:

```
> node exercise-2-to-n-compose-start.js

Assertion failed:  compose3 behaves as expected
Assertion failed:  composeManyUnary works with 3 functions
Assertion failed:  composeManyReduce works with 3 functions
```

Figure 10.26: Running the start file of the exercise

The assertions for **compose3**, **composeManyUnary**, and **composeManyReduce** are all failing, mainly because they're currently aliased to **compose2**.

3. A **compose** for two functions is already implemented:

```
const compose2 = (f, g) => x => f(g(x));
```

compose3 is a naive three-parameter **compose** function that takes the third parameter, calls it first, then calls the second parameter on the output of the first call.

4. Finally, it calls the first parameter on the output of the second parameter, like so:

```
const compose3 = (f, g, h) => x => f(g(h(x)))
```

> **Note**
>
> The function that is the furthest to the right of the parameter definition is called first.
>
> Considering the parameters as an array and that JavaScript has a **reduceRight** function (which traverses an array from right to left while also keeping an accumulator, much like **reduce**), there is a path forward forming.

5. After implementing **compose3**, we can run **npm run Exercise77** again and see that the assertion for **compose3** is not failing anymore:

```
> node exercise-2-to-n-compose-start.js

Assertion failed:  composeManyUnary works with 3 functions
Assertion failed:  composeManyReduce works with 3 functions
```

Figure 10.27: Output after implementing compose3

6. Use parameter rest to allow for an arbitrary number of functions to be composed:

```
const composeManyUnary = (...fns) => x =>
    fns.reduceRight((acc, curr) => curr(acc), x);
```

7. After implementing **composeManyUnary**, the corresponding failing assertion is now passing:

```
> node exercise-2-to-n-compose-start.js

Assertion failed: composeManyReduce works with 3 functions
```

Figure 10.28: Output after implementing compose3 and composeManyUnary

8. Define that compose is using a left-to-right traversal (with **reduce**):

```
const composeManyReduce = (...fns) =>
    fns.reduce((acc, curr) => (...args) => acc(curr(...args)));
```

We can **composeManyReduce** with three functions, that is, **f**, **g**, and **h**. Our implementation will start reducing through the functions. At the first iteration, it will return a function that will take however many arguments (**args**). When called, it will call **f(g(args))**. On the second iteration, it will return a function that takes an arbitrary number of arguments and returns **f(g(h(args)))**. At this point, there are no more functions to iterate through, so the final output of a function that takes a set of arguments and returns **f(g(h(arguments)))** is the output of the **composeManyReduce** function.

After implementing **composeManyReduce**, the corresponding failing assertion is now passing:

```
> node exercise-2-to-n-compose-start.js
```

Figure 10.29: Implementing compose3, composeManyUnary, and composeManyReduce

Function Composition in the Real World with a Simple BFF

A BFF is a server-side component that wraps (API) functionality in a way that is specific to the user interface it serves. This is as opposed to an API that is designed to export general business logic. The backend for frontend might consume an upstream API or the backing service directly, depending on the architecture. A company might have a set of core services to implement business logic and then a BFF for their mobile application, another BFF for their web frontend, and a final BFF for their internal dashboard. Each of the BFFs will have different constraints and data shapes that make the most sense for their respective consumers.

General-purpose APIs tend to have a larger surface area, are maintained by a different team, and have multiple consumers, which in turn leads to the API's shape evolving slowly. The API endpoints are not specific to the user interface, so the frontend application might have to make a lot of API requests just to load up a single screen. A backend for frontend alleviates these issues since each page or screen can have its own endpoint or dataset that it uses. The backend for a frontend will orchestrate the fetching of any relevant data.

To implement the backend for frontend, `micro` will be used. micro is a library for "Asynchronous HTTP microservices" and was built by Zeit. It is very small compared to Express or Hapi. In order to do this, it leverages modern JavaScript features as async/await calls, and its composition model is based on function composition. That is, what would be a middleware in Express or Hapi is a higher-order function that takes a function as a parameter and returns a new function. This is a great opportunity to use `compose` since the interface of the functions that are being composed are function in as a parameter and function out as a return value.

> **Note**
>
> The very brief documentation for micro can be found at https://github.com/zeit/micro. The library itself is barely a couple of hundred lines of JavaScript.

A micro "Hello world" might look as follows. micro accepts a single HTTP handler function that can be async or not. Either way, it is await-ed. It doesn't have a built-in router, which is one of the core APIs that's exposed by Express or Hapi. The output of the handler is sent back as the HTTP response body with a 200 status code:

```
const micro = require('micro');


const server = micro(async () => {

  return '<p>Hello micro!</p>Run this with <code>node example-2-micro-hello.
js</code>';
});


server.listen(3000, () => {
  console.log('Listening on http://localhost:3000');
});
```

Adding request timer logging can be done with the built-in JavaScript `console.time` and `console.timeEnd` functions:

```
// handler and server.listen are unchanged
const timer = fn => async (req, res) => {
  console.time('request');
  const value = await fn(req, res);
  console.timeEnd('request');
  return value;
};


const server = micro(timer(hello));
```

Function composition is the frontend, while the center of micro is the API. Adding a more complex operation such as API key authentication doesn't make integration any more difficult.

The **authenticate** function can have as much complexity as it wants. If it accepts a function parameter and returns a function that takes a **req** (request) and **res** (response) object, it will be compatible with other micro packages and handlers:

```
// handler, timer and server.listen are unchanged
const ALLOWED_API_KEYS = new Set(['api-key-1', 'key-2-for-api']);
const authenticate = fn => async (req, res) => {
  const {authorization} = req.headers;
  if (authorization && authorization.startsWith('ApiKey')) {
    const apiKey = authorization.replace('ApiKey', '').trim();
    if (ALLOWED_API_KEYS.has(apiKey)) {
      return fn(req, res);
    }
  }


  return sendError(
```

```
    req,
    res,
    createError(401, `Unauthorizsed: ${responseText}`)
  );
};
```

```
const server = micro(timer(authenticate(handler)));
```

The micro library leverages function composition so that dependencies between each level of request handling are made obvious.

Exercise 78: Leveraging Compose to Simplify the Micro Server Creation Step

In this exercise, you will refactor the timer and authentication example from the previous section to use **compose**.

> ### Note
>
> Exercise 78 comes with a preconfigured server and a run method alias in the starter files, that is, **exercise-micro-compose-start.js**. The server can be run with **npm run Exercise78**. The working solution for this exercise can be run using the npm run Exercise78 file on GitHub.

Perform the following steps to complete this exercise:

1. Change the current directory to **Lesson10** and run **npm install** if you haven't done so in this directory before.

2. First, run the **node exercise-micro-compose-start.js** command. Then run **npm run Exercise78**. You will see the application starting up, as follows:

```
> node exercise-micro-compose-start.js

Listening on http://localhost:3000
```

Figure 10.30: Running the start file of this exercise

3. Accessing the application with the following **curl** should yield an unauthorized response:

```
curl http://localhost:3000
```

The following is the output of the preceding code:

```
> curl http://localhost:3000
Unauthorized:
Hello authenticated micro!

Run this with node example-api-key-auth.js

## Test requests

Try the following:
  - curl http://localhost:3000 -H 'Authorization: ApiKey api-key-1' -I
which should 200</li>
  - curl http://localhost:3000 -H 'Authorization: ApiKey bad-key' -I wh
ich should 401</li>
  - curl http://localhost:3000 -H 'Authorization: Bearer bearer-token'
-I  which should 401</li>
  - curl http://localhost:3000 -I which should 401
```

Figure 10.31: cURL of the micro application

Note that the compose function is pre-populated in this module.

4. Instead of calling each function on the output of the previous one, we will use compose and call its output to create the server. This will replace the server-creation step:

```
const server = compose(
  micro,
  timer,
  authenticate,
  handler
)();
```

The server-creation step initially looked as follows, which is quite verbose and possibly difficult to read. The **compose** version clearly shows the pipeline that a request will have to come through:

```
const server = micro(timer(authenticate(handler)));
```

5. Restart the application for the changes to take place. Once `npm run Exercise78` is up and running, you should be able to `curl`:

    ```
    curl http://localhost:3000
    ```

    Following is the output of the preceding code:

```
> curl http://localhost:3000
Unauthorized:
Hello authenticated micro!

Run this with node example-api-key-auth.js

## Test requests

Try the following:
  - curl http://localhost:3000 -H 'Authorization: ApiKey api-key-1' -I
 which should 200</li>
  - curl http://localhost:3000 -H 'Authorization: ApiKey bad-key' -I wh
ich should 401</li>
  - curl http://localhost:3000 -H 'Authorization: Bearer bearer-token'
-I  which should 401</li>
  - curl http://localhost:3000 -I which should 401
```

Figure 10.32: cURL of the micro application with compose

In this exercise, we saw that the **compose** refactor didn't affect the functionality of the application. It is possible to try different requests as per the response.

The preceding problem can be sorted with the following code:

```
curl http://localhost:3000 -H 'Authorization: ApiKey api-key-1' -I
```

The following requests will fail with a 401 error since we are not setting a valid authorization header:

```
curl http://localhost:3000 -H 'Authorization: ApiKey bad-key' -I
curl http://localhost:3000 -H 'Authorization: Bearer bearer-token' -I
```

For comparison, here is the equivalent BFF application using Express and its middleware-based composition model. It implements similar functionality to the micro BFF we finished this exercise with:

```javascript
const express = require('express');


const app = express();


const responseText = `Hello authenticated Express!`;


const timerStart = (req, res, next) => {
  const timerName = `request_${(Math.random() * 100).toFixed(2)}`;
  console.time(timerName);
  req.on('end', () => {
    console.timeEnd(timerName);
  });
  next();
};


const ALLOWED_API_KEYS = new Set(['api-key-1', 'key-2-for-api']);
const authenticate = (req, res, next) => {
  const {authorization} = req.headers;
  if (authorization && authorization.startsWith('ApiKey')) {
    const apiKey = authorization.replace('ApiKey', '').trim();
    if (ALLOWED_API_KEYS.has(apiKey)) {
      return next();
    }
  }

  return res.status(401).send(`Unauthorized: <pre>${responseText}</pre>`);
};


const requestHandler = (req, res) => {
```

```
      return res.send(responseText);
   };


   app.use(timerStart, authenticate, requestHandler);


   app.listen(3000, () => {
      console.log('Listening on http://localhost:3000');
   });
```

Knowing about the possibilities that function composition brings will mean more reflection goes into the design of the function interface (inputs and outputs) so that, for example, **compose** can be leveraged. The next section covers immutability and side effects, which are necessary so that we can compose a set of partially applied or pure functions.

Immutability and Side Effects

In a pure function context, the mutation of variables is considered a side effect and therefore a function where the mutation occurs, especially of variables that live beyond the execution of the function, is not pure.

Immutability in JavaScript is hard to enforce but the language gives us good primitives to write in an immutable style. This style leans heavily on operators and functions that create a copy of data instead of mutating in place.

It is possible to write entire sections of applications without using side effects. Any data manipulation is possible without side effects. Most applications, however, need to load the data so that it is displayed from somewhere and possibly save some of the data somewhere as well. These are side effects that need to be managed.

A Look at Redux Action Creators

Action creators create Redux actions. They're useful to abstract the constants and centralize what actions the Redux store supports.

Action creators always return a new action object. Creating and returning a new object is a good way to guarantee the immutability of the return value at least as far as the action creator is concerned. If the action creators returned some version of their parameters, it could make for surprising outputs:

```
const ADD_PRODUCT = 'ADD_PRODUCT';


function addProduct(newProduct) {
```

```
  return {
    type: ADD_PRODUCT,
    newProduct
  };
}
```

Instead of calling **dispatch** with a manually marshaled object, it can be called with the output of an action creator:

```
this.props.dispatch(addProduct(newProduct))
```

Exercise 79: Refactoring the React/Redux Application to Use Action Creators

Action creators are a great way to abstract the action shape from the React component.

> **Note**
>
> Exercise 79 comes with a preconfigured development server and a skeleton for the methods in the starter files, that is, **exercise--refactor-action-creators-start.js** and **exercise-refactor-action-creators-start.html**. The development server can be run with **npm run Exercise79**. The working solution for this exercise can be run using the npm run exercise10 file on GitHub.

In this exercise, you will go from using inline action definitions to using action creators.

Perform the following steps to complete this exercise:

1. Change the current directory to **Lesson10** and run **npm install** if you haven't done so in this directory before. **npm install** downloads the dependencies that are required in order to run this activity (React, Redux, react-redux, and Parcel).

2. First, run **npx parcel serve exercise-refactor-action-creators-start.html**. To see the application during development, run **npm run Exercise79**. You will see the application starting up, as follows:

```
> parcel serve exercise-refactor-action-creators-start.html

Server running at http://localhost:1234
+  Built in 3.40s.
```

Figure 10.33: Running the start file of this exercise

For the development server to live-reload our changes and to avoid configuration issues, edit the **exercise-refactor-action-creators-start.js** file directly.

3. Go to **http://localhost:1234** (or whichever URL the starting script output). You should see the following HTML page:

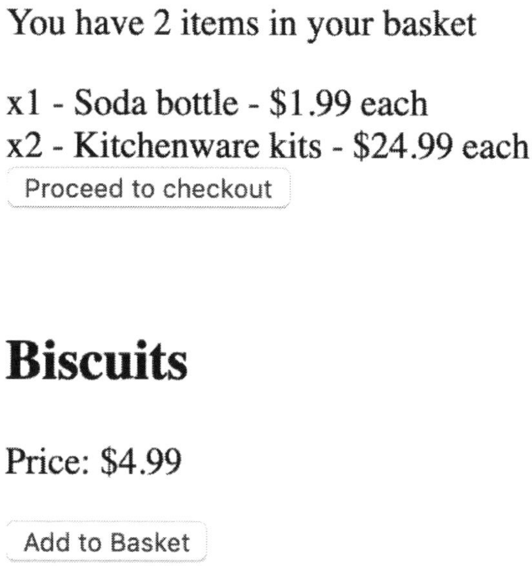

You have 2 items in your basket

x1 - Soda bottle - $1.99 each
x2 - Kitchenware kits - $24.99 each

Proceed to checkout

Biscuits

Price: $4.99

Add to Basket

Figure 10.34: Initial application in the browser

4. Implement the **startCheckout**, **continueShopping**, **done**, and **addProduct** action creators:

```
function startCheckout(items) {
  return {
    type: START_CHECKOUT,
    basket: {
      items
    }
  };
}

function continueShopping() {
  return {
    type: CONTINUE_SHOPPING
  };
}

function done() {
```

```
    return {
      type: DONE
    };
  }

  function addProduct(newProduct) {
    return {
      type: ADD_PRODUCT,
      newProduct: {
        ...newProduct,
        quantity: 1
      }
    };
  }
```

These return the following action types, respectively: **START_CHECKOUT**, **CONTINUE_SHOPPING**, **DONE**, and **ADD_PRODUCT**.

5. Update **handleCheckout** to use the corresponding **startCheckout** action creator:

```
handleCheckout(items) {
  this.props.dispatch(startCheckout(items));
}
```

6. Update **continueShopping** to use the corresponding **continueShopping** action creator:

```
continueShopping() {
  this.props.dispatch(continueShopping());
}
```

7. Update **finish** to use the corresponding **done** action creator:

```
finish() {
  this.props.dispatch(done());
}
```

8. Update **addProduct** to use the corresponding **addProduct** action creator:

```
addProduct(product) {
  this.props.dispatch(addProduct(product));
}
```

4. Create a new selector for **status**:

    ```
    const selectStatus = state => state && state.status;
    ```

5. Create a new selector for **product**:

    ```
    const selectProduct = state => state && state.product;
    ```

6. In **mapStateToProps**, map **items**, **product**, and **status** to their corresponding selectors, which are applied to the state:

    ```
    const mapStateToProps = state => {
      return {
        items: selectBasketItems(state),
        status: selectStatus(state),
        product: selectProduct(state)
      };
    };
    ```

7. Take the functions that call **dispatch** in the App component and extract them to **mapDispatchToProps**, taking care to remove **this.props** from **this.props.dispatch**. Dispatch is the first parameter to **mapDispatchToProps**. Our code should now look as follows:

    ```
    const mapDispatchToProps = dispatch => {
      return {
        handleCheckout(items) {
          dispatch(startCheckout(items))
        },
        continueShopping() {
          dispatch(continueShopping());
        },
        finish() {
          dispatch(done());
        },
        addProduct(product) {
          dispatch(addProduct(product));
        }
      };
    };
    ```

8. Replace the references in **App#render** to **this.handleCheckout**. Instead, call **this. props.handleCheckout**:

```
{status === 'SHOPPING' && (
  <Basket
    items={items}
    renderItem={item => (
      <div>
        x{item.quantity} - {item.name} - $
        {(item.price / 100).toFixed(2)} each{' '}
      </div>
    )}
    onCheckout={this.props.handleCheckout}
    />
)}
```

9. Replace the references in **App#render** to **this.continueShopping** and **this.finish**. Instead, call **this.props.continueShopping** and **this.props.finish**, respectively:

```
{status === 'CHECKING_OUT' && (
  <div>
    <p>You have started checking out with {items.length} items.</p>
    <button onClick={this.props.continueShopping}>
      Continue shopping
    </button>
    <button onClick={this.props.finish}>Finish</button>
  </div>
)}
```

10. Replace the references in **App#render** to **this.addProduct**. Instead, call **this.props. addProduct**:

```
{status === 'SHOPPING' && (
  <div style={{marginTop: 50}}>
    <h2>{product.name}</h2>
    <p>Price: ${product.price / 100}</p>
    <button onClick={() => this.props.addProduct(product)}>
      Add to Basket
    </button>
  </div>
)}
```

```
    }
  ],
  'demo of rest in parameter + spread'
);
```

The array's **rest** and **spread** syntax predate the object's spread/rest since it was part of ECMAScript 2015 (also known as ES6). Much like its object counterpart, it is very useful for creating shallow copies. Another use case we have already seen is converting Array-like objects into fully-fledged Arrays. The same trick can also be used with iterrable such as **Set**.

In the following examples, Array spread is being used to create a copy of an array before sorting it and being used to convert a Set into an Array. Array spread is also being used to create a copy of all but the first element of an array:

```
// Node.js built-in
const assert = require('assert').strict;


const initial = [
  {
    count: 1,
    name: 'Shampoo'
  },
  {
    count: 2,
    name: 'Soap'
  }
];


assert.deepStrictEqual(
  // Without the spread, reverse() mutates the array in-place
  [...initial].reverse(),
  [
    {
      count: 2,
      name: 'Soap'
```

```
    },
    {
       count: 1,
       name: 'Shampoo'
    }
  ],
  'demo of immutable reverse'
);

assert.deepStrictEqual(
  [...new Set([1, 2, 1, 2])],
  [1, 2],
  'demo of spread on Sets'
);

const [first, ...rest] = initial;
assert.deepStrictEqual(first, {count: 1, name: 'Shampoo'});
assert.deepStrictEqual(rest, [
  {
     count: 2,
     name: 'Soap'
  }
]);
```

Object.freeze makes an object read-only if it's running in strict mode.

For example, the following snippets of code will use throw since we're trying to add a property to a frozen object in strict mode:

```
// Node.js built-in
const assert = require('assert').strict;

const myProduct = Object.freeze({
  name: 'Special Sauce',
  price: 1999
```

```
});


assert.throws(() => {
  'use strict';
  myProduct.category = 'condiments';
}, 'writing to an existing property is an error in strict mode');


assert.throws(() => {
  'use strict';
  myProduct.name = 'Super Special Sauce';
}, 'writing a new property is an error in strict mode');
```

Object.freeze is seldom used in practice. JavaScript, as a language designed to run in the browser, is built to be very permissive. Runtime errors exist but should be avoided, especially for something that is bound to be an application issue: writing to a property that is read-only.

What's more, **Object.freeze** only throws in non-strict mode. Take a look at the following example, where accessing and mutating properties on a frozen object is allowed because, by default, JavaScript runs in non-strict mode:

```
// Node.js built-in
const assert = require('assert').strict;


const myProduct = Object.freeze({
  name: 'Special Sauce',
  price: 1999
});


assert.doesNotThrow(() => {
  myProduct.category = 'condiments';
}, 'writing to an existing property is fine in non-strict mode');


assert.doesNotThrow(() => {
  myProduct.name = 'Super Special Sauce';
}, 'writing a new property is fine in non-strict mode');
```

Instead of enforcing immutability, engineering teams often choose to adhere to coding standards that embrace an immutable style.

> **Note**
>
> It is also possible to leverage libraries such as Immutable.js, which provides persistent immutable data structures that are implemented in an efficient manner.

Handling Side Effects in a React/Redux Application React Life Cycle Hooks

The React component's **render()** method should be pure, so it does not support side effects. Being able to predict whether a component needs to re-render based on its inputs (props and state) means a lot of otherwise wasteful updates can be avoided. Since every state or prop update can cause a call to **render**, it is probably not the best spot to place API calls.

What the React documentation suggests is to use the **componentDidMount** life cycle method. **componentDidMount** runs after the component is mounted. In other words, it runs the first time the component is rendered on a page if it wasn't being rendered in the previous state of the React application.

We can use **componentDidMount** to send the HTTP request with **fetch**. The **fetch** Promise's **.then** can be used to update the state from the server response:

```
import React from 'react';


class App extends React.Component {
  constructor() {
    super();
    this.state = {};
  }


  componentDidMount() {
    fetch('https://hello-world-micro.glitch.me')
      .then(response => {
        if (response.ok) {
          return response.text();
        }
```

```
        })
        .then(data => {
          this.setState({
            message: data
          });
        });
    }


    render() {
      return (
        <div>
          <p>Message: {this.state.message}</p>
        </div>
      );
    }
  }
```

Handling Side Effects in a React/Redux Application React Hooks

As a recent addition to React, hooks allow function components to leverage all the features that used to be specific to class components.

The previous example can be refactored into a function component that uses the **useState** and **useEffect** hooks. **useState** is a way we can use state with React function components using a hook. React will re-render the function component when the state from **useState** changes. **useEffect** is a counterpart to `componentDidMount` and is called before the render of the component if the component wasn't being rendered in the application's previous state:

```
import React, {useEffect, useState} from 'react';


const App = () => {
  const [message, setMessage] = useState(null);
  useEffect(() => {
    if (!message) {
      fetch('https://hello-world-micro.glitch.me')
        .then(response => {
```

```
          if (response.ok) {
            return response.text();
          }
        })
        .then(data => {
          setMessage(data);
        });
    }
  });
  return (
    <div>
      <p>Message: {message}</p>
    </div>
  );
};
```

Handling Side Effects in a React/Redux Application Redux-Thunk

A thunk is a way to delay the evaluation of a function. It is a way to do lazy evaluation in languages that don't support it out of the box:

```
let globalState;

function thunk() {
  return () => {
    globalState = 'updated';
  };
}

const lazy = thunk();
console.assert(!globalState, 'executing the thunk does nothing');
lazy();
console.assert(
```

```
  globalState === 'updated',
  'executing the output of the thunk runs the update'
);
```

It is also a way to encapsulate side effects. Since we have first-class functions, we pass the thunk around, which is allowed in pure functions (the thunk is just a function), although calling the thunk itself might have side effects.

redux-thunk is quite simple; instead of passing an action creator that returns an object (with a type field and possibly a payload), the action creator returns a function that takes the store's dispatch and **getState** as parameters.

Inside the thunk, it is possible to access the current store state and dispatch actions, which will be reduced into the store. See the following example with Redux and redux-thunk:

```
// store is set up, App is connected, redux-thunk middleware is applied
import React from 'react';


class App extends React.Component {
  componentDidMount() {
    // this looks like any action creator
    this.props.dispatch(requestHelloWorld());
  }


  render() {
    return (
      <div>
        <p>Message: {this.props.message}</p>
      </div>
    );
  }
}
```

```javascript
function requestHelloWorld() {
  // this action creator returns a function
  return (dispatch, getState) => {
    fetch('https://hello-world-micro.glitch.me')
      .then(response => {
        if (response.ok) {
          return response.text();
        }
      })
      .then(data => {
        dispatch({
          type: 'REQUEST_HELLO_WORLD_SUCCESS',
          message: data
        });
      })
      .catch(error => {
        dispatch({
          type: 'REQUEST_HELLO_WORLD_ERROR',
          error
        });
      });
  };
}
```

Introduction to GraphQL Language Schemas and Queries

GraphQL is a query language. It exposes a typed schema to run queries against. The massive benefit of GraphQL is that the client requests what information it needs. This is a direct effect of having a typed schema.

We will add GraphQL to our BFF using **express-graphql**, which is compatible with micro. We need to provide our GraphQL endpoint with a schema and resolvers so that it can respond to client requests. Such a server is provided in the Exercise 12 start file (change the working directory to **Lesson10**, run **npm install** followed by **npm run Exercise81**, and navigate to **http://localhost:3000** to see it in action).

A sample GraphQL query that returns a basket can work within the following GraphQL schema definition. Note how we have three types, that is, **Query**, **basket,** and **basketItem**. A **basket** contains a list of **basketItems** under an **items** property. The **query** contains the top-level GraphQL query fields, which in this case is just **basket**. To query for **basketItems**, we must load the corresponding **basket** and expand the **items** field:

```
type basket {
  items: [basketItem]
}


"""BasketItem"""
type basketItem {
  name: String
  price: Int
  quantity: Int
  id: String
}


"""Root query"""
type Query {
  basket: basket
}
```

A tool that comes baked into Node.js GraphQL server components is GraphiQL. It is an interface for GraphQL that allows users to go through the schema and provides documentation of the schema.

The query that we entered reads as follows: load the **basket** top-level query field, expand its **items** field, and populate the **name**, **quantity**, and **price** of the **basketItem** elements in the basket's **items** field:

```
GraphiQL  ▶  Prettify  Merge  Copy  History        ‹ Docs

 1 ▾ query{                    ▾ {
 2 ▾   basket {                ▾   "data": {
 3 ▾     items{                ▾     "basket": {
 4         name                ▾       "items": [
 5         quantity            ▾         {
 6         price|                        "name": "Soda bottle",
 7       }                               "quantity": 1,
 8     }                                 "price": 199
 9   }                                 },
10                             ▾         {
                                          "name": "Kitchenware kits",
                                          "quantity": 2,
                                          "price": 2499
                                        }
                                      ]
                                    }
                                  }
                                }
```

Figure 10.38: GraphiQL user interface and a GraphQL query that fetches
fully expanded basket items

Running Updates with GraphQL Mutations and Resolvers

In a query and schema world, one thing that's sorely missing is a way to run write operations. That is where GraphQL mutations come in. Mutations are structured update operations.

Resolvers are a server-side GraphQL implementation detail. A resolver is what resolves a GraphQL query. Resolvers run from the top to the bottom of the schema chain. When resolving a query, fields on an object are executed in parallel; when resolving a mutation, they're resolved in sequence. The following is an example of a mutation being used:

```
const mutation = new GraphQLObjectType({
  name: 'Mutation',
  fields() {
```

```
    return {};
  }
});
```

> **Note**
>
> More guides on GraphQL can be found at https://graphql.org.

Exercise 81: Implementing a BFF Mutation with micro and GraphQL

In this exercise, we will use micro and GraphQL to implement a BFF mutation.

Perform the following steps to complete this exercise:

> **Note**
>
> Exercise 81 comes with a preconfigured server and a skeleton for the methods in the starter file **exercise-graphql-micro-start.js**. The development server can be run with **npm run Exercise81**. The working solution for this exercise can be run using the **npm run Exercise81** file on GitHub.

1. Change the current directory to **Lesson10** and run **npm install** if you haven't done so in this directory before. **npm install** downloads the dependencies that are required so that we can run this activity (micro and **express-graphql**).

2. Run **node exercise-graphql-micro-start.js**. Then, during development, run **npm run Exercise81**. You will see the application starting up, as follows:

```
> node exercise-graphql-micro-start.js

listening on port 3000
```

Figure 10.39: Running the start file of this exercise

3. Go to **http://localhost:3000** (or whichever URL the starting script output). You should see the following GraphiQL page:

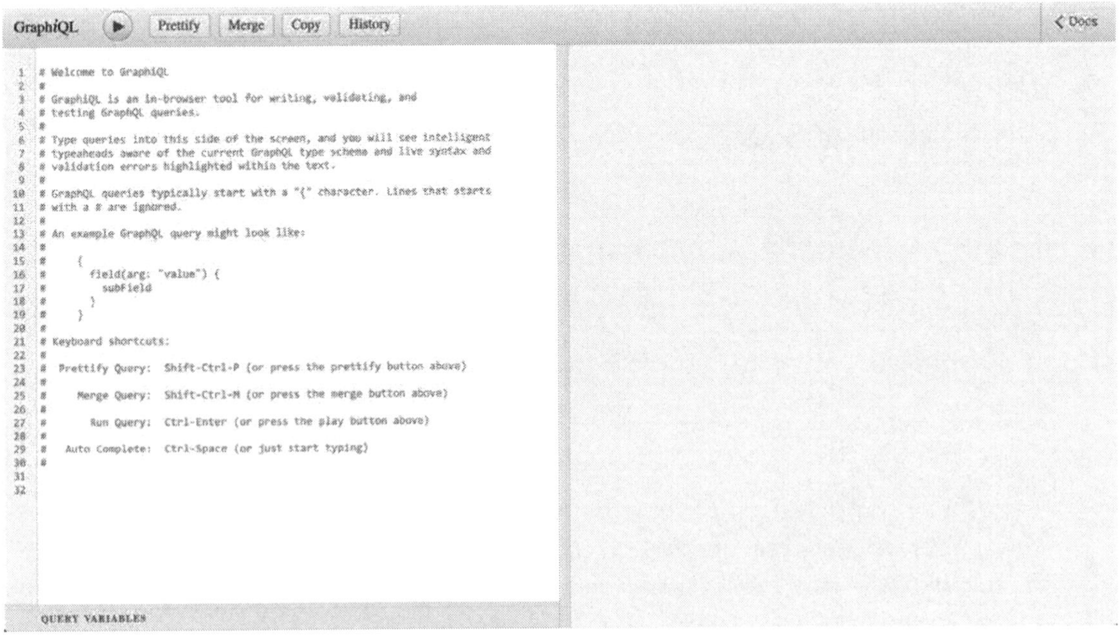

Figure 10.40: Empty GraphiQL user interface

4. Add a **LineItemCost** constant, which is a field definition (plain JavaScript object):

```
const LineItemCost:
= {
  type: GraphQLInt,
  args: {id: {type: GraphQLString}},
  resolve(root, args, context) {
    return 4;
  }
};
```

Our **LineItemCost** should have a **type** property set to **GraphQLInt** since the output of **LineItemCost** calculation is an integer. **LineItemCost** should also have an **args** field, which should be set to **{id: {type: GraphQLString}}**. In other words, our mutation takes an **id** argument that is a string (which is congruent with the sample data we have). For the mutation to return something, it needs a **resolve()** method. For now, it can return any integer. The **resolve** method of a mutations takes the root as the first parameter and the **args** as the second parameter.

5. Let's implement the actual **resolve** method of **LineItemCost** now. First, we need to look up the item from **basketItems** by ID using **.find(el => el.id === args. id)**. Then, we can calculate the cost of the item (**item.price * item.quantity**), as follows:

    ```
    const LineItemCost = {
      type: GraphQLInt,
      args: {id: {type: GraphQLString}},
      resolve(root, args, context) {
        const item = basketItems.find(i => i.id === args.id);
        return item ? item.quantity * item.price : null;
      }
    };
    ```

6. Create a mutation constant that's a **GraphQLObjectType**. See how the query is initialized; its name should be **Mutation**:

    ```
    const mutation = new GraphQLObjectType({
      name: 'Mutation',
      fields() {
        return {};
      }
    });
    ```

7. Add **LineItemCost** to the mutation **fields()** return value. This means that **LineItemCost** is now a top-level mutation. It can be called if **mutation** exists on the GraphQL schema:

    ```
    const mutation = new GraphQLObjectType({
      name: 'Mutation',
      fields() {
        return {LineItemCost};
      }
    });
    ```

8. Add **mutation** to the **GraphQLSchema** schema:

    ```
    const handler = graphqlServer({
      schema: new GraphQLSchema({query, mutation}),
      graphiql: true
    });
    ```

9. Send the following query to your server (through GraphiQL). Enter it on the left-hand side editor and click the **Play** button:

```
mutation {
    cost1: LineItemCost(id: "1")
    cost2: LineItemCost(id: "2")
}
```

> **Note**
>
> This mutation is using what are called GraphQL aliases since we can't run the mutation under the same name twice.

The output should be as follows:

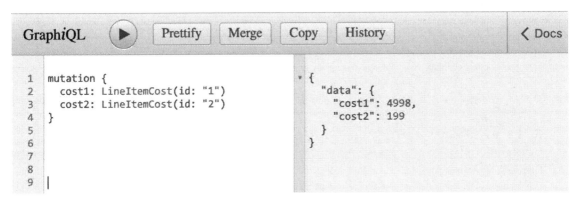

Figure 10.41: GraphiQL with LineItemCost aliased mutation queries for IDs "1" and "2"

To make the basket example more realistic, we will load the initial basket data from the GraphQL BFF, using the GraphQL query, redux-thunk, to handle the side effect, and a new reducer to update the Redux store state. The aim of the next activity is to show you how we can integrate a GraphQL BFF with a React/Redux application with redux-thunk.

Activity 17: Fetching the Current Basket From BFF

In this activity, we will fetch initial basket data from GraphQL BFF to re-render items to the shopping basket, thus updating the initial state of the basket. Let's get started:

> **Note**
>
> Activity 17 comes with a preconfigured development server and a skeleton for the methods in the starter files, that is, **activity-app-start.js** and **activity-app-start.html**. The development server can be run with **npm run Activity17**. The working solution for this activity can be run using the npm run Activity17 file on GitHub.

1. Change the current directory to **Lesson10** and run **npm install** if you haven't done so in this directory before.

2. Run the BFF for Activity 17 and **npx parcel serve activity-app-start.html**. During development, run **npm run Activity17**.

3. Go to **http://localhost:1234** (or whichever URL the starting script output) to check the HTML page.

4. Write a query that will fetch basket items from the BFF. You can use the GraphQL UI at **http://localhost:3000** to experiment with this.

5. Create a **requestBasket** (thunk) action creator that will call **fetchFromBff** with the query from the previous step.

6. Chain a **.then** onto the **fetchFromBff()** call to dispatch a **REQUEST_BASKET_SUCCESS** action with the right **basket** payload.

7. Add a case to the **appReducer** that will reduce a **REQUEST_BASKET_SUCCESS** action with a **basket** payload into the state.

8. Add **requestBasket** to **mapDispatchToProps**.

9. Call **requestBasket**, which is mapped to **dispatch**, in **App#componentDidMount**.

> **Note**
>
> The solution for this activity can be found on page 628.

Summary

First-class functions are part and parcel of using a popular library such as React and its patterns. They also power any and every delegation of implementation, especially on built-ins such as Array. Another core tenet of functional programming is pure functions. Using pure functions for complex data manipulation logic or an abstraction layer around a data structure is a great pattern that was put forward by the popular Redux state management solution. Any side effects and/or dependencies that must be mocked make it that much harder to reason about a complex data manipulation. Higher-order functions and specific techniques such as currying and partial application are widespread in day-to-day JavaScript development. Currying and partial application is a way to design functions with an interface that makes each step of specialization "savable" since it is already a function that has already been applied with a certain number of parameters.

The composition can have real value if a function application pipeline has been spotted. For example, modeling HTTP services as pipelines makes quite a lot of sense. On the other hand, the Node.js HTTP server ecosystem leaders use a middleware-based composition model, micro, which exposes a function composition model. Writing JavaScript in an immutable style allows libraries to have a cheap way to check whether something has changed or not. Side effects in React and Redux are handled outside the regular flow of pure functions, that is, render functions and reducers. Redux-thunk is quite a functional solution to the problem, albeit at the cost of making functions valid actions. Pure Redux actions are JavaScript objects with a type of property.

In this book, we've learned about various frameworks, including React, Angular, and related tools and libraries. It has taught us about the advanced concepts you need to know about to build modern applications. Then, we learned how to represent an HTML document in the Document Object Model (DOM). Later, we combined our knowledge of the DOM and Node.js to create a web scraper for practical situations.

In the next part, we created a Node.js-based RESTful API using the Express library for Node.js. We had a look at how modular designs can be used for better reusability and collaboration with multiple developers on a single project. We also learned how to build unit tests that ensure that the core functionality of our program is not broken over time. We saw how constructors, async/await, and events can load our applications with high speed and performance. The final part of this book introduced you to functional programming concepts such as immutability, pure functions, and higher-order functions.

Appendix

About

This section is included to assist the students to perform the activities in the book.
It includes detailed steps that are to be performed by the students to achieve the objectives of
the activities.

Chapter 1: JavaScript, HTML, and the DOM

Activity 1: Extracting Data from a Page

Solution:

1. Initialize a variable to store the entire content of the CSV:

   ```
   var csv = 'name,price,unit\n';
   ```

2. Query the DOM to find all the elements that represent each product. Notice how we wrap the **HTMLCollection** instance returned in **Array.from** so that we can handle it like a normal array:

   ```
   var elements = Array.from(document.getElementsByClassName('item'));
   ```

3. Iterate over each element found:

   ```
   elements.forEach((el) => {});
   ```

4. Inside the closure, using the **product** element, query to find the price with the unit. Split the string using a slash:

   ```
   var priceAndUnitElement = el.getElementsByTagName('span')[0];
   var priceAndUnit = priceAndUnitElement.textContent.split("/");
   var price = priceAndUnit[0].trim();
   var unit = priceAndUnit[1].trim();
   ```

5. Then query for the name:

   ```
   var name = el.getElementsByTagName('a')[0].textContent;
   ```

6. Append all information to the variable initialized in step 1, separating the values with commas. Don't forget to add newline characters to each line you append to:

   ```
   csv += `${name},${price},${unit}\n`;
   ```

7. Print the variable containing the accumulated data using the **console.log** function:

   ```
   console.log(csv);
   ```

8. Paste the code in the Chrome **Console** tab; it should look like this:

```
> var csv = 'name,price,unit\n';
  var elements = Array.from(document.getElementsByClassName('item'));
  elements.forEach((el) => {
    var priceAndUnitElement = el.getElementsByTagName('span')[0];
    var priceAndUnit = priceAndUnitElement.textContent.split("/");
    var price = priceAndUnit[0].trim();
    var unit = priceAndUnit[1].trim();

    var name = el.getElementsByTagName('a')[0].textContent;

    csv += `${name},${price},${unit}\n`;
  });
  console.log(csv);
```

Figure 1.62: Code ready to run in the Console tab

After pressing *Enter* to execute the code, you should see the CSV printed in the console, as shown here:

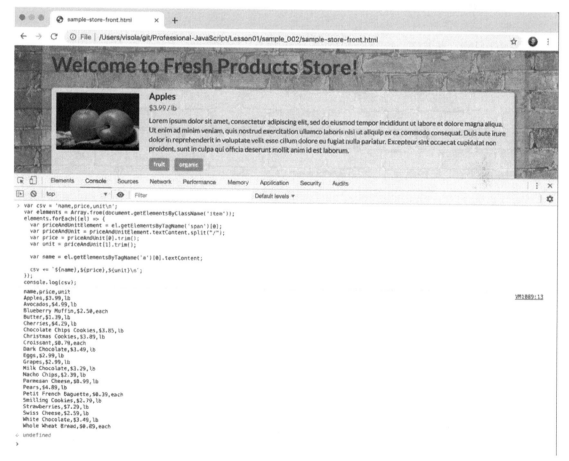

Figure 1.63: The storefront with the code and output in the Console tab

Activity 2: Replacing the Tag Filter with a Web Component

Solution:

1. Start by copying the code from **Exercise07** into a new folder.

2. Create a new file called **tags_holder.js** and in it add a class called **TagsHolder** that extends **HTMLElement**, then define a new custom component called **tags-holder**:

```
class TagsHolder extends HTMLElement {
}

customElements.define('tags-holder', TagsHolder);
```

3. Create two **render** methods: one to render the base state and one to render the tags or some text indicating that no tags are selected for filtering:

```
render() {
  this.shadowRoot.innerHTML = `
  <link rel="stylesheet" type="text/css" href="../css/semantic.min.css" />
  <div>
    Filtered by tags:
    <span class="tags"></span>
  </div>`;
}

renderTagList() {
  const tagsHolderElement = this.shadowRoot.querySelector('.tags');
  tagsHolderElement.innerHTML = '';

  const tags = this._selectedTags;
  if (tags.length == 0) {
    tagsHolderElement.innerHTML = 'No filters';
    return;
  }

  tags.forEach(tag => {
    const tagEl = document.createElement('span');
    tagEl.className = "ui label orange";
    tagEl.addEventListener('click', () => this.triggerTagClicked(tag));
    tagEl.innerHTML = tag;
    tagsHolderElement.appendChild(tagEl);
  });
}
```

4. In the constructor, call **w**, attach the component to the shadow root, initialize the list of selected tags, and call both **render** methods:

```
constructor() {
  super();
  this.attachShadow({ mode: 'open' });
  this._selectedTags = [];
  this.render();
  this.renderTagList();
}
```

5. Create a getter to expose the list of selected tags:

```
get selectedTags() {
  return this._selectedTags.slice(0);
}
```

6. Create two trigger methods: one to trigger the changed event and one to trigger the **tag-clicked** event:

```
triggerChanged(tag) {
  const event = new CustomEvent('changed', { bubbles: true });
  this.dispatchEvent(event);
}
```

```
triggerTagClicked(tag) {
  const event = new CustomEvent('tag-clicked', {
    bubbles: true,
    detail: { tag },
  });
  this.dispatchEvent(event);
}
```

7. Create two **mutator** methods: **addTag** and **removeTag**. These methods receive the tag name and add a tag if not present, or remove tag if present, in the list of selected tags. If the list was modified, trigger the **changed** event and call the method to re-render the list of tags:

```
addTag(tag) {
  if (!this._selectedTags.includes(tag)) {
    this._selectedTags.push(tag);
    this._selectedTags.sort();
    this.renderTagList();
    this.triggerChanged();
  }
}
```

```
   }

   removeTag(tag) {
     const index = this._selectedTags.indexOf(tag);
     if (index >= 0) {
       this._selectedTags.splice(index, 1);
       this.renderTagList();
       this.triggerChanged();
     }
   }
 }
```

8. In the HTML, replace the existing code with the new component. Remove the following lines:

```html
<div class="item">
  Filtered by tags: <span class="tags"></span>
</div>
```

And add:

```html
<tags-holder class="item"></tags-holder>
```

Also add:

```html
<script src="tags_holder.js"></script>
```

> **Note**
>
> You can see the final HTML on GitHub at https://github.com/TrainingByPackt/Professional-JavaScript/blob/master/Lesson01/Activity02/dynamic_storefront.html.

9. In **filter_and_search.js**, do the following:

   At the top, create a reference to the **tags-holder** component:

   ```
   const filterByTagElement = document.querySelector('tags-holder');
   ```

   Add event listeners to handle the **changed** and **tag-clicked** events:

   ```
   filterByTagElement.addEventListener('tag-clicked', (e) =>
   filterByTagElement.removeTag(e.detail.tag));
   filterByTagElement.addEventListener('changed', () => applyFilters());
   ```

   Remove the following functions and all references to them: **createTagFilterLabel** and **updateTagFilterList**.

   In the **filterByTags** function, replace **tagsToFilterBy** with **filterByTagElement.selectedTags**.

   In the **addTagFilter** method, replace the references to **tagsToFilterBy** with **filterByTagElement.addTag**.

Chapter 2: Node.js and npm

Activity 3: Creating a npm Package to Parse HTML

Solution:

1. In an empty folder, use npm to create a new package. You can use all the default values for the options:

```
$ npm init
This utility will walk you through creating a package.json file.
It only covers the most common items, and tries to guess sensible
defaults.

See 'npm help json' for definitive documentation on these fields and exactly
what they do.

Use 'npm install <pkg>' afterwards to install a package and save it as a
dependency in the package.json file.

Press ^C at any time to quit.
package name: (Activity03)
version: (1.0.0)
description:
entry point: (index.js)
test command:
git repository:
keywords:
author:
license: (ISC)
About to write to .../Lesson02/Activity03/package.json:

{
  "name": "Activity03",
  "version": "1.0.0",
  "description": "",
  "main": "index.js",
  "scripts": {
    "test": "echo \"Error: no test specified\" && exit 1"
  },
  "author": "",
```

```
    "license": "ISCs"
}
```

```
    Is this OK? (yes)
```

2. To install **cheerio**, run **npm install**. Make sure that you type the name of the library incorrectly:

```
$ npm install cheerio
npm notice created a lockfile as package-lock.json. You should commit this
file.
npm WARN Activity03@1.0.0 No description
npm WARN Activity03@1.0.0 No repository field.
+ cheerio@1.0.0-rc.3added 19 packages from 45 contributors and audited 34
packages in 6.334s
found 0 vulnerabilities
```

3. Inside this folder, create a file called **index.js** and add the following to it:

```
const cheerio = require('cheerio');
```

4. Create a variable that stores the HTML from the sample code from GitHub (https://github.com/TrainingByPackt/Professional-JavaScript/blob/master/Lesson01/Example/sample_001/sample-page.html). When creating multiline strings, you can use backquotes:

```
const html = `
<html>
  <head>
    <title>Sample Page</title>
  </head>
  <body>
    <p>This is a paragraph.</p>
    <div>
      <p>This is a paragraph inside a div.</p>
    </div>
    <button>Click me!</button>
  </body>
</html>
`;
```

5. Parse the HTML and pass it to cheerio. In cheerio's examples, you are going to see that they name the parsed variable as "**$**" (dollar sign). That is an old convention that was used in the jQuery world. This is what it looks like:

```
const $ = cheerio.load(html);
```

6. Now, we can use that variable to manipulate the HTML. To start, we will add a paragraph to the page with some text in it:

```
$('div').append('<p>This is another paragraph.</p>');
```

We can also query the HTML, similar to what we did in *Chapter 1, JavaScript, HTML, and the DOM,* using CSS selectors. Let's query for all the paragraphs and print their content to the console. Notice that cheerio elements do not behave exactly like DOM elements, but they are very similar.

7. Use the **firstChild** attribute to find the first node of each paragraph and print its content, assuming it will be the text element:

```
$('p').each((index, p) => {
    console.log(`${index} - ${p.firstChild.data}`);
});
```

8. Lastly, inside **index.js**, print the manipulated HTML to the console by calling the **html** function:

```
console.log($.html());
```

Now, you can run your application by calling it from Node.js:

```
$ node index.js
0 - This is a paragraph.
1 - This is a paragraph inside a div.
2 - This is another paragraph.
<html><head>
    <title>Sample Page</title>
    </head>
    <body>
    <p>This is a paragraph.</p>
    <div>
        <p>This is a paragraph inside a div.</p>
    <p>This is another paragraph.</p></div>
    <button>Click me!</button>

</body></html>
```

Figure 2.7: Calling the application from Node.js

Chapter 3: Node.js APIs and Web Scraping

Activity 4 Scraping Products and Prices from Storefront

Solution

1. Start the dynamic server to serve the storefront application using the code from *Exercise 14, Serving Dynamic Content*, in this chapter:

```
$ node Lesson03/Activity04/
Static resources from /path/to/repo/Lesson03/Activity04/static
Loaded 21 products...
Go to: http://localhost:3000
```

2. In a new Terminal, create a new **npm** package, install **jsdom**, and create the **index.js** entry file:

```
$ npm init
...
$ npm install jsdom
+ jsdom@15.1.1
added 97 packages from 126 contributors and audited 140 packages in
12.278s
found 0 vulnerabilities
```

3. Call the **require()** method to load all the modules you will need in the project:

```
const fs = require('fs');
const http = require('http');
const JSDOM = require('jsdom').JSDOM;
```

4. Make an HTTP request to **http://localhost:3000**:

```
const page = 'http://localhost:3000';
console.log(`Downloading ${page}...`);
const request = http.get(page, (response) => {
```

5. Ensure a successful response and collect the data from the body using the data event:

```
if (response.statusCode != 200) {
   console.error(`Error while fetching page ${page}: ${response.
statusCode}`);
   console.error(`Status message: ${response.statusMessage}`);
```

```
    return;
  }

  let content = '';
  response.on('data', (chunk) => content += chunk.toString());
```

6. In the **close** event, parse the HTML using **JSDOM**:

```
response.on('close', () => {
  console.log('Download finished.');
  const document = new JSDOM(content).window.document;
  writeCSV(extractProducts(document));
});
```

The preceding callback calls two functions: **extractProducts** and **writeCSV**. These functions are described in the upcoming steps.

7. Use the **extractProducts** function to query the DOM and fetch product information from it. It stores all the products in an array, which is returned at the end:

```
function extractProducts(document) {
  const products = [];
  console.log('Parsing product data...');
  Array.from(document.getElementsByClassName('item'))
    .forEach((el) => {
      process.stdout.write('.');
      const priceAndUnitElement = el.getElementsByTagName('span')[0];
      const priceAndUnit = priceAndUnitElement.textContent.split("/");
      const price = priceAndUnit[0].trim().substr(1);
      const unit = priceAndUnit[1].trim();

      const name = el.getElementsByTagName('a')[0].textContent;

      products.push({ name, price: parseFloat(price), unit });
    });
  console.log();
  console.log(`Found ${products.length} products.`);
  return products;
}
```

8. Use the **writeCSV** function, which opens the CSV file to write, ensuring that no error occurred:

```
function writeCSV(products) {
  const fileName = 'products.csv';

  console.log(`Writing data to ${fileName}...`);
  fs.open(fileName, 'w', (error, fileDescriptor) => {
    if (error != null) {
      console.error(`Can not write to file: ${fileName}`, error);
      return;
    }
```

9. Now that the file is open, we can write the product data to the file:

```
    // Write header
    fs.writeSync(fileDescriptor, 'name,price,unit\n');
    // Write content
    products.forEach((product) => {
      const line = `${product.name},${product.price},${product.unit}\n`;
      fs.writeSync(fileDescriptor, line);
    });
    console.log('Done.');
  });
}
```

10. In the new Terminal, run the application:

```
$ node .
Downloading http://localhost:3000...
Download finished.
Parsing product data...
....................
Found 21 products.
Writing data to products.csv...
```

Chapter 4: RESTful APIs with Node.js

Activity 5: Creating an API Endpoint for a Keypad Door Lock

Solution

1. Create a new project folder and change the directories going to it to the following:

   ```
   mkdir passcode
   cd passcode
   ```

2. Initialize an **npm** project and install **express**, **express-validator**, and **jwt-simple**. Then, make a directory for **routes**:

   ```
   npm init -y
   npm install --save express express-validator jwt-simple
   mkdir routes
   ```

3. Create a **config.js** file, just as you did in *Exercise 21, Setting Up an Endpoint that Requires Authentication*. This should contain a randomly generated secret value:

   ```
   let config = {};
   // random value below generated with command: openssl rand -base64 32
   config.secret = "cSmdV7Nh4e3gIFTO0ljJlH1f/F0ROKZR/hZfRYTSO0A=";
   module.exports = config;
   ```

4. Make the **routes/check-in.js** file in order to create a check-in route. This can be copied in whole from *Exercise 21, Setting Up an Endpoint that Requires Authentication*:

   ```
   const express = require('express');
   const jwt = require('jwt-simple');
   const { check, validationResult } = require('express-validator/check');
   const router = express.Router();

   // import our config file and get the secret value
   const config = require('../config');
   ```

5. Create a second route file called **routes/lock.js**. Start the file off by importing the required libraries and modules, and create an empty array to hold our valid passcodes:

   ```
   const express = require('express');
   const app = express();
   const { check, validationResult } = require('express-validator/check');
   const router = express.Router();
   ```

```
// Import path and file system libraries for importing our route files
const path = require('path');
const fs = require('fs');

// Import library for handling HTTP errors
const createError = require('http-errors');

// Import library for working with JWT tokens
const jwt = require('jwt-simple');

// import our config file and get the secret value
const config = require('./../config');
const secret = config.secret;

// Create an array to keep track of valid passcodes
let passCodes = [];
```

6. Create a **GET** route for **/code** that requires a **name** value, which is continued after the code in the preceding step in the **routes/lock.js** file:

```
router.get(['/code'], [
    check('name').isString().isAlphanumeric().exists()
  ],
  (req, res) => {
    let codeObj = {};
    codeObj.guest = req.body.name;
    // Check that authorization header was sent
    if (req.headers.authorization) {
      let token = req.headers.authorization.split(" ")[1];
      try {
        req._guest = jwt.decode(token, secret);
      } catch {
        res.status(403).json({ error: 'Token is not valid.' });
      }
      // If the decoded object guest name property
      if (req._guest.name) {
        codeObj.creator = req._guest.name;
```

7. Create another route in **routes/lock.js**. This one will be for **/open** and requires a four-digit code that will be checked against the **passCodes** array to see whether it is valid. Below that route, make sure to export **router**, so that it can be used in **server.js**:

```
router.post(['/open'], [
    check('code').isLength({ min: 4, max: 4 })
  ],
  (req, res) => {
    let code = passCodes.findIndex(obj => {
      return obj.code === req.body.code;
    });
    if(code !== -1) {
      passCodes.splice(code, 1);
      res.json({ message: 'Pass code is valid, door opened.' });
    } else {
      res.status(403).json({ error: 'Pass code is not valid.' });
    }
});

// Export route so it is available to import
module.exports = router;
```

8. Create the main file where our routes will be used in **server.js**. Start by importing the libraries needed and setting URL encoding the JSON:

```
const express = require('express');
const app = express();

// Import path and file system libraries for importing our route files
const path = require('path');
const fs = require('fs');

// Import library for handling HTTP errors
const createError = require('http-errors');


// Tell express to enable url encoding
app.use(express.urlencoded({extended: true}));
app.use(express.json());
```

9. Next, in **server.js**, below the preceding code, import the two routes, implement a **404** catch-all, and tell the API to listen on port **3000**:

```
// Import our index route
let lock = require('./routes/lock');
let checkIn = require('./routes/check-in');

app.use('/check-in', checkIn);
app.use('/lock', lock);

// catch 404 and forward to error handler
app.use(function(req, res, next) {
```

10. Finally, we will test the API to ensure it was done correctly. Start by running your program:

```
npm start
```

11. With the program running, open a second Terminal window and use the **/check-in** endpoint to get a JWT and save the value as **TOKEN**. Then, echo that value to ensure it was successful:

```
TOKEN=$(curl -sd "name=john" -X POST http://localhost:3000/check-in \
  | jq -r ".token")
echo $TOKEN
```

You should get back a long string of letters and numbers like the following:

```
philip@philip-ThinkPad-T420:/$ \
> TOKEN=$(curl -sd "name=john" -X POST http://localhost:3000/check-in \
>   | jq -r ".token")
philip@philip-ThinkPad-T420:/$ echo $TOKEN
eyJ0eXAiOiJKV1QiLCJhbGciOiJIUzI1NiJ9.eyJuYW1lIjoiam9objJ9.vuQgdnNlPJ13ZjGndTElCs
00_vFzRs0dvdMaoI_P6f0
philip@philip-ThinkPad-T420:/$
```

Figure 4.24: Getting TOKEN from the check-in endpoint

12. Next, we will use our JWT to use the **/lock/code** endpoint to get a one-time passcode for Sarah:

```
curl -sd "name=sarah" -X GET \
  -H "Authorization: Bearer ${TOKEN}" \
  http://localhost:3000/lock/code \
  | jq
```

You should get back an object containing a message and a four-digit code like in the following:

```
philip@philip-ThinkPad-T420:/$ \
> curl -sd "name=sarah" -X GET \
>    -H "Authorization: Bearer ${TOKEN}" \
>    http://localhost:3000/lock/code \
>    | jq
{
  "code": "4594",
  "message": "One-time code: 4594, created by john for sarah"
}
philip@philip-ThinkPad-T420:/$ █
```

Figure 4.25: A four-digit one-time code

13. To ensure the code works, send it to the **/lock/open** endpoint. We will send the following command once, expecting it to be successful. We will then send the same command a second time, expecting it to fail since each code is used only once. Run the following twice:

```
# IMPORTANT: Make sure to replace 4594, with your specific passcode!
curl -sd "code=4594" -X POST \
    http://localhost:3000/lock/open \
    | jq
```

Running the preceding command twice should return something like the following:

```
philip@philip-ThinkPad-T420:/$ \
> curl -sd "code=4594" -X POST \
>    http://localhost:3000/lock/open \
>    | jq
{
  "message": "Pass code is valid, door opened."
}
philip@philip-ThinkPad-T420:/$ \
> curl -sd "code=4594" -X POST \
>    http://localhost:3000/lock/open \
>    | jq
{
  "error": "Pass code is not valid."
}
philip@philip-ThinkPad-T420:/$ █
```

Figure 4.26: Running the command twice results in an error

If your result is the same as shown in the preceding figure, then you have successfully completed the activity.

Chapter 5: Modular JavaScript

Activity 6: Creating a Lightbulb with a Flash Mode

Solution:

1. Install the **babel-cli** and **babel** preset as developer dependencies:

   ```
   npm install --save-dev webpack webpack-cli @babel/core @babel/cli @babel/
   preset-env
   ```

2. Add a file called **.babelrc** to the root directory. In it, we will tell Babel to use the preset settings:

   ```
   {
     "presets": ["@babel/preset-env"]
   }
   ```

3. Add a webpack configuration file at **webpack.config.js** in the root directory:

   ```
   const path = require("path");

   module.exports = {
     mode: 'development',
     entry: "./build/js/viewer.js",
     output: {
       path: path.resolve(__dirname, "build"),
       filename: "bundle.js"
     }

   };
   ```

4. Create a new file called **js/flashingLight.js**. This should start as a blank ES6 component that extends **Light**. In the constructor, we will include **state**, **brightness**, and **flashMode**:

   ```
   import Light from './light.js';
   let privateVars = new WeakMap();

   class FlashingLight extends Light {

     constructor(state=false, brightness=100, flashMode=true) {
       super(state, brightness);
       let info = {"flashMode": flashMode};
       privateVars.set(this, info);
       if(flashMode===true) {
   ```

```
        this.startFlashing();
      }
   }
```

5. Add a setter method for the **FlashingLight** object, which will also trigger stop and start flash methods.

```
setFlashMode(flashMode) {
   let info = privateVars.get(this);
   info.flashMode = checkStateFormat(flashMode);
   privateVars.set(this, info);
   if(flashMode===true) {
     this.startFlashing();
   } else {
     this.stopFlashing();
   }
}
```

6. Add a getter method for the **FlashingLight** object:

```
getFlashMode() {
   let info = privateVars.get(this);
   return info.flashMode;
}
```

7. Create a **startFlashing** function that references the parent class's **lightSwitch()** function. This step is tricky because we have to bind it to **setInterval**:

```
startFlashing() {
   let info = privateVars.get(this);
   info.flashing = setInterval(this.toggle.bind(this),5000);
}
```

8. Create a **stopFlashing** function that can be used to turn off the timer:

```
stopFlashing() {
   let info = privateVars.get(this);
   clearInterval(info.flashing);
}
```

9. As the last part of **flashingLight.js**, close the class and export it:

```
}

export default FlashingLight;
```

10. Open **src/js/viewer.js** and modify the button to create a flashing light instead of a colored light:

```
button.onclick = function () {
  new FlashingLight(true, slider.value, true);
}
```

11. Compile the code by running our **build** function with npm:

```
npm run build
```

12. Open up **build/index.html** and set the script location as **bundle.js**:

```
<script src="bundle.js" type="module"></script>
```

13. To test that everything is working as expected, run **npm start** and open **localhost:8000** in your browser. Hit the **build** button to create a full page of lights. If everything has been done correctly, you should see each light blink at 5-second intervals:

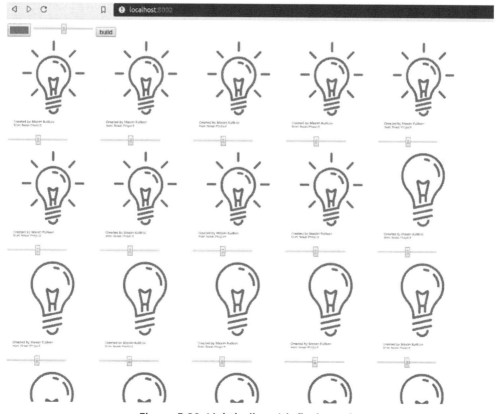

Figure 5.20: Lightbulbs with flash mode

Chapter 6: Code Quality

Activity 7: Putting It All Together

Solution

1. Install the developer dependencies listed in the linting exercise (**eslint**, **prettier**, **eslint-config-airbnb-base**, **eslint-config-prettier**, **eslint-plugin-jest**, and **eslint-plugin-import**):

    ```
    npm install --save-dev eslint prettier eslint-config-airbnb-base eslint-
    config-prettier eslint-plugin-jest eslint-plugin-import
    ```

2. Add an **eslint** configuration file, **.eslintrc**, which contains the following:

    ```
    {
      "extends": ["airbnb-base", "prettier"],
        "parserOptions": {
          "ecmaVersion": 2018,
          "sourceType": "module"
        },
        "env": {
          "browser": true,
          "node": true,
          "es6": true,
          "mocha": true,
          "jest": true
        },
        "plugins": [],
        "rules": {
          "no-unused-vars": [
            "error",
            {
              "vars": "local",
              "args": "none"
            }
          ],
          "no-plusplus": "off",
        }
    }
    ```

3. Add a .**prettierignore** file:

```
node_modules
build
dist
```

4. Add a **lint** command to your **package.json** file:

```
"scripts": {
  "start": "http-server",
  "lint": "prettier --write js/*.js && eslint js/*.js"
},
```

5. Open the **assignment** folder and install the developer dependencies for using Puppeteer with Jest:

```
npm install --save-dev puppeteer jest jest-puppeteer
```

6. Modify your **package.json** file by adding an option telling Jest to use the **jest-puppeteer** preset:

```
"jest": {
  "preset": "jest-puppeteer"
},
```

7. Add a **test** script to **package.json** that runs **jest**:

```
"scripts": {
  "start": "http-server",
  "lint": "prettier --write js/*.js && eslint js/*.js",
  "test": "jest"
},
```

8. Create a **jest-puppeteer.config.js** file containing the following:

```
module.exports = {
  server: {
    command: 'npm start',
    port: 8080,
  },
}
```

9. Create a test file at __tests__/calculator.js that contains the following:

```
describe('Calculator', () => {
  beforeAll(async () => {
    await page.goto('http://localhost:8080');
  })

  it('Check that 777 times 777 is 603729', async () => {
    const seven = await page.$("#seven");
    const multiply = await page.$("#multiply");
    const equals = await page.$("#equals");
    const clear = await page.$("#clear");
    await seven.click();
    await seven.click();
    await seven.click();
    await multiply.click();
    await seven.click();
    await seven.click();
    await seven.click();
    await equals.click();
    const result = await page.$eval('#screen', e => e.innerText);
    expect(result).toMatch('603729');
    await clear.click();
  })

  it('Check that 3.14 divided by 2 is 1.57', async () => {
    const one = await page.$("#one");
    const two = await page.$("#two");
    const three = await page.$("#three");
    const four = await page.$("#four");
    const divide = await page.$("#divide");
    const decimal = await page.$("#decimal");
    const equals = await page.$("#equals");
    await three.click();
    await decimal.click();
    await one.click();
    await four.click();
```

```
      await divide.click();
      await two.click();
      await equals.click();
      const result = await page.$eval('#screen', e => e.innerText);
      expect(result).toMatch('1.57');
    })


  })
```

10. Create a Husky file at .**huskyrc** that contains the following:

```
{
  "hooks": {
    "pre-commit": "npm run lint && npm test"
  }
}
```

11. Install **husky** as a developer dependency by running **npm install --save-dev husky**:

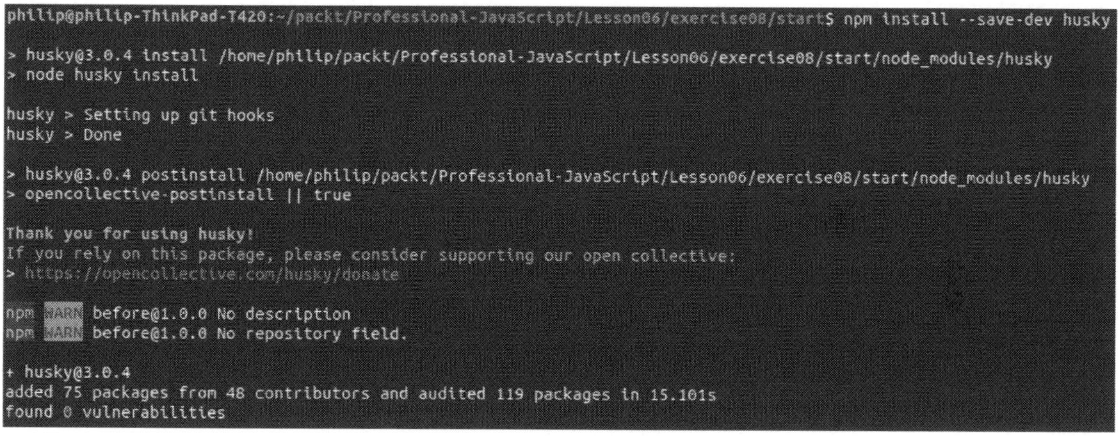

Figure 6.19: Installing Husky

12. Ensure that tests are working correctly using the **npm test** command:

   npm test

   This should return positive results for two tests, as shown in the following figure:

```
philip@philip-ThinkPad-T420:~/packt/Professional-JavaScript/Lesson06/exercise08/start$ npm test

> before@1.0.0 test /home/philip/packt/Professional-JavaScript/Lesson06/exercise08/start
> jest

      console.error node_modules/jest-jasmine2/build/jasmine/Env.js:289
        Unhandled error

      console.error node_modules/jest-jasmine2/build/jasmine/Env.js:290


 PASS  __tests__/calculator.js
  Calculator
    ✓ Check that 777 times 777 is 603729 (190ms)
    ✓ Check that 3.14 divided by 2 is 1.57 (134ms)

Test Suites: 1 passed, 1 total
Tests:       2 passed, 2 total
Snapshots:   0 total
Time:        1.256s
Ran all test suites.
```

Figure 6.20: Showing the positive result of two tests

Ensure the Git hook and linting is working by making a test commit.

Chapter 7: Advanced JavaScript

Activity 8: Creating a User Tracker

Solution

1. Open the **Activity08.js** file and define **logUser**. It will add the user to the **userList** argument. Make sure no duplicates are added:

```
function logUser(userList, user) {
if(!userList.includes(user)) {
userList.push(user);
}
}
```

Here, we used an **includes** method to check whether the user already exists. If they don't, they will be added to our list.

2. Define **userLeft**. It will remove the user from the **userList** argument. If the user doesn't exist, it will do nothing:

```
function userLeft(userList, user) {
const userIndex = userList.indexOf(user);
if (userIndex >= 0) {
    userList.splice(userIndex, 1);
}
}
```

Here, we are using **indexOf** to get the current index of the user we want to remove. If the item doesn't exist, **indexOf** will **return -1**, so we are only using **splice** to remove the item if it exists.

3. Define **numUsers**, which returns the number of users currently inside the list:

```
function numUsers(userList) {
return userLeft.length;
}
```

4. Define a function called **runSite**. We will create a **users** array and call the function we declared previously to test our implementation. We will also invoke the function afterward:

```
function runSite() {
    // Your user list for your website
    const users = [];
    // Simulate user viewing your site
    logUser(users, 'user1');
```

```
        logUser(users, 'user2');
        logUser(users, 'user3');
        // User left your website
        userLeft(users, 'user2');
        // More user goes to your website
        logUser(users, 'user4');
        logUser(users, 'user4');
        logUser(users, 'user5');
        logUser(users, 'user6');
        // More user left your website
        userLeft(users, 'user1');
        userLeft(users, 'user4');
        userLeft(users, 'user2');
        console.log('Current user: ', users.join(', '));
    }
    runSite();
```

After defining the functions, running the preceding code will return the following output:

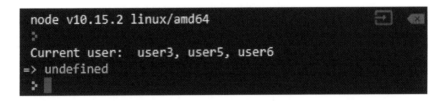

Figure 7.62: Output of running log_users.js

Activity 9: Creating a Student Manager Using JavaScript Arrays and Classes

Solution

1. Create a **School** class that includes all the student's information:

```
class School {
constructor() {
    this.students = [];
}
}
```

In the **School** constructor, we simply initialize a list of students. Later, we will add new students to this list.

2. Create a **Student** class that includes all the relevant information about the student:

```
class Student {
constructor(name, age, gradeLevel) {
    this.name = name;
    this.age = age;
    this.gradeLevel = gradeLevel;
    this.courses = [];
}
}
```

In the student **constructor**, we are storing a list of courses, as well as the student's **age**, **name**, and **gradeLevel**.

3. Create a **Course** class that will include information about the course's **name** and **grade**:

```
class Course {
constructor(name, grade) {
    this.name = name;
    this.grade = grade;
}
}
```

The course constructor simply stores the name of the course and grade in the **object**.

4. Create **addStudent** in the **School** class:

```
addStudent(student) {
this.students.push(student);
}
```

5. Create **findByGrade** in the **School** class:

```
findByGrade(gradeLevel) {
    return this.students.filter((s) => s.gradeLevel === gradeLevel);
}
```

6. Create **findByAge** in the **School** class:

```
findByAge(age) {
return this.students.filter((s) => s.age === age);
}
```

7. Create **findByName** in the **School** class:

```
findByName(name) {
return this.students.filter((s) => s.name === name);
}
```

8. In the **Student** class, create a **calculateAverageGrade** method for calculating the average grade of the student:

```
calculateAverageGrade() {
const totalGrades = this.courses.reduce((prev, curr) => prev + curr.grade,
0);
return (totalGrades / this.courses.length).toFixed(2);
}
```

In the **calculateAverageGrade** method, we use array reduce to get the total grades of all the classes for our student. Then, we divide this by the number of courses in our courses list.

9. In the **Student** class, create a method called **assignGrade**, which will assign a number grade for a course the student is taking:

```
assignGrade(name, grade) {
this.courses.push(new Course(name, grade))
}
```

You should do your work in the **student_manager.js** file and modify the provided method template. You should see the **TEST PASSED** message if you implemented everything correctly:

Figure 7.63: Screenshot showing the TEST PASSED message

Activity 10: Refactoring Functions to Use Modern JavaScript Features

Solution

1. Open **Activity03.js**; it should contain various functions written in legacy JavaScript. When you run **Activity03.js** using Node.js, you should see the following output:

```
node v10.16.0
>
========TEST PASSED========
=> undefined
>
```

Figure 7.64: Output after running Lesson7-activity.js

2. You need to refactor **itemExist**, using the **includes** array:

```
function itemExist(array, item) {
    return array.includes(item);
}


In pushUnique we will use array push to add new item to the bottom
function pushUnique(array, item) {
    if (!itemExist(array, item)) {
        array.push(item);
    }
}

```

3. In **createFilledArray**, we will use **array.fill** to fill our array with an initial value:

```
function createFilledArray(size, init) {
    const newArray = new Array(size).fill(init);
    return newArray;
}


In removeFirst we will use array.shift to remove the first item
function removeFirst(array) {
    return array.shift();
}
```

4. In **removeLast**, we will use **array.pop** to remove the last item:

```
function removeLast(array) {
    return array.pop();
}
```

In cloneArray we will use spread operation to make clone for our array
```
function cloneArray(array) {
    return [...array];
}
```

5. We will refactor our **Food** class using the **ES6** class:

```
class Food {
    constructor(type, calories) {
        this.type = type;
        this.calories = calories;
    }
    getCalories() {
        return this.calories;
    }
}
```

After you have finished the refactor and run the existing code, you should see the same output:

Figure 7.65: Output showing the TEST PASSED message

Chapter 8: Asynchronous Programming

Activity 11: Using Callbacks to Receive Results

Solution:

1. Create a **calculate** function that takes **id** and a **callback** as an argument:

```
function calculate(id, callback) {
}
```

2. We will first call **getUsers** to get all of the users. This will give us the address we need:

```
function calculate(id, callback) {
clientApi.getUsers((error, result) => {
if (error) { return callback(error); }
const currentUser = result.users.find((user) => user.id === id);
if (!currentUser) { return callback(new Error('user not found')); }

});
  }
```

Here, we get all of the users, then we apply the **find** method to the **user** to find the user we want from the list. If that user does not exist, we call the **callback** function with the **User not found** error.

3. Call **getUsage** to get the user's usage:

```
clientApi.getUsage(id, (error, usage) => {
if (error) { return callback(error); }
  });
```

Then, we need to put the call to **getUsage** inside the callback of **getUsers** so it will run after we have finished calling **getUsers**. Here, the callback will be called with a list of numbers, which will be the usage. We will also call the callback with the error object if we receive an error from **getUsage**.

4. Finally, call **getRate** to get the rate of the user we are doing the calculation for:

```
clientApi.getRate(id, (error, rate) => {
if (error) { return callback(error); }
let totalUsage = 0;
for (let i = 0; i < usage.length; i++) {
    totalUsage += usage[i];
}
callback(null, {
```

```
    id,
    address: currentUser.address,
    due: rate * totalUsage
  });
});
```

We will put this call inside the callback for **getUsage**. This creates a nested chain request for all the information we need. Lastly, we will call the callback with the information we are calculating. For the final due amount, we use array reduce to calculate the total usage for that user, and then multiply that by the rate to get the final amount due.

5. When the function is completed, invoke it using an existing ID, as in the following code:

```
calculate('DDW2AU', (error, result) => {
    console.log(error, result);
});
```

You should see output like this:

```
node v10.15.2 linux/amd64
>
=> undefined
null { id: 'DDW2AU', address: '4560 Hickman Street', due: '22.51' }
>
```

Figure 8.43: Invoking the function using an existing ID

6. Invoke the function using an ID that doesn't exist:

```
calculate('XXX', (error, result) => {
    console.log(error, result);
});
```

You should see the following output with the error returned:

```
node v10.15.2 linux/amd64
>
=> undefined
Error: user not found
    at clientApi.getUsers (evalmachine.<anonymous>:62:45)
    at Timeout.setTimeout [as _onTimeout] (evalmachine.<anonymous>:21:13)
    at ontimeout (timers.js:436:11)
    at tryOnTimeout (timers.js:300:5)
    at listOnTimeout (timers.js:263:5)
    at Timer.processTimers (timers.js:223:10) undefined
>
```

Figure 8.44: Invoking a function using an ID that doesn't exist

Activity 12: Refactor the Bill Calculator Using Async and Await

Solution

1. Create the **calculate** function as an **async** function:

   ```
   async function calculate(id) {
   }
   ```

2. Use **await** to call **getUsers** to get the resolved result in **users**:

   ```
   const users = await clientApi.getUsers();
   const currentUser = users.users.find((user) => user.id === id);
   ```

   When we are using the **await** keyword, we must use **async** functions. The **await** keyword will break the control of our program and will only return and continue execution once the promise it is waiting for is resolved.

3. Use **await** to call **getUsage** to get the usage for the user:

   ```
   const usage = await clientApi.getUsage(currentUser.id);
   ```

4. Use **await** to call **getRate** to get the rate for the user:

   ```
   const rate = await clientApi.getRate(currentUser.id);
   ```

5. Lastly, we will call **return** to retrieve **id**, **address**, and **due**:

   ```
   return {
   id,
   address: currentUser.address,
   due: (rate * usage.reduce((prev, curr) => curr + prev)).toFixed(2)
   };
   ```

6. Write the **calculateAll** function as an **async** function:

   ```
   async function calculateAll() {
   }
   ```

7. Use **await** when we call **getUsers** and store the result in **result**:

   ```
   const result = await clientApi.getUsers();
   ```

8. Use a map array to create a list of promises and use **Promise.all** to wrap them. Then, should be use **await** on the promise returned by **Promise.all**:

   ```
   return await Promise.all(result.users.map((user) => calculate(user.id)));
   ```

   Because **await** will work on any promise and will wait until the value is resolved, it will also wait for our **Promise.all**. After it is resolved, the final array will be returned.

9. Call **calculate** on one of the users:

```
calculate('DDW2AU').then(console.log)
```

The output should be as follows:

```
node v10.15.2 linux/amd64
:
{ id: 'DDW2AU', address: '4560 Hickman Street', due: '22.51' }
=> Promise { <pending> }
:
```

Figure 8.45: Calling calculate on one of the users

10. Call the **calculateAll** function:

```
calculateAll().then(console.log)
```

The output should be as follows:

```
node v10.15.2 linux/amd64
:
[ { id: 'DDW2AU', address: '4560 Hickman Street', due: '22.51' },
  { id: 'DV50PD', address: '3445 Red Hawk Road', due: '18.81' },
  { id: 'WCGL6F',
    address: '2355 University Hill Road',
    due: '48.48' } ]
=> Promise { <pending> }
:
```

Figure 8.46: Calling the calculateAll function

As you can see, when we call **async** functions, we can treat them as functions that return a promise.

Chapter 9: Event-Driven Programming and Built-In Modules

Activity 13: Building an Event-Driven Module

Solution:

Perform the following steps to complete this activity:

1. Import the **events** module:

```
const EventEmitter = require('events');
```

2. Create the **SmokeDetector** class that extends **EventEmitter** and set **batteryLevel** to 10:

```
class SmokeDetector extends EventEmitter {
    constructor() {
        super();
        this.batteryLevel = 10;
    }
}
```

In our constructor, because we are extending the **EventEmitter** class and we are assigning a custom property, **batteryLevel**, we will need to call **super** inside the constructor and set **batteryLevel** to **10**.

3. Create a **test** method inside the **SmokeDetector** class that will test the battery level and emit a **low battery** message in the event that the battery is low:

```
test() {
        if (this.batteryLevel > 0) {
            this.batteryLevel -= 0.1;
            if (this.batteryLevel < 0.5) {
                this.emit('low battery');
            }
            return true;
        }
        return false;
    }
```

Our **test()** method will check the battery level and emit a **low battery** event when the battery has less than 0.5 units. We will also reduce the battery level every time we run the **test** method.

4. Create the **House** class, which will store the instances of our event listeners:

```
class House {
    constructor(numBedroom, numBathroom, numKitchen) {
        this.numBathroom = numBathroom;
        this.numBedroom = numBedroom;
        this.numKitchen = numKitchen;
        this.alarmListener = () => {
            console.log('alarm is raised');
        }
        this.lowBatteryListener = () => {
            console.log('alarm battery is low');
        }
    }
}
```

In the **House** class, we are storing some information about the house. We are also storing both of the event listener functions as properties of this object. This way, we can use the function reference to call **removeListener** when we want to detach a listener.

5. Create an **addDetector** method in the **House** class. Here, we will attach the event listeners:

```
addDetector(detector) {
    detector.on('alarm', this.alarmListener);
    detector.on('low battery', this.lowBatteryListener);
}
```

Here, we are expecting the detector that's passed in to be an **EventEmitter**. We are attaching two event listeners to our **detector** argument. When these events are emitted, it will invoke our event emitter inside the object.

6. Create a **removeDetector** method, which will help us remove the alarm event listeners we attached previously:

```
removeDetector(detector) {
    detector.removeListener('alarm', this.alarmListener);
    detector.removeListener('low battery', this.lowBatteryListener);
}
```

Here, we are using the function reference and the alarm argument to remove the listener attached to our listener. Once this is called, the events should not invoke our listener again.

7. Create a **House** instance called **myHouse**. This will contain some sample information about our house. It will also be used to listen to events from our smoke detector:

```
const myHouse = new House(2, 2, 1);
```

8. Create a **SmokeDetector** instance called **detector**:

```
const detector = new SmokeDetector();
```

9. Add our **detector** to **myHouse**:

```
myHouse.addDetector(detector);
```

10. Create a loop to call the test function **96** times:

```
for (let i = 0; i < 96; i++) {
    detector.test();
}
```

Because the testing function will reduce the battery level, we will expect a *low battery* alarm to be emitted if we call it **96** times. This will produce the following output:

Figure 9.50: Low battery alarm emitted

11. Emit an alarm on the **detector** object:

```
detector.emit('alarm');
```

The following is the output of the preceding code:

Figure 9.51: Alarm emitted for the detector object

12. Remove **detector** from the **myHouse** object:

```
myHouse.removeDetector(detector);
```

13. Test this to emit the alarms on the **detector**:

```
detector.test();
detector.emit('alarm');
```

Because we just removed **detector** from our house, we should see no output from this:

```
node v10.16.0
>
=> false
>
```

Figure 9.52: Testing the emit alarms on the detector

Activity 14: Building a File Watcher

Solution:

1. Import **fs** and **events**:

```
const fs = require('fs').promises;
const EventEmitter = require('events');
```

2. Create a **fileWatcher** class that extends the **EventEmitter** class. Use a **modify** timestamp to keep track of the file change.

We need to create a **FileWatcher** class that extends **EventEmitter**. It will take the filename and delay as parameters in the constructor. In the constructor, we will also need to set the last modified time and the timer variable. We will keep them as undefined for now:

```
class FileWatcher extends EventEmitter {
    constructor(file, delay) {
        super();
        this.timeModified = undefined;
        this.file = file;
        this.delay = delay;
        this.watchTimer = undefined;
    }
}
```

This is the most basic way to see whether a file has been changed.

3. Create the **startWatch** method to start watching the changes on the file:

```
startWatch() {
        if (!this.watchTimer) {
            this.watchTimer = setInterval(() => {
                fs.stat(this.file).then((stat) => {
                    if (this.timeModified !== stat.mtime.toString()) {
                        console.log('modified');
                        this.timeModified = stat.mtime.toString();
                    }
                }).catch((error) => {
                    console.error(error);
                });
            }, this.delay);
        }
    }
```

Here, we are using **fs.stat** to get the file's information and comparing the modified time with the last modified time. If they are not equal, we will output **modified** in the console.

4. Create the **stopWatch** method to stop watching the changes on the file:

```
stopWatch() {
        if (this.watchTimer) {
            clearInterval(this.watchTimer);
            this.watchTimer = undefined;
        }
    }
```

The **stopWatch** method is very simple: we will check if we have a timer in this object. If we do, then we run **clearInterval** on that timer to clear that timer.

5. Create a **test.txt** file in the same directory as **filewatch.js**.

6. Create a **FileWatcher** instance and start watching the file every **1000** ms:

```
const watcher = new FileWatcher('test.txt', 1000);
watcher.startWatch();
```

7. Modify some content in **test.txt** and save it. You should see the following output:

```
node v10.16.0
>
(node:127) ExperimentalWarning: The fs.promises API is experimental
=> undefined
modified
modified
modified
>
```

Figure 9.53: Output after modifying the content in the test.txt file

We modified the file twice, which means we are seeing three modified messages. This is happening because when we start the watch, we class this as the file being modified.

8. Modify **startWatch** so that it also retrieves the new content:

```
startWatch() {
    if (!this.watchTimer) {
        this.watchTimer = setInterval(() => {
            fs.stat(this.file).then((stat) => {
                if (this.timeModified !== stat.mtime.toString()) {
                    fs.readFile(this.file, 'utf-8').then((content) => {
                        console.log('new content is: ', content);
                    }).catch((error) => {
                        console.error(error);
                    });
                    this.timeModified = stat.mtime.toString();
                }
            }).catch((error) => {
                console.error(error);
            });
        }, this.delay);
    }
}
```

When we modify **test.txt** and save it, our code should detect it and output the new content:

```
node v10.16.0
>
(node:149) ExperimentalWarning: The fs.promises API is experimental
=> undefined
new content is:  Hello worldssss
new content is:  Hello world2
>
```

Figure 9.54: The modifications that were made in the file can be seen using the startWatch function

9. Modify **startWatch** so that it emits events when the file is modified and an error when it encounters an error:

```
startWatch() {
        if (!this.watchTimer) {
            this.watchTimer = setInterval(() => {
                fs.stat(this.file).then((stat) => {
                    if (this.timeModified !== stat.mtime.toString()) {
                        fs.readFile(this.file, 'utf-8').then((content) => {
                            this.emit('change', content);
                        }).catch((error) => {
                            this.emit('error', error);
                        });
                        this.timeModified = stat.mtime.toString();
                    }
                }).catch((error) => {
                    this.emit('error', error);
                });
            }, this.delay);
        }
    }
```

Instead of outputting the content, we will emit an event with the new content. This makes our code much more flexible.

10. Attach event handlers to **error** and change them on our file **watcher**:

```
watcher.on('error', console.error);
watcher.on('change', (change) => {
    console.log('new change:', change);
});
```

11. Run the code and modify **test.txt**:

```
node v10.16.0
>
(node:171) ExperimentalWarning: The fs.promises API is experimental
=> undefined
new change: Hello world2
new change: Hello world2s
>
```

Figure 9.55: Output after changing our file watcher

Chapter 10: Functional Programming with JavaScript

Activity 15: onCheckout Callback Prop

Solution

1. Change the current directory to **Lesson10** and run **npm install** if you haven't done so in this directory before. **npm install** downloads the dependencies that are required in order to run this activity (React and Parcel).

2. Run **parcel serve activity-on-checkout-prop-start.html** and then execute **npm run Activity15**. You will see the application starting up, as follows:

```
> parcel serve activity-1-on-checkout-prop-start.html

Server running at http://localhost:1234
✦   Built in 9.61s.
```

Figure 10.42: Output after running the start html script

3. Go to **http://localhost:1234** (or whichever URL the start script output). You should see the following HTML page:

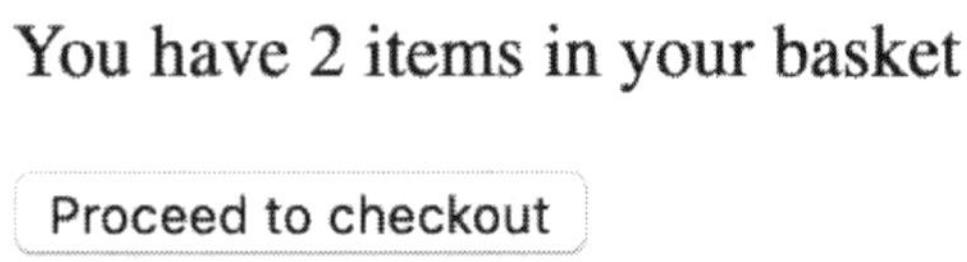

You have 2 items in your basket

    Proceed to checkout

Figure 10.43: Initial application in the browser

4. The **onClick** of the **Proceed to checkout** can be implemented as follows:

```
render() {
  return (
    <div>
      <p>You have {this.state.items.length} items in your basket</p>
      <button onClick={() => this.props.onCheckout(this.state.items)}>
        Proceed to checkout
      </button>
    </div>
  );
}
```

This follows on from the following investigation:

Finding the button in the **Basket** component's **render** method whose text is **Proceed to checkout**.

Noticing its **onClick** handler is currently a function that does nothing when called, **() => {}**.

Replacing the **onClick** handler with the correct call to **this.props.onCheckout**.

5. We should see the following after clicking the **Proceed to checkout** button:

You've started checking out with 2 items.

| Continue shopping | Finish |

Figure 10.44: Output after clicking on the "Proceed to checkout" button

Activity 16: Testing a Selector

Solution

1. Run **npm run Activity16** (or **node activity-items-selector-test-start.js**). You will see the following output:

```
> node activity-2-items-selector-test-start.js

Assertion failed: test not implemented
```

Figure 10.45: Expected output after running the start file of the activity

2. Test that, for empty states, the selector returns **[]**:

```
function test() {
  assert.deepStrictEqual(
    selectBasketItems(),
    [],
    'should be [] when selecting with no state'
  );
  assert.deepStrictEqual(
    selectBasketItems({}),
    [],
    'should be [] when selecting with {} state'
  );
}
```

3. Test that, for an empty basket object, the selector returns []:

```
function test() {
  // other assertions
  assert.deepStrictEqual(
    selectBasketItems({basket: {}}),
    [],
    'should be [] when selecting with {} state.basket'
  );
}
```

4. Test that, if the items array is set but empty, the selector returns []:

```
function test() {
  // other assertions
  assert.deepStrictEqual(
    selectBasketItems({basket: {items: []}}),
    [],
    'should be [] when items is []'
  );
}
```

5. Test that, if the **items** array is not empty and set, the selector returns it:

```
function test() {
  // other assertions
  assert.deepStrictEqual(
    selectBasketItems({
      basket: {items: [{name: 'product-name'}]}
    }),
    [{name: 'product-name'}],
    'should be items when items is set'
  );
}
```

The full test function content after following the previous solution steps:

```
function test() {
  assert.deepStrictEqual(
    selectBasketItems(),
    [],
    'should be [] when selecting with no state'
  );
  assert.deepStrictEqual(
    selectBasketItems({}),
```

```
          [],
          'should be [] when selecting with {} state'
        );
        assert.deepStrictEqual(
          selectBasketItems({basket: {}}),
          [],
          'should be [] when selecting with {} state.basket'
        );
        assert.deepStrictEqual(
          selectBasketItems({basket: {items: []}}),
          [],
          'should be [] when items is []'
        );
        assert.deepStrictEqual(
          selectBasketItems({
            basket: {items: [{name: 'product-name'}]}
          }),
          [{name: 'product-name'}],
          'should be items when items is set'
        );
      }
```

6. There should be no errors in the output of the implemented test:

```
> node activity-2-items-selector-test-start.js
```

Figure 10.46: Final output showing no errors

Activity 17: Fetching the Current Basket From BFF

Solution

1. Change the current directory to **Lesson10** and run **npm install** if you haven't done so in this directory before.

2. Run the BFF for Activity 17 and **npx parcel serve activity-app-start.html**. During development, run **npm run Activity17**. You will see the application starting up, as follows:

```
> concurrently --names GraphQL,React "node activity-3-bff.js" "parcel serve
activity-3-app-start.html"

GraphQL    listening on port 3000
           Server running at http://localhost:1234
+  Built in 3.47s.
```

Figure 10.47: Running the initial start file for the activity

3. Go to **http://localhost:1234** (or whichever URL the starting script output). You should see the following HTML page:

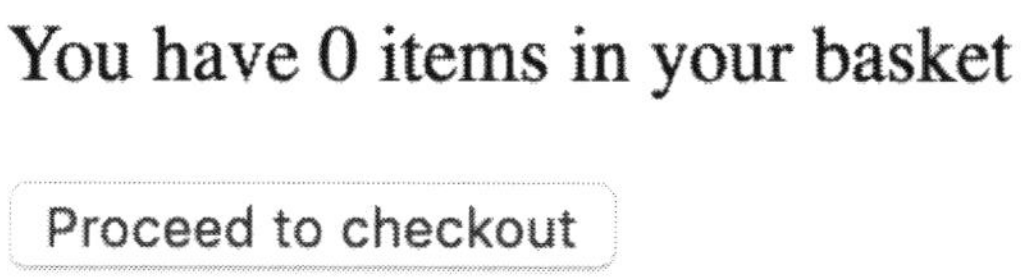

You have 0 items in your basket

Proceed to checkout

Figure 10.48: Initial application in the browser

4. Run the following query in the GraphiQL UI:

```
{
  basket {
    items {
      id
      name
      price
      quantity
    }
  }
}
```

The following is the output of the preceding code:

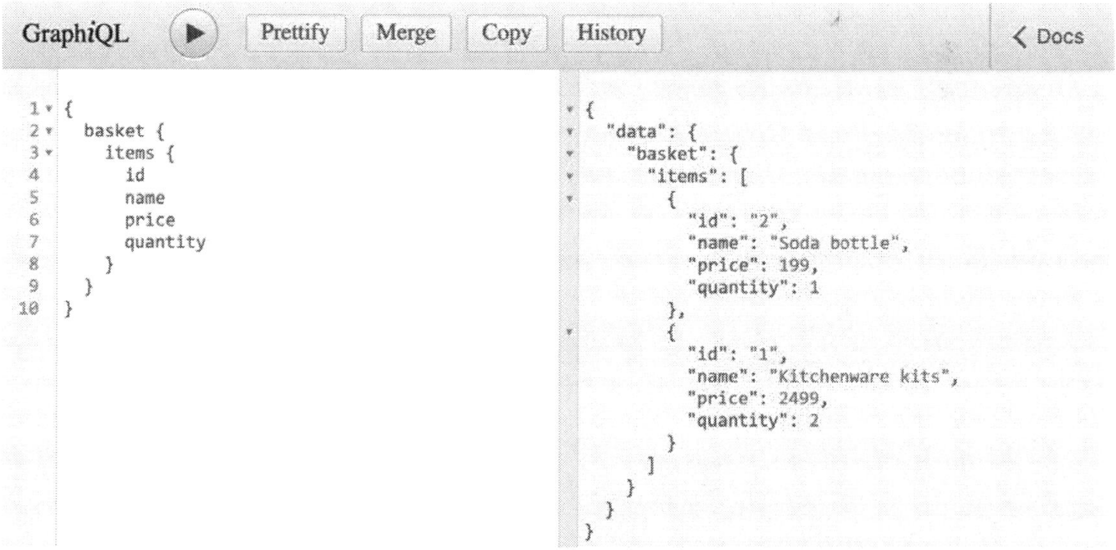

Figure 10.49: GraphiQL UI with basket query

5. Create a new **requestBasket** action creator (that leverages redux-thunk). It calls **fetchFromBff** with the query from the previous step and dispatches a **REQUEST_BASKET_SUCCESS** action with a basket payload extracted from the GraphQL response:

```
function requestBasket() {
  return dispatch => {
    fetchFromBff(`{
      basket {
        items {
          id
          name
          price
          quantity
        }
      }
    }`).then(data => {
      dispatch({
        type: REQUEST_BASKET_SUCCESS,
        basket: data.basket
      });
    });
  };
}
```

6. Reduce the basket data into the store and add the following case to **appReducer** to reduce our new **REQUEST_BASKET_SUCCESS** action's **basket** payload into the state:

```
const appReducer = (state = defaultState, action) => {
  switch (action.type) {
    // other cases
    case REQUEST_BASKET_SUCCESS:
      return {
        ...state,
        basket: action.basket
      };
    // other cases

  }
};3
```

7. Add **requestBasket** in **mapDispatchToProps**, like so:

```
const mapDispatchToProps = dispatch => {
  return {
    // other mapped functions
    requestBasket() {
      dispatch(requestBasket());
    }
  };
};
```

8. Call **requestBasket** on **componentDidMount**:

```
class App extends React.Component {
  componentDidMount() {
    this.props.requestBasket();
  }
  // render method
}
```

When loading up the application with all the preceding steps completed, it flashes with the "You have 0 items in your basket" message before changing to the following screenshot. When the fetch from the BFF completes, it is reduced into the store and causes a re-render. This will display the basket once again, as follows:

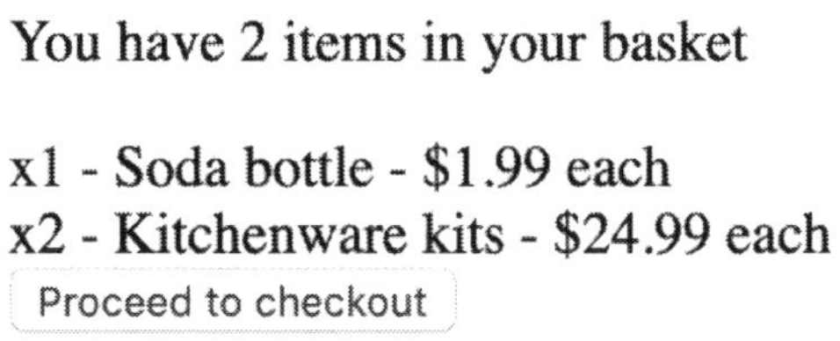

You have 2 items in your basket

x1 - Soda bottle - $1.99 each
x2 - Kitchenware kits - $24.99 each

Proceed to checkout

Figure 10.50: Final application once it has been integrated with the BFF

Index

About

All major keywords used in this book are captured alphabetically in this section. Each one is accompanied by the page number of where they appear.

W

Made in the USA
Middletown, DE
01 July 2020